Rancher Deep Dive

Manage enterprise Kubernetes seamlessly
with Rancher

Matthew Mattox

BIRMINGHAM—MUMBAI

Rancher Deep Dive

Copyright © 2022 Packt Publishing

Group Product Manager: Rahul Nair
Publishing Product Manager: Meeta Rajani
Senior Editor: Athikho Sapuni Rishana
Content Development Editor: Sayali Pingale
Technical Editor: Nithik Cheruvakodan
Copy Editor: Safis Editing
Associate Project Manager: Neil Dmello
Proofreader: Safis Editing
Indexer: Pratik Shirodkar
Production Designer: Sinhayna Bais
Marketing Coordinator: Nimisha Dua
Senior Marketing Coordinator: Sanjana Gupta

First published: June 2022

Production reference: 1070622

Published by Packt Publishing Ltd.
Livery Place
35 Livery Street
Birmingham
B3 2PB, UK.

978-1-80324-609-3

www.packt.com

To my wife, Samantha Mattox, for being my foundation during this life journey. I want to say thank you for putting up with all of the long and late nights, helping when I have writer's block, and always pushing me forward to achieve my goals and aspirations.

– Matthew Mattox

Contributors

About the author

Since 2019, **Matthew Mattox** has served as a SUSE principal support engineer, providing client-focused support. Having experience in both engineering and DevOps, Matthew has a deep understanding of Kubernetes, Docker, Rancher, Longhorn, and OPA Gatekeeper. Apart from designing custom solutions to solve changing problems, he was named "Bullfighter of the Year" for his outstanding work at Rancher Labs. One of his primary goals is to make IT a profit center within your company, not a cost center.

I want to thank all of the people at Rancher/SUSE for all that they have taught me.

In particular, I would like to thank…

Bala Gopalan – Thank you for giving me the tools to succeed.

Ahmad Emneina – Thank you for being a great mentor and always being someone I can count on when I run out of ideas.

Alena Prokharchyk – Thank you for teaching me all of the ins and outs of Rancher; you really inspired me to get into software development.

Hussein Galal – Thank you for teaching me what Kubernetes is and what it can do, and for always being someone I can count on.

Also, thank you to all of the Rancher/SUSE team for their support.

About the reviewer

Lucas Ramage is a co-founder of Infinite Omicron, a company focused on cybersecurity, DevOps, and open source technologies. Prior roles include those of a cyber security consultant and embedded firmware engineer. He also has a bachelor's degree in computer science. For the last 10 years, he has been an active contributor to multiple Linux distributions, including Alpine, Gentoo, and OpenWrt, and also the Android-based distribution, Termux. In addition to maintaining open source projects, he also mentors for Google Summer of Code. He enjoys sharing knowledge and helping others to grow.

I am truly grateful to the open source community and to all of my colleagues and friends who I have been able to learn from over the years. Thank you all for sharing your knowledge with me and the rest of the world. I am also very thankful to my family and my faith for supporting me in life.

About SUSE

Rancher Labs is now part of SUSE.

SUSE is a global leader in innovative, reliable, secure enterprise-grade open source solutions, relied upon by more than 60% of the Fortune 500 to power their mission-critical workloads. SUSE specializes in business-critical Linux, Enterprise container management, and Edge solutions, and collaborates with partners and communities to empower customers to innovate everywhere – from the data center to the cloud, to the edge, and beyond.

SUSE's solutions already power everything from autonomous driving to CAT scan and mammogram machines. Its open source software is embedded inside air traffic control systems, weather forecasting technologies, trains, and satellites.

- **Business-critical Linux**: The SUSE Linux Enterprise family provides a stable, secure, and well-supported Linux operating system for mission-critical workloads such as SAP S/4HANA and other solutions.

- **Enterprise container management**: SUSE Rancher solutions enable customers to standardize cloud-native workload operations across all devices and landscapes, including with end-to-end security meeting the highest standards thanks to SUSE's NeuVector technology.

- **Edge solutions**: The new Edge offerings bring the best of SUSE's Linux and container technologies together. This is helping SUSE to truly innovate at scale by pushing business applications to where they are needed most.

SUSE puts the *open* back in open source, giving customers the agility to tackle innovation challenges today and the freedom to evolve their strategy and solutions tomorrow. The company employs more than 2,000 people globally. SUSE is listed on the Frankfurt Stock Exchange.

Visit suse.com to learn more and follow us on our social handles: @SUSE and @Rancher_Labs.

Table of Contents

Preface

Part 1 – Rancher Background and Architecture and Design

1

Introduction to Rancher and Kubernetes

The history of Rancher Labs as a company	4	What problem is Kubernetes trying to solve?	9
Rancher's earlier products	4	Comparing Kubernetes with Docker Swarm and OpenShift	10
What is Rancher's core philosophy?	5	Kubernetes versus Docker Swarm	10
		Kubernetes versus OpenShift	13
Where did Kubernetes come from?	7	Summary	14

2

Rancher and Kubernetes High-Level Architecture

What is the Rancher server?	16	What do the Cattle agents do?	27
What are RKE and RKE2?	17	How does Rancher provision nodes and clusters?	28
So, what is RKE?	17		
What is RKE2?	19	What are kube-apiserver, kube-controller-manager, kube-scheduler, etcd, and kubelet?	32
What is K3s (five less than K8s)?	20		
What is RancherD?	22	How do the current state and the desired state work?	37
What controllers run inside the Rancher server pods?	22	Summary	39

Part 2 – Installing Rancher

3

Creating a Single Node Rancher

What is a single-node Rancher installation?	44	Starting the Rancher server	51
Requirements and limitations	44	Migration to an HA setup	53
Rules for architecting a solution	46	Backing up the current Rancher server	54
Installation steps	47	Starting cutover to new cluster	56
Installing Docker	47	Cleaning up/rolling back	57
Prepping the SSL certificates	49	Summary	57

4

Creating an RKE and RKE2 Cluster

What is an RKE cluster?	60	Install steps (RKE)	86
Where did RKE come from?	60	Install steps (RKE2)	87
How does RKE work?	60	Configuring an external load balancer (HAProxy)	89
What is an RKE2 cluster?	66	TCP mode	90
What is RancherD?	69	HTTP/HTTPS mode	92
Requirements and limitations	69	Configuring MetalLB	93
Basic requirements	69	Installation	93
Design limitations and considerations	71	Configuration	93
Rules for architecting a solution	73	Summary	94
RKE clusters	74		
RKE2 clusters	81		

5

Deploying Rancher on a Hosted Kubernetes Cluster

Understanding hosted Kubernetes clusters	96	Google's GKE	99
		Azure's AKS	100
Requirements and limitations	98	Rules for architecting a solution	101
Amazon EKS	98	Amazon EKS	102

Google's GKE 104

Azure's AKS 107

Creating a hosted Kubernetes cluster 110

Amazon EKS 110

Google's GKE 113

Azure's AKS 114

Installing and upgrading Rancher 116

Installing Rancher 116

Upgrading Rancher 117

Rancher-Backup-Operator 117

Installation 118

Creating a backup 118

Summary 119

Part 3 – Deploying a Kubernetes Cluster

6

Creating an RKE Cluster Using Rancher

What is a Rancher-managed cluster? 124

Where do Rancher-managed clusters come from? 124

How does Rancher manage nodes? 124

How does Rancher manage a cluster? 125

Requirements and limitations 128

Rancher-created managed nodes 128

Existing nodes 129

Rules for architecting a solution 130

AWS 131

GCP 134

Preparing for nodes to join Rancher 135

Prepping the infrastructure provider 136

The steps for creating an RKE cluster using Rancher 141

Deploying a cluster using node pools 144

Ongoing maintenance tasks 144

Summary 146

7

Deploying a Hosted Cluster with Rancher

How can Rancher manage a hosted cluster? 148

Requirements and limitations 149

Basic requirements 149

Design limitations and considerations 150

Rules for architecting a solution 151

Amazon EKS 152

GKE 153

Microsoft Azure Kubernetes Service (AKS) 155

Prepping the cloud provider   156

Amazon EKS   156

GKE   159

AKS   160

Installation steps   162

Amazon EKS   163

GKE   164

AKS   165

Ongoing maintenance tasks   165

Summary   166

8

Importing an Externally Managed Cluster into Rancher

What is an imported cluster?   168

What is this local cluster in my new
Rancher instance?   168

Why is the local cluster an
imported cluster?   168

Why are some imported clusters
special?   169

What kinds of clusters can be
imported?   169

Why would I import an RKE cluster
instead of creating one in Rancher?   169

What can Rancher do with an
imported cluster?   170

Requirements and limitations   170

Basic requirements   170

Design limitations and considerations   171

Rules for architecting a solution 172

Externally managed RKE   173

Kubernetes The Hard Way   174

k3s cluster   174

RKE2 cluster   175

**How can Rancher access
a cluster?   176**

Summary   178

Part 4 – Getting Your Cluster Production-Ready

9

Cluster Configuration Backup and Recovery

What is an etcd backup?   182

**Why do I need to back up
my etcd?   182**

How does an etcd backup work? 183

RKE clusters   183

RKE2/k3s clusters   184

**How does an etcd
restore work?   185**

RKE clusters   185

RKE2/k3s clusters   186

**When do you need an
etcd restore?   186**

What does an etcd backup
not protect?   188

How do you configure
etcd backups?   189

RKE clusters   189

RKE2/k3s clusters   190

How do you take an
etcd backup?   191

RKE clusters   191

RKE2/k3s clusters   191

How do you restore from an
etcd backup?   192

RKE clusters   192

RKE2/k3s clusters   192

Setting up a lab environment to
test common failure scenarios 193

Summary   193

10

Monitoring and Logging

What is Prometheus
and Grafana?   196

Deploying Rancher's
monitoring stack   198

Adding custom application
metrics to Prometheus   202

Creating alert rules in
Prometheus   205

Creating a Grafana dashboard 207

What is the Banzai Cloud
Logging operator?   208

What is Fluent Bit and Fluentd? 208

Deploying Rancher logging   209

Filtering application logs   210

Writing logs to multiple
log servers   211

Summary   211

11

Bringing Storage to Kubernetes Using Longhorn

What is persistent storage
and why do we need it in
Kubernetes?   214

What is Longhorn?   215

How does Longhorn work?   216

Pros and cons of Longhorn   219

Rules for architecting a
Longhorn solution   220

Smallest   221

Medium with shared nodes   224

Large with dedicated nodes   227

Installing Longhorn   229

How do Longhorn
upgrades work?   231

Critical maintenance tasks for
keeping Longhorn at 100%   231

Troubleshooting common
Longhorn issues   233

Summary   233

12

Security and Compliance Using OPA Gatekeeper

Why should I care about
security in Kubernetes?   236
How do I enforce standards and
security policies in Kubernetes? 238
What is OPA Gatekeeper?   240
How to install OPA Gatekeeper
from the marketplace   243
Best practices and

standard policies   247
How do I scan my cluster for
security issues?   249
How do I lock down my cluster? 250
Deploying Rancher CIS scan   251
Additional security tools for
protecting a cluster   252
Summary   253

13

Scaling in Kubernetes

What is an HPA?   256
When should you use an HPA?   257
When should you not use an HPA? 257
Example – simple web server with
CPU utilization   258

What is a VPA?   259
How does a VPA work?   260
Why do you need a VPA?   260
How to write VPA manifests   261

What is Kubernetes
Node Autoscaler?   263
When should you use a Kubernetes
Node Autoscaler?   264
When should you not use a
Kubernetes Node Autoscaler?   265
How to set up autoscaling with
Rancher-managed clusters   266
How to set up autoscaling with
hosted clusters   266

Summary   266

14

Load Balancer Configuration and SSL Certificates

Why do we need an external
load balancer to support a
Kubernetes cluster?   268
Rules for architecting a solution 268
Round-robin DNS   269
Passive external load balancer   271
Active external load balancer   273

Integrated load balancer   276
Configuring F5 in TCP and
HTTP mode   278
TCP mode   278
HTTP mode   281
Configuring HAProxy to work

with Kubernetes   282
Installing HAProxy on
Ubuntu/Debian systems   282
Red Hat/CentOS   284
TCP mode   285
HTTP mode   286

Installing and
configuring MetalLB   287
What is ingress in Kubernetes? 289
How to add an SSL certificate to
an ingress   291
Summary   292

15
Rancher and Kubernetes Troubleshooting

Recovering an RKE cluster from
an etcd split-brain   294
What is an etcd split-brain?   294
Identifying the common error messages 295

Rebuilding from an
etcd backup   300
How to resolve Pods not being
able to be scheduled due to
OPA Gatekeeper   302
A runaway app stomping
all over a cluster   304

Can rotating kube-ca break
my cluster?   305
How to fix a namespace that is
stuck in terminating status   306
Rancher-created namespaces
getting stuck   306
Custom metrics causing all
namespaces to be stuck   307
The Longhorn system is
stuck terminating   309

General troubleshooting for
RKE clusters   310
Summary   313

Part 5 – Deploying Your Applications

16
Setting Up a CI/CD Pipeline and Image Registry

What is a CI/CD pipeline?   318
Rules for architecting a solution 321
Drone   322
Jenkins   324
GitHub Actions   326

How to deploy Drone and
its runners in Kubernetes
with Rancher   328
Prerequisites   328
Installation steps   328
Connecting to Rancher   331

Injecting secrets into
a pipeline   332

What an image repository is
and the rules for architecting
a solution   335
Docker Hub   335
Image repositories managed by third
parties   337
Self-hosted repo   337

How to deploy Harbor
in Kubernetes   338

Integrating a private registry
into a Kubernetes cluster   340
Collect/publish images   340
Rancher global registry   341
Update RKE/RKE2   341

Summary   342

17

Creating and Using Helm Charts

What is a Helm chart?   344
How does Helm work?   345
How do I create a Helm chart?   353
Deploying a Helm chart   354

Customizing a public
Helm chart   356
Summary   356

18

Resource Management

How to apply resource limits
and quotas to a Pod   358

How namespace limits/quotas
are calculated   361

How to use tools such as
Kubecost to track usage and
cost over time   363
Summary   365

Index

Preface

Rancher and Kubernetes have been driving the wave of DevOps adoption for both on-premises and cloud workloads. This book will guide you through the history of Rancher and Kubernetes and how they came into being. We will dive into how to design, build, and manage your Rancher environment. We will then build upon Rancher, deploying a range of cluster types, including RKE, RKE2, k3s, EKS, and GKE. With each of these cluster types, we will go over how they work, design a solution around them, and finally, deploy them using Rancher.

We will then shift into getting your clusters production-ready. This includes how we back up and restore the different cluster types and monitor the health of our clusters and the application hosted on them. Then, we will dive into how to provide the additional services needed outside of core Kubernetes services, including persistent storage with Longhorn, security/compliance using OPA Gatekeeper, and how to bring dynamic scaling to our clusters.

We will then close the book by covering how to build and deploy our application in a Rancher/Kubernetes ecosystem using tools such as Drone CI for our CI/CD pipeline and Harbor for hosting build artifacts. We will then dive into the deep topic of Helm charts and how they bring package management to our clusters. Finally, we will close by covering resource management and cost reporting to address the goal of turning IT from a black hole into which you throw money into the profit center it can be.

Who this book is for

This book primarily targets DevOps engineers looking to deploy Kubernetes with Rancher, including how Rancher changed how clusters are built and managed using RKE (Rancher Kubernetes Engine) and RKE2/k3s. It is also for people who want to learn more about the Day 2 task part of the Kubernetes and Rancher ecosystem.

What this book covers

Chapter 1, Introduction to Rancher and Kubernetes, explores the history of Rancher and its earlier products, and how Kubernetes changed the whole picture.

Chapter 2, Rancher and Kubernetes High-Level Architecture, discusses the different products that make up the Rancher ecosystem, including the Rancher server, RKE1/2, and k3s.

Chapter 3, Creating a Single Node Rancher, delves into a single node Rancher install, and the limitations of using it in addition to how to migrate to an HA setup.

Chapter 4, Creating an RKE and RKE2 Cluster, looks at RKE1 and 2, how they work, and the rules for architecting a solution using them.

Chapter 5, Deploying Rancher on a Hosted Kubernetes Cluster, covers how to install Rancher on a hosted Kubernetes cluster such as **Google Kubernetes Engine (GKE)**, Amazon **Elastic Container Service (EKS)** for Kubernetes, **Azure Kubernetes Service (AKS)**, or **Digital Ocean's Kubernetes Service (DOKS)**.

Chapter 6, Creating an RKE Cluster Using Rancher, demonstrates how to use Rancher to deploy a downstream RKE cluster along with the rules of architecting this type of cluster.

Chapter 7, Deploying a Hosted Cluster with Rancher, uses cloud providers to deploy hosted Kubernetes clusters using Rancher for managing the cluster over time.

Chapter 8, Importing an Externally Managed Cluster into Rancher, shows how to bring any kind of Kubernetes into Rancher and how Rancher can gain access to imported clusters.

Chapter 9, Cluster Configuration Backup and Recovery, describes how you back up an RKE1/2 cluster using etcd backups in addition to how to restore a cluster from a backup.

Chapter 10, Monitoring and Logging, explains how to use Rancher monitoring to deploy Prometheus, Grafana, and alert manager for monitoring the health of your cluster, in addition to how to use Banzai Cloud Logging to capture your pod logs.

Chapter 11, Bring Storage to Kubernetes Using Longhorn, explores why you would need persistent storage in your Kubernetes cluster and how Longhorn can solve this problem, including how Longhorn works and how to architect a solution using Longhorn.

Chapter 12, Security and Compliance Using OPA Gatekeeper, talks about how to enforce standards and security in your Kubernetes cluster using tools such as OPA Gatekeeper and NeuVector.

Chapter 13, Scaling in Kubernetes, delves into using **Horizontal Pod Autoscaler (HPA)**, **Vertical Pod Autoscaler (VPA)**, and Cluster Autoscaler to dynamically scale your environment.

Chapter 14, Load Balancer Configuration and SSL Certificates, explains how to publish applications hosted in Kubernetes to the outside world using ingresses and load balancers.

Chapter 15, Rancher and Kubernetes Troubleshooting, explains how to recover from some of the most common failures and issues, including how to detect and prevent them in the future along with how to reproduce these issues in a lab environment.

Chapter 16, Setting Up a CI/CD Pipeline and Image Registry, explains what a CI/CD pipeline is and how we can use it to deploy applications in a standardized and controlled process, along with deploying Drone CI and Harbor to support your applications.

Chapter 17, Creating and Using Helm Charts, describes Helm charts and how we can use Helm to package applications both from public and private and then how to publish them in a Kubernetes cluster.

Chapter 18, Resource Management, explains how to manage resources inside your Kubernetes cluster along with monitoring and controlling the cost of hosted applications in Kubernetes.

To get the most out of this book

This book assumes that you have a basic understanding of Linux server administration, including basic Bash scripting, installing packages, and automating tasks at scale. In addition, we are going to assume that you have a basic understanding of most cloud platforms, such as AWS, GCP, vSphere, or Azure.

Software/Hardware covered in the book	OS Requirements
kubectl v1.23+	Windows, macOS, and Linux (any).
Helm v3.8+	A Bash shell is preferred when running scripts.
Rancher v2.5 or v2.6	

It is also recommended to have a lab environment to deploy Rancher and RKE1/2 clusters. An important note: most cloud providers offer trail credits that should be more than enough to spin up small lab clusters.

Finally, Kubernetes and Rancher are ever-changing, so it is important to remember that version numbers will need to be changed as time moves on. So, it is highly recommended to review the release notes of each product and software before picking a version.

Download the color images

We also provide a PDF file that has color images of the screenshots/diagrams used in this book. You can download it here: `https://static.packt-cdn.com/downloads/9781803246093_ColorImages.pdf`.

Download the example code files

You can download the example code files for this book from GitHub at `https://github.com/PacktPublishing/Rancher-Deep-Dive`. In case there's an update to the code, it will be updated on the existing GitHub repository.

We also have other code bundles from our rich catalog of books and videos available at `https://github.com/PacktPublishing/`. Check them out!

Conventions used

There are a number of text conventions used throughout this book.

`Code in text`: Indicates code words in text, database table names, folder names, filenames, file extensions, pathnames, dummy URLs, user input, and Twitter handles. Here is an example: "It is pretty common to rename the local cluster to something more helpful, such as `rancher-prod` or `rancher-west`."

A block of code is set as follows:

```
helm repo add prometheus-community https://prometheus-
community.github.io/helm-charts
helm repo update
helm upgrade –install -n monitoring monitoring prometheus-
community/kube-prometheus-stack
```

Bold: Indicates a new term, an important word, or words that you see on screen. For example, words in menus or dialog boxes appear in the text like this. Here is an example: "With Rancher logging, it is recommended to deploy via the App Marketplace in the Rancher UI by going to **Cluster Tools** and clicking on the **Logging** app."

> **Tips or Important Notes**
> Appear like this.

Get in touch

Feedback from our readers is always welcome.

General feedback: If you have questions about any aspect of this book, mention the book title in the subject of your message and email us at customercare@packtpub.com.

Errata: Although we have taken every care to ensure the accuracy of our content, mistakes do happen. If you have found a mistake in this book, we would be grateful if you would report this to us. Please visit www.packtpub.com/support/errata, selecting your book, clicking on the Errata Submission Form link, and entering the details.

Piracy: If you come across any illegal copies of our works in any form on the internet, we would be grateful if you would provide us with the location address or website name. Please contact us at copyright@packt.com with a link to the material.

If you are interested in becoming an author: If there is a topic that you have expertise in and you are interested in either writing or contributing to a book, please visit authors.packtpub.com.

Share Your Thoughts

Once you've read *Rancher Deep Dive*, we'd love to hear your thoughts! Scan the QR code below to go straight to the Amazon review page for this book and share your feedback.

https://packt.link/r/180324609X

Your review is important to us and the tech community and will help us make sure we're delivering excellent quality content.

Part 1 –
Rancher Background
and Architecture
and Design

By the end of this part of the book, you should be able to architect a Rancher/Kubernetes solution that meets your application's needs.

This part of the book comprises the following chapters:

- *Chapter 1, Introduction to Rancher and Kubernetes*
- *Chapter 2, Rancher and Kubernetes High-Level Architecture*

1
Introduction to Rancher and Kubernetes

This chapter will focus on the history of Rancher and Kubernetes. We will cover what products and solutions came before Rancher and Kubernetes and how they have evolved into what they are today. At the end of this chapter, you should have a good understanding of the origins of Rancher and Kubernetes and their core concepts. This knowledge is essential for you to understand why Rancher and Kubernetes are what they are.

In this chapter, we're going to cover the following main topics:

- The history of Rancher Labs as a company
- Rancher's earlier products
- What is Rancher's core philosophy?
- Where did Kubernetes come from?
- What problem is Kubernetes trying to solve?
- Comparing Kubernetes with Docker Swarm and OpenShift

The history of Rancher Labs as a company

Rancher Labs was founded in 2014 in Cupertino, California, by Sheng Liang, Shannon Williams, Darren Shepherd, and Will Chanas. It was a container management platform before Kubernetes was a thing. From the beginning, Rancher was built on the idea that everything should be open source and community-driven. With Rancher being an open source company, all of the products they have released (including Rancher, RancherOS, RKE, K3s, Longhorn, and more) have been 100% open source. Rancher Lab's flagship product is Rancher. Primarily, Rancher is a management and orchestration platform for containerized workloads both on-premises and in the cloud. Rancher can do this because it has always been vendor-neutral; that is, Rancher can deploy a workload using physical hardware in your data center to cloud VMs in AWS to even a Raspberry Pi in a remote location.

Rancher's earlier products

When Rancher v1.0 was released in March of 2016, it only supported Docker Swarm and Rancher Cattle clusters. Docker Swarm was the early cluster orchestration tool that created a number of the core concepts that we still use today; for instance, the idea that an application should be defined as a group of containers that can be created and destroyed at any time. Another concept is that containers should live on a virtual network that is accessible on all nodes in a cluster. You can expose your containers via a load balancer which, in the case of Docker Swarm, is just a basic TCP load balancer.

While the Rancher server was being created, Rancher Labs was working on their own Docker cluster software, called Cattle, which is when Rancher went **General Availability (GA)** with the launch of Rancher v1.0. Cattle was designed to address the limitations of Docker Swarm, which spanned several different areas.

The first was networking. Originally, Docker Swarm's networking overlay was built on **Internet Protocol Security (IPsec)** with the idea that each node in the cluster would be assigned a subnet; that is, a class C subnet by default. Each node would create an IPsec tunnel to all other nodes in the cluster. It would then use basic routing rules to direct traffic to the node where that container was hosted. For example, let's say a container on node01 with an IP address of 192.168.11.22 wants to connect to another container hosted on node02 with an IP address of 192.168.12.33. The networking swarm uses basic Linux routing to route anything inside the 192.168.12.0/24 subnet to node02 over the IPsec tunnel. This core concept is still in use today by the majority of Kubernetes's CNI providers. The main issue is in managing the health of these tunnels over time and dealing with compatibility issues between the nodes. Cattle addressed this issue by moving IPsec into a container and then wrapping a management layer to handle the creation, deletion, and monitoring of the tunnels.

The second main issue was to do with load balancing. With Docker Swarm, we were limited to very basic TCP/layer4 load balancing. We didn't have sessions, SSL, or connection management. This is because load balancing was all done by iptable rules. Cattle addressed this issue by deploying HAProxy on all nodes in the cluster. Following this, Cattle used a custom container, called `rancher-metadata`, to dynamically build HAProxy's config every time a container was created or deleted.

The third issue was storage. With Docker Swarm, there weren't any storage options outside bind mounting to a host filesystem. This meant that you had to create a clustered filesystem or shared network and then manually map them to all of your Docker hosts. Cattle addressed this by creating `rancher-nfs`, which is a tool that can mount NFS shares inside a container and create a bind mount. As Rancher went on, other storage providers were added, such as AWS and VMware.

Then, as time moved forward at Rancher, the next giant leap was when authentication providers were added, because Rancher provides access to the clusters that Rancher manages by integrating external authentication providers such as Active Directory, LDAP, and GitHub. This is unique to Rancher, as Kubernetes still doesn't integrate very well with external authentication providers.

What is Rancher's core philosophy?

Rancher is built around several core design principles:

- **Open source**: All code, components, and services that make up Rancher or come with Rancher must be open source. Because of this, Rancher has a large community built around it, with users providing feedback, documentation, and contributing code.

- **No lock-ins**: Rancher is designed with no vendor lock-in, including being locked inside Rancher. With containerization evolving so quickly, Rancher needs to enable users to change technologies with as little impact as possible. A core requirement of all products and solutions that Rancher provides is that they can be used with or without the Rancher server. An example of this is Longhorn; there are zero dependencies between Rancher and Longhorn. This means that at any time, a user can uninstall one without impacting the other. This includes the ability to uninstall Rancher without losing your clusters. Rancher does this by having a process in place for a user to take over the management of a cluster directly and kick Rancher out of the picture.

- **Everything is a Kubernetes object**: With the release of Rancher v2.0, which was released in May 2018, after approximately a year and a half of work, Rancher made the switch from storing all of its resources and configurations inside a MySQL database to storing everything as a Kubernetes object. This is done by using custom resources (or CRDs) in Kubernetes. For example, let's consider that the definition of a cluster in Rancher is stored as a **Custom Resource Definition (CRD)** called `clusters.management.cattle.io` and the same with nodes as an object under `nodes.management.cattle.io`, which is scoped to a namespace with the cluster ID. Because of this, users and applications can directly query Rancher objects without needing to talk to Rancher's API. The reason for this change was mainly to do with scalability. With Cattle and MySQL, all cluster-related tasks had to go back to the Rancher server. So, as you scaled up the size of your cluster and the number of clusters, you had to scale up the Rancher server, too. This resulted in customers hitting issues such as "task storms" where a single node rebooting in a cluster causes a flood of requests that are sent to the Rancher server, which, in turn, causes other tasks to timeout, which then causes more requests. In the end, the only thing you can do is to shut everything down and slowly bring it back up.

- **Everything is stateless**: Because everything is a Kubernetes object, there is no need for a database for Rancher. All Rancher pods are stateless, meaning they can be destroyed at any time for any reason. Additionally, Rancher can rely on Kubernetes controllers to simply spin up new pods without needing Rancher to do anything.

- **Controller model**: All Rancher services are designed around the Kubernetes controller model. A control loop is always running, watching the current state, and comparing it to the desired state. And if any differences are found, it applies the application logic to make the current state match the desired state. Alongside this, it uses the same leader election process with Kubernetes core components. This ensures there is only one source of truth and ensures certain controllers will handle failing over after a failure.

Where did Kubernetes come from?

The name **Kubernetes** originates from Greek, meaning **helmsman** or **pilot**. Kubernetes is abbreviated to **k8s** due to the number of letters between the **K** and **S**. Initially, engineers created Kubernetes at Google from an internal project called Borg. Google's Borg system is a cluster manager that was designed to run Google's internal applications. These applications are made up of tens of thousands of microservices hosted on clusters worldwide, with each cluster being made up of tens of thousands of machines. Borg provided three main benefits. The first benefit was the abstraction of resource and failure management, so application designers could focus on application development. The second benefit was its high reliability and availability by design. All parts of Borg were designed, from the beginning, to be highly available. This was done by making applications stateless. This was done so that any component could be destroyed at any time for any reason without impacting availability and, at the same time, could be scaled horizontally to hundreds of instances across clusters. The third benefit was an effective workload; Borg was designed to have a minimal overhead on the compute resources being managed.

Kubernetes can be traced directly back to Borg, as many of the developers at Google that worked on Kubernetes were formerly developers on the Borg project. Because of this, many of its core concepts were incorporated into Kubernetes, with the only real difference being that Borg was custom-made for Google, and its requirements for Kubernetes need to be more generalized and flexible. However, there are four main features that have been derived from Borg:

- **Pods**: A pod is the smallest unit of scheduling in Kubernetes. This object can include one or more containers, with each container in the pods sharing resources such as an IP address, volumes, and other local resources. One of the main design principles is that a pod should be disposable and shouldn't change after creation. Another primary principle is that all application configurations should be handled at the pod level. For example, a database connection string should be defined as part of the pod's definition instead of the application code. This is done so that any changes to the configuration of an application won't require the code to be recompiled and redeployed. Additionally, the pod takes the concept of paired processes from Borg, with the classic example being a log collector. This is because, typically, your container should only have one primary process running inside it.

An example of this is a web server: the server creates logs, but how do you ship those logs to a log server like Splunk? One option is to add a custom agent to your application pod which is easy. But now that you manage more than one process inside a container, you'll have duplicate code in your environment, and most importantly, you now have to do error handling for both your main application and this additional logging agent. This is where sidecars come into play and allow you to bolt containers together inside a pod in a repeatable and consistent manner.

- **Services**: One of Borg's primary roles was the life cycle management of applications and pods. Because of this, the pod name and IP address are ephemeral and can change at any time for any reason. So, the concept of a service was created as an abstraction level wherein you can define a service object that references a pod or pods by using labels. Kubernetes will then handle the mapping of the service records to its pods. These benefits load balance the traffic for a service among the pods that make up that service. Service records allow Kubernetes to add and remove pods without disrupting the applications because the service to pod mapping can simply be changed without the requesting client being aware.

- **Labels**: Because Borg was designed to manage containers at scale, things such as a hostname were impractical for mapping a pod to its running application. The idea was that if you define a set of labels for your application, those can be added to its pods, allowing Kubernetes to track instances at scale. Labels are arbitrary key-value pairs that can be assigned to any Kubernetes resource, including pods, services, nodes, and more. One example set is `"application=web_frontend,"` `"environment=production,"` `"department=marketing"`. Note that each of these keys is a different label selector rule that can create a service record. This has the side benefit of making the reporting and tracking of usage much easier.

- **Every pod has an IP**: When Borg was created, all of the containers on a host would share the host's IP address and then use different ports for each container. This allowed Borg to use a standard IP network. However, this created a burden on infrastructure and application teams, as Borg needed to schedule ports for containers. This required applications to have a set of predefined ports that would be needed for their container.

What problem is Kubernetes trying to solve?

Kubernetes was designed to solve several problems. The primary areas are as follows:

- **Availability**: Everyone, from the application owner to the developers, to the end users, has come to expect 24x7x365 uptime, with work outages and downtime being a four-letter word in IT. With containerization and microservices, this bar has only gotten higher. Kubernetes addresses this issue by scheduling containers across nodes and using the desired state versus the actual state. The idea is that any failures are just a change in the actual state that triggers the controllers to schedule pods until the actual state matches the desired state.

- **CI/CD**: Traditional development was carried out using monolithic developments, with a few significant releases per year. This required a ton of developers working for months to test their releases and build a ton of manual processes to deploy their applications. Kubernetes addresses this issue by being driven by the desired state and config file. This means implementing a DevOps workflow that allows developers to automate steps and continuously integrate, test, and deploy code. All of this will enable teams to fail fast and fix fast.

- **Efficiency**: Traditional IT was a black hole that companies threw money into. One of the reasons behind this was high availability. For one application, you would need at least two servers for each component of your production application. Also, you would require additional servers for each of your lower environments (such as DEV, QAS, Test, and more). Today, companies want to be as efficient with their IT spending as possible. Kubernetes addresses this need by making spinning up environments very easy. With CI/CD, you can simply create a new namespace, deploy your application, run whatever tests you want, and then tear down the namespace to reclaim its resources.

- **Automate scaling**: Traditionally, you would design and build your environment around your peak workload. For instance, let's say your application is mainly busy during business hours and is idle during off-peak hours. You are wasting money because you pay the same amount for your compute resources at 100% and 1%. However, traditionally, it would take days or even weeks to spin up a new server, install your application, config it, and, finally, update the load balancer. This made it impossible to scale up and down rapidly. So, some companies just decided to scale up and stay there. Kubernetes addresses this issue by making it easy to scale up or down, as it just involves a simple change to the desired state.

Let's say that an application currently has two web servers, and you want to add a pod to handle the load. Just change the number of replicas to three because the current state doesn't match the desired state. The controllers kick up and start spinning up a new pod. This can be automated using Kubernetes' built-in **horizontal pod autoscaler (HPA)**, which uses several metrics ranging from simple metrics such as CPU and memory to custom metrics such as overall application response times. Additionally, Kubernetes can use its **vertical pod autoscaler (VPA)** to automatically tune your CPU and memory limits over time. Following this, Kubernetes can use node scaling to dynamically add and remove nodes to your clusters as resources are required. This means your application might have 10 pods with 10 worker nodes during the day, but it might drop to only 1 pod with 1 worker node after hours. This means you can save the cost of 9 nodes for 16 hours per day plus the weekends; all of this without your application having to do anything.

Comparing Kubernetes with Docker Swarm and OpenShift

We will compare both of these in the following section.

Kubernetes versus Docker Swarm

Kubernetes and Docker Swarm are open source container orchestration platforms that have several identical core functions but significant differences.

Scalability

Kubernetes is a complex system with several components that all need to work together to make the cluster operate, making it more challenging to set up and administrate. Kubernetes requires you to manage a database (`etcd`), including taking backups and creating SSL certificates for all of the different components.

Docker Swarm is far simpler, with everything just being included in Docker. All you need to do is create a manager and join nodes to the swarm. However, because everything is baked-in, you don't get the higher-level features such as autoscaling, node provisioning, and more.

Networking

Kubernetes uses a flat network model with all pods sharing a large network subnet and another network for creating services. Additionally, Kubernetes allows you to customize and change network providers. For example, if you don't like a particular canal, or can't do network-level encryption, you can switch to another provider, such as Weave, which can do network encryption.

Docker Swarm networking is fundamental. By default, Docker Swarm creates IPsec tunnels between all nodes in the cluster using IPsec for the encryption. This speed can be good because modern CPUs provide hardware acceleration for AES; however, you can still take a performance hit depending on your hardware and workload. Additionally, with Docker Swarm, you can't switch network providers as you only get what is provided.

Application deployment

Kubernetes uses YAML and its API to enable users to define applications and their resources. Because of this, there are tools such as Helm that allow application owners to define their application in a templatized format, making it very easy for applications to be published in a user-friendly format called **Helm charts**.

Docker Swarm is built on the Docker CLI with a minimal API for management. The only package management tool is Docker Compose, which hasn't been widely adopted due to its limited customization and the high degree of manual work required to deploy it.

High availability

Kubernetes has been built from the ground up to be highly available and to have the ability to handle a range of failures, including pods detecting unhealthy pods using advanced features such as running commands inside the pods to verify their health. This includes all of the management components such as Kube-scheduler, Kube-apiserver, and more. Each of these components is designed to be stateless with built-in leader election and failover management.

Docker Swarm is highly available mainly by its ability to clone services between nodes, with the Swarm manager nodes being in an active-standby configuration in the case of a failure.

Load balancing

Kubernetes pods can be exposed using superficial layer 4 (TCP/UDP mode) load balancing services. Then, for external access, Kubernetes has two options. The first is node-port, which acts as a simple method of port-forwarding from the node's IP address to an internal service record. The second is for more complex applications, where Kubernetes can use an ingress controller to provide layer 7 (HTTP/HTTPS mode) load balancing, routing, and SSL management.

Docker Swarm load balancing is DNS-based, meaning Swarm uses round-robin DNS to distribute incoming requests between containers. Because of this, Docker Swarm is limited to layer 4 only, with no option to use any of the higher-level features such as SSL and host-based routing.

Management

Kubernetes provides several tools in which to manage the cluster and its applications, including `kubectl` for command-line access and even a web UI via the Kubernetes dashboard service. It even offers higher-level UIs such as Rancher and Lens. This is because Kubernetes is built around a REST API that is highly flexible. This means that applications and users can easily integrate their tools into Kubernetes.

Docker Swarm doesn't offer a built-in dashboard. There are some third-party dashboards such as **Swarmpit**, but there hasn't been very much adoption around these tools and very little standardization.

Security

Kubernetes provides a built-in RBAC model allowing fine-grained control for Kubernetes resources. For example, you can grant pod permission to just one secret with another pod being given access to all secrets in a namespace. This is because Kubernetes authorization is built on SSL certifications and tokens for authentication. This allows Kubernetes to simply pass the certificate and token as a file mounted inside a pod. This makes it straightforward for applications to gain access to the Kubernetes API.

The Docker Swarm security model is primarily network-based using TLS (mTLS) and is missing many fine-grained controls and integrations, with Docker Swarm only having the built-in roles of none, view only, restricted control, scheduler, and full control. This is because the access model for Docker Swarm was built for cluster administration and not application integration. In addition to this, originally, the Docker API only supported basic authentication.

Kubernetes versus OpenShift

Both Kubernetes and OpenShift share a lot of features and architectures. Both follow the same core design practices, but they differ in terms of how they are executed.

Networking

Kubernetes lacks a built-in networking solution and relies on third-party plug-ins such as canal, flannel, and Weave to provide networking for the cluster.

OpenShift provides a built-in network solution called **Open vSwitch**. This is a VXLAN--based software-defined network stack that can easily be integrated into RedHat's other products. There is some support for third-party network plugins, but they are limited and much harder to support.

Application deployment

Kubernetes takes the approach of being as flexible as possible when deploying applications to the cluster, allowing users to deploy any Linux distribution they choose, including supporting Windows-based images and nodes. This is because Kubernetes is vendor-agnostic.

OpenShift takes the approach of standardizing the whole stack on RedHat products such as RHEL for the node's operating system. Technically, there is little to nothing to stop OpenShift from running on other Linux distributions such as Ubuntu. Additionally, Openshift puts limits on the types of container images that are allowed to run inside the cluster. Again, technically, there isn't much preventing a user from deploying an Ubuntu image on the Openshift cluster, but they will most likely run into issues around supportably.

Security

Kubernetes had a built-in tool for pod-level security called **Pod Security Policies** (**PSPs**). PSPs were used to enforce limits on pods such as blocking a pod from running as root or binding to a host's filesystem. PSPs were deprecated in v1.21 due to several limitations of the tool. Now, PSPs are being replaced by a third-party tool called **OPA Gatekeeper**, which allows all of the same security rules but with a different enforcement model.

OpenShift has a much stricter security mindset, with the option to be secure as a default, and it doesn't require cluster hardening like Kubernetes.

Summary

In this chapter, we learned about Rancher's history and how it got its start. Following this, we went over Rancher's core philosophy and how it was designed around Kubernetes. Then, we covered where Kubernetes got its start and its core philosophy. We then dived into what the core problems are that Kubernetes is trying to solve. Finally, we examined the pros and cons of Kubernetes, Docker Swarm, and OpenShift.

In the next chapter, we will cover the high-level architecture and processes of Rancher and its products, including RKE, K3s, and RancherD.

2
Rancher and Kubernetes High-Level Architecture

This chapter will cover the high-level processes of **Rancher**, **Rancher Kubernetes Engine (RKE)**, **RKE2** (also known as **RKE Government**), **K3s**, and **RancherD**. We will discuss the core design philosophy of each of these products and explore the ways in which they are different. We'll dive into Rancher's high-level architecture and see how Rancher server pods communicate with downstream clusters using the Cattle agents, which include both the Cattle-cluster-agent and the Cattle-node-agent. We'll also look at how the Rancher server uses RKE and how Rancher-machine provisions downstream nodes and Kubernetes (**K8s**) clusters. After that, we'll cover the high-level architecture of K8s, including **kube-api-server**, **kube-controller-manager**, and **kube-scheduler**. We'll also discuss how each of these components maintains the state of the cluster. Finally, we'll examine how an end user can change the desired state and how the controllers can update the current state.

In this chapter, we're going to cover the following main topics:

- What is the Rancher server?

- What are RKE and RKE2?

- What is K3s (five less than K8s)?

- What is RancherD?

- What controllers run inside the Rancher server pods?

- What does the Cattle agent do?

- How does Rancher provision nodes and clusters?

- What are kube-apiserver, kube-controller-manager, kube-scheduler, etcd, and kubelet?

- How do the current state and the desired state work?

What is the Rancher server?

The **Rancher server** forms the core of the Rancher ecosystem, and it contains almost everything needed by any other component, product, or tool depending on or connecting to the Rancher server via the Rancher API. The *Rancher server* is usually shortened to just *Rancher*, and in this section, when I say *Rancher*, I will be talking about the *Rancher server*.

The heart of Rancher is its API. The **Rancher API** is built on a custom API framework called **Norman** that acts as a translation layer between the Rancher API and the K8s API. Everything in Rancher uses the Rancher or K8s API to communicate. This includes the Rancher **user interface** (**UI**), which is 100% API-driven.

So, how do you connect to the Rancher API? The Rancher API is a standard **RESTful API**. This means that a request flows from an external HTTP or TCP load balancer into the ingress controller, and then the request is routed to one of the Rancher server pods. Norman then translates the request into a K8s request, which then calls a `CustomResource` object. Of course, because everything is being stored in a `CustomResource` object in K8s, the Rancher request flow is stateless and doesn't require session persistence. Finally, once the `CustomResource` object is created, changed, or deleted, the controller for the object type will take over and process that request. We'll go deeper into the different controllers later in this chapter.

What are RKE and RKE2?

What do I need, RKE or RKE2? Traditionally, when building a K8s cluster, you would need to carry out several steps. First, you'd need to generate a root **CA key** as well as the certificates for the different K8s components and push them out to every server that was part of the cluster. Second, you'd then install/configure **etcd**, and this would include setting up the **systemd** service on your management nodes. Next, you would need to bootstrap the etcd cluster and verify that all etcd nodes were communicating and replicating correctly. At this point, you would install kube-apiserver and connect it back to your etcd cluster. Finally, you would need to install kube-controller-manager and kube-scheduler and connect them back to the kube-apiserver objects. If you wanted to bring up the control plane for your cluster, even more steps would be needed to join your worker nodes to the cluster.

This process is called *K8s the hard way*, and it's called that for a reason, as this process can be very complicated and can change over time. And in the early days of K8s, this was the only way to create K8s clusters. Because of this, users needed to make large scripts or **Ansible Playbooks** to create their K8s clusters. These scripts would need lots of care and feeding to get up and running, with even more work required to keep them working as K8s continually changed.

Rancher saw this issue and knew that for K8s to become mainstream, it needed to be *crazy easy* to build clusters for both end users and the Rancher server. Initially, in the Rancher v1.6 days, Rancher would build K8s clusters on its container clustering software called **Cattle**. Because of this, everything needed had to run as a container, and this was the starting point of RKE.

So, what is RKE?

RKE is Rancher's cluster orchestration tool for creating and managing **Cloud Native Computing Foundation** (**CNCF**)-certified K8s clusters on a wide range of operating systems with a range of configurations. The core concept of RKE is that everything that makes up the K8s cluster should run entirely within **Docker** containers. Because of this, RKE doesn't care what operating system it's deployed on, as long as it's within a Docker container. This is because RKE is not installing binaries on the host, configuring services, or anything similar to this.

How does RKE work?

RKE is a **Golang** application that runs on most **Linux/Unix**-based systems. When a user wants to create a K8s cluster using RKE, they must first define the cluster using a file called `cluster.yml` (see *Figure 2.1*). RKE then uses that configuration file to create all of the containers needed to start the cluster, that is, etcd, kube-apiserver, kube-controller-manager, kube-scheduler, and kubelet. Please see the *How does Rancher provision nodes and clusters?* section in this chapter for further details on nodes and clusters.

```
! cluster.yaml
 1    nodes:
 2      - address: 172.27.7.21
 3        user: root
 4        hostname_override: a1ubrancherl01
 5        internal_address: 172.27.7.21
 6        role: [controlplane,worker,etcd]
 7      - address: 172.27.7.22
 8        user: root
 9        hostname_override: a1ubrancherl02
10        internal_address: 172.27.7.22
11        role: [controlplane,worker,etcd]
12      - address: 172.27.7.23
13        user: root
14        hostname_override: a1ubrancherl03
15        internal_address: 172.27.7.23
16        role: [controlplane,worker,etcd]
17
18    services:
19      etcd:
20        backup_config:
21          enabled: true      # enables recurring etcd snapshots
22          interval_hours: 12 # time increment between snapshots
23          retention: 6       # time in days before snapshot purge
24          s3backupconfig:
25            access_key: "ABCDEFGHIJKLMNPO..."
26            secret_key:  "123456789abcdefghijklmpo..."
27            bucket_name: "etcd-backups"
28            folder: "Cluster-Name-Here"
29            endpoint: "s3.us-west-1.wasabisys.com"
30            region: "us-west-1"
31
32    dns:
33      provider: coredns
34      upstreamnameservers:
35      - 172.27.2.23
36      - 172.27.2.24
```

Figure 2.1 – A code snippet from the cluster.yaml file

What is RKE2?

RKE2 is Rancher's next-generation K8s solution and is also known as RKE Government. RKE2 was designed to update and address some of the shortfalls of RKE, and it also brought the *crazy easy* setup methods from K3s to improve its functionality. RKE2 is also a fully CNCF-certified K8s distribution. But RKE2 was created specifically for Rancher's US federal government and their customers, as they have several special requirements for their K8s use – the first being that it is highly secure by default.

When setting up RKE, you must follow a hardening guide and take several manual steps to comply with **CIS benchmarks**. RKE2, on the other hand, is designed to be secure with little to no action required by the cluster administrator. US federal customers need their K8s clusters to be **FIPS-enabled** (**FIPS** stands for the United States **Federal Information Processing Standards**). Also, because RKE2 is built on K3s, it inherits a number of its features – the first being the support of **ARM64**-based systems. So, you could set up RKE2 on a **Raspberry Pi** if you chose to. This provides users with the flexibility to mix and match ARM64 and **AMD64** nodes in the same cluster and that means customers can run workloads such as multiple arch builds using the **Drone Continuous Integration (CI)** platform inside their cluster. This also provides support for low-power and cost-effective ARM64 nodes.

The second feature inherited from K3s is **self-bootstrapping**. In RKE, you would need to define the cluster as YAML and then use the RKE binary to try to create and manage the cluster. But with RKE2, once the first node has been created, all of the other nodes simply join the cluster using a registration endpoint running on the master nodes. Note that this does require an external load balancer or a round-robin DNS record to be successful. Because RKE2 can manage itself, it allows you to do very cool tasks, such as defining a K8s upgrade with kubectl and just letting the cluster take care of it for you.

The third feature that RKE2 inherited from K3s was built-in **Helm** support. This is because RKE2 was built with Rancher's **fleet** feature in mind, where all of the cluster services (such as cert-manager, **Open Policy Agent (OPA) Gatekeeper**, and more) should be deployed in an automated process using Helm. But the most significant change from RKE in RKE2 was the move from Docker to **containerd**. With RKE, you must have Docker installed on all nodes before RKE can manage them. This is because the core K8s components like etcd and kube-apiserver are static containers that are deployed outside the K8s cluster. RKE2 leverages what are known as **static pods**. These are unique pods that are managed directly by kubelet and not by kube-controller-manager or kube-scheduler. Because these pods don't require the K8s cluster to be up and running in order to start, the core K8s components such as etcd and kube-apiserver can just be pods – just like any other application in the cluster. This means that if you run `kubectl -n kube-system get pods`, you can see your etcd containers, and you can even open a shell to them or capture logs, just like you would with any other pod.

Last but not the least, the most crucial feature of RKE2 is that it's fully open source with no paywall – just like every other Rancher product.

What is K3s (five less than K8s)?

K3s is a fully CNCF-certified K8s distribution. This means that in K3s, the YAML you would deploy is just a standard K8s cluster deployed in a K3s cluster. K3s was created because traditional K8s clusters – or even RKE clusters – were designed to run at scale, meaning that they would require three etcd nodes, two control plane nodes, and three or more worker nodes for a standard configuration. In this case, the minimum size for nodes would be around four cores, with 8 gigabits of RAM for the etcd objects and control plane nodes, with the worker nodes having two cores and 4 gigabits of RAM. These would just be the background requirements when talking about K8s clusters at the scale of an IE 50 node cluster, with the worker nodes having 64 cores and 512 GB of RAM. But when you start looking at deploying K8s at the edge, where physical space, power, and compute resources are all at a premium, standard K8s and RKE are just too big. So, the question is: *how do we shrink K8s?*

K3s was based on the following core principles: no legacy code, duplicate code, or extras. With RKE and other standard K8s distributions, each component exists as its separate code with its own runtime. At Rancher, they asked themselves a question:

Hey, there is a lot of duplicate code running here. What if we just merged kube-apiserver, kube-controller-manager, kube-scheduler, and kubelet into a single binary?

And that was how K3s was born. K3s only has *master* and *worker* nodes, with the master node running all of the core components. The next big breakthrough was what they did with etcd. The etcd object is not small. It eats memory like it's going out of style and doesn't play nice when it's in a cluster of one. This is where **kind** comes into the picture.

The kind database adapter makes standard **SQL** databases such as **SQLite3**, **MySQL**, or **Postgres** look like an etcd database. So, as far as kube-apiserver knows, it's talking to an etcd cluster. The CPU and memory footprint is much smaller because you can run a database like SQLite3 in place of etcd. It is important to note that Rancher does not customize any of the standard K8s libraries in the core components. This allows K3s to stay up to date with upstream K8s. The next big area of saving in K3s was in-tree storage drivers and cloud providers. Upstream K8s has several storage drivers built into the core components. For example, RKE has storage drivers to allow K8s to connect to the **AWS** API and use **Amazon EBS** volumes to provide storage directly to pods. This is great if you are running in AWS, but if you are running in **VMware** then this code is just wasting resources. It's the same the other way round, with VMware's **vSphere** having a storage provider for mounting **Virtual Machine Disks (VMDKs)** to nodes. The idea was that most of these storage and cloud providers are not used. For example, if I'm running a cluster on Amazon, why do I need libraries and tools for Azure? Plus there are out-of-tree alternatives that can be deployed as pods instead of being baked in. Also, most of the major storage providers are moving to out-of-tree provisioning anyway. So, K3s removes them. This eliminates a significant overhead. Because of all these optimizations, K3s clusters can fit on a 40 MB binary file and run on a node with only 512 MB of RAM.

The other significant change in K3s to K8s was the idea that it should be *crazy easy* to spin up a K3s cluster. For example, creating a single-node K3s cluster only requires the `curl -sfL https://get.k3s.io | sh -` command to run, with the only dependency being that it's within a Linux ARM64 or AMD64 operating system with `curl` installed. Because of this ease of use, K3s is frequently deployed in single-node clusters where a user wants to use all of the management tools that K8s provides but without the scale. For example, a developer might spin up a K3s cluster on their laptop using a **virtual machine (VM)** to deploy their application just as they would in their production K8s cluster.

Another great use case for K3s is deploying to a retail environment where you might have hundreds or even thousands of locations all over the country (or world) and have a single K3s node running on a small PC at each location. K3s helps in this situation because it is so tiny, so common problems such as slow internet connections are not that big of a problem, and also K3s can keep running even if it loses its connection back to a corporate data center. An even more extraordinary kind of deployment for K3s is a wind turbine in the middle of nowhere with only a **Long-Term Evolution (LTE)** connection for internet access. These are the kinds of deployments K3s was built for.

What is RancherD?

RancherD is a marriage between Rancher and K3s/RKE2. Initially, when you wanted to install Rancher, you would first be required to create a K8s cluster using RKE, and then you would be required to install Rancher by using Helm on the RKE cluster. RancherD takes a lot of the ideas from K3s and RKE2 but is built for Rancher specifically. In a similar vein to K3s and RKE2, RancherD is a single binary that can be easily installed using the `curl -sfL https://get.rancher.io | sh` – command on a Linux AMD64 or ARM64 server. This binary is similar to RKE2 but has been optimized to host the Rancher server. RancherD also includes extra tools to support the Rancher server application. For example, the `rancherd reset-admin` command will reset the administrator password for the Rancher server.

To change this password with a normal RKE or RKE2 cluster, you would need to find the Rancher server pod and open a shell into the container. Then you would run the `reset-admin` command. The main idea behind RancherD is to make it very easy to manage Rancher. It does this by using the RKE2 Helm operator to handle deploying the Rancher server pods. And because it uses the same Helm chart that you would use in an RKE cluster, all of the customization options are still available (the best feature being the ease of management of SSL certificates). In a standard Rancher server deployment, you must configure and manage the SSL certificates that support the Rancher API. This can be a pain when using internally signed certificates, as you need to edit a secret inside the cluster, which can be difficult for new K8s users. RancherD solves this problem by simply having the user drop the certificate files into `/etc/rancher/ssl/` on one of the RancherD nodes, at which point it takes over the process and handles the update for you. Most of the time, you'll use RancherD when you don't want to manage the K8s cluster that hosts Rancher but can't use a hosted K8s option such as **AWS EKS**, **Azure AKS**, or **Google GKE**, or if you need to manage a large number of different Rancher installations. For example, if you were running a hosted environment where you were providing *Rancher as a service*, you might use RancherD to simplify the management of these clusters at scale.

What controllers run inside the Rancher server pods?

Rancher is made of a set of pods – three pods by default – that run in a K8s cluster. These pods can service requests from the ingress controller – **ingress-nginx** by default – using Norman to translate the Rancher API requests into the K8s API requests to access the custom resource objects that Rancher uses. But the Rancher server pods also host several controllers, with the primary controllers as follows:

- **Rancher Authentication Controller**: This controller is responsible for managing the users and permissions in Rancher and the downstream clusters that Rancher manages. This controller is required for Rancher to manage and synchronize a user's/group's permissions to the downstream K8s clusters. Rancher needs to provide this service because – by default – K8s doesn't have integrations with external authentication providers such as **GitHub** or **Okta**, as most of the current external authentication providers are built on top of **webhooks,** for example, **Lightweight Directory Access Protocol (LDAP)**. By default, kube-apiserver doesn't know or understand what LDAP is. If you want to use LDAP as your external authentication provider, you are required to stand up a Go webhook service to listen for `TokenReview` requests from K8s. This service then calls the LDAP server and validates the username and password. If it passes the validation, the service will respond with a `200 OK` response, with all other response codes representing a failed authentication. Because of this, the setup process can be very complex and unreliable. As a result, Rancher chose the approach of building its controller to validate the username and password with external authentication providers such as LDAP, AD, GitHub, Okta, and more. Once the user has been validated, Rancher will give the user a bearer token that they can use to authenticate directly to the K8s API. The controller does this by creating matching service accounts, roles, and role bindings on the downstream clusters ahead of time. The controller also provides some higher-level controls via the Rancher concept of *projects*. You can define a group of namespaces called a *project* and manage permissions at the project level instead of managing them only at the cluster or namespace level.

- **Rancher Catalog Controller**: This controller is responsible for managing the catalogs inside Rancher. But what is a *catalog*? Rancher uses the concept of *catalogs* that are repositories for Helm charts. Rancher calls them catalogs because they give users a catalog of applications to deploy to their cluster. The default catalogs have several great applications including **WordPress**, **MySQL**, **Rancher Longhorn**, the **Datadog Cluster Agent**, and many more. All of these catalogs come together in Rancher under what is called the **Apps and Marketplace** feature, allowing users to deploy Helm-based applications to your cluster. You can also add your repository as a catalog, which is excellent for DevOps teams that want to provide their application teams with standardized toolsets. For example, if an application team wanted their own monitoring systems, they could modify and tune the system based on their preferences. You might create a **Prometheus** Helm chart with a basic configuration that the application team could simply click to deploy on their cluster.

Another great example of the use of a Helm chart is for environments where there might be one primary application – for example, the core application for the business that other teams must write their applications to connect to and work with. You can create a Helm chart for the monolithic application that an application team can quickly spin up to do integration testing with and then spin down to save costs. In this case, all of this would be managed by the Rancher catalog controller, which handles caching the catalogs (for speed reasons) and for legacy applications, deploying the application, that is, running the `helm install` command inside the Rancher server pod.

But with Rancher v2.6, this process has been moved over to Fleet to handle the deployment process, where Fleet will spin up a Helm operator pod on the downstream cluster and run the Helm commands. Note that this is excellent for speed, scalability, and flexibility, as Fleet gives you many options for customizing the Helm chart and is part of Rancher's DevOps at scale. Fleet is designed to manage up to a million clusters at once. It is important to note that the Rancher catalog controller only runs on the Rancher leader pod. If that is deleted or lost, the cache will need to be rebuilt, but this process usually only takes a few minutes. This controller also synchronizes the cache on a schedule (6 hours by default), but the syncing process can be forced to update, with this process running the `helm repo update`... command but as Go code instead.

- **Rancher Cluster Controller**: This controller is responsible for managing any RKE cluster that Rancher has provisioned. This includes custom clusters and Rancher-deployed clusters with this controller being built on top of the Go code that makes up RKE. This controller manages your `cluster.yaml` and `cluster.rkestate` files for you and handles running `rke up` from inside the Rancher leader pod. Note that when troubleshooting the cluster if it is stuck when updating status issues, this is the controller we'll look at the most. Please see the *How does Rancher provision nodes and clusters?* section later in this chapter for more details on how this controller works.

- **Rancher Node Controller**: This controller is responsible for managing the Rancher-provisioned nodes. This controller is only used for Rancher-provisioned clusters on virtualized platforms such as **Amazon EC2**, **Google GCP**, VMware vSphere, and so on. This controller is built on top of the Go code that makes up a Rancher machine, which in turn is built on top of **Docker Machine**. This controller's main function is to handle the creation and deletion of VMs in a node pool. Please see the *How does Rancher provision nodes and clusters?* section later in this chapter for more details about this process. Note, when troubleshooting node provisioning errors such as SSH timeout or configuration validation errors, this is the controller we'll look at the most.

- **Rancher Pipeline Controller**: This controller manages Rancher's built-in **CI/CD** pipeline system, which is built on top of **Jenkins**. This controller is mostly used as a wrapper for handling the creation and deployment of Jenkins on the cluster along with handling the configuration of webhooks and code repositories such as GitHub, **GitLab**, and **Bitbucket**. The heavy lifting of running jobs is done by Jenkins, but the Rancher UI integrations allow users to manage and review their pipelines without going into the Jenkins UI. Rancher also provides Jenkins with access to the K8s cluster to deploy workloads. The controller handles querying the code repository and using the `rancher-pipelines.yml` file to configure the pipeline.

> **Note**
>
> As of Rancher v2.5, Git-based deployment pipelines are now recommended to handle Rancher Continuous Delivery, powered by Fleet. As a result, this controller was removed in Rancher v2.6.

- **Rancher Monitoring Controller**: This controller manages the integration between the monitoring systems in the Rancher UI and the rancher-monitoring application, which is built on top of **Prometheus**, **Grafana**, **Alertmanager**, **Prometheus Operator**, and **Prometheus Adapter**. The rancher-monitoring application allows you to monitor the state of your cluster and its nodes, along with the K8s components (etcd, kube-apiserver, and so on) and your application deployments. Because of this, you can create alerts based on metrics collected by Prometheus, which can be sent to alert services such as **Slack**, **PagerDuty**, email, and more. Also, because the rancher-monitoring application deploys the custom metrics API adapter from Prometheus, you can use custom metrics such as application response times or work queue depths for your **Horizontal Pod Autoscaler (HPA)** to scale up and down your applications using metrics outside of CPU and memory usage. This controller primarily handles syncing the settings and configurations between Rancher and the rancher-monitoring application. Note that in Rancher v2.5 and the rancher-monitoring application v2 this process is changing to use a `vanilla` upstream Prometheus monitoring stack deployment instead of a Rancher customized Prometheus deployment.

- **Rancher Logging Controller**: This controller manages the integration between the logging systems in the Rancher UI and the **Banzai Cloud Logging** operator. This controller is a translation layer that allows users to define logging Flows and ClusterFlows via the Rancher UI, which get translated into **Custom Resource Definition (CRD)** objects that the Banzai Cloud Logging operator uses for configuring both applications and cluster-level logging. Before Rancher v2.5, Rancher used several different logging providers, including **Syslog**, **Splunk**, **Apache Kafka**, and **Fluentd**. However, this was a custom Rancher solution and wasn't very flexible. So, as part of the logging v2 migration, everything was moved over to Banzai to be better aligned with where the industry is heading to.

- **Rancher Istio Controller**: This controller manages the integration between the Rancher UI and the **Istio** deployment on the downstream cluster. This is needed because Istio has migrated away from using Helm for installation to using the `istioctl` binary or the Istio operator. This controller also handles deploying **Kiali** for graphing traffic flows throughout the service mesh. This allows users to see what applications connect to other applications, including the traffic rates and latencies between pods. This can be extremely valuable for application owners and teams.

- **Rancher CIS Scan Controller**: This controller handles installing and configuring the **rancher-cis-benchmark** tool that is built on top of kube-bench, an open source tool from **Aqua Security**. This tool is used to check that your K8s cluster is compliant with the CIS standards. It does this by using the **Sonobuoy** plugin to collect the configuration settings of the different K8s components, for example, if you have the `--insecure-bind-address` flag set to something besides `localhost` on kube-apiserver. Note that this setting allows requests to bypass the authentication and authorization modules, and they must not be exposed outside the node. In this case, Sonobuoy would collect this setting and then kube-bench would flag that value as a failed check. Finally, the **rancher-cis-benchmark** tool would collect all of the checks together in an excellent report that can be sent off by email to the security team.

What do the Cattle agents do?

The Cattle agents that Rancher deploys on downstream clusters (that is, clusters that Rancher is managing) provide Rancher with access to the cluster and its nodes. This is done using two different sets of pods:

- **Cattle-cluster-agent**: This runs as a deployment with a scale of one on your workers. When this pod starts up, it creates a **WebSocket** connection to the Rancher API. Once that connection is made, the Cattle-cluster-agent will create a TCP tunneled connection over the WebSocket connection back to the Rancher leader pod. Inside that pod, it will bind to a random port on `localhost`. This tunnel will then allow connections for the Rancher server pod to the downstream cluster. Because of this, Rancher does not need firewall rules to open from the Rancher servers to the downstream cluster, including the need to port-forward, which can be a security issue. This WebSocket connection is held open by Rancher and the Cattle-cluster-agent, as if this connection drops, Rancher will lose access to the cluster until the connection can be restored.

- **Cattle-node-agent**: This runs as a **DaemonSet** on all nodes with a toleration that ignores just about everything. This pod uses the same kind of WebSocket connection as the previous example, with a TCP tunnel back to Rancher. Still, RKE uses this connection inside the Rancher server pod to provide a socket connection to the Docker Engine running on the node. This is needed for RKE to spin up the non-K8s containers that make up an RKE cluster.

> **Note**
>
> Cattle-node-agent is only used in clusters where Rancher manages the cluster, that is, when Rancher built the cluster using RKE. For imported clusters, such as an Amazon EKS cluster, the Cattle-node-agent is not needed.

Both agents use HTTPS to connect to the Rancher API. They do this by passing some environment variables into the pods. The first variable is `CATTLE_SERVER`; this variable is the hostname of the Rancher API. An example hostname is `rancher.example.com`. Note that there is no HTTP or HTTPS in this variable, as it is a requirement for the agents to connect to Rancher over an HTTPS connection. The second variable is `CATTLE_CA_CHECKSUM`, a **SHA-256** checksum of the certificate chain for the Rancher API. If you use a self-signed or internally signed certificate as a default, the pod will not trust that certificate, as the image will not have that root CA certificate stored inside it. The agents work around this issue by decoding the certificate chain from the Rancher API and hashing it using SHA-256. Then, by comparing the hash to the `CATTLE_CA_CHECKSUM` variable, so long as they match, the agents will trust that HTTPS connection. It's important to note that if you renew the certificate in place, that is, without changing the chain, the `CATTLE_CA_CHECKSUM` variable will not change if you change certificates to a different authority – for example, if you are switching from a self-signed certificate to a publicly signed certificate from a company such as **DigiCert**, **GoDaddy**, and so on. This will cause the `CATTLE_CA_CHECKSUM` variable to have longer matches, thereby requiring manual work to update the agents. This process is documented at `https://github.com/rancherlabs/support-tools/tree/master/cluster-agent-tool`.

How does Rancher provision nodes and clusters?

Rancher can provision a number of different nodes and clusters using the following methods. There are three main types of clusters in Rancher. *Rancher-created clusters using RKE*, *Rancher-created clusters using a hosted provider*, and *imported clusters*. Each of these types has subtypes, which we will describe in detail here.

The Rancher-created clusters using RKE are as follows:

- **Rancher-created nodes**: One of the great things about Rancher is that if you choose Rancher, it can build the cluster for you, and they can manage the VMs themselves. This is done by using a tool called **Rancher-machine**. This tool is based on Docker Machine, which lets you create VMs and install Docker. Docker Machine does this by using driver plugins. These driver plugins act as a translation layer between Docker Machine and the virtualization provider – for example, **Amazon AWS**, **Linode**, **OVHcloud**, or VMware vSphere.

How Docker Machine works is that you give it credentials to your virtualization provider and define the specifications on the VM, such as how many cores, how much RAM, and so on. Then, the driver plugin takes over to call the cloud provider's API endpoint to provision the VM. Docker Machine then creates an SSH key pair for each VM and then uses the driver plugin to push the SSH key to the VM. It then waits for the SSH connection to become available.

Once the SSH connection has been created, Docker Machine then installs Docker. This is where Rancher-machine comes into the picture. Rancher-machine builds on top of Docker Machine by adding additional driver plugins such as **DigitalOcean** and **Rackspace**. It then provides additional features such as implementing cloud-init. You can run other steps during the node provisioning process such as creating a filesystem for Docker or applying customizations to Docker Engine. Rancher provides higher-level functions such as defining node templates to deploy nodes in a repeatable process that is expanded even more by defining node pools (a group of nodes using node templates). Node pools allow Rancher to add and remove nodes from the group at will. For example, if a node crashes in the pool and doesn't recover during the default 15-minute timeout (customized), Rancher can create a new replacement VM and destroy the crashed node. This process can also be used to perform a rolling replacement of nodes for use cases where you don't want to *patch in place* but want to update your base image and recreate all of your nodes in a rolling fashion.

- **Bring your own nodes**: These nodes are for use cases where you would like or need to create the VMs yourself or use physical servers. In this case, you will define your cluster configuration in Rancher. Then, Rancher will create a command for you to run that looks like the following:

```
docker run -d --privileged --restart=unless-stopped
--net=host -v /etc/kubernetes:/etc/kubernetes -v /
var/run:/var/run  rancher/rancher-agent:v2.6.0
--server https://rancher-lab.support.tools --token
abcdefghijkmn123456789 --etcd --controlplane --worker.
```

Let's break down this command. First, this is a Docker command that can run on any Linux host that has Docker installed. The next part is `run`, which says to create a new container, with the next flag being `-d`, which says to run in *detached* mode. This will start the container and put it in the background. The `-privileged` flag then tells Docker that it will be a privileged container – meaning that this container can access all of the devices on the host. Think of it like running the process directly on the host operating system with little to no limits. The `--restart=unless-stopped` flag just tells Docker to keep restarting this container until we tell it to stop. Next is the `--net=host` flag, which gives the container the same network as the host. Therefore, the container's IP will be the host's IP. The next two flags pass the `/etc/kubernetes` and `//var/run` directories inside the container. The `/etc/kubernetes` directory is used to store node-level configuration files and, most importantly, the SSL certificates used for the K8s components.

The following section is the container image and tag. This image will match the Rancher version, and this image includes all of the binaries that will be needed to bootstrap this node. The `--server` flag is the Rancher API server path. This will be passed into the container, creating and tunneling back to the Rancher leader pod (please see the *What do the Cattle agents do?* section earlier in this chapter for more details). Next, we have the `-token` flag. This is used to authenticate the agent to the Rancher server and tie this agent to a cluster. Each cluster will have a unique token, but all of the agents in a cluster will share the same token. Finally, we have the `role` flags. These flags are used to assign the different roles of the RKE cluster to the node. Note that nodes can have more than one role, but a cluster requires at least one node for each role: one etcd node, one control plane, and one worker node. You can mix and match roles as you choose, but there are best practices for this that should be followed.

In both Rancher-created nodes and *bring your own nodes*, once the bootstrap agent has been successfully started on the node, the agent will tunnel back to the Rancher leader pod and register the new node in Rancher RKE. It then uses the registered nodes to dynamically create the `cluster.yaml` file using the registered or registering nodes to the cluster. If this cluster has already been successfully started once before, Rancher will also pull `cluster.rkestate` from the CRD `clusters.management.cattle.io` object. This file includes the current state of the cluster, the root and server certificates, and the authentication tokens that RKE will use to communicate to the cluster. Then, the cluster controller will use the port binding on the Rancher leader pod to connect the Docker engines on the nodes. At this point, RKE will create the certificates and configuration files, deploy them to the nodes, and start creating/updating the etcd cluster. RKE performs this process in a serial fashion, working on only one node at a time, and if RKE runs into any issues, it will throw an error and exit the function. Also, an etcd backup is taken on each etcd node for existing clusters before making any changes. Once the etcd plane has been successfully started, RKE will begin working on the control plane, where RKE will start up the kube-apiserver objects, kube-controller-manager, and kube-scheduler, working again in a serial fashion by running one node at a time and running health checks as it goes. And again, if any step in this process fails, RKE will fail too. Finally, RKE will come to the worker plane. This process is different, because it is designed to create a parallel to doing multiple worker nodes at once, and it will continue even if a failure happens, so long as the settings defined in the `zero downtime` configuration have not been violated. The default settings are only one etcd or control plane node down at any given time, with up to 10% of the worker nodes down. Note, this number is rounded down to the nearest node, with a minimum of one node per batch:

- **Rancher-created clusters using a hosted provider**: One of the nice things about Rancher is you can use a hosted K8s cluster such as AWS EKS, Google GKE, or Azure AKS if you don't want to deal with VMs and just want to let your cloud provider manage the VMs for you. Rancher can help by using the cloud provider's **software development kit** (**SDK**) to provide the cluster for you. This is mainly for reasons of convenience and consistency, as there are no unique or hidden options that Rancher has that you can't do yourself. As part of its new hosted cluster option in v2, Rancher also allows for the three-way synchronization of configurations between Rancher, the cloud provider, and the end user. What is remarkable is that if you want to change some settings for your AWS EKS cluster, you can manage it directly in the AWS console and your changes will be reflected in Rancher. Note that this can be done for RKE clusters too but requires a few extra steps.

- **Imported K8s clusters**: Finally, if you don't want Rancher to manage your clusters whatsoever, but you do want Rancher to be a friendly web UI for your cluster, you can utilize the excellent *convenience features* of Rancher such as **Active Directory (AD)** authentication, web kube-proxy access, and more. You can import the cluster where Rancher will deploy the cluster-Cattle-agent on the cluster but will not have access to items such as etcd, kubelet, the Docker CLI, and more. In this instance, Rancher will only be able to access the kube-apiserver endpoint. Note that Rancher supports any certificated K8s distribution for the imported cluster option, and this can include *K8s the hard way*, EKS, a self-managed RKE cluster, or even a K3s/RKE2 cluster. As of Rancher v2.6.0, K3s and RKE2 clusters are unique in that they can be imported into Rancher and Rancher can then take over management of the cluster moving forward. Please note that this is still a new process and has its limitations and bugs.

What are kube-apiserver, kube-controller-manager, kube-scheduler, etcd, and kubelet?

The etcd object is a distributed and consistent key-value pair database. **CoreOS** initially developed etcd to handle OS upgrades in cluster management systems and store configuration files in 2013. Because of this, etcd needed to be highly available and consistent. The etcd object is currently affiliated with the CNCF and has been widely adopted in the industry. An etcd cluster is based on the idea of maintaining consistency across nodes – most clusters contain three or five nodes, and there is a requirement that there be an odd number of nodes. This is due to the requirements of the Raft consensus algorithm. This algorithm selects a master node, which etcd calls the *leader*. This node is responsible for synchronizing data between nodes. If the leader node fails, another election will happen, and another node will take over this role. The idea here is that etcd is built on the concept of a *quorum*. This means that more than half of the nodes in the cluster must be in consensus. In a standard three-node cluster, the etcd cluster will continue to accept writes if a single node fails, but if two nodes fail, the surviving etcd node will take the safest option and go into read-only mode until a quorum can be restored in the cluster. A five-node cluster is the same, but it requires three of the five nodes to fail to lose service. All write processes go to the etcd leader node, which are written to the Raft log and then broadcast to all cluster nodes during operations. Once the majority of the nodes have successfully acknowledged the write (that is, two nodes in a three-node cluster and threes nodes in a five-node cluster), the Raft log entry is committed, and the write is acknowledged back to the client. If a majority of the nodes do not acknowledge the write, then the write will fail and will not be committed. Because of Raft, adding more nodes to the cluster will increase the fault tolerance, but this also increases the load on the leader node without improving performance.

For now, etcd stores the data because etcd is built on top of **BoltDB**, which writes its data into a single memory-mapped file. This means the operating system is responsible for handling the data caching and will keep as much data in memory as possible – this is why etcd can be a *memory hog* and requires a high-speed disk, preferably an **SSD** or **NVME**. Then for the data, etcd uses **multiversion concurrency control (MVCC)** to handle concurrent write operations safely. The MVCC works in conjunction with Raft, where every write is tracked by a revision. By keeping a history of the revisions, etcd can provide the version history of all of the keys. This impacts read performance because key-value pairs are written to disk in the order created in the transaction log, not by an index (as in a traditional database). This means that key-value pairs written simultaneously are faster to read than key-value pairs written at different times. However, with etcd keeping revisions over time, the disk and memory usage can grow very large. Even if you delete a large number of keys from etcd, the space will continue to grow since the prior history of those keys will still be retained. This is where etcd compaction and defragmenting come into the picture wherein etcd will drop superseded revisions, that is, older data that has been *overwritten,* where the memory-mapped file will have several holes so etcd will then run a defrag to release free pages back to the operating system. However, it is essential to note that all incoming reads and writes will be blocked during a defragmentation.

kube-apiserver is a critical component in a K8s cluster, as it is the server that provides the REST API endpoint for the whole cluster. kube-apiserver is the only K8s component that connects to the etcd cluster and acts as an access point for all of the other K8s components. Now, kube-apiserver is intended to be relatively simple, with most of the business logic being done by other controllers and plugins. But one of its primary responsibilities is authentication and **RBAC (role-based access control)**. The default access control behavior is that all clients should be authenticated to interact with kube-apiserver.

The other central role that kube-apiserver serves is managing secret encryption. By default, K8s stores secrets in plain text inside the etcd database. This can be a security issue, as secrets store items like passwords, database connection strings, and so on. To protect secrets, kube-apiserver supports an encryption provider. What happens is, any time a secret is created or updated, kube-apiserver will call the encryption provider to access the encryptions algorithm and keys to encrypt the data, then send this data to the etcd cluster. Then whenever a secret is read from the etcd cluster, kube-apiserver uses the reverse process to decrypt the data before sending the response back to the client. Because of this, the clients are unaware that secrets are encrypted, with the only impact being performance. The standard for Rancher is to use `aescbc` for its encryption algorithm, as this provides a good balance between performance and strength, and also has the added benefit that most modern CPUs support AES with CBC mode in hardware. As a result, encryption and decryption performance are usually not an issue.

Another one of the critical things to remember about kube-apiserver is that it's stateless; besides some in-memory caching, kube-apiserver stores no data. This means kube-apiserver is great for horizontal scaling. It also has no leader election process as there is no leader node. So, typically, clusters will have at least two nodes running kube-apiserver, but you can have more with larger clusters. You also don't have the limitation of old numbers of nodes in the way you do with etcd. The kube-apiserver is also where a lot of core cluster configuring happens. For example, when using a cloud provider such as AWS or VMware vSphere, you need to create a configure file and pass that file path into the kube-apiserver component as a command-line flag. Note, kube-apiserver does not support hot changing settings and requires a restart to alter its configurations.

The K8s controller manager, kube-controller-manager, is the core controller for K8s and is typically called the *controller for controllers*, as its main job is to sit in a non-terminating loop that regulates the state of the cluster. It connects to the kube-apiserver component and creates several watch handles that monitor the current state of the cluster and compare it to the desired state. The kube-controller-manager component does this by having several smaller controllers.

The first of these smaller controllers is the *replication controller*. This controller ensures that the specified number of pods in a **ReplicaSet** are running at any given time. An example of this is if a ReplicaSet has five pods in the desired state, but it only has hour pods in the current state. The replication controller will create a new pod object in the unscheduled state, thereby bringing the ReplicaSet back up to the required five pods. Another example is when a node fails – here, the replication controller will see that the pod has been disabled, deleted, or terminated, and it will create a new pod object again. The replication controller also handles terminating pods when the current state is greater than the desired state. There is some business logic built inside the termination process. Here, the main rule is that pods that are currently not in the ready status, that is, they are pending or failed, are the first pods to be set for terminations, with the oldest pods being the next in line. Note that the replication controller does not delete pods or call nodes directly, or even connect to other controllers. All communication happens between the controller and kube-apiserver.

The second controller is the *endpoints controller*, which is responsible for maintaining the endpoints that join services and their assigned pods, with endpoint and service records being part of the cluster DNS system. K8s needs to track pods being created and deleted in the cluster to update those records with the correct IP addresses.

The third controller is the *service account and token controller*. This controller is responsible for creating and managing service accounts in the cluster and creating tokens for the service accounts to use to authenticate the kube-apiserver component. Note that the tokens are stored as secrets in the namespace where the service accounts are hosted.

The fourth controller is the *node controller*. This controller is responsible for watching the status of the nodes in the cluster by watching the node leases that kubelet is periodically updating by sending a heartbeat. Suppose a node lease violates the node timeout that is five minutes by default. The node controller will decide that this node must be down and start the pod eviction process wherein the controller updates the pods running on that node with the status of Unknown and will taint the node object with the taint of unschedulable. This will trigger the replication controller to begin deleting pods that cannot tolerate that taint. It is essential to remember the following things about this process. First, K8s has no way of knowing if a node is genuinely down or if it's just having issues communicating with the kube-apiserver, which means if a kubelet on the node crashes or locks up, then the pods running on the node will continue to run without issue, even though the node controller has flagged them and the replication controller has deleted them. And also, because K8s has no way for the cluster to block I/O to the failed node, you could run into a split-brain issue with the same pod/application running in two locations simultaneously. You also must remember that pods that have tolerations for the unschedulable taint will not be rescheduled.

An example of this is a canal pod that has a toleration for any taint placed on a node, meaning this pod will be scheduled on a node no matter what. The next thing to remember is that the eviction process does have rate limiting, which, by default, will evict pods at a rate of ten pods per second. This is to prevent a flood of pods from being rescheduled in the cluster. Finally, only a single kube-controller-manager is allowed to be active at any one time. It does this by using a leader election process. All kube-controller-manager processes try to grab a lease in kube-apiserver. One process becomes the leader, allowing the other controllers to start taking action in the cluster. The leader will continue to refresh this lease while the other nodes continue monitoring the lease, comparing the last renewal timestamp to the expiration timestamp. If the lease is ever allowed to expire, the standby kube-controller-manager will race to become the new leader. All this being said, scaling the kube-controller-manager horizontally only improves fault tolerance and will not improve performance.

kube-scheduler is the controller that handles assigning pods to nodes. It does this by watching for unscheduled pods, at which point kube-scheduler is evaluating nodes. kube-scheduler first builds a list of nodes that meets all of the requirements. For example, if a pod requires a node selector rule, only nodes with that label will be added to the node candidate list. Next, kube-scheduler will evaluate the taints and tolerations of the nodes and pods. For example, by default, a pod will not tolerate the node with taint scheduling disabled. This taint is typically applied to master, etcd, or control-plane nodes. In this case, the node wouldn't be added to the node candidate list. Next, kube-scheduler will create what it calls a node *score*. This score is based on the availability of the resources, such as CPU, memory, disk, network, and more, that are available on the node. For example, a node that is underutilized, that is, with a lot of CPU and memory available will score higher than a node that is highly utilized, that is, with little to no CPU or memory available. Once all of the scores are calculated, kube-scheduler will sort them from the highest to lowest. If there is only one node with the highest score, then that node wins. If there is a tie, kube-scheduler will randomly pick a winner from the nodes that tied. Finally, kube-scheduler will update the pod object in kube-apiserver with its node assignment. An important thing to remember is kube-scheduler can be tuned and even replaced with other third-party schedulers. This is mainly done for environments with burst workloads where many pods will be created at once. This is because kube-scheduler doesn't know about resource utilization and its pods over time. It only gets whatever the current value is at scheduling. So, what can happen is one node will get flooded with new pods and fall over. Those pods are then rescheduled on a new node, which in turn knocks that node over as well. But during that event, the first node is recovered, and so now all of the new pods will go to that node because it is empty, and the process repeats repeatedly. There is also an essential idea to understand here, kube-scheduler only touches a pod at the time of creation. Once the pod has been scheduled to a node, that's it. The kube-scheduler component does not rebalance or move pods around. There are also tools like kube-descheduler that can fill in this gap and help you balance your cluster.

In simple terms, kubelet is the node agent in K8s. kubelet runs on every worker node, and in the case of RKE, all nodes. kubelet has several different roles and responsibilities. The first is taking the pod specifications in kube-apiserver that have the node assignments of the node where kubelet is running. kubelet then compares that pod specification to the current state of the node. kubelet does this by connecting to Docker or containerd to gather what containers are currently running on the node. Then, if there is a difference, kubelet will create or destroy the containers for them to match. The kubelet component's second responsibility is *pod health*.

Pods can have *probes* defined as a part of their specifications. These include *liveness probes*, which are responsible for checking whether the application inside a pod is healthy. These checks are simple **Bash** commands or HTTP requests that run inside kubelet. An example of these checks could be if you had an NGINX web server running inside a pod and you wanted to perform an HTTP GET request to / every 5 seconds to confirm that NGINX is up and responding to requests.

> **Note**
>
> The kubelet component only accepts 200 OK responses as evidence of a healthy request. All other response codes will return a failure. Another type of probe is called the *startup probe*. This probe is similar to the liveness probe but mainly tells kubelet that a pod has successfully started.

An example might be a database inside a pod where the database could take a few minutes to fully start up. If you just used the liveness probes, you would need to space out your schedule to allow the database to start before kubelet killed the pod entirely. So, you'd want to use a *startup probe* with a delay of a minute or two, then, once that is successful, the liveness probe could take over and run every few seconds. Finally, the *readiness probe* is very similar to the startup probe, but it is used for controlling when K8s can start sending traffic to a pod. An example of this could be a web server that might start up and be healthy but can't connect to a backend database. In this case, you don't want kubelet to kill the pod, as it is fine, but you also don't want to start sending traffic to the pod until it can connect to the database.

How do the current state and the desired state work?

Desired state is one of the core concepts of Rancher and K8s. The idea is that you should declare the state of an object (for example, a pod, deployment, or volume) as you would like it to be. Then, the cluster should report the current state of the object, at which point it's the role of the controller (the kube-controller-manager component in the case of most of K8s core objects) to compare these two states. If no difference is found, don't do anything, but if a discrepancy is found, the controller's job is to create a *plan* for making the current state match the desired state.

For example, if you had a deployment with a replica of three pods deployed in a cluster, the ReplicaSet controller will see that the replica count is set to three (desired state) with an image of *v2*. The controller will then call the kube-apiserver component and pull a copy of the current and desired state for that ReplicaSet at which point, the controller will start comparing settings. In this example, the current state will now have three healthy pods using the *v1* image tag, because pods can't be modified after being created. The controller will need to create new replacement pods and will need to destroy the old pods. It does this by creating a new pod object with the updated image tag. This pod object will have the status of *waiting to be scheduled*. At this point, kube-scheduler takes over to assign that pod to a node. Then, kubelet takes over to create the container(s), IP address, mount volumes, and so on that are needed for the pod. Then, once everything has been started and the probes are successful, kubelet will update the pod object to the state of `Ready`. This takes us back to the ReplicaSet controller, which will then detect that one of the number pods has successfully been started. If yes, pick the oldest pod that doesn't meet the spec and terminate that pod by setting the status to terminating. This will trigger kubelet to destroy the pod and its resources. Then, once everything is cleaned up, kube-controller-manager will remove the terminated pod object in kube-apiserver. This process then starts again and will repeat until all of the pods in the ReplicaSet match the desired state.

The controllers are designed to always aim to have the current state matching the desired state. If the controllers run into an issue, such as the new pods keep crashing, the image can't be pulled, or a `configmap` object is missing, then after several failed attempts, the controller will keep trying, but it will put that object in a **CrashLooping** status. This tells the controller to stop fixing that state for a set amount of time (the default is 5 minutes). The controller does this to prevent spamming the cluster with requests for failing resources (for example, if you had entered a typo in the image tag). We don't want the controller to keep creating and deleting the same pod over and over again as fast as it can, as this will put a load on kube-apiserver, etcd, kube-scheduler, and so on, which would create an extreme case of a large number of pods all crashlooping at the same time, and this could take the cluster down.

Summary

In this chapter, we learned about Rancher, RKE, RKE2, K3s, and RancherD. We went over some of the pros and cons of each product. We then went over how they were designed and how they work. Next, we covered all of the controllers that make up Rancher and explored how they work behind the scenes. After that, we dove into how Rancher uses its Cattle agents for communicating with its clusters and nodes. Finally, we went into detail on the different core components of K8s, including kube-apiserver, kube-controller-manager, and kube-scheduler.

In the next chapter, we will see how to install Rancher in a single-node environment.

Summary

Part 2 – Installing Rancher

This part will cover all the different ways to deploy Rancher, ranging from a single-node POC to a complete enterprise solutions and even how to deploy Rancher on a hosted cluster.

This part of the book comprises the following chapters:

- *Chapter 3, Creating a Single Node Rancher*
- *Chapter 4, Creating an RKE or RKE2 Cluster*
- *Chapter 5, Deploying Rancher on a Hosted Kubernetes Cluster*

3
Creating a Single Node Rancher

This chapter will cover the process of installing Rancher as a single Docker container. This is an excellent option for proof of concept, development, or testing purposes. This chapter will cover the requirements and limitations of a single-node Rancher and the core architecture rules needed to create a proper enterprise solution. Finally, it will cover migrating to a **High Availability (HA)** cluster.

In this chapter, we're going to cover the following main topics:

- What is a single-node Rancher installation?
- Requirements and limitations
- Rules for architecting a solution
- Installation steps
- Migration to an HA setup

What is a single-node Rancher installation?

Rancher can be installed by running a single Docker container. This process goes back to the roots of Rancher v1.6 when the Rancher server was a Java-based application that ran as a Docker container using an external MySQL database or in single node mode using a MySQL server running inside the Rancher server container. With the move to Rancher v2.x, everything in Rancher moved to use the Kube-apiserver and **Custom Resource Definitions (CRDs))**. Because of this, Rancher needs a Kubernetes cluster to work correctly. In the earlier Rancher v2.x releases, this was done by embedding the Kubernetes services such as **etcd**, **Kube-apiserver**, **kube-scheduler**, **kube-controller-manager**, **kubelet**, and **kube-proxy** into the Rancher server code. When Rancher first tries to detect, the environment variable KUBECONFIG is set. Kubernetes sets this variable by default in all pods, so if it's missing, then Rancher knows that it must be running in single-node mode. At which point, the Rancher server process will start checking whether there are SSL certificates for the Kubernetes components if they are missing or expired. Rancher will handle creating them. Next, Rancher will start etcd in a cluster of one and start Kube-apiserver and the required controllers. The big note here is this cluster is very stripped down. For example, this cluster does not have CoreDNS, ingress-controller, or even a **Container Network Interface** (**CNI**) such as Canal, simply because Rancher doesn't need them because this setup was not a true cluster and was any kind of standard configuration. Several problems came up with the earlier versions. For example, before Rancher v2.3.x, there was no way to rotate the certificates inside the Rancher server container, and initially, Rancher would create certificates with an expiration of 1 year. This meant that after a year, your Rancher server would crash and wouldn't start up because none of the Kubernetes components work with expired certificates, this being a safety measure in the Go library to not allow any HTTPS connection to an endpoint without a validated certificate. And, of course, an expired certificate is not a validated certificate. In Rancher v2.3.x, a process was added to Rancher to look for expired or expiring certificates and rotate them. This was done by spinning up a unique K3s cluster inside a Docker container and deploying the Rancher server as a pod.

Requirements and limitations

The following items are **requirements** for a single-node Rancher:

- A Linux host running Docker 18.06.3, 18.09.x, 19.03.x, 20.10.x

- Minimum of two cores but four cores is highly recommended

- 8 GB of RAM

- 10 GB of SSD storage with a latency under 10ms

- Inbound TCP ports `80` and `443` between the end users and the managed clusters

The following items are not required but are **highly recommended**:

- A DNS record such as `rancher.example.com` in place of using the server hostname

- A certificate signed by a recognized Certificate Authority (CA), such as DigiCert and GoDaddy

- An HTTP or TCP load balancer placed in front of the Rancher server

- Server backups, which can be a file or snapshot-level backups

- A dedicated filesystem/disk for the Docker filesystem `/var/lib/docker`

- A dedicated filesystem/disk for the Rancher persistent data `/var/lib/rancher`

- The Linux host should be a **virtual machine** (**VM**) where the hypervisor or cloud provider will be providing redundancy in the event of hardware failure.

The following items are the known **limitations** of a single-node Rancher:

- A single-node Rancher is recommended only for development and testing purposes. Do not use it in production.

- Only the Rancher server should be installed on this host. This server should not be hosting any other applications.

- A single-node Rancher is not designed for **HA.**

- Migrating from a single node to HA is not officially supported and is not guaranteed to work.

- The single-node Rancher feature will be removed at some point and will no longer be available.

- Rancher v2.5.x and higher requires the privileged option, so you cannot run Docker in rootless mode.

- A single-node Rancher can be installed on a desktop/laptop, but there are issues when the IP address of the host changes along with requiring DNS records to be created.

Rules for architecting a solution

The **pros** are as follows:

- A single-node Rancher is very simple to set up as you just need to deploy a single container.

- It's very fast to spin up. A single-node Rancher only takes a few minutes to start compared with RKE, which can take 10-15 minutes to start.

- It has low resource utilization, compared to RancherD and a complete RKE cluster. A single-node Rancher uses a lot less CPU, memory, and storage.

- There is no need for a load balancer or DNS if you want just the server hostname or IP address.

- A single-node Rancher can be run on a laptop. (Note: Rancher Desktop is a better product for this solution.)

The **cons** are as follows:

- A single-node Rancher is not designed for production.

- Rancher official and community support is very limited.

- There are limited troubleshooting options as the K3s settings are baked into the code and cannot be changed without building a new release.

- The long-term future of single-node Rancher is uncertain and will be removed in a future release.

- There's no scalability or redundancy if the host goes offline. Rancher is down.

- By default, a single-node Rancher stores its data inside the container, and if that container is lost, the data will be lost.

- There's no built-in backup solution; RKE, RKE2, K3s, and RancherD can back up to local disk or S3.

The **architecture rules** are as follows:

- You should plan for migrating from a single-node Rancher to HA.

- Rancher requires an SSL certificate and will not work without a certificate.

- Using publicly signed certificates can make scripts and tools easier as the Rancher URL will be trusted by default.

- All clusters/nodes that Rancher will be managing need to connect to the Rancher URL over SSL.

- Rancher does support air-gapped environments, but it will require additional steps to provide proxied access to the internet, or you will need to offer Docker images and catalogs via internally hosted services.

Installation steps

We are going to assume the following:

- That you already have a Linux VM that has been created and patched (in this example, we'll be using a VMware VM running Ubuntu 20.04).

- That the Linux VM has internet access and doesn't require an HTTP proxy for access. Note, if you do not have internet access, please see the air-gap steps located at `https://rancher.com/docs/rancher/v2.5/en/installation/other-installation-methods/air-gap/`.

- That you have SSH and root access to the Linux VM.

- That you are installing Docker using a default configuration and storage location.

- That the filesystems `/var/lib/docker` and `/var/lib/rancher` have already been created and mounted.

- That you have already created a DNS record for Rancher. In this example, we'll be using `rancher.support.tools` and an associated SSL certificate signed by a recognized CA.

Installing Docker

In this section, we'll be installing and configuring Docker:

1. SSH into the Linux VM and become root using the `sudo su -` command.

2. Run the `curl https://releases.rancher.com/install-docker/20.10.sh | bash` command to install Docker.

3. Set Docker to start at system boot by running `systemctl enable docker`.

4.   Verify Docker is running by running `docker info`. The output should look like the following:

```
root@a1ubranl00:~# docker info
Client:
 Context:    default
 Debug Mode: false
 Plugins:
  app: Docker App (Docker Inc., v0.9.1-beta3)
  buildx: Build with BuildKit (Docker Inc., v0.6.1-docker)

Server:
 Containers: 0
  Running: 0
  Paused: 0
  Stopped: 0
 Images: 0
 Server Version: 20.10.8
 Storage Driver: overlay2
  Backing Filesystem: extfs
  Supports d_type: true
  Native Overlay Diff: true
  userxattr: false
 Logging Driver: json-file
 Cgroup Driver: cgroupfs
 Cgroup Version: 1
 Plugins:
  Volume: local
  Network: bridge host ipvlan macvlan null overlay
  Log: awslogs fluentd gcplogs gelf journald json-file local logentries splunk syslog
 Swarm: inactive
 Runtimes: io.containerd.runc.v2 io.containerd.runtime.v1.linux runc
 Default Runtime: runc
 Init Binary: docker-init
 containerd version: e25210fe30a0a703442421b0f60afac609f950a3
 runc version: v1.0.1-0-g4144b63
 init version: de40ad0
 Security Options:
  apparmor
  seccomp
   Profile: default
 Kernel Version: 5.4.0-86-generic
 Operating System: Ubuntu 20.04.3 LTS
 OSType: linux
 Architecture: x86_64
 CPUs: 4
 Total Memory: 7.748GiB
 Name: a1ubranl00
 ID: KRPX:O5TH:3XMS:GS5L:UPP3:CEBZ:X25W:QCTA:RBJN:IG76:6L2U:JZC2
 Docker Root Dir: /var/lib/docker
 Debug Mode: false
 Registry: https://index.docker.io/v1/
 Labels:
 Experimental: false
 Insecure Registries:
  127.0.0.0/8
 Live Restore Enabled: false

WARNING: No swap limit support
root@a1ubranl00:~#
```

Figure 3.1 – Docker information output

Text output: https://raw.githubusercontent.com/PacktPublishing/ Rancher-Deep-Dive/main/ch03/install_steps/01_installing_ docker/example_output.txt

5. Configure log rotation – we'll want to enable log rotation of the Docker logs. Create/ edit the /etc/docker/daemon.json file to have the following content:

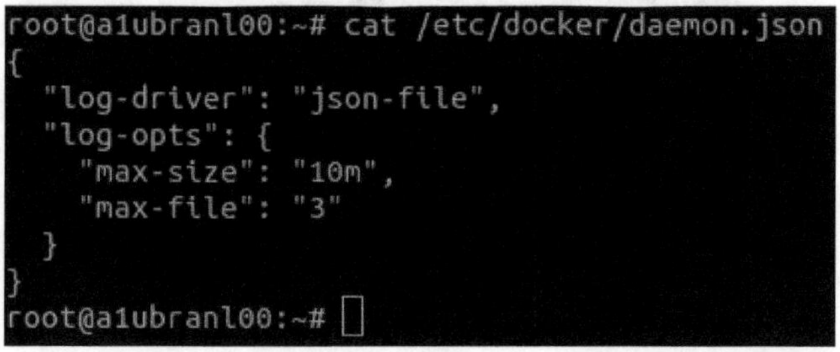

```
root@a1ubran100:~# cat /etc/docker/daemon.json
{
  "log-driver": "json-file",
  "log-opts": {
    "max-size": "10m",
    "max-file": "3"
  }
}
root@a1ubran100:~# 
```

Figure 3.2 – Enabling log rotation of the Docker logs

Test version: https://raw.githubusercontent.com/PacktPublishing/ Rancher-Deep-Dive/main/ch03/install_steps/02_configure-log- rotation/daemon.json

6. Restart Docker to apply the change using the systemctl restart docker command.

Prepping the SSL certificates

In this section, we'll be preparing the SSL certificate and key for use by the Rancher server. These files will be called tls.crt and tls.key. The steps are as follows:

1. To create tls.crt, we'll need a full certificate chain. This includes the root and intermediate certificates. Most public root authorities publish these certificates on their website.

2. We'll want all certificates files to be in the **Privacy Enhanced Mail** (**PEM**) format. Note that sometimes this is called **Base64**. If your certificate is in a different format, you should go to https://knowledge.digicert.com/solution/ SO26449.html for more details about converting between formats.

3. Once all files are in the PEM format, we'll want to create a file with the content of each certificate in the following order. Note that some certificates might have multiple intermediate certificates. If you have questions, please work with your CA. Also, if you are using an internal CA, you might not have an intermediate certificate. You might just have the root and server certificate.

```
-----BEGIN CERTIFICATE-----
Root certificate
-----END CERTIFICATE-----
-----BEGIN CERTIFICATE-----
Intermediate certificate
-----END CERTIFICATE-----
-----BEGIN CERTIFICATE-----
Server certificate
-----END CERTIFICATE-----
```

Figure 3.3 – Creating a file to store the certificates

Text example: `https://raw.githubusercontent.com/PacktPublishing/Rancher-Deep-Dive/main/ch03/install_steps/03_prepping_ssl_certs/example_certs/tls.pem`

4. For the private key, we'll want to make sure it does not have a passphrase. We do this by reviewing the top of the file; see the following examples for details.

These are examples of keys that have a passphrase:

```
-----BEGIN RSA PRIVATE KEY-----
Proc-Type: 4,ENCRYPTED DEK-Info: DES-EDE3-CBC,
....
-----END RSA PRIVATE KEY-----
```

Figure 3.4 – Example 1 of a passphrase

```
-----BEGIN ENCRYPTED PRIVATE KEY-----
MIIJnDBOBgkqhkiG9w0BBQ0wQTApBgkqhkiG9w0BBQwwHAQIupZ5LBxkx4wCAggA
....
0+S3p1U3GAYMxdbZAcMtKnQzSVI4AalbF7a+7C1bFS4JIWBg/W1jkzZP/lc6klKq
b1J+hEz5rSoD+E/2ccsLpg==
-----END ENCRYPTED PRIVATE KEY-----
```

Figure 3.5 – Example 2 of a passphrase

This is an example of a key that does not have a passphrase:

```
-----BEGIN RSA PRIVATE KEY-----
MIIJKQIBAAKCAgEAuozVjS468biRJAwRr0+LLW+fxoucw4u5vsI4UyFnLA2KnNMV
vc8idiTLTyOjukxgUYCABGxu0jzk5QP9Fgqs7p2+MmZn+lDBPF9zLAP/SJQVL2Jx
....
Br8vCDapjAgW2pazmpzDCv67C3G6yO4WTqBAphSpk4AIy7YJUgDQxnf3sfMgCiqV
ZIPf77ywmSOF5Ou6EyTYqglsGRXYXfUrR1j+HmqQ+EdMNEY1Kk9lWk1vIZ/p
-----END RSA PRIVATE KEY-----
```

Figure 3.6 – Example of a key without a passphrase

5. If your key has a passphrase, you'll need to remove it using the `openssl rsa -in original.key -out tls.key` command and enter your passphrase during the prompt.

6. Once this process is done, you should have two files, `tls.crt` and `tls.key`.

7. You'll want to create the `/etc/rancher/ssl/` directory using the `mkdir -p /etc/rancher/ssl/` command and place both files in this directory. Note that these files should be owned by root.

Starting the Rancher server

In this section, we'll create the `docker run` command and start the Rancher server.

The following is an example command:

```
docker run -d \
--name rancher_server \
--restart=unless-stopped \
-p 80:80 \
-p 443:443 \
-v /etc/rancher/ssl/tls.crt:/etc/rancher/ssl/cert.pem \
-v /etc/rancher/ssl/tls.key:/etc/rancher/ssl/key.pem \
--privileged \
rancher/rancher:v2.5.8 \
--no-cacerts
```

Figure 3.7 – Example of docker run command

Text version: https://raw.githubusercontent.com/PacktPublishing/Rancher-Deep-Dive/main/ch03/install_steps/04_rancher_run_command/example01.txt

We'll now break down this command:

1. `docker run -d` will create a new container and start it in detached mode.

2. `--name rancher_server` will set the name of the container to be `rancher_server`. This is makes future commands easier because, without it, Docker will generate a random name.

3. `--restart=unless-stopped` will tell Docker to make sure this container stays running unless you manually stop it.

4. `-p 80:80` will map port 80 (HTTP) on the host to port 80 inside the container.

5. `-p 443:443` will map port 443 (HTTPS) on the host to port 443 inside the container. Note that if you are doing SSL offloading at the load balancer, this is not needed.

6. The `v /etc/rancher/ssl/tls.crt:/etc/rancher/ssl/cert.pem` and `-v /etc/rancher/ssl/tls.key:/etc/rancher/ssl/key.pem` flags will pass the certificate files we created earlier into the Rancher server.

7. The `-v /var/lib/rancher:/var/lib/rancher` flag will bind the data directory for Rancher to the host filesystem.

8. `--privileged` will give the Rancher server container root capabilities on the host. This is needed because we'll be running K3s inside the container, which will have additional containers.

9. `rancher/rancher:v2.5.8` will set the Rancher image, which will set the Rancher server version.

10. `--no-cacerts` will disable the certificate generation process in the Rancher server as we will be bringing our own.

11. Finally, once we start the Rancher server, we'll need to wait a few minutes for Rancher to start fully.

12. You can watch the server start by running the `docker logs -f rancher_server` command.

13. You'll then need to open your Rancher URL in a browser. Note that if you are planning to use a CNAME or load balancer, you should be using that URL instead of using the IP/hostname of the host.

14. To get the admin password, you'll need to run the `docker logs rancher_server 2>&1 | grep "Bootstrap Password:"` command:

```
root@a1ubran100:~# docker logs rancher_server 2>&1 | grep "Bootstrap Password:"
2021/09/28 01:40:54 [INFO] Bootstrap Password: p7brsdjzs4bnfbldxn6rqhq2mfgffz5ghdjddj7ptw5vkmjkqm7q2g
root@a1ubran100:~# 
```

Figure 3.8 – Snippet of step 14

15. Once you have logged into Rancher, you'll want to set the password and URL:

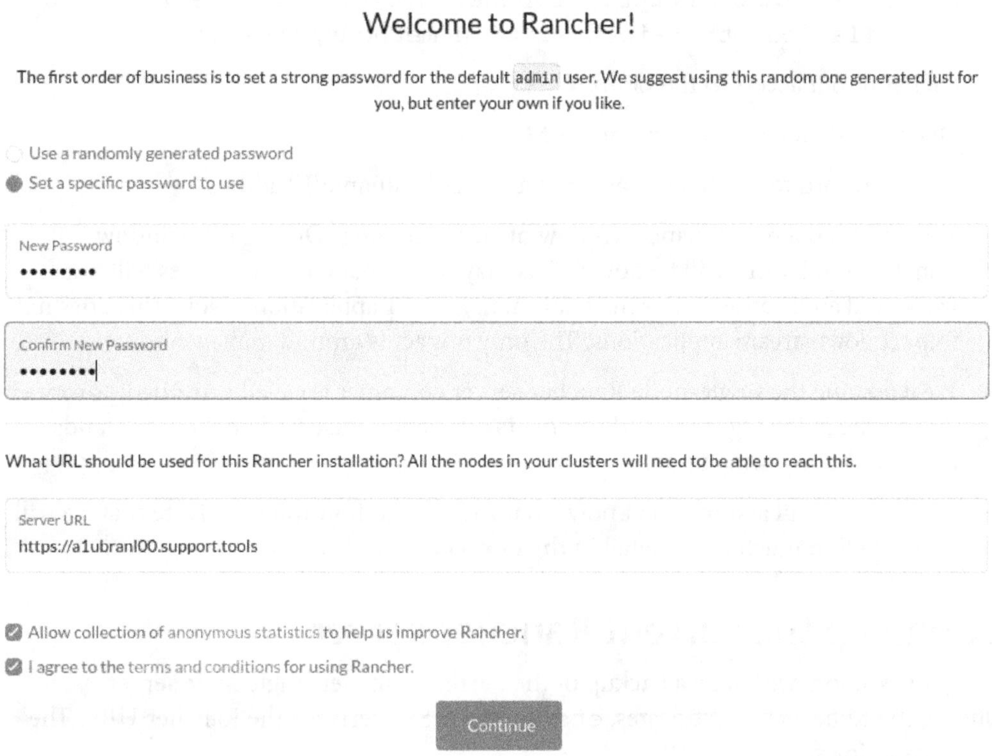

Welcome to Rancher!

The first order of business is to set a strong password for the default `admin` user. We suggest using this random one generated just for you, but enter your own if you like.

○ Use a randomly generated password

● Set a specific password to use

New Password
••••••••

Confirm New Password
••••••••

What URL should be used for this Rancher installation? All the nodes in your clusters will need to be able to reach this.

Server URL
https://a1ubranl00.support.tools

☑ Allow collection of anonymous statistics to help us improve Rancher.

☑ I agree to the terms and conditions for using Rancher.

Continue

Figure 3.9 – Rancher login page

It is important you set the URL to something you would like to keep, as changing the URL is difficult and time-consuming. For the password, this will be the password for the local admin, which is a root-level account that has full access to Rancher. This should be a secure password.

Migration to an HA setup

To migrate from a single-node Rancher to an HA installation, we'll need the following:

- You should be running the latest version of Rancher and RKE.

- You already have three new Linux VMs (in this example, we'll be using a VMware VM running Ubuntu 20.04). Note that at the end of this process, the original VM can be reclaimed.

- We will assume that the Linux VMs have internet access and don't require an HTTP proxy for access. Note that if you do not have internet access, please see the air-gap steps located at `https://rancher.com/docs/rancher/v2.5/en/installation/other-installation-methods/air-gap/`.

- SSH and root access to the Linux VMs.

- Docker installed on the three new VMs.

- A DNS record for Rancher that is not a server hostname/IP address.

- You will need a maintenance window of 30-60 minutes. During this window, Rancher and its API will be down. This may mean that CICD pipelines will not work, and application teams may not manage their applications. Note, this does not impact downstream applications. The only impact is around management.

- We'll assume the single-node Rancher server container is called `rancher_server` during the following steps. If the name is different, please update the commands listed in the following steps.

- This section will assume you know what RKE is and how to use it. Note that we will cover RKE in much more detail in the next chapter.

Backing up the current Rancher server

During this section, we'll take a backup of the current Rancher single node server, including the Kubernetes certificates, `etcd`, and the SSL certs for the Rancher URL. The steps are as follows:

1. SSH into the current Rancher server node.

2. Become root using the `sudo su -` command.

3. Stop the current Rancher server using the `docker stop rancher_server` command.

4. Create a volume from the current server using the `docker create --volumes-from rancher_server --name rancher-data-<DATE> rancher/rancher:<RANCHER_CONTAINER_TAG>` command. Please replace the date and tag placeholder values.

5. Create a `tar.gz` file backup using the `docker run --volumes-from rancher-data-<DATE> -v $PWD:/backup:z busybox tar pzcvf /backup/rancher-data-backup-<RANCHER_VERSION>-<DATE>.tar.gz /var/lib/rancher` command. Please replace the date and tag placeholder values.

6. Verify the backup file has been created using the `ls -lh` command. The backup file will be created in the current directory.

7. Restart the Rancher server backup using the `docker start rancher_server` command.

8. Open a shell into the Rancher server container using the `docker exec -it rancher_server /bin/bash` command.

9. Backup the current certificated using the `tar -zcvf pki.bundle.tar.gz /etc/kubernetes/ssl` command.

10. Leave the shell using the `exit` command.

11. Copy the backup file out of the Rancher server using the `docker cp rancher_server:/var/lib/rancher/pki.bundle.tar.gz` command.

12. Create a temporary container using the `docker run --net=container:rancher_server -it -v $(pwd):/cwd --name etcd-utility rancher/rke-tools:v0.1.20` command.

13. Set up certificates for `etcd` using the `mkdir ssl; cd ssl; cp /cwd/pki.bundle.tar.gz .; tar -zxvf pki.bundle.tar.gz --strip-components 3` commands.

14. Take an `etcd` backup using the `cd /; ETCDCTL_API=3 etcdctl snapshot save --cacert=/ssl/kube-ca.pem --cert=/ssl/kube-etcd-127-0-0-1.pem --key=/ssl/kube-etcd-127-0-0-1-key.pem single-node-etcd-snapshot` command.

15. Exit the shell using the `exit` command.

16. Copy the `etcd` backup out of the temporary container using the `docker cp etcd-utility:/single-node-etcd-snapshot` command.

17. Stop the current Rancher server using the `docker stop rancher_server` command.

18. Copy the `pki.bundle.tar.gz` and `single-node-etcd-snapshot` files to whatever server/workstation you will be using to run the `rke` commands from. Some people will use the first node in the cluster for this task.

Starting cutover to new cluster

At this point, we're going to start restoring the backup into the new cluster and migrate over the Rancher URL:

1. You should update the DNS or your load balancer to redirect traffic from the old single-node Rancher server to the new cluster. Note, the DNS might take some time to propagate fully, so we'll want to do that now.

2. We do want to modify the `cluster.yaml` file only to include the first node. We're going to assume that the hostname is `node01` for the rest of the steps. You can use the example located at `https://raw.githubusercontent.com/PacktPublishing/Rancher-Deep-Dive/main/ch03/migrating_from_single_to_ha/cluster.yml`.

3. SCP over the `single-node-etcd-snapshot` and `pki.bundle.tar.gz` files to `node01`.

4. SSH into the node01 host and become root using the `sudo su -` command.

5. Create the directory snapshot directory using the `mkdir -p /opt/rke/etcd-snapshots` command.

6. Move the two backup files into the `/opt/rke/etcd-snapshots` directory. These files should be owned by root.

7. You can now leave the SSH terminal on `node01`.

8. Start the restore using the `rke etcd snapshot-restore --name single-node-etcd-snapshot --config cluster.yaml` command.

    This process might take 5-10 minutes to complete. Example command output is located at `https://raw.githubusercontent.com/PacktPublishing/Rancher-Deep-Dive/main/ch03/migrating_from_single_to_ha/restore_command_output.txt`.

9. At this point, you can start the cluster using the `rke up --config cluster.yaml` command.

10. If you run into any errors, try running the `rke up` command a second time.

11. Once it completes successfully, you can edit the `cluster.yaml` file to include `node02` and `node03`.

12. Run `rke up` again to add the additional nodes.

13. At this point, you can log in to Rancher and verify everything is accessible and healthy. Note that it might take a few minutes for downstream clusters to reconnect and become *active* in the UI.

14. It is important to note that any cluster-level changes such as creating a new cluster, editing an existing cluster, or deleting a cluster should be avoided until you are sure that you will not be rolling back to the old server.

Cleaning up/rolling back

In the event of an unsuccessful migration, use the following steps:

1. Change the DNS record for the Rancher URL back to the original server.

2. Start the Rancher single node container using the `docker start rancher_ server` command.

3. It is important to note that it is currently not possible to migrate changes made in HA back to a single node. So, in the event of a rollback, all changes since shutting the single Rancher node will be lost.

4. After a few days of *burn-in*, you can delete the old VM or clean up the old server using the script at `https://raw.githubusercontent.com/ rancherlabs/support-tools/master/extended-rancher-2- cleanup/extended-cleanup-rancher2.sh`.

Summary

In this chapter, we learned about how a single-node Rancher works and its pros and cons. We then went over the steps and commands needed to install Rancher in single node mode. We finally went into detail about migrating to an HA setup, including backing up the current data and restoring it.

In the next chapter, we will cover RKE and RKE2, including where they came from, how they work, and how to design a solution using them.

4

Creating an RKE and RKE2 Cluster

The standard way of deploying Rancher is by creating an **Rancher Kubernetes Engine (RKE)** cluster then using Helm to install Rancher on the cluster. The new way to deploy Kubernetes clusters using RKE2 is built on K3s and the new internal cluster management model. By doing so, Rancher can manage the cluster it lives on directly without requiring an external tool such as RKE. This chapter will cover when using RKE2 over RKE makes sense, and how to bootstrap the first node and join additional nodes to the cluster. At this point, we'll install Rancher on the cluster using the **Helm** tool, which installs the Rancher server workload on the cluster. Finally, we'll cover how to configure a load balancer to support the Rancher URL.

In this chapter, we're going to cover the following main topics:

- What is an RKE cluster?
- What is an RKE2 cluster?
- What is RancherD?
- Requirements and limitations
- Rules for architecting a solution
- Install steps (RKE)

- Install steps (RKE2)
- Configuring an external load balancer (HAProxy)
- Configuring MetalLB

Let's get started!

What is an RKE cluster?

RKE is Rancher's Kubernetes distribution that runs entirely inside Docker containers. Of course, RKE is a CNCF-certified distribution, so all the standard Kubernetes components and API resources are available. The easiest way to understand RKE clusters is to know where it originated and how it works.

Where did RKE come from?

Originally, when Rancher first started creating Kubernetes clusters, Rancher used its clustering software called **Cattle**, with the idea being Kubernetes was just another application in the cluster. This caused several problems ranging from kubelet and Cattle fighting to control the containers to even needing a custom load balancer solution built on top of HAProxy. But for most components, the most significant issue was that the Rancher server managed the Cattle side of the cluster, and Kubernetes managed the pod side. This meant that the cluster had a dependency on Rancher to get pod IPs and needed Rancher to update the load balancer when pod changes happened. This all changed with Rancher v2.x and the creation of RKE, the idea being RKE will create and manage the cluster independent of the Rancher server. Of course, some of the core ideas of Cattle were brought forward into RKE, with the main idea being if everything is just a container, then Rancher doesn't need to care about the OS. RKE doesn't need any libraries or packages. At its core, RKE manages standalone Docker containers for core Kubernetes services. These include etcd, kube-apiserver, kube-scheduler, kube-controller-manager, kubelet, and kube-proxy.

How does RKE work?

One of the core design principles is that RKE has desired state configuration in the form of a configuration file called `cluster.yaml`. With this file, RKE knows what kind of cluster you want to build, what nodes to use, and how each Kubernetes component should be configured. This file is a YAML formatted file, so you will need to follow the YAML standard when creating/editing this file with a common trap for new players being tabs. YAML uses spaces and not taba, even though they look the same. If you start running into syntax errors, it might be because of tabs. What follows is an example `cluster.yaml` with the next section. We'll break down the different parts of the config file.

```
nodes:
  - address: node01.support.tools
    hostname_override: node1
    internal_address: 192.168.1.101
    user: ubuntu
    role:
      - controlplane
      - worker
      - etcd
  - address: node02.support.tools
    hostname_override: node2
    internal_address: 192.168.1.102
    user: ubuntu
    role:
      - controlplane
      - worker
      - etcd
  - address: node03.support.tools
    hostname_override: node3
    internal_address: 192.168.1.103
    user: ubuntu
    role:
      - controlplane
      - worker
      - etcd

cluster_name: examplecluster
kubernetes_version: v1.21.5-rancher1-1

ingress:
  provider: nginx

services:
  kube-api:
    audit_log:
      enabled: true
  etcd:
    backup_config:
      enabled: true          # enables recurring etcd snapshots
      interval_hours: 3      # time increment between snapshots
      retention: 72          # time in days before snapshot purge
      # Optional S3
      s3backupconfig:
        access_key: "ABCDE....."
        secret_key:  "12345679....."
        bucket_name: "etcd"
        folder: "examplecluster"
        endpoint: "s3.us-west-1.amazonaws.com"
        region: "us-west-1"
```

Figure 4.1 – Example cluster.yml

Full config: https://raw.githubusercontent.com/PacktPublishing/
Rancher-Deep-Dive/main/ch04/example_configs/simple_3_node_
cluster.yml

The first section is nodes. In this section, you'll define the nodes used to create the cluster. If we break down the node definition, we'll see the first line, which is address. This is the hostname or IP address that RKE will use to connect to the node. It is pretty standard to use a server's **FQDN (Fully Qualified Domain Name)**.

> **Important Note**
> The server where RKE is being run from must be able to resolve the hostname.

This address should not be changed without removing the node from the cluster first then rejoining it as a new node. The address field is required when defining a node.

The following section is hostname_override, which sets the node name in Kubernetes. Most people will set this to be the short hostname. This name does not have to be in DNS as it is just a label in Kubernetes. For example, AWS uses the naming convention of ip-12-34-56-78.us-west-2.compute.internal, but you might want to override this to be something more helpful such as etcd01 or prod-worker01.

> **Note**
> Just like the address field, the hostname field should not be changed after a node has been configured.

If you would like to change the hostname, IP address, or role, you should remove, clean it, and rejoin it. If this field is not set, RKE will default to using the address field.

The following field is user. This field is used by RKE when creating its SSH tunnel to the nodes. This account should have permission to run the docker command without sudo. This user must be a member of the group Docker or be root. If a user is not defined at the node level, RKE will default to the currently running user. It is standard for this to be root or a service account. Rancher recommends typically not using a personal account as you will need to set up SSH keys.

This brings us to the next field: `ssh_key_path`. This should be the path to the SSH private key for connecting to a node. RKE does require SSH keys to be set up between the server running the RKE binary and all of the nodes. When you SSH to the nodes, you get prompted with a password or **2FA (two-factor authentication)**. You will need to work with your Linux server team to change this. If `ssh_key_path` is not set at the node level, it will default to the cluster's default option as defined in the **Global settings** section. If `ssh_key_path` is not set, RKE will default to `~/.ssh/id_rsa`.

This ties into the next section, `port`, which is the port that RKE will use for connecting to the SSH server. RKE will default to port 22. Usually, this is not changed, but in rare cases, when using port forwarding, multiple servers can share the same public IP address without RKE needing direct IP access to the nodes. The following field is `docker_socket`, which is the file path to the Docker socket. This file is a Unix domain socket, sometimes called an IPC socket. This file provides API access to dockerd.

Note that this API does not have authentication or encryption and has complete control over Docker and its containers. This file must be protected; hence, by default, this file is owned by the root user and the Docker group. RKE uses this file to connect to Docker Engine to run commands, create containers, and so on.

Finally, we get to the `role` fields. These fields define what role (`etcd`, `controlplane`, or `worker`) is assigned to a node. You can mix and match these role assignments as you want. For example, the standard three-node cluster has all three nodes having all three roles. We will go into more detail in the *Rules for architecting a solution* section.

The following section is what I call the global settings section. This section is where you can define cluster-level settings. We'll be covering the most common settings, with the complete list of cluster settings being located at `https://rancher.com/docs/rke/latest/en/config-options/`. The first field is `cluster_name`, which is used for setting the name of your cluster. This setting doesn't affect the cluster, with the only real change being the `kubeconfig` file that RKE generates will have the cluster name in it, which can make mapping kubeconfig to a cluster much more straightforward. By default, RKE will set this to local, and this setting can be changed at any time.

The next most common setting is `ignore_docker_version`. This setting tells RKE if it should ignore an unsupported Docker version on a node. RKE has a built-in metadata file that maps all the supported versions that have been tested and approved by Rancher. It is expected that Docker will be upgraded with the operating system as part of standard patching, which can cause RKE not to upgrade a cluster if the RKE release is not as up to date. It is pretty common to set this setting to `true` so that RKE will still throw a warning message in the logs, but it will continue building the cluster.

The next field is probably the most important setting you can set, which is `kubernetes_version`. By default, when RKE is created, it will have a default Kubernetes version set. This is usually the highest officially supported version at build time. For example, RKE v1.2.3 will default the Kubernetes version `v1.19.4-rancher1-1`, which is fine when the cluster is created. But if later, someone upgrades RKE to v1.3.1, which has the new default of `v1.21.5-rancher1-1`, suppose you didn't set your Kubernetes versions in your `cluster.yaml` file. The next RKE upgrade event will cause what I call an accidental upgrade. This can be fine but has been known to cause problems. We don't want to upgrade a cluster without testing and planning. Hence, Rancher usually recommends setting `kubernetes_version` in your `cluster.yaml` as a safety measure.

> **Note**
> This setting also sets the image version tags of all the Kubernetes components such as etcd, kube-apiserver, canal, ingress-nginx-controller, and so on.

This brings us to the next field, `system_images`. This section has a list of all the Docker images and their tags for all the different components. For example, the line `etcd: rancher/coreos-etcd:v3.1.12` sets the Docker image to use for etcd. Note that, by default, Docker pulls images without a registry name from Docker Hub. You can change the behavior using the `--registry-mirror` flag to force Docker to use a private registry instead. This is usually used in air-gapped environments where your servers cannot pull images from Docker Hub. If you want to learn more about setting this up, please see Rancher's documentation at `https://rancher.com/docs/rke/latest/en/config-options/system-images/#air-gapped-setups`.

Finally, we come to the `services` section. In this section, we'll define the settings for each of the Kubernetes components, for e.g., if you want to configure etcd backups. Note that you should have etcd backups turned on, and newer RKE versions turn local backups on by default. You go to services, etcd, and `backup_config`. There you can enable recurring etcd snapshots by setting `enabled` to `true`. You can also set the backup schedule using `interval_hours`. RKE doesn't use a schedule like cron for its backup schedule. The schedule is based on when the `etcd-tools` container is started. The basic process is that `etcd-tools` will take a backup as soon the container starts, then sleep for X number of hours as defined in `interval_hours` until taking another backup and repeating this process. Currently, there is no way of telling RKE to take a backup at a scheduled time.

The next setting is `retention`, which sets how many hours `etcd-tools` will keep a snapshot before purging them. The current default is 6 hours. But it is common to increase this setting to something like 72 hours. This is mainly to stop backups from rolling off too quickly. For example, if a change was made late on a Friday, you might not catch it until Monday. With the default setting, you will have lost that recovery point. But if you set it to 72 hours, you still have a chance. It is important to note that etcd snapshots are complete copies of the database, so if your etcd database is 1 GB in size, your backup will be 1 GB before compression, with most backups being in the 100~200 MB range after compression. By default, RKE will back up locally on the etcd nodes to the directory /opt/rke/etcd-snapshots with each etcd node having a full copy of the backups. This is great for ease of use but leads to the problem that you are storing your backups on the same server you are backing up. You can, of course, set up `rsync` scripts to copy this data off another server or use a backup tool such as TSM to back up this directory, or even use a tool such as Veeam to take an image backup of the whole server. But what I usually recommend is to use the S3 backup option.

This leads us into the next section, which is `s3backupconfig`. These settings allow you to configure `etcd-tools` to send its etcd snapshots to an S3 bucket instead of local storage. This helps in disaster recovery cases where you lose a data center or when someone deleted all your etcd nodes in vCenter by mistake, because with `cluster.yaml`, `cluster.rkestate`, and an etcd backup, we can rebuild a cluster from nothing. Please have a look at my Kubernetes Master Class on Disaster Recovery located at `https://github.com/mattmattox/Kubernetes-Master-Class/tree/main/disaster-recovery` for more details on this process. It's also important to note that just because this is S3, it doesn't mean you have to use AWS's S3 offering. Any S3 provider will work assuming they are following the S3 standard.

What is an RKE2 cluster?

RKE2, also known as RKE Government, is Rancher's new Kubernetes distribution. RKE2 differs from RKE in several ways, the first being its focus on security.

> **Note**
>
> To make things easier in this section, we will call the original RKE distribution **RKE1**, with the new distribution being called **RKE2**.

Originally in RKE1 clusters, the cluster was not entirely secure by default, meaning you had to take steps (The Rancher Hardening Guide: `https://rancher.com/docs/rancher/v2.6/en/security/#rancher-hardening-guide`) to pass the CIS Kubernetes Benchmark. Both because of the difficulty of the process and the fact that some people didn't even know about it meant a good number of RKE1 clusters were left insecure. RKE2 flips that model around by being secure by default and requiring you to go through several complex steps to make it less secure. RKE2 also passes the CIS Kubernetes Benchmark v1.5 and v1.6 like RKE1 does and FIPS 140-2 compliance. Finally, on the security side, the RKE2 process has been built from the start with CVE scanning as part of the build pipeline, making it very difficult to include known CVE issues in the product.

The second big difference is the conversion from Docker to containerd. With RKE1, everything was built around Docker and Docker-based commands/APIs. And with the announcement of removing support for the Docker runtime in Kubernetes v1.22, this migration is a must in the long-term supportability of Kubernetes. I will note that Dockershim, an adapter between the Kubernetes **CRI (Container Runtime Interface)** and Docker, has allowed people to keep using Docker with Kubernetes for the foreseeable future. Rancher is also going to maintain a fork of cri-dockerd. Please see `https://github.com/rancher/rancher/issues/30307` for more details and the official statement. With all that being said, RKE2 and K3s moved to containerd because of speed and management overhead. Docker brings a lot of tools and libraries into the picture that are not needed by a Kubernetes host and wastes resources. This is because Docker is running containerd under the hood, so why not remove that layer and just let kubelet directly manage containerd?

The third significant change was moving from running everything in containers to allowing some low-level components such as kubelet to run as a binary directly on the host. Because items such as kubelet are outside of containterd, kubelet can do tasks such as upgrading containerd without running into the chicken and the egg issue as you would in RKE1. Kubelet can't upgrade Docker because the first step is to stop Docker, which stops kubelet, which stops the upgrade. As you can see in the following diagram shown, RKE2 has **Managed processes**, which run directly on the operating system and not as containers.

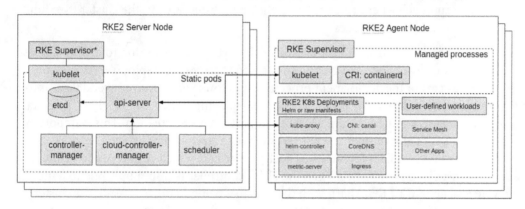

Figure 4.2 – RKE2 server and agent high-level diagram

The fourth significant change was no more containers that are not pods. In RKE1, most of the core components such as the kubelet, etcd, kube-apiserver, kube-controller-manger, and kube-scheduler were Docker containers but were not Kubernetes pods. This was because these containers were created and managed by the RKE binary and not by kubelet. With RKE2, kubelet is a binary on the host operating system, and kubelet can use static pods. These pods are unique because they can be created and started without etcd, kube-apiserver, and so on. This is done by making the manifest files that include all the items usually provided by the cluster ahead of time, such as the pod name, IP, MAC address, secrets, volumes, and so on, at which point, kubelet can start and manage the pod just like any other pod. Once kubelet can connect to the cluster, that pod can be discovered and added into etcd.

This leads us to the most significant change in RKE2 over RKE1: moving from centralized control to a distributed control model. With RKE1, all the core cluster management tasks were managed by the RKE1 binary itself. Even when Rancher is managing the cluster, it creates the `cluster.yml` file and runs the RKE1 binary inside the Rancher server. Because of this, with RKE1, you must update `cluster.yaml` and run an `rke up` command. This process then causes the RKE1 binary to reconcile the cluster. RKE2 takes this process and moves it into the cluster, meaning an RKE2 cluster can manage itself. RKE2 uses an approach where you bootstrap the first master node in the cluster then join the other master and worker nodes.

As part of moving to a distributed model with RKE1, you had the option to deploy simple YAML files as an add-on job. RKE2 builds on this to allow you to deploy YAML files and Helm charts as part of the deployment process. This allows you to move several tasks into the cluster creation process. For example, you are deploying Rancher's Longhorn product, which provides a distributed storage provider, as part of cluster creation. This is important as a good number of environments will need storage to start deploying over services such as Prometheus. RKE2 integrates K3s' Helm controller, which allows you to define a Helm chart installation via YAML. Then the Helm controller will spin up a pod to handle deploying and upgrading that chart, with the end goal being to move most of the cluster tasks, such as adding and removing nodes to and from clusters, from a process inside the Rancher server to a process on the downstream cluster itself. This helps Rancher support managing clusters at a mass scale (1 million+ clusters for a single Rancher deployment), including better data handling for edge clusters by lowering traffic between the Rancher servers and the edge cluster.

Finally, the process of joining a node to an existing RKE2 cluster is a lot different than an RKE1 cluster. With RKE1, the binary handles deploying the containers to the new node. With RKE2, there is a simple process where the first node is started with a special flag, `cluster-init`. This tells RKE2 to create a new cluster. This includes creating a new etcd cluster and creating a fresh root CA (kube-ca), and if it is not set, RKE2 will generate a token for the cluster. Once the first node has been created, the Kubernetes API should be available and used by the rest of the nodes to join the cluster. This is why you need a round-robin DNS record or a load balancer for your Kubernetes API endpoint. Moving forward, you need to set the RKE2 cluster token on each new node in the cluster along with the server endpoint. Both these settings are required for RKE2 even to start. These settings are defined in the file `/etc/rancher/rke2/config.yaml`. Note that with RKE2, this file configures RKE2 in general. So if you want to define kubelet settings, node labels/taints, and so on, this file must be protected as the token stored in that file is used for several security-related tasks such as Kube-API access and etcd encryption. So, the token should be treated as a password, that is, it should be unique, random, and long. The default length is 32 characters. You should also avoid using special control characters such as the dollar sign, backslash, quotemarks, and so on.

What is RancherD?

RancherD is a special binary designed to bootstrap a Kubernetes cluster (K3s/RKE2) and Rancher. The idea is to simplify the creation of the K3s/RKE2 cluster that directly supports the Rancher server application and its components. RancherD is designed only to be run once on a node, at which point RancherD takes care of setting up K3s/RKE2 and the manifest files needed for Rancher. This process can be beneficial when you want to deploy large numbers of Rancher deployments. For example, if you wish each of your Kubernetes clusters to have its own Rancher dashboard, environments do not share a single Rancher deployment. This is seen a lot with hosting companies that provide Rancher as a service to their customers.

It is important to note that RancherD uses RKE2 behind the scenes, so the same requirements and limitations apply. We'll be covering those requirements and limitations in the next section.

Requirements and limitations

In this section, we'll discuss the basic requirements for RKE and RKE2 clusters along with their limitations.

Basic requirements

Let's have a look at the basic requirements for **RKE** first:

- RKE requires Docker to be installed on the host before RKE can join it to the cluster.

- RKE runs on almost any Linux OS, but you should refer to the Rancher Support Matrix located at `https://rancher.com/support-maintenance-terms/`.

- RKE requires SSH access to all nodes in the cluster using an SSH key.

- RKE requires permissions to run Docker commands without sudo or a password.

- All nodes in a cluster must be routable to all other nodes, meaning you can have nodes on direct subnets, but you must be able to connect between nodes directly without using an NAT.

- RKE requires firewall rules to be opened between nodes depending on the role of the node. Please see `https://rancher.com/docs/rke/latest/en/os/#ports` for more details.

- An RKE cluster requires at least one node for each role in the cluster, with the roles being etcd, controlplane, and worker. The cluster will not come online until this requirement is met. Note that a node can have multiple roles, including having all three roles.

- RKE only requires a minimum of one core, which changes with cluster size and node role selection. It's recommended to at least have two cores, with the standard size being four cores.

- The memory requirement is based on the node's role, with the etcd role needing about 4 GB, kube-apiserver needing 4 GB, and the worker role needing about 2 GB.

- For storage, you'll need around 10 GB of tier 1/2 storage (SSD is preferred but not required).

- For the filesystem, RKE relies on Docker storage drivers, so please review Docker's documentation at `https://docs.docker.com/storage/storagedriver/`.

- RKE doesn't require its own filesystem, but it's recommended that `/var/lib/docker` be on its own filesystem/disk to prevent Docker from filling up the root filesystem.

- On etcd nodes, the database is stored in a bind mount located at `/var/lib/etcd` and is not required to be on its own dedicated disk. Also, with larger clusters, it is recommended for this data to be stored on tier 1 storage as etcd can be sensitive to storage latency.

- If you are using RKE's local backup option, the `/opt/rke/etcd-snapshots` directory should be its own filesystem or an NFS share for safety reasons.

The following are the requirements of **RKE2**:

- RKE2 runs on almost any Linux OS, but you should refer to the Rancher Support Matrix located at `https://rancher.com/support-maintenance-terms/`.

- Installing and configuring RKE2 requires root-level permissions on the host.

- All nodes in a cluster must be routable to all other nodes, meaning you can have nodes on direct subnets, but you must be able to connect between nodes directly without using an NAT.

- RKE2 requires firewall rules to be opened between nodes depending on the role of the node. Please see `https://rancher.com/docs/rancher/v2.5/en/installation/requirements/ports/` for more details.

- RKE2 requires a master and worker node in the cluster. Note that both roles can be on the same node.

- RKE2 only requires a minimum of one core, which changes with cluster size and node role selection. It's recommended to have at least have two cores, with the standard size being four cores.

- The memory requirement is based on the node's role, with the master role needing 4 GB and the worker/agent role requiring about 2 GB.

- RKE2 stores its data under the mount point `/var/lib/rancher`, which includes containerd data, images, etcd, and so on.

- For master nodes, etcd is stored under `/var/lib/rancher/rke2/server/ db/etcd`; it is recommended that this data be stored on tier 1 storage as etcd can be sensitive to storage latency.

- RKE2 has etcd backups turned on by default and stores the backups under `/var/ lib/rancher/rke2/server/db/snapshots,` which should be its own filesystem or can be an NFS share for safety reasons.

Design limitations and considerations

Now, let's discuss the design limitations for both clusters.

The following lists the design considerations for RKE:

- After creating a cluster, you cannot change the network provider (CNI), called the network plugin in the RKE documentation located at `https://rancher.com/ docs/rancher/v2.5/en/faq/networking/cni-providers/`.

- By default, RKE will use the subnets `10.42.0.0/16` and `10.43.0.0/16` for the pod overlay and service network. This cannot be changed after cluster creation, so if these networks overlap with your current network, you'll need to choose different subnets for your cluster.

- Support for Windows worker nodes is currently limited to Rancher-managed RKE clusters. You cannot use RKE directly to join a Windows node.

- RKE currently doesn't provide support for the ARM64 OS.

- RKE supports an air-gapped environment, but you are required to do some additional steps, which are located at `https://rancher.com/docs/rke/ latest/en/config-options/system-images/#air-gapped-setups.`

- Switching an RKE to an air-gapped environment can be done by reconfiguring the cluster, deployments, and applications.

- RKE clusters can be built across data centers so long as there is an odd number of data centers with an etcd and control plane node in each data center.

- Network latency between etcd nodes should be less than 10 ms.

The following are the design considerations for RKE2:

- After creating a cluster, you cannot change the network provider (CNI), called the network plugin in the RKE2 documentation located at `https://docs.rke2.io/install/network_options/`.

- By default, RKE2 will use the subnets `10.42.0.0/16` and `10.43.0.0/16` for the pod overlay and service network. This cannot be changed after cluster creation so if you are currently using one of these subnets in your current network, you should change this setting.

- As of writing, RKE2 provides experimental support for Windows nodes, but you still need to provide a Linux node in the cluster.

- As of writing, RKE2 doesn't provide support for the ARM64 OS even though K3s does.

> **Note**
>
> There is an open feature request (`https://github.com/rancher/rke2/issues/1946`) to offer ARM64 support.

- RKE2 supports an air-gapped environment, but you are required to do some additional steps, which are located at `https://docs.rke2.io/install/airgap/`.

- RKE2 in an air-gapped environment can work in private registry mode and tarball mode with the steps located at `https://docs.rke2.io/install/airgap/`.

- RKE2 clusters can be built across data centers so long as there is an odd number of data centers with a master node in each data center.

- Network latency between etcd nodes should be less than 10 ms.

Now that we understand the limitations of RKE1 and RKE2, we'll be using these along with a set of rules and examples to help us design a solution using RKE1 and RKE2.

Rules for architecting a solution

In this section, we'll cover some standard designs and the pros and cons of each. It is important to note that each environment is unique and will require tuning for the best performance and experience. It's also important to note that all CPU, memory, and storage sizes are recommended starting points and may need to be increased or decreased by your workloads and deployment processes.

Before designing a solution, you should be able to answer the following questions:

- Will multiple environments be sharing the same cluster?

- Will production and non-production workloads be on the same cluster?

- What level of availability does this cluster require?

- Will this cluster be spanning multiple data centers in a metro cluster environment?

- How much latency will there be between nodes in the cluster?

- How many pods will be hosted in the cluster?

- What are the average and maximum size of pods you will be deploying in the cluster?

- Will you need GPU support for some of your applications?

- Will you need to provide storage to your applications?

- If you need storage, do you need only **RWO (Read Write Once)**, or will you need **RWX (Read Write Many)**?

RKE clusters

The following are designs for RKE clusters.

Single-node clusters

In this design, we will be deploying an RKE cluster on a single node with all roles.

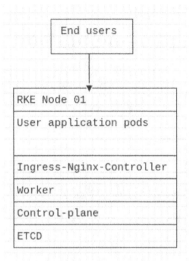

Figure 4.3 – RKE single-node cluster

Example config: `https://github.com/PacktPublishing/Rancher-Deep-Dive/blob/main/ch04/standard_designs/rke/00_single_node_cluster/cluster.yaml`

The **pros** of a single-node cluster are listed as follows:

- Simple to set up.

- Fast and easy to create.

- No external load balancer is needed.

- A great cluster for CI/CD pipelines that need a Kubernetes cluster for testing that can be destroyed later.

- Useful for sandbox testing where HA and scale is not needed.

- Can be installed on a developer's laptop where resources are minimal.

- A single-node RKE cluster can be converted to an HA cluster later.

The **cons** are listed as follows:

- No HA.

- Downtime is required during patching and upgrades.

- Can encourage bad application behavior by using the server's IP or hostname for the application endpoint instead of VIP or CNAME.

- Many Kubernetes components get their HA features from the cluster itself, so a lot of the components won't be able to handle failures as cleanly as they would in an HA cluster.

- User applications share the same nodes as management services, meaning that a runaway application can take down the cluster.

The following are the **hardware requirements**:

- Servers(s): 1 physical/virtual server

- CPU: 4 cores

- Memory: 4-8GB

Small three-node clusters

In this design, we will be deploying the smallest RKE cluster with full HA, a three-node cluster with all nodes having all roles.

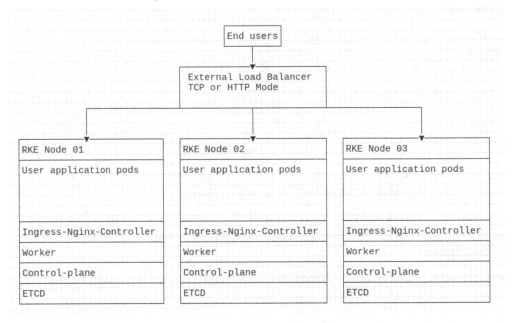

Figure 4.4 – Standard three-node RKE cluster

Example config: `https://github.com/PacktPublishing/Rancher-Deep-Dive/blob/main/ch04/standard_designs/rke/01_small_cluster/cluster.yaml`

The **pros** of a small three-node cluster are listed as follows:

- Full HA – you can lose any node in the cluster and still have full cluster and application availability.

- Simple to manage as all nodes have the same roles, so all nodes are the same.

- No required downtime during patching and upgrades. Please see Rancher's zero downtime documentation for more details at `https://rancher.com/docs/rke/latest/en/upgrades/maintaining-availability/`.

The **cons** are listed as follows:

- An external load balancer or a round-robin DNS record is needed for external application access.

- User applications share the same nodes as management services, meaning that a runaway application can take down the cluster.
- Only N+1 of availability, so during maintenance tasks, you cannot suffer a failure of a node without loss of service.

The following are the **hardware requirements**:

- Servers(s): 3 physical/virtual servers
- CPU: 4 cores per server
- Memory: 4-8GB per server

Medium clusters

In this design, we will be deploying the standard RKE cluster where we have migrated the core management services for Kubernetes to their nodes. This is done because as clusters grow in size, protecting the management services for Kubernetes becomes even more critical. This design tries to balance HA with cost. This is done by having etcd and the control plane share the same nodes but with the change of moving the worker roles to their own set nodes. This design works for 2 to 10 worker node clusters.

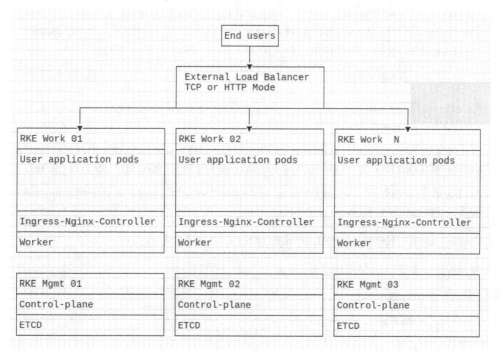

Figure 4.5 – RKE cluster with separate nodes for management services

Diagram: `https://github.com/PacktPublishing/Rancher-Deep-Dive/ blob/main/ch04/standard_designs/rke/02_medium_cluster/README. md`

Example config: `https://github.com/PacktPublishing/Rancher-Deep-Dive/blob/main/ch04/standard_designs/rke/02_medium_cluster/ cluster.yaml`

The **pros** of a medium cluster are listed as follows:

- Full HA – you can lose any one of the management nodes (etcd and control plane) in the cluster and still have complete cluster management.

- User workloads and management services run on different nodes, stopping runaway applications from taking down the cluster.

- Due to the scalable limitations of etcd, having more than five etcd nodes causes a decrease in performance. So it is normally recommended to scale the design vertically instead of horizontally.

- More than one worker node can fail without loss of service, assuming you have enough CPU and memory available on the remaining workers.

- No required downtime during patching and upgrades. Please see Rancher's zero downtime documentation for more details at `https://rancher.com/docs/ rke/latest/en/upgrades/maintaining-availability/`.

The **cons** are listed as follows:

- An external load balancer or a round-robin DNS record is needed for external application access.

- Only N+1 of availability, so during maintenance tasks, you cannot suffer a failure of a node without loss of service at the management plane (etcd and control plane).

- Additional complexity when creating nodes as you might need to size management nodes differently than worker nodes.

The following are the **hardware requirements** for etcd and the control plane:

- Servers(s): 3 physical/virtual servers

- CPU: 8 cores per server

- Memory: 8-16 GB

> **Note**
> Worker node sizing should be based on your workload and its requirements.

Large clusters

In this design, we're expanding on the design for a medium cluster but breaking up etcd and the control plane and then changing the node sizing and node count.

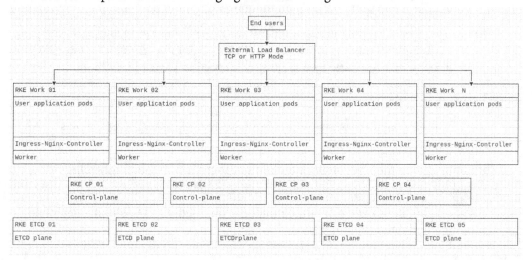

Figure 4.6 – RKE cluster with separate nodes for etcd and control plane

Diagram: `https://github.com/PacktPublishing/Rancher-Deep-Dive/raw/main/ch04/standard_designs/rke/03_large_cluster/README.md`

Example config: `https://github.com/PacktPublishing/Rancher-Deep-Dive/raw/main/ch04/standard_designs/rke/03_large_cluster/cluster.yaml`

The **pros** of large clusters are listed as follows:

- Full HA – you can lose any two management nodes (etcd and control plane) in the cluster and still have complete cluster management.

- User workloads and management services run on different nodes, stopping runaway applications from taking down the cluster.

- Due to the scalable limitations of etcd because having more than five etcd nodes causes slowness. So it is normally recommended to as etcd to design to scale vertically instead of horizontally.

- The control plane isn't designed to scale by adding more nodes because kube-apiserver is active on all nodes, but each node has a caching layer to increase performance so scaling horizontally makes the caching less efficient.

- N+2 of availability, so during maintenance tasks, you can suffer a failure of a node without loss of service at the management plane (etcd and control plane).

- More than one worker node can fail without loss of service, assuming you have enough CPU and memory available on the remaining workers.

- No required downtime during patching and upgrades. Please see Rancher's zero downtime documentation for more details at `https://rancher.com/docs/rke/latest/en/upgrades/maintaining-availability/`.

The **cons** are listed as follows:

- An external load balancer or a round-robin DNS record is needed for external application access.

- The controllers in the control plane are not scalable, with only one controller being the leader at a time.

- Additional complexity when creating nodes as you might need to size management nodes differently than worker nodes.

The following are the **hardware requirements**:

- **etcd plane**:

  - Servers(s): 5 physical/virtual servers.

  - CPU: 8-16 cores per server.

  - Memory: 32-64 GB per server for the management plane.

  - Storage: NVME storage is recommended.

- **Control plane**:

  - Servers(s): 4 physical/virtual servers.

  - CPU: 8-16 cores per server.

  - Memory: 32-64 GB per server for the management plane. Note: It is recommended for the control plane node to match the size of etcd nodes as a starting point.

> **Note**
> Worker node sizing should be based on your workload and its requirements.

RKE2 clusters

The following are design recommendations for RKE2 clusters.

Single-node clusters

In this design, we will be deploying an RKE2 cluster on a single node with all roles.

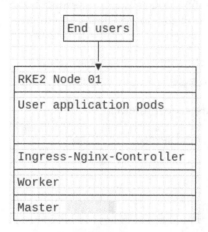

Figure 4.7 – Single-node RKE2

Diagram: `https://github.com/PacktPublishing/Rancher-Deep-Dive/raw/main/ch04/standard_designs/rke2/00_single_node_cluster/README.md`

The **pros** are as follows:

- Simple to set up.

- Fast and easy to create.

- No external load balancer needed.

- Great for CI/CD pipeline jobs that need a Kubernetes cluster to test their deployments with, after which the cluster will be destroyed.

- Great for sandbox testing where HA and scale are not needed.

- Can be installed on a developer's laptop environments where resources are minimal.
- A single-node RKE2 cluster can be converted to an HA cluster at a later date.

The **cons** are as follows:

- No HA.
- Downtime is required during patching and upgrades.
- Can encourage bad application behavior by using the server's IP or hostname for the application endpoint instead of VIP or CNAME.
- Many Kubernetes components get their HA features from the cluster itself, so a lot of the components won't be able to handle failures as cleanly as they would in an HA cluster.
- User applications share the same nodes as management services, meaning that a runaway application can take down the cluster.

The following are the **hardware requirements**:

- Servers(s): 1 physical/virtual server
- CPU: 2 cores
- Memory: 4 GB

Small three-node clusters

In this design, we will be deploying the smallest RKE2 cluster with full HA, a three-node cluster with all nodes having all roles.

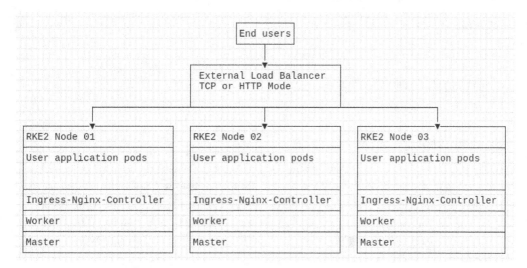

Figure 4.8 – Three-node RKE2 cluster with HA

Diagram: `https://github.com/PacktPublishing/Rancher-Deep-Dive/blob/main/ch04/standard_designs/rke2/01_small_cluster/README.md`

Example commands: `https://github.com/PacktPublishing/Rancher-Deep-Dive/blob/main/ch04/standard_designs/rke2/01_small_cluster/commands.md`

The **pros** are as follows:

- Full HA – you can lose any node in the cluster and still have full cluster and application availability.

- Simple to manage as all nodes have the same roles, so all nodes are the same.

- No required downtime during patching and upgrades. Please see Rancher's zero downtime documentation for more details at `https://rancher.com/docs/rke/latest/en/upgrades/maintaining-availability/`.

The **cons** are as follows:

- An external load balancer or a round-robin DNS record is needed for external application access and RKE2 management.

- User applications share the same nodes as management services, meaning that a runaway application can take down the cluster.

- Only `N+1` of availability, so during maintenance tasks, you cannot suffer a failure of a node without loss of service.

The following are the **hardware requirements**:

- Servers(s): 3 physical/virtual servers
- CPU: 2-4 cores per server
- Memory: 4-8 GB per server

Medium clusters

In this design, we will be deploying the standard RKE2 cluster where we have migrated the core management services for Kubernetes to their own nodes. This is done because as clusters grow in size, protecting the management services for Kubernetes becomes even more critical. This design tries to balance HA with cost. This is done by having the master role on its own nodes with the worker roles on their own nodes. This design works for 2 to 10 worker node clusters.

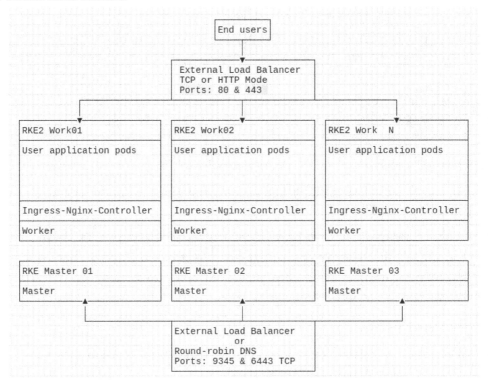

Figure 4.9 – RKE2 cluster with separate nodes for management services

Diagram: https://github.com/PacktPublishing/Rancher-Deep-Dive/raw/main/ch04/standard_designs/rke2/02_medium_cluster/README.md

Example commands: `https://github.com/PacktPublishing/Rancher-Deep-Dive/blob/main/ch04/standard_designs/rke2/02_medium_cluster/commands.md`

The **pros** are as follows:

- Full HA – you can lose any one of the master nodes in the cluster and still have complete cluster management.

- User workloads and management services run on different nodes, stopping runaway applications from taking down the cluster.

- Due to the scalable limitations of etcd, having more than five etcd nodes causes a decrease in performance. So it is normally recommended to scale the design vertically instead of horizontally.

- More than one worker node can fail without loss of service, assuming you have enough CPU and memory available on the remaining workers.

- No required downtime during patching and upgrades. Please see Rancher's zero downtime documentation for more details at `https://rancher.com/docs/rke/latest/en/upgrades/maintaining-availability/`.

The **cons** are as follows:

- An external load balancer or a round-robin DNS record is needed for external application access and RKE2 management.

- Only N+1 of availability, so during maintenance tasks, you cannot suffer a failure of a node without loss of service at the management plane (etcd and control plane).

- Additional complexity when creating nodes as you might need to size management nodes differently than worker nodes.

The following are the **hardware requirements**:

- Master node:

  - Servers(s): 3 physical/virtual servers

  - CPU: 4 cores per server

  - Memory: 8 GB

> **Note**
>
> Worker node sizing should be based on your workload and its requirements.

Large clusters

For a larger cluster with RKE2, you are limited in your design because in an RKE2 cluster, etcd and control plane services are tied together and cannot be separated into different planes. The only real change that can be made is to increase the master node count from 3 to 5 then start increasing the size of the node.

Install steps (RKE)

Once you have created `cluster.yaml`, you have RKE create a cluster for you. This is done by running the `rke up --config cluster.yaml` command. RKE will look for the `cluster.rkestate file`. If it cannot find that file, RKE will assume that you are creating a new cluster, which causes RKE to create a new root CA certificate called **kube-ca** along with all the other certificates needed in the cluster. RKE will verify that all are valid and rotate and create the certificates for the different Kubernetes components as required if the cluster already has certificates. RKE then verifies the dialer has access to all the nodes in the cluster. The dialer will create an SSH tunnel to each node and bind to the Docker socket file. RKE will then use a file-deployer container to push the certificates to each node in the `/etc/kubernetes/ssl directory`.

RKE will then check if any etcd nodes are being added or removed from the cluster. Suppose RKE detects that the downtime settings for etcd are currently violated. By default, RKE only allows one etcd node to be down. RKE then handles the process of removing etcd nodes by stopping the etcd container and removing the etcd member from the etcd leader. RKE will then take care of adding any new etcd nodes to the cluster. It is important to note that this process is designed to be slow and safe – RKE will only do one etcd node at a time and take an etcd snapshot before changing each node.

Once the etcd plane has been completed successfully, RKE will take care of starting the controlplane. This process includes kube-apiserver, kube-controller-manager, and kube-scheduler. RKE will start each component on each control plane node one at a time. RKE will test that its health check endpoint is available for each component, which for most components is `/healthz`. It is vital to note RKE follows the same process as the etcd plane of verifying the max unavailable settings are not currently violated. Suppose the settings become violated during this process. RKE will stop and fail with an error.

Next, RKE will handle creating the worker plane. This process is different than the etcd and control plane because it's designed to be done in parallel. This is mainly done for larger clusters where you might have hundreds of worker nodes in the cluster. So, by default, RKE will process 10% of the worker nodes at once. For the existing node, RKE will cordon the node to prevent changes to the node. It is important to note that the application pods continue to run during this process, with the only impact being that the CNI provider might need to be restarted. The effect is like unplugging the NIC from the node for a few seconds before plugging it back in. This can affect applications that use long-lived connections that need to be held open. This is typically seen with applications that use database connection pooling, where the application will create several database connections then keep them open. Depending on the application, these connections might not reconnect automatically and may need to be restarted.

Install steps (RKE2)

RKE2 handles the process of cluster creation very differently compared to RKE1. With RKE2, the first master node in the cluster is unique because it handles bootstrapping the cluster. The bootstrap process creates a root CA certificate, and if the cluster token has not been set, RKE2 will handle creating one. Then RKE2 will initialize the etcd cluster. Finally, RKE2 will create the etcd encryption key based on the cluster token. RKE2 then stores the cluster state in a unique bootstrap key pair in etcd called bootstrap. This bootstrap data includes the Kubernetes certificates, private keys, and the etcd encryption keys. Once the cluster has been bootstrapped, the additional master nodes can join the cluster using the Kubernetes API endpoint to connect to the first node in the cluster. The RKE2 will use the cluster token to authenticate and decrypt the bootstrap data. Finally, once all the master nodes have been created, the same process is done for the worker nodes, with the only difference being the INSTALL_RKE2_TYPE="agent" install option, which tells RKE2 to configure this node as a worker node.

The following are some example commands for creating a standard three master node cluster with worker nodes. More details about these commands can be found at https://docs.rke2.io/install/ha/.

```
# 1st master node
curl -sfL https://get.rke2.io | sh -
mkdir -p /etc/rancher/rke2/
cat << EOF > /etc/rancher/rke2/config.yaml
kube-apiserver-arg: "kubelet-preferred-address-types=InternalIP
,ExternalIP,Hostname"
tls-san:
```

```
  - mgmt01.support.tools
  - mgmt02.support.tools
  - mgmt03.support.tools
  - rke2-vip.support.tools
node-taint:
  - "CriticalAddonsOnly=true:NoExecute"
EOF
systemctl enable rke2-server.service
systemctl start rke2-server.service
```

This preceding code handles bootstrapping the first node in the cluster along with setting up the SAN certificate for the Kubernetes API endpoint and the node taint to prevent user workloads from running on this server.

```
# Capture the node token from the first node
cat /var/lib/rancher/rke2/server/node-token`
```

We need this token in the preceding code block in order for the other nodes to join the cluster.

```
# 2nd, 3rd master nodes
curl -sfL https://get.rke2.io | sh -
mkdir -p /etc/rancher/rke2/
cat << EOF > /etc/rancher/rke2/config.yaml
kube-apiserver-arg: "kubelet-preferred-address-types=InternalIP
,ExternalIP,Hostname"
tls-san:
  - mgmt01.support.tools
  - mgmt02.support.tools
  - mgmt03.support.tools
  - rke2-vip.support.tools
node-taint:
  - "CriticalAddonsOnly=true:NoExecute"
server: https://<<Cluster DNS record>>:9345
token: <<Node Token goes here>>
EOF
systemctl enable rke2-server.service
systemctl start rke2-server.service
```

This preceding code handles joining the additional master nodes to the existing cluster.

```
# Worker nodes
curl -sfL https://get.rke2.io | INSTALL_RKE2_TYPE="agent" sh -
mkdir -p /etc/rancher/rke2/
cat << EOF > /etc/rancher/rke2/config.yaml
server: https://<<Cluster DNS record>>:9345
token: <<Node Token goes here>>
EOF
systemctl enable rke2-agent.service
systemctl start rke2-agent.service
```

This preceding code then handles joining the worker nodes to the cluster we just built.

Example commands: `https://github.com/PacktPublishing/Rancher-Deep-Dive/blob/main/ch04/standard_designs/rke2/02_medium_cluster/commands.md`

Now that we have successfully created the cluster, the next step will be to prepare an external load balancer to act as a frontend endpoint for the cluster. In the next section, we'll be configuring HAProxy in both HTTP and TCP mode. These settings are fairly standard, and you should be able to use them as a template for other load balancer technologies, for example, F5 or A10.

Configuring an external load balancer (HAProxy)

With RKE/RKE2 clusters, you will get an ingress-nginx-controller. This is a daemonset that, by default, runs on all worker nodes. And by default, nginx will listen on ports 80 and 443. Nginx will then act as a layer 7 (HTTP/HTTPS mode) load balancer for applications hosted inside the Kubernetes cluster. This is great for load balancing applications inside the cluster, but the issue you run into is how you provide redundancy across nodes. The simplest way is to create a **DNS A** record with all the worker nodes' IP addresses in the cluster and just use round-robin DNS to load balance between the nodes and handle fault-tolerance. The downside is round-robin DNS can be very slow to update, and you must rely on the clients operating the failover. In the real world, this process can be very unreliable. To solve this issue, we're going to place an HAProxy server in front of the cluster. This process would be very similar for other load balancers, such as A10, F5, nginx, and so on. Next, we're going to cover two different ways for configuring HAProxy.

TCP mode

This mode is only responsible for transferring data at the transport protocol layer, and in this case, we're only looking at TCP/80 and TCP/443. HAProxy is not terminating the connection, so things such as host-based routing and SSL are not available. Because of this, TCP mode is sometimes called *Layer 4* load balancing because it's just passing traffic. So, in this case, we will have a frontend **Virtual IP Address (VIP)** that does a one-to-one mapping for the TCP ports. It is important to note that by default, TCP mode doesn't have any session management enabled. It is normal to allow sticky sessions in TCP mode using source IP matching. This can be needed for applications that use server-based session management.

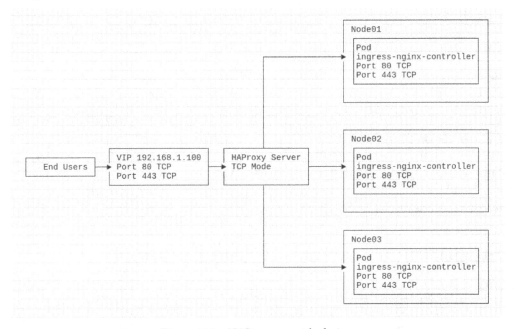

Figure 4.10 – HAProxy example design

Diagram: `https://github.com/PacktPublishing/Rancher-Deep-Dive/blob/main/ch04/haproxy/diagrams/tcp_mode.md`

Here's a sample configuration:

```
frontend prometheus
    bind *:8404
    option http-use-htx
    http-request use-service prometheus-exporter if { path /metrics }
    stats enable
    stats uri /stats
    stats refresh 10s

listen stats
    bind :9000
    mode http
    stats enable
    stats hide-version
    stats realm Haproxy\ Statistics
    stats uri /
    stats auth admin:Passw0rd

listen http
    bind *:80
    mode tcp
    balance leastconn
    stick match src
    stick-table type ip size 200k expire 30m
    server node01 192.168.1.101:80 check
    server node02 192.168.1.102:80 check
    server node03 192.168.1.103:80 check

listen https
    bind *:443
    mode tcp
    balance leastconn
    stick match src
    stick-table type ip size 200k expire 30m
    server node01 192.168.1.101:443 check ssl verify none
    server node02 192.168.1.102:443 check ssl verify none
    server node03 192.168.1.103:443 check ssl verify none
```

Figure 4.11 – Example HAProxy config when in TCP mode

Full config: `https://github.com/PacktPublishing/Rancher-Deep-Dive/blob/main/ch04/haproxy/config/tcp.cfg`

Note that in this example config, I have the two additional endpoints exposed in HAProxy, the first being the Prometheus metrics endpoint, which allows a Prometheus server to scrape HAProxy for metrics. Please see `https://www.haproxy.com/blog/haproxy-exposes-a-prometheus-metrics-endpoint/` for more details.

The second is the `stats` endpoint, enabling you to view the current status of the frontend and backend sections. This can be very helpful when troubleshooting an issue. Please see `https://www.haproxy.com/blog/exploring-the-haproxy-stats-page/` for more details. It is important to note that these endpoints should be protected by a basic user login page and firewall rules.

HTTP/HTTPS mode

This mode is responsible for terminating the HTTP and SSL connection. Because of this, HAProxy can modify the request or make routing decisions. For example, `dev.example.com` can be routed to the dev RKE cluster, with `prod.example.com` being routed to the production RKE cluster even though they share the same VIP.

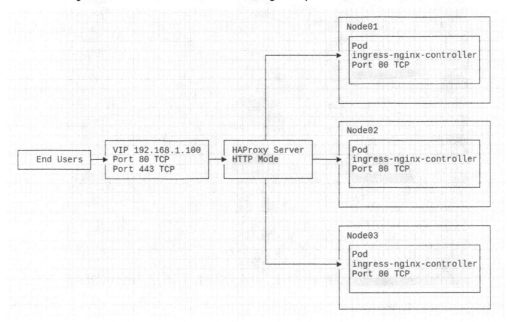

Figure 4.12 – Example HAProxy config when in HTTP mode

Diagram: `https://github.com/PacktPublishing/Rancher-Deep-Dive/blob/main/ch04/haproxy/diagrams/http_mode.md`

For environments where you don't want an external load balancer, MetalLB is an alternative option, and in the next section, we'll cover installing and configuring MetalLB in the simplest form, which is in Layer2 mode.

Configuring MetalLB

MetalLB replaces the need for an external load balancer. It does this by announcing external IP addresses using a **VIP** or **Border Gateway Protocol (BGP)**, then using port mapping to forward the traffic to the Kubernetes service. Each service exposed by MetalLB has its own IP address, which is pulled from a pool of IP addresses defined in the ConfigMap. MetalLB uses a daemonset called **speaker** to handle assigning the IP address on nodes, with the controller handling the orchestration. For more details about how this process works, please see the MetalLB documentation at `https://metallb.universe.tf/concepts/`.

Installation

The following steps will install MetalLB's controller and its speaker. More details about this process can be found at `https://metallb.universe.tf/installation/`:

```
kubectl apply -f https://raw.githubusercontent.com/metallb/
metallb/v0.10.3/manifests/namespace.yaml
kubectl apply -f https://raw.githubusercontent.com/metallb/
metallb/v0.10.3/manifests/metallb.yaml
```

Configuration

In this step, we'll define the IP address pool. More details about this process can be found at `https://metallb.universe.tf/configuration/`.

Create a configmap with the following values:

```
apiVersion: v1
kind: ConfigMap
metadata:
  namespace: metallb-system
  name: config
data:
  config: |
    address-pools:
    - name: default
      protocol: layer2
      addresses:
      - 192.168.1.240-192.168.1.250
```

Finally, to add a MetalLB IP to a cluster service, simply add the following annotation to the service definition. More details about this process can be found at `https://metallb.universe.tf/usage/`:

```
annotations:
  metallb.universe.tf/address-pool: default
```

Summary

In this chapter, we learned about RKE, RKE2, and RancherD, including how each of these tools works. We then went over the requirements and limitations of each tool. We covered the rules of architecting RKE and RKE2 clusters, including some example configs and the pros and cons of each solution. We finally went into detail about the steps for creating clusters using the configs we made earlier. We then ended the chapter by covering how to install and configure HAProxy and MetalLB as a load balancer for both RKE and RKE2 clusters. After completing this chapter, you should be able to design a solution that meets your environment needs, then deploy the cluster types. Also, by understanding how each of the clusters operate, you should be able to troubleshoot most basic issues.

In the next chapter, we will cover how to deploy Rancher on a hosted cluster and some of the limitations and rules that need to be followed.

5

Deploying Rancher on a Hosted Kubernetes Cluster

One of the great things about Rancher is it can be deployed on any certified Kubernetes cluster. This means that Rancher can be installed on a hosted Kubernetes cluster such as **Google Kubernetes Engine (GKE)**, Amazon **Elastic Container Service (EKS)** for Kubernetes, **Azure Kubernetes Service (AKS)**, or **Digital Ocean's Kubernetes Service (DOKS)**. This can simplify management on Rancher, but there are some limitations with hosted Kuberenetes solutions. We will then cover the rules for designing the hosted Kubernetes cluster along with some standard designs. At which point, we'll install Rancher on the cluster using the **Helm** tool to install the Rancher server workload on the cluster. Finally, we'll cover how to back up Rancher with a hosted Kubernetes cluster.

In this chapter, we're going to cover the following main topics:

- Understanding hosted Kubernetes clusters
- Requirements and limitations
- Rules for architecting a solution

- Creating a hosted Kubernetes cluster
- Installing and upgrading Rancher
- Rancher-Backup-Operator

Let's dive in!

Understanding hosted Kubernetes clusters

One of the questions that always comes up when deploying a Kubernetes cluster in the cloud is not just about using a hosted Kubernetes cluster, but what a hosted Kubernetes cluster is. In short, it's a cluster that is deployed and managed by an outside party. Usually, this kind of cluster is provided as a service by a cloud provider such as Amazon's AWS, Google's GCP, Microsoft's Azure, and so on. This kind of service is sometimes called **Kubernetes as a Service** (**KaaS**) because these types of clusters are provided as a service. As a consumer, there are some limitations with a hosted Kubernetes cluster versus one you build yourself:

- **Control**: When using a hosted Kubernetes cluster, you are an end user. You do not have complete control of the cluster. Tasks such as upgrading Kubernetes to a newer version are something your provider handles for you. Usually, this is triggered by you going into the cloud provider's dashboard and selecting a more recent Kubernetes version. Still, most cloud providers have the option to force an upgrade without your input. For example, in early 2020, EKS started to deprecate Kubernetes v1.14 with official support ending by 11/2020. As soon as the end-of-support date passed, Amazon began to upgrade clusters automatically, and there was little to nothing you could do to stop the upgrade. If the upgrade broke your application, there was no going back and no downgrading. Your only option was to fix your application. Google and Azure have the same process in place, with their argument being the cluster endpoints are on the public internet (in most cases) so keeping up to date with security patches is a must.

- **Access**: With a hosted Kubernetes cluster, you'll get access to the Kube API endpoint for tools such as kubectl, Helm, and even Rancher. But in most cases, you will not get access to the Kubernetes node itself. So, you can't just SSH into the node and install software such as monitoring agents and backup software. Plus, even if the cloud provider gives you SSH access to the nodes, it's typically only to the worker nodes for troubleshooting issues. Their support team will not support any customizations you make to the nodes. Also, you shouldn't be making any changes in the first place because cloud providers can and do replace nodes as needed with little to no notification beforehand.

> **Note**
>
> All major cloud providers allow you to set up a preferred maintenance window, but they can do emergency maintenance outside that window if needed.

This is generally for tasks such as replacing a failed node or applying a critical security fix.

- **Customization**: With most hosted Kubernetes clusters, the cloud provider defines items such as **etcd**, **kube-apiserver**, and **kubelet**. So, for example, if your application is hitting the Kube API endpoint, creating a high number of requests, with a self-hosted Kubernetes cluster, you can just increase the CPU and memory available to kube-apiserver. With a hosted Kubernetes cluster, there is no option to change that because the cloud provider owns that service. The same goes for customizing security settings such as etcd encryption. With a self-hosted Kubernetes cluster, you can set up the encryption however you like. With a hosted Kubernetes cluster, you are limited to whatever they provide. For example, EKS supports etcd encryption using AWS **Key Management Service (KMS)**. But with AKS, Azure turns on encryption by default but gives you no way to change or force rotate the key. And with other cloud providers such as DigitalOcean, they don't have etcd encryption at all.

> **Note**
>
> The preceding statement is valid as of writing, but Azure has stated this is on the roadmap, so this might change in the future.

- **Backups**: The cloud provider owns the etcd services and does not provide access to etcd to you. So, you have no way of taking an etcd backup. This means, if you have a catastrophic failure and lose the cluster, you have no way to restore the cluster without redeploying all your applications quickly, or you'll need to use a third-party tool such as Velero to take a YAML backup of all your Kubernetes objects. And for applications like Rancher that store their data as Kubernetes objects, the data must be backed up. This was the main reason that Rancher didn't support hosted clusters because Rancher has no way to be downgraded besides doing an etcd restore. Rancher v2.5 addressed this by creating the Rancher Backup Operator tool, which walks through all the Kubernetes objects that Rancher uses, exports them as JSON files, and packages them up into a `tarball` file, then pushes it to a backup location.

Now that we understand what a hosted Kubernetes cluster is, next, we're going to go into the requirements and limitations of some of the most popular cloud providers.

Requirements and limitations

In this section, we'll be discussing the basic requirements of Rancher on various clusters along with their limitations and design considerations.

Amazon EKS

The **basic requirements** for Amazon EKS are as follows::

- Rancher requires at least two worker nodes in the cluster, but three nodes are highly recommended.

- Each worker node should have at least two cores with 4 GB of memory.

- Rancher requires a network load balancer for accessing the Rancher console.

- Once the EKS cluster has been created, you'll need to follow the procedure located at `https://docs.aws.amazon.com/eks/latest/userguide/create-kubeconfig.html` to generate a kubeconfig file for accessing the cluster.

- Rancher requires EKS to have nginx-ingress-controller installed on the cluster. Please follow the steps located at `https://rancher.com/docs/rancher/v2.5/en/installation/install-rancher-on-k8s/amazon-eks/#5-install-an-ingress` for more details.

- The inbound port `443/TCP` should open for all downstream nodes, clusters, and end users that need Rancher UI/API access.

> **Note**
>
> Port `80` will redirect end users to the HTTPS URL. So, port `80` is not required but is recommended for the convenience of end users.

The **design limitations and considerations** are as follows:

- The cluster should span across three availability zones.

- EKS, by default, uses the DNS servers that are defined in the VPC. If you need to access on-premise resources via DNS, you should follow the procedure located at `https://docs.aws.amazon.com/vpc/latest/userguide/vpc-dns.html`.

- Suppose you are blocking outbound internet access for the cluster. In that case, you will need to provide a private registry for the images if you plan to use Amazon **Elastic Container Registry (ECR)** for this role. You'll need to configure the IAM permissions for the cluster using the procedure located at `https://docs.aws.amazon.com/AmazonECR/latest/userguide/ECR_on_EKS.html`.

- You can use node auto-scaling groups, but the scaling up and down of the cluster can cause disruptions to the Rancher UI and cause cluster operations to fail for a short period of time, including the loss of access to the downstream cluster via the Rancher API.

- If you use AWS Certificate Manager, you should pick a certificate that auto-renews with the same root CA This is because Rancher will need the checksum of the root CA for the agents. So, changing the root CA does require a good amount of work, which we will cover in a later chapter.

- The Rancher server does have ARM64 based images. So, you could use ARM64 nodes in the cluster, but you might still require an AMD64 node for other services and containers such as Prometheus, which currently doesn't have ARM64 support.

- EKS does not automatically recover from kubelet failures and can require user intervention.

- EKS limits the number of pods per node based on the size of the node. Please see Amazon's documentation, located at `https://github.com/awslabs/amazon-eks-ami/blob/master/files/eni-max-pods.txt`, for more details.

Google's GKE

The **basic requirements** for GKE are as follows:

- Rancher requires at least two worker nodes in the cluster, but three nodes are highly recommended.

- Each worker node should have at least two cores with 4 GB of memory.

- Rancher requires a network load balancer for accessing the Rancher console.

- Once the GKE cluster has been created, you'll need to follow the procedure located at `https://cloud.google.com/kubernetes-engine/docs/how-to/cluster-access-for-kubectl` to generate a kubeconfig file for accessing the cluster.

- Rancher requires GKE to have nginx-ingress-controller installed on the cluster. Please see the steps located at `https://rancher.com/docs/rancher/v2.5/en/installation/install-rancher-on-k8s/gke/#5-install-an-ingress` for more details.

- The inbound port 443/TCP should open for all downstream nodes, clusters, and end users that need Rancher UI/API access. Note: port 80 will redirect end users to the HTTPS URL. So, it is not required but is recommended for convenience.

The **design limitations and considerations** are as follows:

- The cluster should span three availability zones.

- You cannot customize your server configuration. You must use one of the two server types they offer: Container OS or Ubuntu. You don't get to pick the Kubernetes versions or kernel versions.

- Cluster add-on services such as Kube-DNS and ip-masq-agent are very limited when it comes to their configurability.

- GKE currently has no support for ARM64.

Azure's AKS

The **basic requirements** for AKS are as follows:

- Rancher requires at least two worker nodes in the cluster, but three nodes are highly recommended.

- Each worker node should have at least two cores with 4 GB of memory.

- Rancher requires a network load balancer for accessing the Rancher console.

- Once the AKS cluster has been created, you'll need to follow the procedure located at `https://cloud.google.com/kubernetes-engine/docs/how-to/cluster-access-for-kubectl` to generate a kubeconfig file for accessing the cluster.

- Rancher requires AKS to have nginx-ingress-controller installed on the cluster. Please see the steps located at `https://rancher.com/docs/rancher/v2.5/en/installation/install-rancher-on-k8s/gke/#5-install-an-ingress` for more details.

- The inbound port 443/TCP should open for all downstream nodes, clusters, and end users that need Rancher UI/API access. Note: port 80 will redirect end users to the HTTPS URL. So, it is not required but is recommended for convenience.

The **design limitations and considerations** are as follows:

- The cluster should span three availability zones.

- AKS is relatively new compared to EKS and GKE, so many features are still not **General Availability (GA)**.

- The only choices for the operating system are Ubuntu and Windows Server.

> **Note**
> The Rancher server does not work on Windows nodes.

- Node upgrades are not automated like GKE and require manual work to be applied.

- AKS does not automatically recover from kubelet failures and can require user intervention.

- AKS currently has no support for ARM64.

We now understand the limitations of running Rancher on a hosted Kubernetes cluster. Next, we'll be using this and a set of rules and examples to help us design a solution using the major cloud providers.

Rules for architecting a solution

In this section, we'll cover some standard designs and the pros and cons of each. It is important to note that each environment is unique and will require tuning for the best performance and experience. It's also important to note that all CPU, memory, and storage sizes are recommended starting points and may need to be increased or decreased based on the number of nodes and clusters to be managed by Rancher.

Before designing a solution, you should be able to answer the following questions:

- Will you be separating non-production and production clusters into their own Rancher environments?

- For a hybrid cloud environment, will you be separating clusters by their provider? For example, will you deploy one instance of Rancher server for all AWS clusters and another instance of Rancher server for all on-prem clusters?

- Will you require both public and private IP addresses for your Kubernetes nodes?

- Will you be hosting any additional applications on the Rancher cluster? If so, what are the CPU, memory, and storage requirements?

- Do you require site-to-site replication between regions?

- How many nodes and clusters are you planning on supporting?

> **Note**
> Rancher's official server sizing guide can be found at `https://rancher.com/docs/rancher/v2.5/en/installation/requirements/#rke-and-hosted-kubernetes`.

Amazon EKS

In this section, we're going to cover some of the major cluster designs for EKS clusters.

EKS small clusters

In this design, we will be deploying the smallest EKS cluster that can still run Rancher. Note that this design is only for testing or lab environments and is not recommended for production deployments and can only handle a couple of clusters with a dozen or so nodes each.

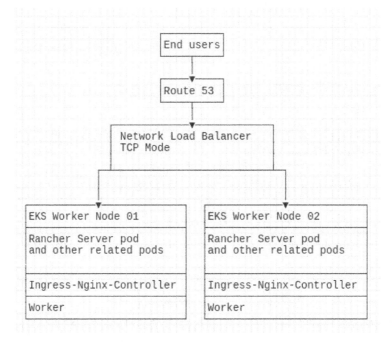

Figure 5.1 – EKS small cluster with two worker nodes

The **pros** are as follows:

- Node-level redundancy; you can lose a worker without an outage to Rancher.
- No required downtime during EKS patching and upgrades. Please see https://docs.aws.amazon.com/eks/latest/userguide/update-managed-node-group.html for more details.

The **cons** are as follows:

- If you are running additional applications such as Prometheus or Grafana, the nodes can run out of resources.

- Only `N+1` of resource availability, so during maintenance tasks, you cannot suffer a failure of a node without loss of service.

> **Note**
> During node group upgrades, Amazon will add a new node before removing the old one.

- You do need to customize the Rancher install to only use one replica instead of the default three.

The **node sizing** requirements are as follows:

- One node group with two nodes in the group
- CPU: 2 cores per node
- Memory: 4 GB per node

EKS using a typical cluster size with Availability Zone redundancy

In this design, we will expand upon the EKS small design by adding a worker, giving us three worker nodes. We'll also leverage AWS's **Availability Zone** (**AZ**) redundancy by having a worker node in one of three AZs. By doing this, the cluster can handle the failure of an AZ without impacting Rancher. We will also increase the size of the worker nodes to manage up to 300 clusters with 3,000 nodes.

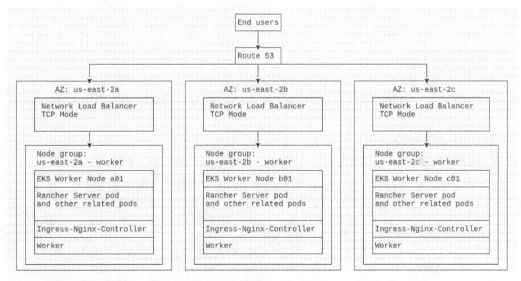

Figure 5.2 – EKS standard with three worker nodes and AZ redundancy

The **pros** are as follows:

- Node-level redundancy: You can lose a worker without an outage in Rancher.

- AZ redundancy: You can lose a whole AZ without an outage in Rancher; this also includes at the load balancer level.

- No required downtime during EKS patching and upgrades. Please see `https://docs.aws.amazon.com/eks/latest/userguide/update-managed-node-group.html` for more details.

- N+2 of availability: During maintenance tasks, you can suffer a failure of a node without loss of service.

The **cons** are as follows:

- Additional cost for the additional worker node.

- Additional complexity during setup because each AZ has its node group.

- Additional complexity with the NLB because it must have an interface in each AZ.

- Additional complexity during an upgrade as each node group needs to upgrade on its own.

The **node sizing** requirements are as follows

- Three node groups with one node in each group

- CPU: 8 cores per node

- Memory: 16 GB per node

Google's GKE

In this section, we're going to cover some of the major cluster designs for GKE clusters.

GKE small clusters

In this design, we will be deploying the smallest GKE cluster that can still run Rancher. Note that this design is only for testing or lab environments, is not recommended for production deployments, and can only handle a couple of clusters with a dozen or so nodes each.

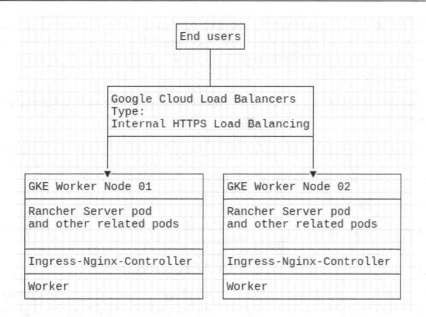

Figure 5.3 – GKE small cluster with two worker nodes

The **pros** are as follows:

- Node-level redundancy: You can lose a worker without an outage in Rancher.

- No required downtime during GKE patching and upgrades. Please see `https://cloud.google.com/kubernetes-engine/docs/concepts/cluster-upgrades` for more details.

The **cons** are as follows:

- If you are running additional applications such as Prometheus or Grafana, the nodes can run out of resources.

- Only `N+1` of availability, so during maintenance tasks, you cannot suffer the failure of a node without loss of service.

> **Note**
> During cluster upgrades, Google will add a new node before removing the old one.

- Using GCP's cluster upgrade autopilot, it can get stuck terminating the Rancher server pods. If the maintenance window is too small, the upgrade will be paused, leaving the cluster in a partially upgraded state. I recommend a maintenance window of at least 4 hours.

- You do need to customize the Rancher install to only use one replica instead of the default three.

The **node sizing** requirements are as follows:

- One node pool with two nodes in the pool

- CPU: 2 cores per node

- Memory: 4 GB per node

GKE using a typical cluster size with AZ redundancy

In this design, we will expand upon the GKE small design by adding a worker, giving us three worker nodes. We'll also leverage GCP's zone redundancy by having a worker node in one of three zones. By doing this, the cluster can handle the failure of an AZ without impacting Rancher. We will also increase the size of the worker nodes to manage up to 300 clusters with 3,000 nodes.

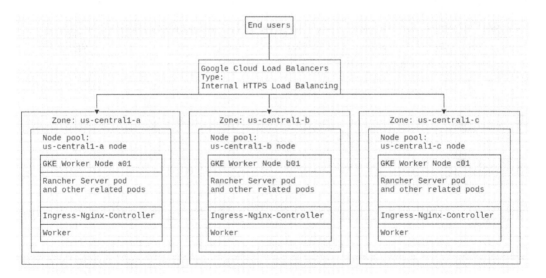

Figure 5.4 – GKE standard with three worker nodes and zone redundancy

The **pros** are as follows:

- Node-level redundancy: You can lose a worker without an outage in Rancher.

- Zone redundancy: You can lose a whole AZ without an outage in Rancher; this also includes at the load balancer level.

- No required downtime during GKE patching and upgrades. Please see `https://cloud.google.com/kubernetes-engine/docs/concepts/cluster-upgrades` for more details.

- `N+2` of availability: During maintenance tasks, you can suffer a failure of a node without loss of service.

- No additional complexity during an upgrade as autopilot will take care of the upgrades for you.

The **cons** are as follows:

- Additional cost for the additional worker node.

- Additional complexity during setup because each zone has its node pool.

The **node sizing** requirements are as follows:

- Three node pools with one node in each pool

- CPU: 8 cores per node

- Memory: 16 GB per node

Azure's AKS

In this section, we're going to cover some of the major cluster designs for AKS clusters.

AKS small clusters

In this design, we will be deploying the smallest AKE cluster that can still run Rancher. AKS is a little special in the fact that it support clusters with only one node. As mentioned earlier, this design is only for testing or lab environments, is not recommended for production deployments, and can only handle a couple of clusters with a dozen or so nodes each. It is important to note that AKS does support Windows node pools, but Rancher must run on a Linux node.

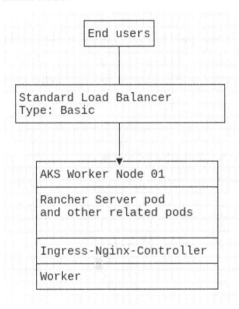

Figure 5.5 – AKS single-node cluster

The **pros** are as follows:

- Lower costs as you are only paying for a single node.
- Azure does support node surges during an upgrade, which is where Azure will provide a new node to the cluster before cordoning and draining the old node.

The **cons** are as follows:

- You cannot suffer a failure of a node without loss of service.

> **Note**
> During cluster upgrades, Azure will add a new node before removing the old one.

- If you are running additional applications such as Prometheus or Grafana, the node can run out of resources.

- If the node drain fails, Azure will stop the upgrade without rolling back.

- You do need to customize the Rancher install to only use one replica instead of the default three.

The **node sizing** requirements are as follows:

- One node pool with one node in the pool
- CPU: 2 cores per node
- Memory: 4 GB per node

AKS using a typical cluster size with zone redundancy

In this design, we will expand upon the AKS single-node design by adding two workers, giving us three worker nodes. We'll also leverage Azure's zone redundancy by having a worker node in one of three zones. By doing this, the cluster can handle the failure of an AZ without impacting Rancher. We will also increase the size of the worker nodes to manage up to 300 clusters with 3,000 nodes.

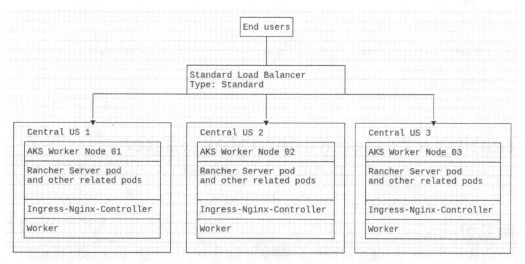

Figure 5.6 – AKS standard cluster with three nodes

The **pros** are as follows:

- Node-level redundancy: You can lose a worker without an outage in Rancher.

- Zone redundancy: You can lose a whole zone without an outage in Rancher; this also includes the load balancer level.

- No required downtime during AKS patching and upgrades. Please see `https://docs.microsoft.com/en-us/azure/aks/upgrade-cluster` for more details.

- `N+2` of availability: During maintenance tasks, you can suffer a failure of a node without loss of service.

The **cons** are as follows:

- Additional cost for the additional worker node.

- Additional complexity during setup because each zone has its node pool.

- Zone availability support is limited to only some regions. Please see `https://docs.microsoft.com/en-us/azure/aks/availability-zones#limitations-and-region-availability` for more details.

- If you are using Azure Disk Storage, volumes cannot be attached across zones. Please see `https://docs.microsoft.com/en-us/azure/aks/availability-zones#azure-disks-limitations` for more details.

The **node sizing** requirements are as follows:

- Three node pools with one node in each pool

- CPU: 8 cores per node

- Memory: 16 GB per node

Now that we have a design for our cluster, in the next section, we'll be covering the steps for creating each of the major cluster types.

Creating a hosted Kubernetes cluster

In this section, we are going to walk through the commands for creating each of the hosted Kubernetes clusters.

Amazon EKS

This section will cover creating an EKS cluster with an ingress by using command-line tools.

> **Note**
> The following steps are general guidelines. Please refer to `https://aws-quickstart.github.io/quickstart-eks-rancher/` for more details.

Prerequisites

You should already have an AWS account with admin permissions along with a VPC and subnets created.

The following tools should be installed on your workstation:

- **AWS CLI v2**: Please refer to `https://docs.aws.amazon.com/cli/latest/userguide/install-cliv2.html` for more details.

- **eksctl**: Please refer to `https://docs.aws.amazon.com/eks/latest/userguide/eksctl.html` for more information.

- **kubectl**: Please refer to `https://docs.aws.amazon.com/eks/latest/userguide/install-kubectl.html` for more information.

- **Helm**: Please refer to `https://helm.sh/docs/intro/install/` for more information.

Creating the cluster

Let's look at the steps next:

1. Run the `aws configure` command and enter your access and secret keys. This will provide you with access to the AWS account.

2. Run the following command to create the EKS cluster:

```
eksctl create cluster  --name rancher-server  --version
1.21  --without-nodegroup
```

> **Note**
>
> In this example, we'll be making a standard three-node cluster with one node in each AZ.

3. Run the following command to add the first node pool to the cluster:

```
eksctl create nodegroup --cluster=rancher-server
--name=rancher-us-west-2a --region=us-west-2 --zones=us-
west-2a --nodes 1 --nodes-min 1 --nodes-max 2
```

This will create the node pool in `us-west-2a`.

4. Run the following command to add the second node pool to the cluster:

```
eksctl create nodegroup --cluster=rancher-server
--name=rancher-us-west-2b --region=us-west-2 --zones=us-
west-2b --nodes 1 --nodes-min 1 --nodes-max 2
```

This will create the node pool in us-west-2b.

5. Run the following command to add the third node pool to the cluster:

```
eksctl create nodegroup --cluster=rancher-server
--name=rancher-us-west-2c --region=us-west-2 --zones=us-
west-2c --nodes 1 --nodes-min 1 --nodes-max 2
```

This will create the node pool in us-west-2c.

6. To verify the cluster, run the following command:

```
eksctl get cluster
```

> **Note**
> It might take 5 to 10 mins for the cluster to come online.

7. Next, install nginx-ingress-controller using the following commands:

```
helm repo add ingress-nginx https://kubernetes.github.io/
ingress-nginx
helm repo update
helm upgrade --install \
    ingress-nginx ingress-nginx/ingress-nginx \
    --namespace ingress-nginx \
    --set controller.service.type=LoadBalancer \
    --version 3.12.0 \
    --create-namespace
```

Creating the load balancer

If you are just testing, you can run the kubectl get service ingress-nginx-controller -n ingress-nginx command to capture the external DNS record. Then you can create a CNAME DNS record to point to this record.

> **Note**
> This should not be used for production environments.

For creating the frontend load balancer, please see https://docs.aws.amazon.com/Route53/latest/DeveloperGuide/routing-to-elb-load-balancer.html for more details.

At this point, the cluster is ready for Rancher to be installed. We'll cover this step in the next section.

Google's GKE

This section will cover creating a GKE cluster with an ingress by using command-line tools.

> **Note**
>
> The following steps are general guidelines. Please refer to `https://cloud.google.com/kubernetes-engine/docs/quickstart` for more details.

Prerequisites

You should already have a GCP account with admin permissions. This section will use Cloud Shell, which has most of the tools already installed.

Setting up Cloud Shell

1. Go to the upper-right corner of the GCP console and click the **Terminal** button.
2. Run the `gcloud components install kubectl` command to install the kubectl client in your GCP terminal.
3. Run the `gcloud init` command to configure the permissions.

Creating the cluster

1. To create a node in each zone, run this command:

    ```
    gcloud container clusters create rancher-server --zone
    us-central1-a --node-locations us-central1-a,us-central1-
    b,us-central1-c --num-nodes=3
    ```

2. Grab the `kubeconfig` file using the following command:

    ```
    gcloud container clusters get-credentials rancher-server
    ```

    It might take 5 to 10 mins for the cluster to come online.

3. Install `nginx-ingress-controller` using the following commands:

    ```
    helm repo add ingress-nginx https://kubernetes.github.io/
    ingress-nginx
    ```

```
helm repo update
helm upgrade --install \
  ingress-nginx ingress-nginx/ingress-nginx \
  --namespace ingress-nginx \
  --set controller.service.type=LoadBalancer \
  --version 3.12.0 \
  --create-namespace
```

Creating the load balancer

If you are just testing, you can run the `kubectl get service ingress-nginx-controller -n ingress-nginx` command to capture the external IP. Then you can create a DNS record to point to this IP.

> **Note**
>
> This should not be used for production environments.

For creating the frontend load balancer, please see `https://cloud.google.com/kubernetes-engine/docs/concepts/ingress` for more details.

At this point, the cluster is ready for Rancher to be installed. We'll cover this step in the next section.

Azure's AKS

This section will cover creating an AKS cluster with an ingress by using command-line tools.

> **Note**
>
> The following steps are general guidelines. Please refer to `https://docs.microsoft.com/en-us/azure/aks/kubernetes-walkthrough-portal` for more details.

Prerequisites

You should already have an Azure account with admin permissions.

The following tools should be installed on your workstation:

- The Azure CLI: Please refer to `https://docs.microsoft.com/en-us/cli/azure/` for more details.

- kubectl: Please refer to `https://kubernetes.io/docs/tasks/tools/#kubectl` for more information.
- Helm: Please refer to `https://helm.sh/docs/intro/install/` for more information.

Logging in to Azure

Run the `az login` command. This command is used to log in to Azure.

> **Note**
>
> You might need to log in to a web browser if you are using **two-factor authentication (2FA)**.

Creating the cluster

1. Run the following command to create a resource group:

    ```
    az group create --name rancher-server --location eastus
    ```

2. Next, run the following command to create the cluster:

    ```
    az aks create  --resource-group rancher-server  --name
    rancher-server  --kubernetes-version 1.22.0  --node-count
    3  --node-vm-size Standard_D2_v3
    ```

3. Grab the `kubeconfig` file using the following command:

    ```
    az aks get-credentials --resource-group rancher-server
    --name rancher-server
    ```

    It might take 5 to 10 mins for the cluster to come online.

4. Install `nginx-ingress-controller` using the following commands:

    ```
    helm repo add ingress-nginx https://kubernetes.github.io/
    ingress-nginx
    helm repo update
    helm upgrade --install \
      ingress-nginx ingress-nginx/ingress-nginx \
      --namespace ingress-nginx \
      --set controller.service.type=LoadBalancer \
      --version 3.12.0 \
      --create-namespace
    ```

Creating the load balancer

If you are just testing, you can run the `kubectl get service ingress-nginx-controller -n ingress-nginx` command to capture the external IP. Then you can create a DNS record to point to this IP.

> **Note**
>
> This should not be used for production environments.

For creating the frontend load balancer, please see `https://docs.microsoft.com/en-us/azure/aks/load-balancer-standard` for more details.

At this point, the cluster is ready for Rancher to be installed. We'll cover this step in the next section.

Installing and upgrading Rancher

In this section, we are going to cover installing and upgrading Rancher on a hosted cluster. This process is very similar to installing Rancher on an RKE cluster but with the difference being the need for Rancher Backup Operator, which we will cover in the next section.

Installing Rancher

1. Run the following command to add the Helm Chart repository:

   ```
   helm repo add rancher-latest https://releases.rancher.
   com/server-charts/latest
   ```

2. Run the `kubectl create namespace cattle-system` command to create the namespace for Rancher.

   > **Note**
   >
   > The namespace name should always be `cattle-system` and cannot be changed without breaking Rancher.

3. We are now going to install Rancher. In this case, we'll be deploying Rancher with three pods, and we'll be using the load balancers to handle SSL certificates:

   ```
   helm upgrade --install rancher rancher-latest/rancher \
       --namespace cattle-system \
       --set hostname=rancher.example.com \
   ```

```
      --set ingress.tls.source=external \
      --set replicas=3 \
    --version 2.6.2
```

Please see `https://rancher.com/docs/rancher/v2.5/en/installation/` `install-rancher-on-k8s/#install-the-rancher-helm-chart` for more details and options for installing Rancher.

Upgrading Rancher

Before starting an upgrade, you should do a backup using the backup steps mentioned in the next section:

1. Run the `helm repo update` command to pull down the latest Helm Charts.

2. To grab your current values, run the following command:

   ```
   helm get values rancher -n cattle-system
   ```

   > **Note**
   >
   > If you saved your `install` command, you could reuse it as it has the `upgrade --install` flag, which tells the Helm CLI to upgrade the deployment if it exists. If the deployment is missing, install it. The only thing you need to change is the version flag.

Please see `https://rancher.com/docs/rancher/v2.5/en/installation/` `install-rancher-on-k8s/upgrades/` for more details and options for upgrading Rancher.

At this point, we have Rancher up and running. In the next section, we'll be going into some common tasks such as backing up Rancher using the Rancher Backup Operator.

Rancher-Backup-Operator

Because we don't have access to the etcd database with hosted Kubernetes clusters, we need to back up Rancher data differently. This is where the Rancher-Backup-Operator comes into the picture. This tool provides the ability to back up and restore Rancher's data on any Kubernetes cluster. It accepts a list of resources that need to be backed up for a particular application. It then gathers these resources by querying the Kubernetes API server, packages them to create a `tarball` file, and pushes it to the configured backup storage location. Since it gathers resources by querying the API server, it can back up applications from any type of Kubernetes cluster.

Installation

Let's look at the steps to install this tool:

1. Run the following command to add the Helm Chart repository:

    ```
    helm repo add rancher-charts https://raw.
    githubusercontent.com/rancher/charts/release-v2.5/
    ```

2. Run the `helm repo update` command to pull down the latest charts.

3. To install the CRDs needed by Rancher-Backup-Operator, run the following command:

    ```
    helm install --wait --create-namespace -n cattle-
    resources-system rancher-backup-crd rancher-charts/
    rancher-backup-crd
    ```

4. Finally, install the application using this command:

    ```
    helm install --wait -n cattle-resources-system rancher-
    backup rancher-charts/rancher-backup
    ```

Creating a backup

To configure the backup schedule, encryption, and storage location, please see the documentation located at https://rancher.com/docs/rancher/v2.5/en/backups/configuration/backup-config/.

Take a one-time backup – before doing maintenance tasks such as upgrading Rancher, you should take a backup:

1. Create a file called `backup.yaml` with the following content:

    ```
    apiVersion: resources.cattle.io/v1
    kind: Backup
    metadata:
      name: pre-rancher-upgrade
    spec:
      resourceSetName: rancher-resource-set
    ```

2. Run the `kubectl apply -f backup.yaml` command to back up the Rancher data.

You can find additional examples at https://github.com/rancher/backup-restore-operator/tree/master/examples.

Summary

In this chapter, we learned about hosted Kubernetes clusters such as EKS, GKE, and AKS, including the requirements and limitations of each. We then covered the rules of architecting each type of cluster, including some example designs and the pros and cons of each solution. We finally went into detail about the steps for creating each type of cluster using the design we made earlier. We ended the chapter by installing and configuring the Rancher server and Rancher Backup Operator. At this point, you should have Rancher up and ready to start deploying downstream clusters for your application workloads.

The next chapter will cover creating a managed RKE cluster using Rancher IE, a downstream cluster. We will cover how Rancher creates these clusters and what the limitations are.

Part 3 – Deploying a Kubernetes Cluster

This part will cover all the different types of Kubernetes clusters that Rancher can build and manage, along with all the limitations and requirements of these clusters.

This part of the book comprises the following chapters:

- *Chapter 6, Creating an RKE Cluster Using Rancher*

- *Chapter 7, Deploying a Hosted Cluster with Rancher*

- *Chapter 8, Importing an Externally Managed Cluster into Rancher*

6

Creating an RKE Cluster Using Rancher

One of the first things you'll do after installing Rancher is to start building downstream clusters. There are three main types of clusters in Rancher: Rancher-managed **Rancher Kubernetes Engine** (**RKE**) clusters, Rancher-managed hosted clusters, and imported clusters.

In this chapter, we'll be covering how to deploy a downstream cluster to use existing servers running Docker. We'll see how Rancher uses a set of agents to provide access to these servers for Rancher to create an RKE cluster. Then, we'll cover the requirements and limitations of this type of cluster. We will then cover the rules for designing a Rancher-managed RKE cluster, at which point, we'll go through the process of registering nodes in Rancher. Finally, we'll cover the maintenance tasks needed for the ongoing cluster management.

In this chapter, we're going to cover the following main topics:

- What is a Rancher-managed cluster?
- Requirements and limitations
- Rules for architecting a solution
- Preparing for nodes to join Rancher
- Prepping the infrastructure provider
- Steps for creating an RKE cluster using Rancher
- Deploying a cluster using node pools
- Ongoing maintenance tasks

What is a Rancher-managed cluster?

Rancher can manage a cluster on behalf of end users. This can be done by using existing nodes or Rancher-created nodes. It is important to note that, at the time of writing, Rancher v2.6 has RKE2 support as a technical preview feature. But we will be talking about Rancher-managed clusters using RKE in this chapter.

Where do Rancher-managed clusters come from?

Since the beginning, Rancher has always used the technique of defining a cluster inside Rancher and then using the Rancher agents to provide access to the downstream nodes for cluster creation. In Rancher v1.6, this was used to deploy the `Cattle` clusters, and with Rancher v2.x, this same idea was advanced to deploy RKE clusters.

How does Rancher manage nodes?

In some environments, you don't want to manage the **Virtual Machines** (**VMs**). To solve this, Rancher has what are called **node drivers**. These drivers allow Rancher to launch and manage the VMs that Rancher will use to create the cluster. A node driver that Rancher uses is called the Rancher machine, which is based on Docker Machine. The main idea is that Docker Machine has several different **Software Development Kits** (**SDKs**) for most major infrastructure providers such as **Amazon Web Services** (**AWS**), Azure, DigitalOcean, and vSphere.

The basic process is that the cluster controller creates a machine object that defines the server being created. The machine controller takes over to handle calling the Rancher machine to start making the API calls to the infrastructure provider using the node templates defined in Rancher. As a part of the node creation process, Rancher creates an **SSH (Secure Shell Protocol)** key pair for each node. Note that each node will have a unique key. The Rancher machine then uses `cloud-init` to customize the base image and push the SSH keys to the server. It is important to note that the base image uses Ubuntu as default, but this image can be changed to any supported OS found at `https://www.suse.com/suse-rancher/support-matrix/all-supported-versions/`. The main requirement is that it supports `cloud-init` and Docker. Once `cloud-init` has been completed successfully, Rancher will SSH into the node to run the `docker run` command to handle pushing the Rancher agent to the node.

How does Rancher manage a cluster?

In Rancher v2.x, once you have defined the cluster (which we'll cover later in this chapter), Rancher will create a `docker run` command. Please see the example in the following figure. We're now going to break this command down into its parts:

```
Run this command on one or more existing machines already running a supported version of Docker.
sudo docker run -d --privileged --restart=unless-stopped --net=host -v /etc/kubernetes:/etc/kubernetes -v /var/run:/var/run
rancher/rancher-agent:v2.4.4 --server https://example.rancher.com --token qkg67qfzzlqx8p4xg2gr2czt5ft52xqmmqtjfhwldtq52pb6s645lj
--ca-checksum 2bf373829900ec0c3f3539849577a122126040dccaea01556231b0eea813817d --worker
```

Figure 6.1 – The docker run command for joining a node to the cluster

First, the `docker run` command will create a new container. This is normally called the **bootstrap agent**. Next is the `-d` flag, which tells Docker to start this container in the background, with the next flag being `--privileged`. This flag is important because the Rancher agent will need access to the host and its resources to spin up the additional tools and containers needed by Rancher and RKE. The `--restart=unless-stopped` flag is to keep this container running even if it crashes. Then, the next flag, `--net=host`, tells Docker to use the host network for this container. This is needed to be able to get items such as the host's IP address and hostname.

We then come to the `-v /etc/kubernetes:/etc/kubernetes` and `-v /var/run:/var/run` flags. These two flags will create a bind mount for the host filesystem in the bootstrap container. The first directory is used to store SSL certificates used by the RKE components and some `config` files. The second directory is used to provide access to several host-level commands. This includes the Docker **Command-Line Interface (CLI)** access, which Rancher uses for creating additional containers.

The next section is the `image` tag. This will, of course, match the version of Rancher. The next section is the command-line options that are passed to the Rancher agent binary. The first option is `-server`, which is Rancher's API endpoint and should be used when it connects back to Rancher. It is important to note that this must be an HTTPS URL. The next option is `--token`, a special token used by Rancher to authenticate an agent and tie it to a cluster. It is important to note that this token will be the same for all nodes in the cluster. Also, this token should be treated like a password.

The next option is `--ca-checksum`, which is a SHA256 checksum of the root certificate of Rancher's API endpoint. This is used because it is common for users to use self-signed or privately signed certificates for their Rancher servers, and because the root certificates that are inside the container might not be up to date. The Rancher agent will request the root certificate from the Rancher URL and compare that certificate's checksum to the `--ca-checksum` and assume they match. The agent will assume that the root certificate can be trusted. It is important to note that these only handle trusting the root certificate. The rest of the certificate must still be valid – that is, the certificate has not expired with the correct hostname. This is why it's important not to change the root CAs of your Rancher API endpoint. Officially, there is no support to change the Rancher API endpoint or the root CA, but Rancher support does have tools such as the **cluster agent** tool that can take care of this for you. The tool is located at `https://github.com/rancherlabs/support-tools/tree/master/cluster-agent-tool`.

Finally, at the end of the command, we get to the section that will need to be customized based on the role and settings of the node. In the example shown in *Figure 6.2*, we have some of the standard agent options that users use, with the first being `--node-name`, which is an option that lets you override the hostname of the node. This is because, by default, the Rancher agent will use the short hostname of the server as the node name in both Rancher and Kubernetes. For some environments, this is fine, and the option can be skipped, but in cloud environments such as AWS, where a server hostname such as `ip-10-23-24-15` can be hard to read and doesn't match what the server is named in the console, it can be helpful to set the node name to something more user-friendly.

It is important to note that Rancher and RKE do not use this hostname for networking communications, so the node name does not need to be a valid DNS record, but it is recommended that it be valid to help with future troubleshooting. Also, it is essential to remember that a hostname shouldn't be changed after a node is registered into Rancher, as the hostname is used as a key, and changing the hostname will cause Rancher to try registering it as a new node. This can break the cluster, as it is in an unknown state, so it is recommended that if you want to change the name of a node, remove it from the cluster, clean it using the cleanup script located at `https://github.com/rancherlabs/support-tools/blob/master/extended-rancher-2-cleanup/extended-cleanup-rancher2.sh`, and then rejoin the node as a new node to the cluster.

The next option is --address, which sets the external IP address of the node. Usually, this is only needed when a node is behind a **Network Address Translation (NAT)**, with the chassis example being AWS, where a VM is assigned a private IP with a one-to-one NAT for the public IP. The agent will try to auto-detect this IP. You can find out more about this process by going to https://rancher.com/docs/rancher/v2.5/en/cluster-provisioning/rke-clusters/custom-nodes/agent-options/#dynamic-ip-address-options. This leads us to the next option, which is --internal-address, with this setting being used to set the IP address used by Kubernetes for inter-host communication. If a node has more than one **Network Interface Controller (NIC)**, it is imperative that this setting is used to avoid the network being misrouted.

An example is you have 1 GB NIC for management and 10 GB NIC for data. We would want RKE/Kubernetes to use the 10 GB NIC IP address to improve speed. If this option is not set, the kubelet will try to auto-detect the correct IP for the node by using the default gateway and the DNS record for the node's hostname. It is recommended to set these manually if a node has more than one IP.

There are additional flags that can be set at the agent level. For example, --labels will set the node's labels and –taints will set the node's taints at node creation, but it is important to note that these options are locked in at this point and can cause problems if they need to be changed at a later date. The rest of the agent options can be found at https://rancher.com/docs/rancher/v2.5/en/cluster-provisioning/rke-clusters/custom-nodes/agent-options/.

At the very end of the command, we have the role options. These flags tell Rancher/RKE what role is assigned to this node, such as --etcd, --controlplane, and --worker. When the node is registering with Rancher for the first time, the role options are sent to Rancher and are used by it when generating the cluster configuration. It is important to note that these roles should not be changed after registering a node in Rancher. If you need to change a node's role, it is recommended to remove the node, clean it, and rejoin it:

```
Run this command on one or more existing machines already running a supported version of Docker.

sudo docker run -d --privileged --restart=unless-stopped --net=host -v /etc/kubernetes:/etc/kubernetes -v /var/run:/var/run
rancher/rancher-agent:v2.4.4 --server https://example.rancher.com --token qkg67qfzzlqx8p4xg2gr2czt5ft52xqmmqtjfhwldtq52pb6s645lj
--ca-checksum 2bf373829900ec0c3f3539849577a122126040dccaea01556231b0cea813817d --node-name example-hostname --address 1.1.1.1 --
internal-address 10.0.0.1 --etcd --controlplane --worker
```

Figure 6.2 – A docker run command with node customizations

What happens after a node has been registered? Once the Rancher agent has been successfully started, it will register the node in Rancher, and the node will go into the `Waiting to register with Kubernetes` state. At this point, the agent will create a WebSocket connection and wait. This triggers the cluster controller inside Rancher to update the cluster configuration. The object is equivalent to the `cluster.yaml` and `cluster.rkestate` files used by RKE but inside the Rancher container instead. This is because the cluster controller uses the same code as RKE. There are mostly minor differences, with the biggest one being the addition of a dialer to handle tunneling the Docker socket connection over WebSocket. The cluster controller will follow the same process as the RKE command.

Now that we understand what a Rancher-managed cluster is, let's look into the requirements and limitations of these types of clusters.

Requirements and limitations

In this section, we'll be discussing the basic requirements of Rancher on various nodes along with its limitations and design considerations.

Rancher-created managed nodes

These are the **basic requirements**:

- A supported OS. The official supported OSes can be found at `https://www.suse.com/suse-rancher/support-matrix/all-supported-versions/`.

- Rancher-created nodes have a special requirement that the Rancher servers must be able to SSH into the node.

- The required firewall rules and ports can be found at `https://rancher.com/docs/rancher/v2.5/en/installation/requirements/ports/#ports-for-rancher-launched-kubernetes-clusters-using-node-pools`.

- Docker is not required to be already installed.

These are the **design limitations and considerations**:

- The base image used to create the nodes should be as small as possible and should be started in less than 10 minutes.

- Rancher does not have an IP address pool or integration with any **IP Address Management (IPAM)** solutions. Rancher relies on the infrastructure provider to handle assigning an IP address to nodes. If you are using **Dynamic Host Configuration Protocol (DHCP)**, the IP addresses assigned to these nodes should have very long leases and be effectively static – that is, these IP addresses should not change.

- The hostname of the nodes is defined at the node pool level, with the node names being sequential by adding a number to the end of the template name and incrementing by one each time a node is created.

> **Important Note**
> Rancher will reuse old hostnames that have been successfully reclaimed.

- If the nodes are being deployed in an air-gapped environment, Rancher will require a proxy server to be configured in `cloud-init`, or the package manager should be able to pull packages such as curl and Docker from its repository. Even if these packages are already installed, Rancher will still run either the `yum install curl` or `apt install curl` commands.

- Auto should be set to `0` for node pools with etcd and controlplane nodes.

Existing nodes

These are the **basic requirements**:

- A supported OS. The official supported OSes can be found at `https://www.suse.com/suse-rancher/support-matrix/all-supported-versions/`.

- The required firewall rules and ports can be found at `https://rancher.com/docs/rancher/v2.5/en/installation/requirements/ports/#ports-for-rancher-launched-kubernetes-clusters-using-custom-nodes`.

- Docker should already be installed on the node(s), and we recommend using the installation script located at `https://github.com/rancher/install-Docker`.

- If you are using auto-scaling groups, it's essential to ensure that only one etcd node or controlplane node is taken offline at once. You want to ensure that you don't lose a quorum for etcd or get stuck in a cluster update because multiple controlplane nodes are down.

These are the **design limitations and considerations**:

- When registering nodes in a new cluster, Rancher requires at least one node with each of the roles, such as etcd, controlplane, and worker. This can be a single node or separate nodes for each role or a mix of any roles.

- When adding nodes to a cluster, it is crucial to ensure that new etcd and controlplane nodes are added one at a time. You can technically add them all at once, but you can run into stability issues with new clusters.

- If you are using a private registry for hosting the Docker images used by Rancher, you should configure the registry setting in the cluster using the steps listed at `https://rancher.com/docs/rke/latest/en/config-options/private-registries/`.

We now understand the requirements and limitations. In the next section, we are going to use this knowledge, along with additional rules and example designs, to help us architect a solution that meets our needs.

Rules for architecting a solution

In this section, we'll cover some standard designs and the pros and cons of each. It is important to note that each environment is unique and will require tuning for the best performance and experience. It's also important to note that all CPU, memory, and storage sizes are recommended starting points and may need to be increased or decreased by your workloads and deployment processes. Also, we'll be covering designs for the major infrastructure providers (AWS and **Google Cloud Platform** (**GCP**)), but you should be able to translate the core concepts for other infrastructure providers.

Before designing a solution, you should be able to answer the following questions:

- Will multiple environments be sharing the same cluster?

- Will production and non-production workloads be on the same cluster?

- What level of availability does this cluster require?

- Will this cluster be spanning multiple data centers in a metro cluster environment?

- How much latency will there be between nodes in the cluster?

- How many pods will be hosted in the cluster?

- What are the average and maximum sizes of pods deployed in the cluster?

- Will you need GPU support for some of your applications?

- Will you need to provide storage to your applications?

- If you need storage, do you need only **Read Write Once** (**RWO**), or will you need **Read Write Many** (**RWX**)?

> **Note**
>
> Rancher's official server sizing guide can be found at `https://rancher.com/docs/rancher/v2.5/en/installation/requirements/#rke-and-hosted-kubernetes`.

AWS

In this design, we will be deploying a standard size cluster on AWS using the Rancher EC2 node driver, using a very similar design to the one that we created in *Chapter 4*, *Creating an RKE and RKE2 Cluster*, for the medium-size RKE cluster. The basic idea is to try and balance **High Availability** (**HA**) with cost and use the fact that AWS intro-zone network speed and latency are so good that we can treat it like a single data center.

> **Note**
>
> This needs to be tested because some regions are slower than others, and some users have reported much higher latency.

This design works for 2 to 50 worker nodes in the clusters. This is higher than a medium RKE cluster because the **Non-Volatile Memory** (**NVM**) storage in AWS can handle more throughput than most on-premises storage.

Note

You might need to scale up the management nodes, depending on the environment.

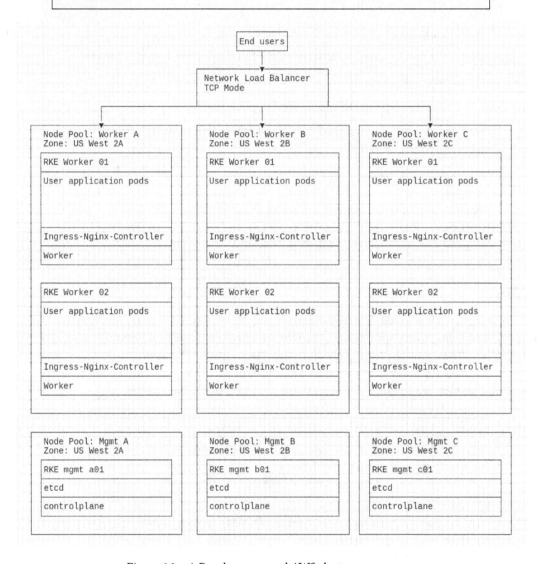

Figure 6.3 – A Rancher-managed AWS cluster across zones

Diagram: `https://github.com/PacktPublishing/Rancher-Deep-Dive/blob/main/ch06/standard_designs/AWS/README.md`

The **pros** are as follows:

- Node-level redundancy – you can lose a worker without an application outage.
- Full HA – you can lose any one of the management nodes (etcd and controlplane) in the cluster and still have complete cluster management.
- User workloads and management services run on different nodes, stopping runaway applications from taking down the cluster.
- Availability zone redundancy – you can lose a whole Availability Zone without an outage.
- Safer patching and upgrades for the master nodes because the node pools are across zones. So, we can simply scale up all three node pools from one node to two in parallel, and then scale down each pool one at a time.
- Uses zone anti-affinity rules to make sure applications are being spread across different zones using Pod topology spread constraints, which you can learn more about here: `https://kubernetes.io/docs/concepts/workloads/pods/pod-topology-spread-constraints/`.

The **cons** are as follows:

- Additional cost for the additional worker node.
- Additional complexity during setup because each Availability Zone has its own node group.
- Additional complexity with the NLB because it must have an interface in each Availability Zone.
- Additional complexity during an upgrade as each availability node group needs to upgrade on its own.
- AWS doesn't support **Elastic Block Storage** (**EBS**) volumes in different zones, so if you plan to use AWS's storage class, you'll need to ensure that application data is stored redundantly across Availability Zones. You can use AWS's EFS, but the cost can be very prohibitive.

The **node sizing** requirements are as follows:

- Servers(s): three EC2 instances
- CPU: eight cores per server
- Memory: 8-16 GB
- Storage: **Solid-State Drive** (**SSD**) or **Non-Volatile Memory Express** (**NVMe**) 10-15 GB

> **Important Note**
>
> The latency is the most important metric we want to monitor when it comes to etcd.
>
> Worker node sizing should be based on your workload and its requirements.

GCP

In this design, we'll deploy a standard size cluster on GCP as we did with AWS:

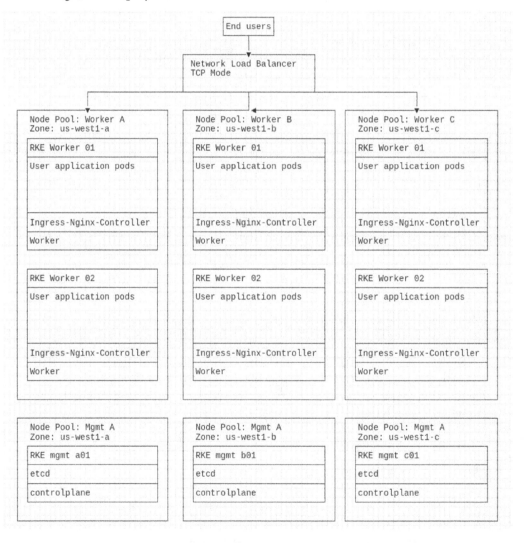

Figure 6.4 – A Rancher-managed AWS cluster across zones

Diagram: `https://github.com/PacktPublishing/Rancher-Deep-Dive/blob/main/ch06/standard_designs/GCP/README.md`

> **Note**
>
> The pros, cons, and node sizing requirements for GCP are exactly the same as that of AWS. You can refer to the *Amazon's AWS* section for more details on this.

Now we have the design for our cluster created. In the next section, we are going to start the process of creating the cluster, with the first step being to prepare the nodes.

Preparing for nodes to join Rancher

Before creating the cluster, we need to prepare the nodes/images that we'll use to create the cluster. This section will assume that you are using an Ubuntu or Red Hat-/CentOS-based image/node, as these are the two most common ones used.

For Rancher-managed nodes, we need to create a base image cloned and deployed in the environment. There are two main ways to create this image:

- The first is to start from a public image such as the Ubuntu ServerW cloud images, which can be found at `https://cloud-images.ubuntu.com/focal/current/`. Note that this image must come from a trusted source directly from the Ubuntu site or your infrastructure provider's official images. These images are designed to be small and lightweight, as they only have the essential tools and pre-installed packages. And for most people, that is the end of the process, as most of the customization you will want to make can be done through the `cloud-init` tool. If you need to install any additional tools or require changes to settings, you should refer to your infrastructure provider's documentation for opening that image and customizing it.

  We usually recommend changing as little as possible and not installing tools such as Puppet, Chef, or backup clients because these servers are designed to be disposable and easily replaced. Also, we usually recommend patching the base image for minor updates. Still, we would recommend going back to the official image source and pulling down the new version for major upgrades instead. Finally, we recommend not updating/upgrading the node in the `cloud-init` file, as we want all nodes deployed from that image to be the same. In addition, Rancher has a 10-minute timeout during the node creation process, and updating/patching can cause the node to exceed that window.

- The second is to start from a golden image that you or your team already use in your environment for other applications. For example, if your Linux team already has a Red Hat-based image with all the customization needed for your environment, there is no sense in reinventing the wheel, and you can simply use that existing image. Note that you might need to do additional testing and tuning of that image to ensure it is fully supported.

> **Note**
>
> You should still follow the same recommendations as listed under the public image option as far as the `cloud-init` settings.

In addition, we should make sure that any tools for automating patching are disabled because we don't want the node to change after its creation.

The process is much different for custom nodes because Rancher has nothing to do with the node creation process or the OS. In this case, you or your Linux team are responsible for creating the server, configuring it, installing Docker, and registering it with Rancher. This has the upside of giving you a great deal of control over the server. You should still follow the same recommendations as listed under the public image option. The difference is that tools such as Puppet or Chef are supported because Rancher is not managing the OS.

At this point, you should have your nodes built and ready to go if you are planning to bring your own nodes to Rancher. In the next section, we'll be covering the steps if we want Rancher to build the nodes for us.

Prepping the infrastructure provider

Now that we have the node image created, we have to configure that image in Rancher.

> **Note**
>
> This is only applicable to Rancher-managed clusters. If you are using existing nodes, then this section can be skipped.

The first step is to create a service account in the infrastructure provider that has the permissions that Rancher needs to create, manage, and delete the nodes. For security reasons, we recommend this to be a dedicated account not shared with other applications or users and that the permissions for this account be limited to only what is needed. Details for the permissions of each of the different infrastructure providers can be found at `https://rancher.com/docs/rancher/v2.5/en/cluster-provisioning/rke-clusters/cloud-providers/`.

It is important to remember that Rancher and the infrastructure provider are still evolving, so these permissions might change over time. Once you have that account created, you'll need to log into the Rancher v2.6.x UI and go to the **Cluster management** page and select the **Cloud Credential** page. This brings up a setup wizard, as shown in *Figure 6.5*.

> **Note**
> The Rancher UI will test that the credentials are correct but will not validate that the account has all the permissions that Rancher will need.

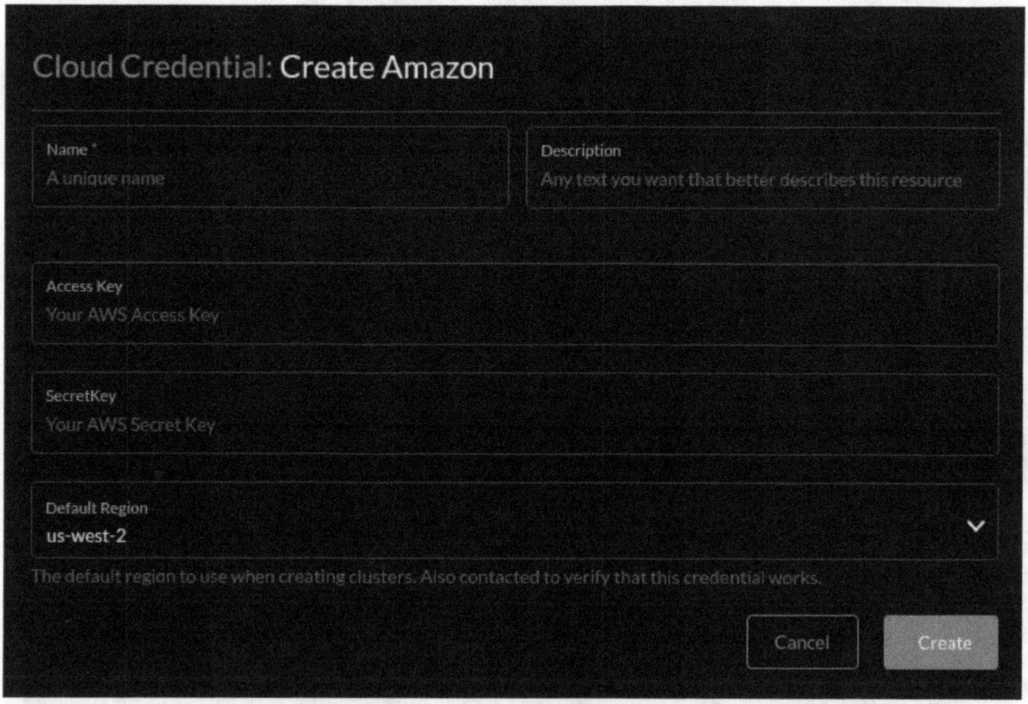

Figure 6.5 – The Cloud Credential setup wizard for Amazon

For more details about the cloud credentials, please go to https://rancher.com/ docs/rancher/v2.5/en/user-settings/cloud-credentials/.

The next step is to create the node template. This is how we define a node configuration. This includes selecting the image, location, and any other infrastructure settings.
We do this by going to the **Cluster Management** page, expanding **RKE1 Configuration**, and then choosing **Node templates**. This will bring up a setup wizard, as shown in the following screenshot.

> **Note**
>
> The Rancher UI will dynamically query the infrastructure provider as you click through different pages.

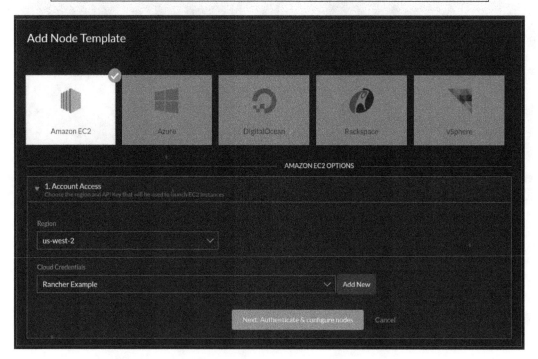

Figure 6.6 – The node template wizard for Amazon – step one

The following two pages are different, based on the infrastructure provider.

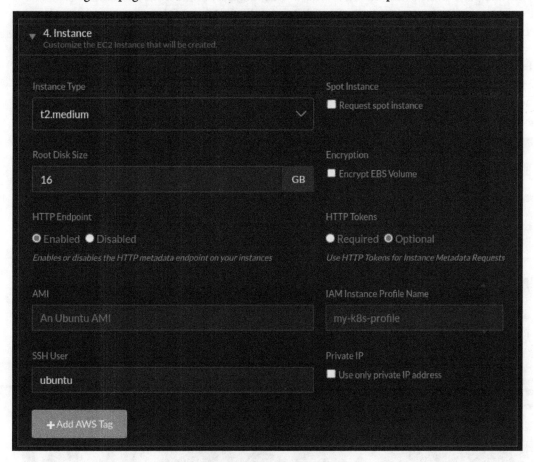

Figure 6.7 – The node template wizard for Amazon – Instance settings

The final page of the setup wizard is where you'll do most of the node customization – for example, setting the server size, root disk size, and tags. Most of these settings can be left to the default values; the only setting I usually recommend changing is **Root Disk Size**, which defaults to 16 GB. This is great for a lab/sandbox, but for actual production nodes, I would recommend going with 30-40 GB. Also, the **Name** field is usually not changed, so I recommend using a very descriptive name. There also is a **Description** field for entering notes. Finally, the **Labels** field can be a little confusing (refer to *Figure 6.8*). The bottom section of the page is for setting the Docker/Kubernetes labels, taints, and engine options:

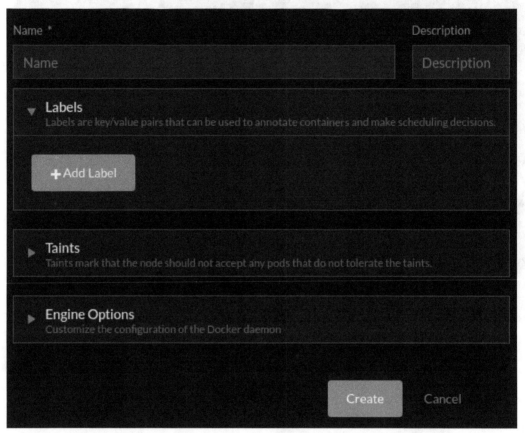

Figure 6.8 – The node template wizard for Amazon – the node settings

For more details about the node templates, please go to `https://rancher.com/docs/rancher/v2.5/en/user-settings/node-templates/`.

At this point, we have done all the preparation work that is needed for Rancher to create and manage our nodes for us. In the next section, we'll be starting the process of actually creating the cluster in Rancher.

The steps for creating an RKE cluster using Rancher

In this section, we're going to create a custom cluster mainly using default settings. In the next section, we'll cover creating an RKE cluster using an infrastructure provider.

The first step is to go to the Rancher UI and the **Cluster Management** page. From there, go to the **Clusters** page and click the **Create** button in the top right corner of the page. This brings you to a page that shows you all the major cluster types. Please see the following figure for an example. From this page, we are going to click the **Custom** button:

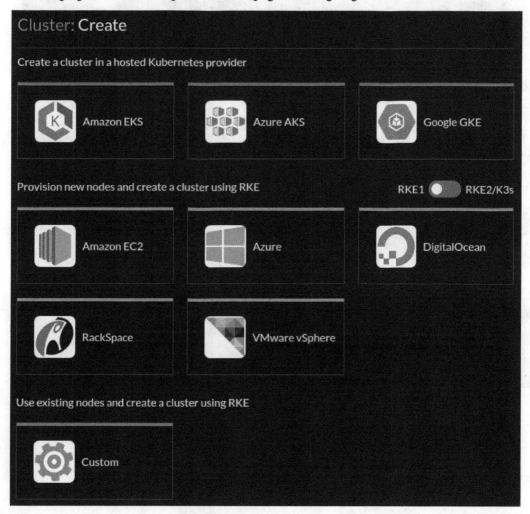

Figure 6.9 – The cluster creation page

The next page is where you can define the cluster. The first field that you'll fill out is **Cluster Name**. The cluster name is limited to a maximum of 253 characters, all lowercase and alphanumeric, with dots and dashes. For more details about the rest of the other settings on this page, refer to `https://rancher.com/docs/rancher/v2.5/en/cluster-provisioning/rke-clusters/custom-nodes/`:

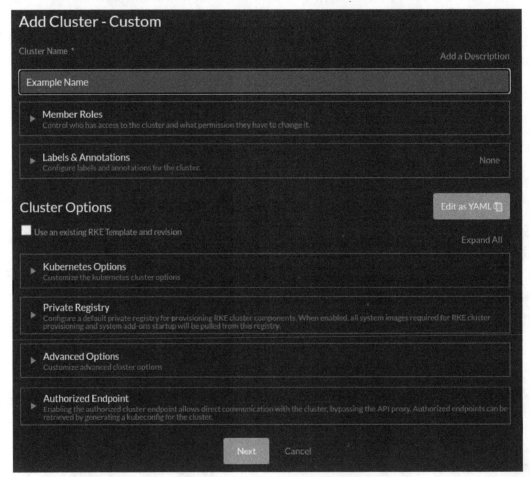

Figure 6.10 – The cluster settings page

Now that we have a cluster, we need to start adding nodes to the cluster. Because we're creating a custom cluster, the next page will be the **Customize Node Run Command** wizard. From here, we can generate the `docker run` commands that we'll need to join the different kinds of nodes. This page can be retrieved later by going to the **Cluster Management** page and selecting **Cluster** from the list:

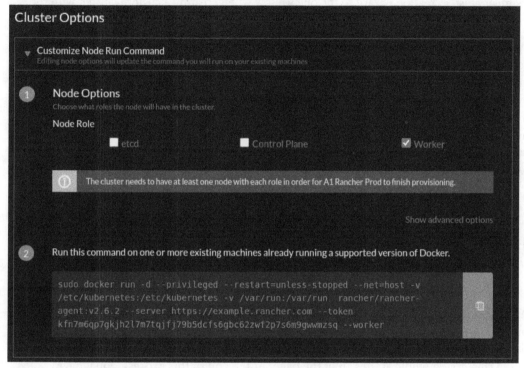

Figure 6.11 – The Customize Node Run Command wizard

At this point, Rancher should be creating our new cluster. You can monitor the process via the Rancher UI by clicking on the cluster dashboard or the **Nodes** tab. At the end of this process, you will have a Kubernetes cluster. In the next section, we'll cover creating a cluster using node pools.

Deploying a cluster using node pools

Now that we have a custom cluster, we will follow the same steps for creating a cluster with node pools. To start with, instead of selecting **custom**, you'll want to choose the infrastructure provider you wish to use, which will be used for this cluster. This brings you a similar cluster creation wizard to the one we saw when creating a custom cluster, with the difference being the additional **Node Pool** section and no docker run command wizard.

With this wizard, you'll add a node pool for each different type of node you want to configure, with the important field being **Name Prefix**, which is used to set the hostnames on the nodes in this pool. It is essential that these names are meaningful and do not overlap. The other main fields are the roles' checkboxes. The UI will warn you about the minimum number of nodes required for each type of node. If this is not met, Rancher will not allow you to create the cluster:

Figure 6.12 – The node pool creation wizard

At this point, Rancher will take over to start the process of creating servers and provisioning RKE on top of them. You can monitor the creation of the nodes by going to the **Nodes** tab and watching status messages for each node. The same applies to the status of the cluster as a whole at the top of the page. At the end of this process, you'll have a Kubernetes cluster ready to start deploying applications to. In the next section, we'll be covering some of the tasks that we'll need to do in order to keep the cluster healthy.

Ongoing maintenance tasks

After creating a cluster, a few ongoing maintenance tasks need to be done to keep the cluster running in a healthy state.

The first task that I recommend setting up is the scheduled etcd backups, which in Rancher v2.4 and beyond are enabled by default. The default behavior is to have each etcd node take an etcd snapshot and store it locally in `/opt/rke/etcd-snapshots`. The etcd backup is a point-in-time snapshot of the etcd database that stores the configuration of the cluster. This backup is critical when recovering from a failure. So, it is pretty common to configure the backup to the S3 option, as we don't want to store the backups on the same server that is being backed up. You can find a detailed list of the S3 settings at `https://rancher.com/docs/rke/latest/en/etcd-snapshots/recurring-snapshots/#options-for-the-etcd-snapshot-service`.

> **Note**
>
> Rancher/RKE supports any S3-compatible storage. So, for on-premises environments, you can use a tool such as MinIO. If you already have an enterprise storage solution, you might want to review it and see whether it has S3 support, as several newer enterprise storage subsystems provide S3 out of the box.

The second task that I recommend testing and documenting is how you will patch/upgrade the nodes in the cluster. The two main ways are to patch in place or replace the node. The most common way for custom clusters is to patch in place, with the high-level process being the creation of a script walk-through of all nodes in the cluster and using the following steps:

1. Drain and cordon the node.

2. Then, apply any patches/upgrades/reboots that are needed on the node.

3. Once all tasks have been completed, the node is un-cordoned, and the next node is processed. An example script can be found at `https://github.com/PacktPublishing/Rancher-Deep-Dive/blob/main/ch06/cluster_patching/rolling_reboot.sh`.

> **Note**
>
> This script is designed to have a lot of sleep periods, as it was intended to be run in unattended mode. For clusters with node pools, you'll typically replace the nodes instead of changing the existing nodes. This is done by scaling up the node pool and then removing the old nodes one at a time and replacing them.

The third task that I recommend testing and documenting is how to upgrade Kubernetes. The basic process is to review the release notes for the new version. Then, when it comes to upgrading the cluster, you'll want to take an etcd snapshot, as this is the only way to roll back an upgrade. The rules and process for this upgrade can be found at `https://github.com/mattmattox/Kubernetes-Master-Class/tree/main/rancher-k8s-upgrades#rke-upgrade--prep-work` along with a masterclass that does a deep dive into the subject.

Summary

In this chapter, we learned about the different types of Rancher-managed clusters, including the requirements and limitations of each. We then covered the rules of architecting each type of cluster, including some example designs and the pros and cons of each solution. Finally, we went into detail about the steps for creating each type of cluster using the design we made earlier. We ended the chapter by going over the major maintenance tasks.

The next chapter will cover how to create a hosted cluster in Rancher – that is, a downstream cluster. We will cover how Rancher creates these clusters and what the limitations are.

7
Deploying a Hosted Cluster with Rancher

For teams that don't want to manage any servers, Rancher provides the ability to deploy and manage hosted Kubernetes services such as **Google Kubernetes Engine (GKE)**, **Amazon Elastic Container Service for Kubernetes** (**Amazon EKS**), or **Azure Kubernetes Service** (**AKS**). This chapter will cover the pros and cons of using a hosted cluster versus an RKE cluster. Then, we'll cover the requirements and limitations of this type of cluster. At that point, we'll go through the process of prepping the cloud provider. Then, we'll go over setting up EKS, GKE, and AKS clusters using Rancher. Finally, we'll cover the maintenance tasks needed for ongoing cluster management.

In this chapter, we're going to cover the following main topics:

- How can Rancher manage a hosted cluster?
- Requirements and limitations
- Rules for architecting a solution
- Prepping the cloud provider
- Installation steps
- Ongoing maintenance tasks

How can Rancher manage a hosted cluster?

One of the first questions I get is, *what is a hosted cluster?* The short answer is that it's a Kubernetes cluster created and managed by a cloud provider such as Google, Amazon, or Azure but with Rancher managing the configuration of the cluster. Rancher uses a cloud provider's API and their SDK to create the cluster the same way you would as an end user through their web console or a command-line tool. As of Rancher v2.6, the current list of supported cloud providers is as follows:

- **GKE**
- **Amazom EKS**
- **AKS**
- **Alibaba Cloud Container Service for Kubernetes) (Alibaba ACK)**
- **Tencent Kubernetes Engine (Tencent TKE)**
- **Huawei Cloud Container Engine (Huawei CCE)**

Rancher does this by having a set of controllers in the Rancher leader pod. Each cloud provider has its controller, and each controller uses a Go library for communicating with the cloud provider. Rancher uses a process wherein Rancher stores the cluster's configuration as a specification in the cluster object. For example, EKS is stored under `Spec.EKSConfig`. For this section, we will go over the v1 controllers first and then the new v2 controllers.

With the original v1 controllers, which are found in Rancher v2.0–2.4, the cluster config was stored in this object and was only updated when Rancher or a user changed. If you were to create an EKS cluster in Rancher and then make a change in the AWS console, that change wouldn't be reflected in Rancher, which would overwrite your change during the next update event. This means the source of truth for these types of clusters is Rancher, and at the time of writing, these clusters cannot be detached from Rancher and managed externally.

The new v2 controllers are only available for EKS and GKE, added to Rancher v2.5.8 and later. The idea of configuration synchronization was added to allow changes made outside Rancher to be synced to it. This is done by two operators called eks-operator and gke-operator. The operator stores the configuration for the cloud provider as `Spec.EKSStatus` and `Spec.GKEStatus`. These objects are refreshed every 5 minutes from the cloud provider. The local configuration of the cluster is stored as `Spec.EKSConfig` and `Spec.GKEConfig`, which represent the desired state of the cluster with most of the fields in the `config section` being `NULL`. Rancher keeps these values `NULL` until they are set in Rancher. Once the value has been set in Rancher, the operator uses the cloud provider's SDK to update the cluster. Once the cloud has been updated, the `Status` specs will get updated. If you change the cluster outside Rancher, that change will get picked up by it, and if the managed field is different, it will get overwritten.

One question that always comes up is, *what is the difference between building a hosted cluster in Rancher and building it outside Rancher and then importing it?* The answer to this question depends on the type of cluster. If it's an EKS or GKE cluster, you'll import the cluster, and Rancher will detect the cluster type. Then, assuming Rancher has the correct permissions, Rancher will *convert* this cluster into a hosted cluster. At that point, the cluster can be managed in the same manner it would be if Rancher created it. We will be covering more about importing clusters into Rancher in the next chapter.

Requirements and limitations

Now that we understand what a hosted cluster is and how it works in Rancher, we will move on to the requirements and limitations of a hosted cluster in Rancher, along with the design limitations and constraints when choosing a hosted cluster.

Basic requirements

Rancher needs permissions from a cloud provider to be able to create a cluster and its related services. The required permissions will vary, depending upon the cloud provider. The links to the official Rancher documentation for each cloud provider type are listed as follows:

- Google Kubernetes Engine: `https://rancher.com/docs/rancher/v2.6/en/cluster-provisioning/hosted-kubernetes-clusters/gke/`.

- Amazon EKS: `https://rancher.com/docs/rancher/v2.6/en/cluster-provisioning/hosted-kubernetes-clusters/eks/`.

- AKS: `https://rancher.com/docs/rancher/v2.6/en/cluster-provisioning/hosted-kubernetes-clusters/aks/`.

- The rest of the cloud providers can be found at `https://rancher.com/docs/rancher/v2.6/en/cluster-provisioning/hosted-kubernetes-clusters/`.

It is recommended that Rancher be configured using a dedicated service account with the least permissions possible.

Rancher will need access to a cloud provider's API endpoint, which means that Rancher will need internet access directly or via an HTTP(S) proxy. If you are using a private API such as AWS's API gateway, that will need to be configured in Rancher.

Rancher will need access to the Kubernetes-API endpoint for the cluster from the Rancher servers.

It is recommended that cloud service accounts are configured in Rancher under a dedicated service account such as local admin, and this account should be the admin permissions in Rancher.

Design limitations and considerations

Some settings such as the available regions are hardcoded in Rancher, meaning that if a cloud provider adds a new region, it might not be available in the Rancher UI until you upgrade Rancher.

> **Important Note**
> For the v2 controllers, you can work around the limitations in the Rancher UI by creating the cluster outside Rancher and then importing it.

The Kubernetes versions that are available in the Rancher UI may not match what the cloud provider allows. For example, if you are running an older version of Rancher, you might have v1.13 available in the drop-down menu, but because Amazon no longer supports this version, you will get an error in Rancher stating that the cluster creation failed.

More cloud providers will assume that the cluster being built will have public internet access and public IP addresses assigned to the nodes, load balancers, and a Kube-API endpoint if you want to set up an air-gapped or private IP-only cluster. You will need to work with the cloud provider to configure the additional firewall rules, routes, and other settings required for this cluster. The following are the documentations for using the private endpoints in Rancher:

- For EKS private-only endpoints, Rancher provides documentation for the additional steps needed, which are located at `https://rancher.com/docs/rancher/v2.5/en/cluster-admin/editing-clusters/eks-config-reference/#private-only-api-endpoints`.

- For the GKE private endpoint, you can find the documentation at `https://rancher.com/docs/rancher/v2.5/en/cluster-admin/editing-clusters/gke-config-reference/#private-cluster`.

> **Note**
> At the time of writing, this type of configuration is not very mature and has several bugs.

Snapshots and backups are not a thing. Unlike an RKE/2 cluster, most of the hosted clusters do not provide you access to the etcd backup and do not provide an etcd backup option. If the cluster is lost or a user makes a mistake (for example, deleting the wrong namespace), your only option is to redeploy. There are third-party tools such as Velero that can address this shortcoming, and we will cover them later on in this chapter.

The permissions Rancher requires can be too great for some security teams to approve. Rancher does provide a list of the minimum EKS permissions, located at `https://rancher.com/docs/rancher/v2.5/en/cluster-provisioning/hosted-kubernetes-clusters/eks/permissions/`. It is important to note that some features may not work with a lower set of permissions, and it may require tuning.

The cost of load balancers with hosted clusters can be greater than an RKE/2 cluster. This is because most cloud providers will deploy an external load balancer instead of the shared load balancer, the Ingress NGINX Controller, that RKE/2 uses. Note that you can work around this limitation by deploying nginx-ingress with an external load balancer in front of it.

In this section, we have covered the requirements and limitations. In the next section, we are going to use that knowledge along with additional rules and example designs to help us architect a solution that meets your needs.

Rules for architecting a solution

In this section, we'll cover some of the standard designs and the pros and cons of each. It is important to note that each environment is unique and will require tuning for the best performance and experience. It's also important to note that all CPU, memory, and storage sizes are recommended starting points and may need to be increased or decreased by your workloads and deployment processes. Also, we'll be covering designs for the major infrastructure providers (Amazon EKS and GKE), but you should be able to translate the core concepts for other infrastructure providers.

Before designing a solution, you should be able to answer the following questions:

- Will multiple environments be sharing the same cluster?
- Will production and non-production workloads be on the same cluster?
- What level of availability does this cluster require?
- Will this cluster be spanning multiple data centers in a metro cluster environment?
- How much latency will there be between nodes in the cluster?
- How many pods will be hosted in the cluster?
- What are the average and maximum size of pods for deployment in the cluster?
- Will you need GPU support for some of your applications?

- Will you need to provide storage to your applications?
- If you need storage, do you need only `ReadWriteOnce` (RWO) or will you need `ReadWriteMany` (RWX)?

Let's start with Amazon EKS.

Amazon EKS

EKS is the most mature cloud provider when it comes to **Kubernetes as a Service** (**KaaS**). Because of this, EKS is one of the most flexible solutions, but some limitations and rules need to be followed when creating an EKS cluster in Rancher.

The **pros** of Amazon EKS are as follows:

- EKS supports enormous clusters, with the current limits being 3,000 nodes per cluster with 737 pods per node (depending on node size).

- EKS supports third-party **Container Network Interface** (**CNI**) providers such as Calico.

- EKS natively supports **Elastic Block Store** (**EBS**) for high-speed `ReadWriteOnce` storage. The provisioner comes pre-installed. You can find more details about this storage class at `https://docs.aws.amazon.com/eks/latest/userguide/ebs-csi.html`.

- For workloads that require `ReadWriteMany`, EKS supports **Elastic File System** (**EFS**), managed by NFS share from Amazon. You can find more details about this at `https://docs.aws.amazon.com/eks/latest/userguide/efs-csi.html`.

- Because Amazon controls both the cloud networking and the cluster overlay network, you can assign IP addresses from your **Virtual Private Cloud** (**VPC**) directly to pods inside your cluster. This allows other Amazon services to communicate with pods directly. You can find more details about this at `https://docs.aws.amazon.com/eks/latest/userguide/pod-networking.html`.

- EKS has direct integration between EKS and AWS load balancers. This allows you to deploy both an **Application Load Balancer** (**ALB**) as a layer 7/HTTP(S) load balancer and a **Network Load Balancer** (**NLB**) as a layer 4/TCP load balancer.

The **cons** of Amazon EKS are as follows:

- EKS limits the number of pods per node based on the node size. For example, `t2.nano` only supports four pods per node. With so few available pods, most services such as the CNI, node exporters, and log collectors will use up all available slots of the node before any application pods can be started. `t2.large` or larger is generally recommended. You can find a list of all the node sizes versus the maximum pod count at `https://github.com/awslabs/amazon-eks-ami/blob/master/files/eni-max-pods.txt`.

- At the time of writing, EKS doesn't have an automatic node repair process, so if a node crashes and doesn't recover, that node will not be replaced until you force a replacement. You can find more details about this limitation at `https://aws.amazon.com/premiumsupport/knowledge-center/eks-node-status-ready/`.

- Several manual steps are required when doing upgrades. Amazon has these steps documented at `https://docs.aws.amazon.com/eks/latest/userguide/update-cluster.html`.

Now, let's talk about GKE.

GKE

GKE is the second-most mature cloud provider when it comes to KaaS. This is because Google created Kubernetes and still drives a lot of the integration and development work for core Kubernetes.

The **pros** of GKE are as follows:

- GKE has the broadest range of supported Kubernetes (three significant releases), and GKE is typically very up to date with new releases. You can find more details about the release schedule and versions at `https://cloud.google.com/kubernetes-engine/docs/release-notes#latest_versions`.

- With GKE, you can enable Autopilot on your cluster, and with that, you can fully automate the upgrade process for your cluster. This includes both the control plane and the worker node level. You can find the documentation for Autopilot at `https://cloud.google.com/kubernetes-engine/docs/concepts/autopilot-overview`.

- You can set the release channel for your cluster to be rapid, which gives you releases every couple of weeks to the regular channel (which is the default option) and provides an update every 2 to 3 months. Finally, you can select the stable channel, which is very similar to regular, the difference being that it is the last channel to get updates. This allows even more time for accurate user testing. You can find more details about this at `https://cloud.google.com/kubernetes-engine/docs/concepts/release-channels`.

- GKE provides automatic node repair; if a node fails, GKE can and will automatically replace it. It does this using the node status, which helps if kubelet crashes when the OS stays running, but the node is effectively dead in the cluster. You can learn more about this process at `https://cloud.google.com/kubernetes-engine/docs/how-to/node-auto-repair`.

- GKE is unique because you can select Google's container-optimized OS, a stripped-down OS designed for security and stability. Alternatively, you can choose an Ubuntu-based image. You can also mix and match inside a cluster. The complete list of node images is available at `https://cloud.google.com/kubernetes-engine/docs/concepts/node-images`.

- GKE supports Windows Server containers. This is done by adding Windows workers nodes to your GKE cluster. The limitation of Windows nodes in GKE can be found at `https://cloud.google.com/kubernetes-engine/docs/concepts/windows-server-gke`.

- GKE allows you to remotely access worker nodes using an SSH client, which is excellent for troubleshooting node and application issues.

The **cons** of GKE are as follows:

- GKE will only provide 99.95% of the **service-level agreement** (**SLA**) if you use regional clusters, which costs extra. The details about this cost can be found at `https://cloud.google.com/kubernetes-engine/pricing#cluster_management_fee_and_free_tier`.

- At the time of writing, GKE does not have a government cloud option. All the currently supported regions can be found at `https://cloud.google.com/compute/docs/regions-zones`.

Lastly, we'll talk about AKS.

Microsoft Azure Kubernetes Service (AKS)

AKS is the new kid on the block when it comes to KaaS, but Microsoft has been investing a lot in AKS and has closed the feature gap very quickly.

The **pros** of AKS are as follows:

- AKS follows Microsoft's standard monthly patch schedule as they do with their OSes. They also publish their releases on their GitHub page, which is located at `https://github.com/Azure/AKS/releases`.

- AKS has automatic node repair whereas Microsoft Azure uses both node agents and the node status in the cluster to trigger a repair. Azure's restoration process is less advanced than the other cloud providers, as it will try rebooting the node before reimaging it and then giving up. Finally, if that fails, an Azure engineer will investigate the issue. You read more about this process at `https://docs.microsoft.com/en-us/azure/aks/node-auto-repair`.

- AKS fully supports integration with **Azure Active Directory** (**Azure AD**). This allows you to assign permissions inside your cluster using Azure AD users and groups. For more details, visit `https://docs.microsoft.com/en-us/azure/aks/managed-aad`.

- AKS has Visual Studio Code extensions that allow developers to run and debug their code directly on their laptop as if it was part of the AKS cluster. Bridge to Kubernetes is basically like creating a VPN connection in your cluster so that pods running on your computer can directly communicate with the clusters and other pods running in the cluster. You can learn more about how this works at `https://docs.microsoft.com/en-us/visualstudio/bridge/overview-bridge-to-kubernetes?view=vs-2019`.

The **cons** of AKS are as follows:

- The upgrade process for AKS has some manual steps.

> **Note**
> The automatic cluster upgrade is in public preview. You can see the current status at `https://azure.microsoft.com/en-us/updates/public-preview-automatic-cluster-upgrades-in-aks/`.

- Some settings such as network policies can only be set when creating clusters and cannot be enabled afterward. You can find more details at `https://docs.microsoft.com/en-us/azure/aks/use-network-policies#create-an-aks-cluster-and-enable-network-policy`.

- AKS will only provide 99.95% of the SLA if you use regional clusters, which increases the cost of the cluster. Details about this cost can be found at `https://azure.microsoft.com/en-us/pricing/details/bandwidth/`.

Now that we understand the pros and cons of each of the major hosted providers, we are going to dive into getting everything set up in the cloud provider and in Rancher so that we can start creating clusters.

Prepping the cloud provider

Before creating a hosted cluster in Rancher, we need to prepare the cloud provider for Rancher. In this section, we'll be covering setting up permissions in the three major hosted Kubernetes clusters, which are EKS, GKE, and AKS.

We'll start with Amazon EKS.

Amazon EKS

The prerequisites are as follows:

- You should already have an AWS subscription created and available to use.

- You'll need permissions in AWS to be able to create **Identity and Access Management (IAM)** policies.

- Your Rancher server(s) should be able to reach AWS API public or private endpoints. You can read more about Amazon's API Gateway private endpoint at `https://aws.amazon.com/blogs/compute/introducing-amazon-api-gateway-private-endpoints/`.

- EKS will require a VPC to be created, and you should work with your networking team to make it. Amazon has a tutorial located at `https://docs.aws.amazon.com/eks/latest/userguide/create-public-private-vpc.html` that covers creating a VPC.

- You should have a dedicated service account in AWS for Rancher.

- You should have a dedicated service account in Rancher, and this account should have admin-level permissions. You can use the local admin account for this role. For this section, we will assume that you will be using the local admin account.

Setup permissions

Here are the setup permissions for Rancher:

1. If you do not already have a dedicated service account in AWS, you should follow the steps at `https://docs.aws.amazon.com/IAM/latest/UserGuide/id_users_create.html`. For this section, we are going to use the name `rancher` for this service account.

2. Now that we have the service account, we will assign an IAM policy to that account. This policy gives Rancher the permissions it needs to create an EKS cluster. The minimum required permissions can be found at `https://rancher.com/docs/rancher/v2.6/en/cluster-provisioning/hosted-kubernetes-clusters/eks/#minimum-eks-permissions`, and the steps for creating an IAM policy and attaching it to a service account can be found at `https://docs.aws.amazon.com/eks/latest/userguide/EKS_IAM_user_policies.html`.

3. We now need to create access and secret key pair, and the process for doing this can be found at `https://docs.aws.amazon.com/IAM/latest/UserGuide/id_credentials_access-keys.html#Using_CreateAccessKey`. It is important to note that as per Amazon's best practices guide for access keys, you should set an expiration time for the access key. This will require you to rotate it though. The best practices guide can be found at `https://docs.aws.amazon.com/general/latest/gr/aws-access-keys-best-practices.html`, and you can find the documentation for rotating access keys at `https://docs.aws.amazon.com/IAM/latest/UserGuide/id_credentials_access-keys.html#rotating_access_keys_console`. You should also store this key in a safe place if it is needed in the future.

4. At this point, you should log into the Rancher web UI as the local admin or your dedicated service account.

5. For the web UI, navigate to **Cluster Management** and then to **Cloud Credentials**.

6. Then, click on the **Create** button and select **Amazon** from the list.

7. Fill in the following form. You should give this credential a name that lets you know it's for Amazon and what subscription it's a part of – for example, you might call it AWS-Prod. The Rancher UI will test whether the credentials are correct but will not validate that the account has all the permissions that Rancher will need. Also, the default region doesn't matter and can be changed at any time. It is also important to note that the access key will be visible, but the secret key is encrypted and cannot be quickly recovered from Rancher:

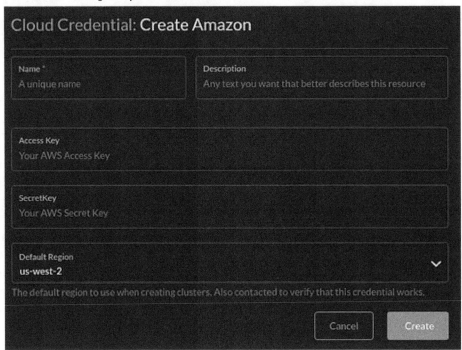

Figure 7.1 – The Cloud Credential setup wizard for Amazon

For more details about the cloud credentials, please go to https://rancher.com/docs/rancher/v2.5/en/user-settings/cloud-credentials/.

Now, let's move on to GKE.

GKE

The prerequisites are as follows:

- You should already have a Google cloud project created and available to use.

- You'll need permissions in GCP to be able to create and assign roles.

- Your Rancher server(s) should be able to reach the GCP API public or private endpoints. You can read more about private access options for services at `https://cloud.google.com/vpc/docs/private-access-options`.

- As with AWS, you should have dedicated service accounts in both GCP and Rancher.

- If you want to use a private GKE cluster, you should review Rancher's documentation, `https://rancher.com/docs/rancher/v2.6/en/cluster-admin/editing-clusters/gke-config-reference/private-clusters/`, for all the additional steps and costs required for this type of cluster.

Setup permissions

Here are the setup permissions for Rancher:

1. If you do not already have a dedicated service account in GCP, you should follow the steps located at `https://cloud.google.com/compute/docs/access/create-enable-service-accounts-for-instances`. For this section, we are going to use the name `rancher` for this service account.

2. Now that we have the service account, we will assign the following default roles to the rancher service account: `compute.viewer`, `viewer`, `container.admin`, and `iam.serviceAccountUser`.

3. Instead of an API key pair, GCP uses a private key for service accounts. You'll need to save the key in JSON format. You can find a detailed set of instructions at `https://cloud.google.com/iam/docs/creating-managing-service-account-keys#creating_service_account_keys`. You must keep this key for future use.

4. At this point, you should log into the Rancher web UI as the local admin or your dedicated service account.

5. Navigate to **Cluster Management** for the web UI and then to **Cloud Credentials**.

6. Then, click on the **Create** button and select **Google** from the list.

7. Fill in the following form. You should give this credential a name that lets you know it's for Google and what project it's a part of – for example, you might call it GCP-Prod. The Rancher UI will test whether the credentials are correct but will not validate that the account has all the permissions that Rancher will need:

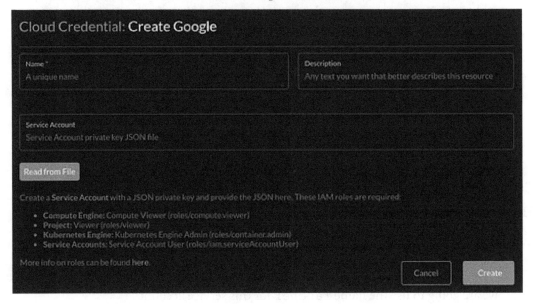

Figure 7.2 – The Cloud Credential setup wizard for Google

Lastly, let's delve into AKS.

AKS

The prerequisites are as follows:

*   You should already have an Azure subscription created and available to use.

*   You'll need permissions in Azure AD to be able to create an app registration.

- Your Rancher server(s) should be able to reach the Azure API public or private endpoints. You can read more about private access options for services at `https://docs.microsoft.com/en-us/azure/api-management/api-management-using-with-internal-vnet?tabs=stv2`.

- Azure doesn't need a dedicated service account, but as with AWS and GCP, Rancher should have one.

- You should have the Azure command-line tool already installed.

- You should have a resource group created for the AKS clusters and related services.

Setup permissions

Here are the setup permissions for Rancher:

- Run the following command. You'll want to document the output, as we'll need it later:

```
az ad sp create-for-rbac --skip-assignment
```

- We now want to assign the contributor role to the service principal using the following command. Please note that you'll need the app and subscription ID from the previous command:

```
az role assignment create --assignee $appId --scope /
subscriptions/$<SUBSCRIPTION-ID>/resourceGroups/$<GROUP>
--role Contributor
```

- At this point, you should log into the Rancher web UI as the local admin or your dedicated service account.

- Navigate to **Cluster Management** for the web UI and then to **Cloud Credentials**.

- Then, click on the **Create** button and select **Azure** from the list.

- Fill in the following form. You should give this credential a name that lets you know it's for Azure and what project it's a part of – for example, you might call it AZ-Prod. The Rancher UI will test that the credentials are correct but will not validate that the account has all the permissions that Rancher will need. For the **Environment** field, **AzurePublicCloud** is the most common option unless you are using a government subscription:

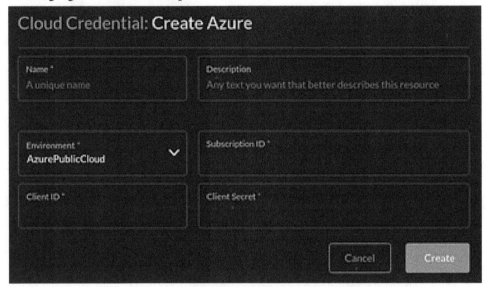

Figure 7.3 – The Cloud Credential setup wizard for Azure

For the other cloud providers, you can find the steps at `https://rancher.com/docs/rancher/v2.6/en/cluster-provisioning/hosted-kubernetes-clusters/`. At this point, Rancher should have access to the cloud provider. In the next section, we will go through creating some hosted clusters.

Installation steps

In this section, we're going to create a hosted cluster, mainly using the default settings. For the examples, we will be continuing to use EKS, GKE, and AKS. Most of these settings can be translated for other cloud providers. It is important to note that you must already have the cloud credentials for each provider and environment you want to configure. It is also recommended that you keep Rancher up to date as cloud providers are constantly changing, and you might run into a bug simply because you are on an older version of Rancher. The latest stable versions can be found at `https://github.com/rancher/rancher#latest-release`.

We'll start with Amazon EKS.

Amazon EKS

The following steps show you how to set up EKS using Rancher:

1. Log into Rancher using the service account that we used during the cloud credentials creation step.

2. Browse the **Cluster Management** page, click on **Clusters,** and then click the **Create** button.

3. Then, from the list, select **Amazon EKS**, at which point you should be prompted with a cluster setup wizard.

4. You'll want to give the cluster a name. This name can be changed later, but it is recommended not to change it, as that can lead to a name mismatch, which would then lead to a user deleting the wrong resource. Also, the description field is a freeform field that can provide additional information such as who owns this cluster or who should be contacted about this cluster; some users will use this field to post maintenance messages such as Scheduled maintenance every Friday at 7 PM CDT. This can be changed at any time. The bottom section assigns the cloud credential to this cluster:

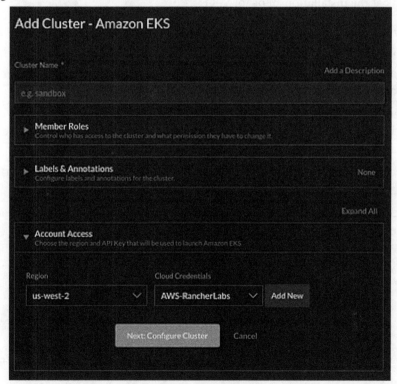

Figure 7.4 – The cluster creation wizard for Amazon EKS

5. The rest of the wizard will fill in the default values. You can change them as you see fit, but you should know what you are changing.

6. The final step is to define the node groups. This includes settings such as the size of the node, the **Amazon Machine Image** (**AMI**) image, and the pool size. After defining the cluster, you should click the **Create** button, at which point Rancher will start the cluster creation process.

7. The details for all the different settings can be found at `https://rancher.com/docs/rancher/v2.6/en/cluster-admin/editing-clusters/eks-config-reference/`.

8. The cluster will go into the **Updating** status, depending on the cluster's size and Amazon's request queue. This process can take anywhere from 2 to 60 minutes. Please note that the wait is primarily dependent on Amazon and how busy they are.

Let's move on to GKE.

GKE

Now, let's look at the installation steps for GKE:

1. Follow the same steps as you did for EKS, but this time, select **Google GKE** from the options menu.

2. The main difference is the **Account access** section, as it may ask you to re-enter the cloud credentials and Google project ID.

3. The details for all the different settings can be found at `https://rancher.com/docs/rancher/v2.6/en/cluster-admin/editing-clusters/gke-config-reference/`.

4. Again, the final step of clicking the **Create** button will cause Rancher to start the cluster creation process.

5. The cluster will go into the **Updating** status, depending on the cluster's size and Google request queue. This process usually takes around 15 minutes.

Lastly, let's look into AKS.

AKS

Lastly, the installation procedure for AKS is as follows:

1. Follow the same steps for EKS and GKE, but this time, select **Azure AKS** from the options menu.

2. The details for all the different settings can be found at `https://rancher.com/docs/rancher/v2.6/en/cluster-admin/editing-clusters/aks-config-reference/`.

3. It is important to note that the network policy is a setting that can only be enabled when creating clusters. You can find details about the different options at `https://docs.microsoft.com/en-us/azure/aks/use-network-policies#differences-between-azure-and-calico-policies-and-their-capabilities`.

4. Again, the final step of clicking the **Create** button will cause Rancher to start the cluster creation process.

5. The cluster will go into the **Updating** status, depending on the cluster's size and Microsoft's request queue. This process usually takes around 60 minutes. From experience, the first cluster in a subscription takes the longest, with additional clusters being faster.

At this point, we should have a Kubernetes cluster from one or more of the cloud providers and be able to easily repeat this process for as many different clusters as we need. This leads us into the final section on what do you do after your cluster is up and running.

Ongoing maintenance tasks

After creating a cluster, a few ongoing maintenance tasks need to be done to keep it running in a healthy state.

The first recommended task is setting up backups. But because these are hosted clusters, we can't take an etcd backup as we would with an RKE1/2 cluster. So, we'll need to use a third-party tool such as **Velcro** or **Kasten**. These tools follow the same basic process of querying the Kube-API endpoint to grab a list of objects in the cluster. Then, they will export the different types of Kubernetes objects, IE deployments, ConfigMaps, secrets, and so on as a JSON or YAML file, the idea being that the restore process is running `kubectl apply` on the backup files. We will be covering these tools in an upcoming chapter.

The second recommended task is testing and documenting how an upgrade impacts your applications. As most cloud providers will do a force drain of a node during a scheduled upgrade, you'll want to test how your application handles this kind of drain. For example, if you are using a multi-master database such as MariaDB Galera Cluster, do your database pods rebuild faster than the worker nodes are drained? A typical way to test this is by changing the node image to simulate the effects of a Kubernetes upgrade. This is because most providers don't allow you to downgrade your clusters. So, being able to repeat this test over and over again is not possible.

Summary

In this chapter, we learned about the different types of hosted clusters that Rancher can deploy, including the requirements and limitations of each. We then covered the rules of architecting each type of cluster, including some of the pros and cons of each solution. We finally went into detail about the steps for creating each type of cluster. We ended the chapter by going over the major ongoing maintenance tasks.

The next chapter will cover importing an externally managed cluster into Rancher.

8

Importing an Externally Managed Cluster into Rancher

In the previous chapters, we covered Rancher-created clusters and hosted clusters. This chapter will cover Rancher-imported clusters, and requirements and limitations when doing this. We'll then dive into a few example setups, with us finally ending the chapter by diving into how Rancher accesses an imported cluster.

In this chapter, we're going to cover the following main topics:

- What is an imported cluster?
- Requirements and limitations
- Rules for architecting a solution
- How can Rancher access a cluster?

What is an imported cluster?

After creating your first **Rancher Kubernetes Engine** (RKE) cluster and installing Rancher on the cluster, one of the first questions is this: *What is this local cluster in my new Rancher instance, and why is it an imported cluster?* To understand what that cluster is and why it is an imported cluster, we first need to answer the question of what an imported cluster in Rancher is. The short answer is that an imported cluster is a Kubernetes cluster built and managed outside of Rancher. Rancher only has access to the resources inside the cluster but not the cluster itself, which means that Rancher can create deployments, ConfigMaps, ingress, and so on, just as any other end user would be able to do. However, tasks such as upgrading the Kubernetes version, adding a node to a cluster, and taking an etcd backup are not available to Rancher. The reason for this is that Rancher only has access to clusters via the kube-api endpoint. Rancher doesn't have direct access to nodes, etcd, or anything deeper in a cluster.

What is this local cluster in my new Rancher instance?

Rancher will automatically import the cluster on which Rancher is installed. It is important to note that this is the default behavior. In the versions before Rancher v2.5.0, there was a Helm option called addLocal=false that allowed you to disable Rancher from importing the local cluster. But in Rancher v2.5.0, that feature was removed and replaced with the restrictedAdmin flag, which restricts access to the local cluster. It is also important to note that the local cluster is called local by default, but you can rename it just as you would do with any other cluster in Rancher. It is pretty common to rename the local cluster to something more helpful such as rancher-prod or rancher-west. For the rest of this section, we will be calling this cluster the local cluster.

Why is the local cluster an imported cluster?

The local cluster was built outside Rancher, and Rancher doesn't manage it. This is because you run into the chicken-and-egg problem. How do you install Rancher if you don't have a Kubernetes cluster, but you need Rancher to create a cluster? So, to address this, we'll explain it further. Before Rancher v2.5.0, you would have needed to create an RKE cluster (for a detailed set of instructions about installations to create an RKE cluster, please refer to *Chapter 4, Creating an RKE and RKE2 Cluster*). But because this cluster was being managed by RKE and not by Rancher, the local cluster needed to be an imported cluster.

Why are some imported clusters special?

Now, with Rancher v2.5.0+ and RKE2, this picture has changed. When Rancher is installed on an RKE2 cluster, you can import the RKE2 cluster into Rancher and allow Rancher to take control of the cluster. This is because of a new tool called the **System Upgrade Controller**, which helps RKE2 and k3s clusters be managed inside the cluster itself using a set of **Custom Resource Definitions** (**CRDs**) called **plans**. The controller allows you to define actions such as upgrading the node's operating system in the cluster, upgrading Kubernetes versions, and even managing the new k3OS operating system. These settings are just Kubernetes objects that you can modify as you see fit. More details about the System Upgrade Controller can be found at `https://github.com/rancher/system-upgrade-controller`.

What kinds of clusters can be imported?

With Rancher, you can import any **Cloud Native Computing Foundation** (**CNCF**)-certified Kubernetes cluster, as long as the cluster follows the standard defined in the official Kubernetes repository located at `https://github.com/kubernetes/kubernetes`. This includes a fully custom cluster such as **kubernetes-the-hard-way**, a Kubernetes cluster built 100% manually with no tooling such as RKE doing the heavy lifting for you. Note that this kind of cluster is optimized for learning and should not be viewed as production-ready. You can find more details and the steps for creating this cluster type at `https://github.com/kelseyhightower/kubernetes-the-hard-way`. Besides a fully custom cluster, you can import a cluster built using RKE or VMware's Tanzu Kubernetes product built on their vSphere product, or even **Docker Kubernetes Service** (**DKS**), which is made by Docker's enterprise solution. It is important to note that Kubernetes distributions such as OpenShift are not 100% CNCF-certified. It may still work, but Rancher does not officially support it. You can find more details about OpenShift and Rancher at `https://rancher.com/docs/rancher/v2.5/en/faq/`.

Why would I import an RKE cluster instead of creating one in Rancher?

The answer to this question comes down to control. Let's suppose you want complete control over your Kubernetes clusters and don't want Rancher to define your cluster for you. This includes importing legacy clusters that might not be supported anymore by Rancher or a third-party cluster from a hosted cloud provider that Rancher doesn't currently support.

What can Rancher do with an imported cluster?

Even though there are some limitations when importing a cluster into Rancher, Rancher can still provide value to the cluster, with the first benefit being a single pane of glass for all your Kubernetes clusters. We will be covering the limitations in the next section. The Rancher **user interface** (**UI**) gives users access to all their clusters via a web interface. The second benefit is a centralized authentication and access source. Even with an imported cluster, Rancher will still sync users, groups, and their permissions down to the imported cluster, just as with a Rancher-launched cluster with the Rancher **application programming interface** (**API**) proxy giving users access to their clusters via `kubectl`, even if they don't have direct access to the cluster.

Requirements and limitations

Now that we understand what an imported cluster is and how it works in Rancher, we will move on to the requirements and limitations of a hosted cluster in Rancher, along with the design limitations and constraints when choosing a hosted cluster.

Basic requirements

In this section, we'll be covering the basic requirements of a Kubernetes cluster that is needed by Rancher. These are outlined here:

- Rancher requires full administrator permissions to the cluster, with the default cluster role of `cluster-admin` being the recommended level of permissions.
- The imported cluster will need access to the Rancher API endpoint.
- If you are importing an **Elastic Kubernetes Service** (**EKS**) or **Google Kubernetes Engine** (**GKE**) cluster, the Rancher server should have a service account and the required permissions to the cloud provider. Please see the previous chapter for details about hosted clusters and the required permissions.
- Rancher publishes a list of the current supported Kubernetes versions for each Rancher release. You can find this list at `https://www.suse.com/suse-rancher/support-matrix/all-supported-versions/`.
- `cattle-node-agent` will use the host's network and **Domain Name System** (**DNS**) settings to connect to the Rancher API endpoint. Because of this, it is recommended that services such as `systemd-resolved` and `dnsmasq` be disabled. Also, `/etc/resolv.conf` should have the DNS server configured and not the `127.0.0.1` loopback address.
- For k3s and RKE2 clusters, you will need to have a `system-upgrade-controller` installed on the cluster before importing the cluster into Rancher.

- Harvester clusters can be imported too, as of Rancher v2.6.1. However, for this, the feature flag must be enabled using the steps located at `https://rancher.com/docs/rancher/v2.6/en/virtualization-admin/#feature-flag`.

Let's look at the design considerations next.

Design limitations and considerations

In this section, we'll be going over the limitations and considerations for clusters that will be imported into Rancher. These are outlined here:

- A cluster should only be imported in a single Rancher install at a time.

- Clusters can be migrated between Rancher installs, but projects and permissions will need to be recreated after the move.

- If you are using a **HyperText Transfer Protocol/Secure (HTTP/S)** proxy for providing access to your Rancher API endpoint, you will need to add additional agent environment variable details, which can be found at `https://rancher.com/docs/rancher/v2.5/en/cluster-provisioning/registered-clusters/`.

- If the cluster has **Pod Security Policy (PSP)** enabled, then `cattle-cluster-agent` and `cattle-node-agent` will require an unrestricted policy as the node agent will be mounting host filesystems, including the root filesystem. The cluster agent will need access to all objects in the cluster.

- If the cluster has **Open Policy Agent (OPA)** Gatekeeper installed, adding the `cattle-system` namespace to the *ignore* list is recommended. This is because the agents will not set limits and requests, and any changes made after the deployment will be overwritten. For more details, please see the OPA Gatekeeper documentation at `https://github.com/open-policy-agent/gatekeeper` and `https://www.openpolicyagent.org/docs/latest/kubernetes-tutorial/`.

- It is important to note that as of Rancher v2.6.2, k3s and RKE2 clusters are still in technical preview, therefore they might be missing features and have breaking bugs.

- The RKE2 configuration settings defined in the `/etc/rancher/rke2/config.yaml` file cannot be overwritten by Rancher, so you should try to make as little customization to this file as possible.

- For imported k3s clusters that use an externally managed database such as MySQL, Postgres, or a non-embedded `etcd` database, Rancher and k3s will not have the access and tools needed to take database backups. Such tasks will need to be managed externally.

- If a cluster has been imported into Rancher and then re-imported into another Rancher instance, any applications deployed via the Rancher catalog will be imported and will need to be redeployed or managed directly using Helm.

- If the imported cluster is using Rancher Monitoring v1, you are required to uninstall and clean up all monitoring namespaces and CRDs before re-enabling monitoring in the Rancher UI.

Let's suppose you have a fleet deployed on the cluster before it has been imported into Rancher. The fleet should be uninstalled before importing it to Rancher v2.6.0 as the fleet is baked into Rancher, and the two different fleet agents will be fighting with each other.

At this point, we have all the requirements and limitations of importing an externally managed cluster into Rancher. We'll be using this in the next section to start creating our cluster design.

Rules for architecting a solution

In this section, we'll cover some of the standard designs and the pros and cons of each. It is important to note that each environment is unique and will require tuning for the best performance and experience. It's also important to note that all **central processing unit (CPU)**, memory, and storage sizes are recommended starting points and may need to be increased or decreased by your workloads and deployment processes. Also, we'll be covering designs for externally managed RKE clusters and Kubernetes The Hard Way, but you should be able to translate the core concepts for other infrastructure providers.

Before designing a solution, you should be able to answer the following questions:

- Will multiple environments be sharing the same cluster?

- Will production and non-production workloads be on the same cluster?

- What level of availability does this cluster require?

- Will this cluster be spanning multiple data centers in a metro cluster environment?

- How much latency will there be between nodes in the cluster?

- How many pods will be hosted in the cluster?

- What will be the average and maximum size of the pods you will be deploying in the cluster?

- Will you need **graphics processing unit** (**GPU**) support for some of your applications?

- Will you need to provide storage to your applications?

- If you need storage, do you only require **Read Write Once** (**RWO**) or will you need **Read Write Many** (**RWX**)?

Externally managed RKE

In this type of cluster, you use the RKE tool along with a `cluster.yaml` file to manually create and update your Kubernetes cluster. At its heart, both Rancher-launched clusters and externally managed RKE clusters use the RKE tool, with the difference being who oversees the cluster and its configuration files. Note that if these files are lost, it can be challenging to manage the cluster moving forward, and you will be required to recover them.

The **pros** are outlined here:

- Control because you are manually running RKE on your cluster. You are in control of nodes being added and removed.

- The cluster is no longer dependent on the Rancher server, so if you want to remove Rancher from your environment, you can follow the steps located at `https://rancher.com/docs/rancher/v2.5/en/faq/removing-rancher/` to kick Rancher out without needing to rebuild your clusters.

The **cons** are outlined here:

- You are responsible for keeping the RKE binary up to date and ensuring the RKE version matches your cluster. RKE can do an accident upgrade or downgrade, which can break your cluster if you don't adhere to this.

- You are responsible for maintaining the `cluster.yaml` file as nodes are added and removed.

- You must have a server or workstation with **Secure Shell** (**SSH**) access to all the nodes in the cluster.

- After any cluster creation or update event, you are responsible for protecting `cluster.rkestate`, which holds the secrets and certificate keys for the cluster. Without this file, RKE will not work correctly. Note that you can recover this file from a running cluster using the steps at `https://github.com/rancherlabs/support-tools/pull/63`.

Kubernetes The Hard Way

This cluster is designed for people who want to learn Kubernetes and do not want to automate cluster creation and maintenance. This is seen a lot in lab environments where you might need to run very non-standard configurations. The details and steps for this kind of cluster can be found at `https://github.com/kelseyhightower/kubernetes-the-hard-way`.

The **pros** are outlined here:

- **Knowledge**—Since Kubernetes The Hard Way is optimized for learning, you will be taking care of each step in the cluster creation and management process. This means that there is no *man behind the curtain* taking care of the cluster for you.

- **Customization**—Because you are deploying each component, you have complete control to pick the version, all the settings, or even replace a standard component with a customized solution.

- The ability to run cutting-edge releases, as most Kubernetes distributions have a lag time from when upstream Kubernetes releases a version to when it's available to end users. This is because of testing, code changes needing to be made, release schedules, and so on.

The **cons** are outlined here:

- Kubernetes The Hard Way is not designed for production and has minimal support from the community.

- Maintenance of the cluster is tough, as distributions such as RKE provide several maintenance services such as automated `etcd` backups, certificate creation, and rotation. With Kubernetes The Hard Way, you are responsible for scripting out these tasks.

- **Version matching**—With Kubernetes The Hard Way, you pick the versions of each of the components, which requires a great deal of testing and validation. The distributions take care of this for you.

k3s cluster

This cluster is a fully certified Kubernetes distribution designed for the edge and remote locations. The central selling point is ARM64 and ARMv7, allowing k3s to run on a Raspberry Pi or other power-efficient server. Details about k3s can be found at `https://rancher.com/docs/k3s/latest/en/` and `https://k3s.io/`. We also covered k3s in a more profound and detailed manner in earlier chapters.

The **pros** are outlined here:

- As of writing, k3s is the only Rancher distribution that supports running on ARM64 and ARMv7 nodes. RKE2 should be adding full support for ARM64 in the future.

> **Important Note**
> Official support is being tracked under `https://github.com/rancher/rke2/issues/1946`.

- k3s is designed to be very fast when it comes to cluster creation. So, you can create a k3s cluster, import it into Rancher, run some tests, then delete the cluster all as part of a pipeline that can be used for testing cluster software such as special controllers and other cluster-level software.

- Suppose you deploy k3s at a remote location with a poor internet connection. You can still import it into Rancher to provide a single glass pane and other related features, but if the connection between the k3s cluster and Rancher is lost, the cluster will continue running with the applications not noticing anything.

The **cons** are outlined here:

- Imported k3s clusters are still in technical preview as of Rancher v2.6.2 and are still missing features such as node creation.

- The k3s cluster must still be built outside of Rancher first then imported into Rancher, which requires additional work and scripting.

RKE2 cluster

This kind of cluster is the future of Kubernetes clusters for Rancher, as RKE2 was designed from the ground up to move the management of clusters from external to internal. By this, I mean that with RKE, you used an external tool (the RKE binary), and you were responsible for the configuration files and the state files, which caused a fair amount of management overhead. Rancher originally addressed this by having the Rancher server take over that process for you, but the issue with that is scale. If you have tens of thousands of clusters being managed by Rancher, just keeping all those connections open and healthy becomes a nightmare, let alone running `rke up` for each cluster, as they change over time. RKE2 used the bootstrap process created for k3s to move this task into the cluster itself. In the previous chapters, we dove deeper into RKE2.

The **pros** are outlined here:

- As of Rancher v2.6.0, you can create an RKE2 cluster outside of Rancher, import it, and have Rancher take over the management of the cluster.

- By importing an RKE2 cluster, you no longer need `cattle-node-agent` as `rke2-agent` replaces this functionally, and that agent doesn't need Rancher to work.

- An RKE2 cluster can be imported into Rancher and removed without impacting the cluster.

The **cons** are outlined here:

- RKE2 is still in technical preview with limited support and features.

- You still need to bootstrap the first node in the cluster before importing it into Rancher, which requires additional tooling/scripting.

- RKE2 doesn't support the k3OS operating system, but with Harvester, this feature is currently in progress. You can find more details at `https://github.com/harvester/harvester/issues/581`.

- Imported RKE2 clusters do have official support for Windows nodes as of this writing. You can find a documented process for joining a Windows worker to an RKE2 cluster at `https://docs.rke2.io/install/quickstart/#windows-agent-worker-node-installation`. If you are importing this cluster into Rancher, you must have a Linux node in the cluster to support the Cattle agents.

By this point, we should have our design locked in and be ready to deploy our cluster and import it into Rancher.

How can Rancher access a cluster?

Before we dive into how Rancher accesses imported clusters, we first need to cover the steps for importing a cluster into Rancher. The process is pretty easy in the fact that you'll go to **Cluster Management** in the Rancher UI and click the **Import Existing** button. At this point, you'll select if you are importing a hosted cluster that is part of the Rancher v2-hosted cluster controller (that is, Amazon EKS, **Azure Kubernetes Service** (**Azure AKS**), or Google's GKE. If you are importing any other cluster type, you'll want to select the **Generic** type. You'll then give the cluster a name, and Rancher will give you a `kubectl` command to run on the cluster. This command will deploy the required agents on the cluster.

Imported clusters access downstream clusters the same way Rancher does with other cluster types. The `cattle-cluster-agent` process runs on one of the worker nodes in the downstream cluster. This agent then connects the Kubernetes API endpoint, with the default being to use the internal service record, but this can be overwritten by the `KUBERNETES_SERVICE_HOST` and `KUBERNETES_PORT` environment variables. However, this is usually not needed. The cluster agent will connect to the kube-api endpoint using the credentials defined in the Cattle service account. If the agent fails to connect, it will exit, and the Pod will retry until it can make the connection. It is crucial to note, though, that the pods will not be rescheduled to a different node during this process, assuming the node is still in a `Ready` status. This can lead to issues with zombie nodes that don't report their node status correctly. For example, if DNS is broken on a node, the cluster agent will have issues making that connection, but the node might still be in a `Ready` status. It is important to note that with Rancher v2.6.0, two cluster agents have node-scheduling rules that make sure they are on different worker nodes.

Once the cluster agent has been able to connect to the Kubernetes API endpoint, the agent will connect to the Rancher API endpoint. The agent does this by first making an HTTPS request to the `https://RancherServer/ping` **Uniform Resource Locator (URL)**, a unique endpoint in the Rancher server that always responds with a code of `200 OK` and an output of `pong`. This is done to verify that the Rancher server is up and healthy and ready for connections. As part of making this connection, the agent requires that the connection be HTTPS with a valid certificate, which is fine if you are using a publicly signed certificate from a known root authority. However, issues arise when you are using a self-signed or internally signed certificate or if the base image of the agent doesn't trust that authority. In such cases, the connection will fail. To address this issue, the agents use an environment variable called `CATTLE_CA_CHECKSUM`, which is a **Secure Hash Algorithm 256 (SHA256)** checksum of the root authority certificate. The agent will capture the root certificate chain from the Rancher API endpoint if this variable is detected. The agent will then take a SHA256 checksum of just the root certificate and compare it against `CATTLE_CA_CHECKSUM` and check if they are the same. Then, the agent will add that root certificate to its trusted list of root authority certificates, allowing the connection process to continue. If this check fails, the agent will sleep for 60 seconds and try again. This is why it's important not to change root authorities for your Rancher server without updating the agents first.

> **Note**
> If you want to change the root authority certificate for the Rancher server, please follow the documented process at `https://github.com/rancherlabs/support-tools/tree/master/cluster-agent-tool`. This script will redeploy the agents with the updated values.

Once the agent has successfully connected to Rancher, the agent will then send the cluster token to Rancher, using that token to match the agent to its cluster and handle the authentication. At this point, the agent will create a WebSocket connection into Rancher and will use this connection to bind to a random loopback port inside the Rancher leader pod. The agent will then open that connection by sending probe requests to prevent connection timeouts. This connection should not disconnect, but if it does, the agents will automatically try reconnecting and keep retrying until it succeeds. The Rancher server then uses the loopback port for connecting to the downstream cluster.

Summary

In this chapter, we learned about imported clusters and how they work, including how agents work differently on imported clusters than on other clusters. We learned about the limitations around this type of cluster and why you might want such limitations. We then covered some of the pros and cons of each solution. We finally went into detail about the steps for creating each type of cluster. We ended the chapter by going over how Rancher provides access to imported clusters.

The next chapter will cover how to manage the configuration of a cluster in Rancher over time and at scale.

Part 4 – Getting Your Cluster Production-Ready

This part will cover all the steps for bringing a blank Kubernetes cluster into a production-ready cluster. This includes maintenance tasks such as etcd backups and Kubernetes upgrades, monitoring your cluster health, collecting application logs, and extending a cluster's functionality using tools such as OPA Gatekeeper and Longhorn.

This part of the book comprises the following chapters:

- *Chapter 9, Cluster Configuration Backup and Recovery*
- *Chapter 10, Monitoring and Logging*
- *Chapter 11, Bringing Storage to Kubernetes Using Longhorn*
- *Chapter 12, Security and Compliance Using OPA Gatekeeper*
- *Chapter 13, Scaling in Kubernetes*
- *Chapter 14, Load Balancer Configuration and SSL Certificates*
- *Chapter 15, Rancher and Kubernetes Troubleshooting*

9
Cluster Configuration Backup and Recovery

The previous chapters covered importing externally managed clusters into Rancher. This chapter will cover managing RKE1 and RKE2 clusters in Rancher when it comes to backup and recovery of the cluster. This includes some of the best practices for setting up your backups. Then, we'll walk through an etcd restore, finally covering the limitations of an etcd backup.

In this chapter, we're going to cover the following main topics:

- What is an etcd backup?
- Why do I need to back up my etcd?
- How does an etcd backup work?
- How does an etcd restore work?
- When do you need an etcd restore?

- What does an etcd backup not protect?
- How do you configure etcd backups?
- How do you take an etcd backup?
- How do you restore from an etcd backup?
- Setting up a lab environment to test common failure scenarios

What is an etcd backup?

As we covered in *Chapter 2, Rancher and Kubernetes High-Level Architecture*, etcd is the database for Kubernetes where the cluster's configuration is stored. Both RKE1 and RKE2 use etcd for this role, but other distributions, such as k3s, can use different databases, such as MySQL, PostgreSQL, or SQLite. For this chapter, we'll only be focusing on etcd. With Kubernetes, all components are designed to be stateless and not store any data locally. The significant exemption to that rule is etcd as its only job is to store persistent data for the cluster. This includes all the settings for the cluster and definitions of all your Deployments, Secrets, and ConfigMap. This means that if the etcd cluster is ever lost, you lose the whole cluster, which is why it's crucial to protect the etcd cluster from an availability viewpoint, which we covered in *Chapter 2, Rancher and Kubernetes High-Level Architecture*, and *Chapter 4, Creating an RKE and RKE2 Cluster*.

Why do I need to back up my etcd?

One of the questions that always comes up when people start their Kubernetes journey is "Why do I need to back up, etcd?" The next question is then "Can't I just redeploy the cluster if anything happens?" How I answer that question is "Yes, in an ideal world, you should be able to rebuild your cluster from zero by just simply deploying everything. But we don't live in a perfect world. It is tough to redeploy 100% of our applications in the real world if you lose a cluster."

The scenario I always give is, let's say it's late on a Friday night, you just did a Kubernetes upgrade, and now everything is failing. Applications are crashing, and you can't find a fix to fail forward with the upgrade. If you have an etcd backup from before the upgrade, with Rancher, it's a few clicks to roll the cluster back to a state it was in before the upgrade, versus you spending hours spinning up a new cluster and then spending hours deploying all your core services, such as monitoring, logging, and storage, on the cluster. Then, who knows how fast you can redeploy all your applications, assuming the standup process is fully documented or still working.

It is highly recommended to take etcd backups no matter the environment, including development and testing environments, as it simply gives you options. I always follow the rule *No one ever got fired for having too many backups*. It is important to note that backups are turned on by default with Rancher-deployed clusters. This was done for the simple fact that an etcd backup usually only takes up a couple hundred megabits of storage and is so valuable during a disaster.

One of the questions that come up is, "Do I need etcd backups if I have a VM snapshot?" While having additional backups is always great, the issue is recovering etcd after restoring from a snapshot. The problem is that all nodes must be in sync at the time of the snapshot for the restore to be successful. If it is the only option you have, you can still recover etcd from a VM snapshot, but you'll need to restore one of the etcd nodes, clean the other etcd nodes, and resync the etcd data from the restored node. You can find this process and scripts at `https://github.com/rancherlabs/support-tools/tree/master/etcd-tools`. It is essential to know this process can be very difficult and time-consuming, and it is not an officially supported solution.

How does an etcd backup work?

In this section, we'll look at how etcd backups work for RKE and RKE2 clusters.

RKE clusters

For RKE clusters, the process for one-time snapshots is controlled by the RKE binary, with scheduled snapshots being managed by a standalone container that is deployed by RKE called `etcd-rolling-snapshots`. Both processes follow the same basic steps, with the first step being to go to each etcd node in the cluster one at a time and start a container called `etcd-snapshot-once` or `etcd-rolling-snapshots`, depending on the type of backup. This container is what is going to do most of the heavy lifting in this process. It is important to note that this is a Docker container outside Kubernetes, and customization on this container is minimal. Once the container is started, it runs a tool called `rke-etcd-backup`, which is part of Rancher's rke-tools, which can be found at `https://github.com/rancher/rke-tools/`.

This tool is mainly a utility script that handles finding the certificates files, at which point it will run the `etcdctl snapshot save` command. This command will export the whole etcd database as a single file. It is important to note that this is a full backup and not an incremental or differential backup. Also, etcd does not have translation logs like other databases, so the snapshot file contains the whole database as a single file.

Once the database is backed up, RKE will backup some additional files to make cluster restores easier. This includes extracting the `cluster.rkestate` file from `configmap full-cluster-state` in the `kube-system` namespace. In versions of RKE before v1.0.0, RKE would back up the `/etc/kubernetes/ssl/` certificate folder, but this is no longer needed as the `rkestate` file has all the certificates and their private keys as part of the JSON. Once all the files have been created, rke-tools will zip up all the files into a single backup file stored in `/opt/rke/etcd-snapshots/` on the host. Then, if you have configured S3 backups, rke-tools will upload the backup file to the S3 bucket.

> **Important Note**
> By default, rke-tools will leave behind a local copy of the backup just in case.

Finally, rke-tools will purge backups. This is done by counting the total number of scheduled backup files. Then, if that count is greater than the retention setting, which is 6 by default, it will start deleting the oldest backup until it meets the retention settings. It is important to note that any one-time snapshots will not be counted and deleted. So, it is common for these backups to stay on the nodes until they are manually cleaned up. Once this process is finished, RKE will start on the next etcd node in the cluster.

> **Note**
> There is a known design quirk that for S3 backups, a backup will be taken on all etcd nodes in the cluster, and each node will upload its backup file to the S3 bucket with the same name. This means that the file will be overwritten multiple times during a backup.

RKE2/k3s clusters

With RKE2 and k3s clusters, they share the code for an etcd backup and restore it. The main difference from RKE is that the etcd backup process is directly built into the `rke2-server` binary instead of a separate container. With RKE2/k3s, etcd backups are turned on by default and are configured with server options, which we will cover later in this chapter. The other main difference is with RKE2; the only file that is backed up is just an etcd snapshot file as RKE2 doesn't need the `rkestate` file as RKE did. With the cluster status for RKE2 being stored in the bootstrap key is stored in the etcd database directly. It is important to note that the bootstrap key is encrypted using an AES SHA1 cipher using the server token as the encryption key, not stored in etcd. You are required to store and protect the token outside the backup process. If you lose the token, there is no way of recovering the cluster without breaking the encryption.

The other difference is how backups are configured because each master node is configured independently, meaning that you can set different backup schedules on each node. This also includes how the scheduled snapshot is run in the fact it uses the cronjob format, which allows you to force the backup to happen at set times, for example, nightly at midnight or every hour on the hour. To address the S3 overwrite issue that RKE has, RKE2 uses the hostname of the node in the backup filename. This means that every node in the cluster will still take an etcd backup and upload it to the S3 bucket, but it will not be overwritten. Because of this, you will have duplicate backups in your S3 bucket, meaning if you have three master nodes in the RKE2 cluster, you will have three copies of the etcd backup file stored in S3. Again, in etcd, backups are usually tiny, so the increased storage is usually just background noise.

How does an etcd restore work?

Next, let's look at how an etcd restore works for the different clusters.

RKE clusters

For RKE clusters, the process of restoring etcd is done using the `rke etcd snapshot-restore` command, which uses the same standalone container with rke-tools as the RKE binary uses for the backups. The main difference is that all etcd nodes will need the same backup file for the restore. This means when you give the RKE binary the snapshot name, all nodes in the cluster must have a copy of that file.

The first step in the restore process is to create an MD5 hash of the file on each node and compare the hashes to verify that all nodes are in agreement. If this check fails, the restore will stop and require the user to copy the backup file between nodes manually. A flag called `--skip-hash-check=true` can be added to the RKE `restore` command, but this is a safety feature that shouldn't be disabled unless you know what you are doing. If you are using the S3 option, RKE will download the backup file from the S3 bucket on each node before running this process, at which point the hash verification process is the same.

Once the backup files have been verified, RKE will tear down the etcd cluster, meaning that RKE will stop all the etcd and control plane containers on all nodes, at which point RKE will start a standalone container called `etcd-restore`, which will restore the etcd data directory on each node. This is why all nodes must have the same snapshot file. Once the restore container has been completed successfully on all nodes, RKE will run a standard RKE up process to build the etcd and control plane back up, including creating a new etcd cluster and then starting the control plane services.

Finally, it ends the process by updating the worker nodes. During this task, the cluster will be offline for about 5 to 10 minutes while the restore process is running. Most application Pods should continue to run without impact, assuming they do not depend on the kube-api service. For example, the ingress-nginx-controller will stay up and running during a restore but will have a stall configuration.

RKE2/k3s clusters

The restore process is very different in RKE2/k3s because in RKE, one master server in the cluster will be used as a new bootstrap node to reset the cluster. This process stops the rke2-server service on all master nodes in the cluster. The new bootstrap node, rke2, will run the following command:

```
rke2 server --cluster-reset --cluster-reset-restore-path=<PATH-TO-SNAPSHOT>
```

This will create a new etcd cluster ID and restore the etcd snapshot into the new single-node etcd cluster. At this point, rke2-server will be able to start. The rest of the rke2 master nodes need to be cleaned and rejoined to the cluster as *new* nodes. Once all the master nodes are back up and healthy, the worker nodes should rejoin automatically on their own, but it can be slow and unreliable, so it is standard practice to restart the rke2-agents after the restore.

> **Important Note**
>
> It is important to note that the whole cluster will be rolled back for both restore processes. This includes any Deployments, ConfigMaps, Secrets, and so on. So, if you are restoring to resolve an application issue, you will need to reapply any changes to any other applications in the cluster.

When do you need an etcd restore?

Of course, the following questions always comes up: "When should I do an etcd restore?" and "Is an etcd restore only for emergencies?". The general rule of thumb is that an etcd restore is mainly for disaster recovery and rolling back a Kubernetes upgrade. For example, you accidentally delete most or all the etcd nodes in a cluster or have an infrastructure issue such as a power outage or storage failure. If the cluster does self-recover on its own, doing an etcd restore from the last backup before the event will be the fastest way to restore service to the cluster.

The other main reason for doing a restore is a failed Kubernetes upgrade. As with RKE, there is no way to downgrade a cluster without restoring the cluster from an etcd backup before the upgrade. This is the way it is always recommended to take a snapshot right before the upgrade. It is important to note that the RKE binary will allow you to set an older Kubernetes version and will try to push out that version to cluster. This process will generally break the cluster and is highly unsupported. In both these cases, the cluster is down or in a failed state, and our goal is to restore service as soon as possible.

Of course, the next question is, "When should I not do an etcd restore?" The answer is, you shouldn't be doing a restore to roll back a failed application change. For example, an application team pushes out a change to their application that fails, that is, there is a bug in their code, or they misconfigured something in their application. Doing an etcd restore from before the change will work to roll back the changes, but you are also impacting all the other applications deployed in the cluster and recycling the cluster to roll back a change that really should just be fixed by redeploying the application with the older code/settings.

> **Note**
>
> Having processes in place for your application teams to roll back a Deployment should be required in your environment. Most CI/CD systems usually have a way to select an older commit and push it out.

The other main reason not to do an etcd restore is to restore an old snapshot. For example, if you restore from a backup that is a few weeks old, there is a good chance that the tokens will be expired, and because of this, the cluster will not come up after the restore. Resolving this will require manual work to refresh the tokens for the broken services. Plus, the biggest issue is "What has changed in this cluster since that backup?" Who knows what upgrades, deployment, code changes, and more have changed in this cluster since that snapshot was taken. You could be fixing one team's problem but breaking everyone else's application in the process. The rule that I follow is 72 hours. If a snapshot is older than 72 hours, I need to weigh my options of restoring it, that is, is most of that time over the weekend when no changes are being made? Great, I have no problem recovering a snapshot from Friday on Monday. But if I know that application teams like to deploy on Thursdays and I'm restoring from a Wednesday snapshot, I should probably stop and talk to the application teams before moving forward.

Finally, when restoring after a Kubernetes upgrade, my rule is an upgrade is a line in the sand for restores that should only be crossed shortly after the upgrade. For example, say I upgraded my cluster from v1.19 to v1.20, and within minutes, my applications started having issues. Then great, let's restore to the snapshot right before the upgrade. But if I did that upgrade on Friday night, and on Tuesday, an application team member comes to me and says, "Hey, we are seeing some weird errors. Can you roll back that upgrade?" My answer is going to be "No." Too much time has passed since the last upgrade and rolling back will cause too much impact on the cluster. Of course, my next question to them would be, "Why didn't your smoke test catch this after the upgrade?", as it is a standard process to smoke test applications after a significant change to the environment.

What does an etcd backup not protect?

Of course, an etcd backup does not cover all data in a cluster, as we covered earlier in this chapter; etcd stores the cluster's configuration. But there is additional data in the cluster that is not stored in etcd. The main one is volumes and the data stored inside the volume data. Suppose you have a **PersistentVolumeClaim** (**PVC**) or **PersistentVolume** (**PV**) with data inside the volume. That data is not stored in etcd but is stored in the storage device, that is, **Network File System** (**NFS**), local storage, Longhorn, and so on. The only thing stored in etcd is the definition of the volume, that is, the name of the volume, size, configuration, and more. This means if you restore from an etcd backup of a cluster after a volume was deleted, depending on the storage provider and its retain policy, the data inside that volume is lost. So, even if you do an etcd restore, the cluster will create a new volume to replace the deleted volume, but the volume will be empty with no data inside it. If you need to backup volumes or other higher-level backup functions, you should look at tools such as Veeam's Kasten or VMware's Velero.

The other big item that doesn't get backed up in an etcd backup is the container images, which means a deployment with a custom image. etcd only stores the image configuration, that is, the image example: `docker.io/rancherlabs/swiss-army-knife:v1.0`. But this does include the image data itself. This typically comes up when someone deploys an app with a custom image then loses access to the image down the road. A great example is hosting your container images in a repository server such as Harbor or JFrog inside the cluster that needs them to start.

How do you configure etcd backups?

Let's look at how to configure etcd backups for RKE and RKE2 clusters.

RKE clusters

For RKE clusters, the etcd backup configuration is stored in the `cluster.yml` file. There are two main types of etcd backups with RKE. The first is a one-time backup that is triggered manually by a user event, such as manually running the `rke etcd snapshot-save` command, upgrading the Kubernetes versions, or making a change to an etcd node in the cluster. The second type is recurring snapshots that are turned on by default with the release of RKE v0.1.12. The default process is to take a backup of everything every 12 hours. It is important to note that this schedule is not fixed like a cronjob where it will always run at the same time but instead is based on how much time has passed since the last scheduled backup.

Following is a set of example `cluster.yaml` files for both local and S3 etcd backups:

- Local backup only – `https://github.com/PacktPublishing/Rancher-Deep-Dive/blob/main/ch09/rke/local-backups.yaml`

- Local and S3 backup – `https://github.com/PacktPublishing/Rancher-Deep-Dive/blob/main/ch09/rke/s3-backups.yaml`

- For the full list of options and settings, please see the official Rancher documentation at `https://rancher.com/docs/rke/latest/en/etcd-snapshots/recurring-snapshots/#options-for-the-etcd-snapshot-service`.

RKE2/k3s clusters

As we talked about earlier in this chapter, RKE2 and k3s handle etcd backups at a node level instead of a cluster level, which means that you define your etcd backup schedule and other settings on each master node in the cluster instead of defining it at the cluster level. This allows you to do some cool things, such as shifting your backup schedule for each node, for example, the first node backups at 12 A.M., 3 A.M., 6 A.M., and so on. The second node backups at 1 A.M., 4 A.M., 7 A.M., and so on, with the third node having a schedule of 2 A.M., 5 A.M., 8 A.M. Note that this is usually only done in large clusters to prevent all etcd nodes from being backed up simultaneously as there is a slight dip in performance for etcd during the backup. So, we want only to impact one etcd node at a time. You can also only configure backups on a first node for lower environments where backups are excellent but not required.

For the complete list of options and settings, please see the official Rancher documentation for RKE2 at `https://docs.rke2.io/backup_restore/` or k3s. Please see `https://rancher.com/docs/k3s/latest/en/backup-restore/` for the official documentation for k3s. It is important to note that embedded etcd in k3s is still experimental.

> **Note**
>
> If you need an HTTP proxy to access your S3 bucket, please configure the proxy setting as stated in the documentation located at `https://docs.rke2.io/advanced/#configuring-an-http-proxy`.

Following is a set of example rke2 configuration file for both local and S3 etcd backups:

- Local backup only – `https://github.com/PacktPublishing/Rancher-Deep-Dive/blob/main/ch09/rke2/local-backups.yaml`

- Local and S3 backup – `https://github.com/PacktPublishing/Rancher-Deep-Dive/blob/main/ch09/rke2/s3-backups.yaml`

How do you take an etcd backup?

In this section, we'll look at taking an etcd backup for RKE and RKE2 clusters.

RKE clusters

For custom clusters, you can make a one-time backup using the following command:

```
rke etcd snapshot-save --config cluster.yml --name snapshot-
name
```

The first option sets the `cluster.yml` filename. This is only needed if you are not using the default filename of `cluster.yml`. The second option specifies the name of the backup. This is technically optional, but it is highly recommended to set this to something meaningful, such as `pre-k8s-upgrade` and `post-k8s-upgrade`. It is also highly recommended to avoid using special characters in the filename. If you use S3 backups, the settings will default to whatever is defined in the `cluster.yml` file. You can override these settings using the command-line flags, which are documented at `https://rancher.com/docs/rke/latest/en/etcd-snapshots/one-time-snapshots/#options-for-rke-etcd-snapshot-save`. If you are using an RKE cluster deployed via Rancher, please see the documentation at `https://rancher.com/docs/rancher/v2.6/en/cluster-admin/backing-up-etcd/`.

RKE2/k3s clusters

Both RKE2 and k3s use the same commands for taking backups by replacing `rke2` with `k3s` for k3s clusters. For a one-time backup, you'll run the following command:

```
rke2 etcd-snapshot save -name snapshot-name
```

The `name` flag has the same rules as RKE, but with the main difference being you might get an error about `FATA[0000] flag provided but not defined: ...` for all options in `config.yaml` that are not related to the S3 settings. To work around this issue, it is recommended to copy only the S3 settings to a new file called `s3.yaml` in `/etc/rancher/rke2/` and add the `-config /etc/rancher/rke2/s3.yaml` flag to the command.

How do you restore from an etcd backup?

Let's now look at how to restore data from an etcd backup.

RKE clusters

For restores in RKE, you'll need to run the `rke etcd snapshot-save --config cluster.yml --name snapshot-name` command. It is imperative you set the snapshot name to be the filename of the snapshot you want to restore minus the `.zip` file extension. Suppose you are restoring from a scheduled snapshot. In that case, the filename will have some control characters as part of the timestamp, so it's recommended that you wrap the filename in single quotes again, making sure to remove the file extension.

> **Note**
>
> If you are restoring an etcd backup into a new cluster, that is, all new nodes, you'll run into some token issues and need to address this issue. You can use the script at `https://github.com/PacktPublishing/Rancher-Deep-Dive/blob/main/ch09/rke/restore-into-new-cluster.sh.sh` to delete the secret and recycle the services. This script was designed for a three-node cluster and assumes using the default settings.

RKE2/k3s clusters

For restores in RKE2, there is a little more work than RKE. The first step is to stop `rke2-server` on all master nodes using the `systemctl stop rke2-server` command. Then, from one node master, you'll reset the cluster and restore the etcd database using the `rke2 server --cluster-reset --cluster-reset-restore-path=<PATH-TO-SNAPSHOT>` command. Once the restore is finished, you'll run the `systemctl start rke2-server` command to start the *new* etcd cluster. You'll then need to go to other master nodes in the cluster and run the `rm -rf /var/lib/rancher/rke2/server/db` command to remove the etcd data stored on the node, at which point we can restart `rke2-server` using the `systemctl start rke2-server` command to rejoin the cluster. This will cause a new etcd member to join the etcd cluster and sync the data from the bootstrap node. It is recommended that you only rejoin the nodes one at a time, allowing the node to go into a *Ready* status before rejoining the next node. Finally, once all the master nodes have rejoined, the worker nodes should recover. But after 5 minutes, you might want to restart the rke2-agent using the `systemctl restart rke2-agent` command to speed up the recovery process.

Setting up a lab environment to test common failure scenarios

Finally, we'll end this chapter by practicing some common failure scenarios. I created a Kubernetes masterclass on this subject called *Recovering from a disaster with Rancher and Kubernetes*, which can be found at `https://github.com/mattmattox/Kubernetes-Master-Class/tree/main/disaster-recovery`, with the YouTube video located at `https://www.youtube.com/watch?v=qD2kFA8THrY`. I cover some of the training scenarios that I have created in this class. Each scenario has a script for deploying a lab cluster and breaking it. I then dive into troubleshooting and restoring/recovering steps for each scenario. Finally, it ends with some preventive tasks. I usually recommend new customers go through these scenarios at least once before rolling Rancher/RKE into production. It should be something you are comfortable with and have a documented process for. This includes verifying you have the correct permissions or have a documented process for getting them. Typically, you'll need root/sudo permissions on all etcd, control plane, and master nodes.

Summary

In this chapter, we learned about RKE, RKE2, k3s, and etcd backups and recovery. This includes how the backup and restore process works. We learned about the limitations of etcd backups. We then covered how to configure scheduled backups. We finally went into detail about the steps for taking a one-time backup and restoring from a snapshot. We ended the chapter by talking about the *Recovering from a disaster with Rancher and Kubernetes* masterclass. At this point, you should be comfortable backing up and restoring your cluster, including using etcd backups to recover from catastrophic failure.

The next chapter will cover monitoring and logging in Rancher.

10

Monitoring and Logging

The previous chapters covered cluster configuration, backup, and recovery. This chapter will cover Rancher monitoring and how Rancher uses Prometheus and Grafana to collect metrics for a cluster and then appoint them. Then, we will cover Rancher logging and how Rancher uses the Banzai Cloud Logging operator and Fluent Bit to collect the logs from the Kubernetes components and collect application logs, including filtering logs.

In this chapter, we're going to cover the following main topics:

- What is Prometheus and Grafana?
- Deploying Rancher's monitoring stack
- Adding custom application metrics to Prometheus
- Creating alert rules in Prometheus
- Creating a Grafana dashboard
- What is the Banzai Cloud Logging operator?

- What is Fluent Bit?
- Deploying Rancher logging
- Filtering application logs
- Writing logs to multiple log servers

What is Prometheus and Grafana?

In this section, we'll be covering the most popular monitoring solution for Kubernetes clusters.

Prometheus is an open source monitoring and alerting framework that the Kubernetes community has widely adopted. Prometheus was initially created by SoundCloud back in 2012 before it was accepted by the **Cloud Native Computing Foundation** (**CNCF**) as its second incubated project after Kubernetes. Prometheus was built from the ground up to work with Kubernetes, the core idea being that everything should be discoverable via the Kubernetes API. At this point, Prometheus will pull the metrics and store them as time-series key-value pairs.

Of course, the first question that always comes up is, *what are metrics?* In the simplest terms, it's a numerical measurement of a resource. For example, it can be the current memory usage of a pod or the current number of connections to a database server. It is important to note that Prometheus doesn't support anything but an integer or floating-point number for the values. You can't set a value to something such as the words *up* or *down* for the value of a metric. For example, if you want to check whether a job was successful or failed, you might output that value as 0 for a successful status and 1 for a failed status.

The other central point with metrics is they should be a point-in-time value. For example, you might want the average number of connections at a given time. So, you would define a metrics endpoint at the pod level. One of the traps for new players is to add the metric endpoint to a service record. This might be easier but is not recommended for the long term because you might want a different rule in the future. For example, you start with just finding an average number of connections over the last 5 minutes, and then you want to change that to 15 minutes. Do you change the value of the current metric, which might affect historical reporting, or do you add another metric, which then means you are collecting duplicate data? The best approach is to output the raw data as a metric and then process it inside Prometheus and Grafana.

The next question that comes up is, *how does Prometheus get its data?* Because Prometheus uses a `pull` instead of a `push` model, this is done by running a web server that exports the metrics as a simple text output of key-value pairs. This is commonly called an exporter in Prometheus. These exporters can be built directly into your application, as in the case of most of the core components of Kubernetes. For example, etcd has a built-in metrics exporter that runs on a different port, `2379`. It is common to run metrics on a different port than the main application because Prometheus, by default, will try making a `GET` request without authentication. Prometheus can query an endpoint that requires authentication, but setting up the tokens or credentials requires additional work and maintenance. So, most users will avoid it and use the fact that metrics are only exposed internally to the cluster and not to the public as *good enough* security.

Of course, Prometheus uses exporters to collect metrics, so the question of what exporters are available comes up. And luckily, because of the open source community, there are a significant number of third-party exporters for most standard applications. For example, almost all major open source databases have an exporter such as MySQL, CouchDB, MongoDB, MSSQL, Oracle DB, and PostgreSQL. You can find the official list at `https://prometheus.io/docs/instrumenting/exporters/#databases`. It's the same with standard web servers such as Apache and NGINX, with the complete list available at `https://prometheus.io/docs/instrumenting/exporters/#http`. And, of course, almost all Kubernetes native applications such as CoreDNS, Longhorn, Linkerd, and OPA Gatekeeper have Prometheus exporters built right into the application.

For application developers, there are several libraries available for Go, Java/JVM, Python, and Node.js that allow even custom applications to add built-in support for Prometheus. Of course, if you can't find a premade exporter for your application, upstream Prometheus provides excellent resources for writing your exporter, including naming standards, example code, and different technical aspects for handling use cases. All this can be found at `https://prometheus.io/docs/instrumenting/writing_exporters/`.

Finally, one of the newer features added to Prometheus is alerting. Because Prometheus is already collecting your environment and applications data, it makes sense to add alerting into Prometheus using AlertManager. The core concept is that you define a set of queries that will run inside the Prometheus server that, if violated, will trigger an alert, which will be sent to Alertmanager, which will forward that alert to several external services such as email, Slack, and PagerDuty. Later in this chapter, we'll cover creating alerts in Prometheus along with some examples.

The one main feature that Prometheus is missing is a way to visualize your data. This is where Grafana comes into the picture. Grafana allows you to visualize data stored in Prometheus and other data sources such as MySQL, Loki, and InfluxDB. The main idea behind Grafana is that you create a dashboard that will query a data source (Prometheus, in this case) and then use this data to develop a range of graphs, charts, gauges, and so on. It is important to note that Gradana doesn't store any data outside of caching query results. Grafana also supports exploring logs from sources such as Loki and Elasticsearch. It also has a notification system that can trigger alerts based on queries, as Prometheus does. This can be helpful for application teams to create custom alerts.

Deploying Rancher's monitoring stack

With Rancher, there are two main versions of monitoring, v1 and v2. The original v1 monitoring that came with Rancher 2.0 to 2.4 is based on Prometheus and Grafana. But with the Rancher server and UI managing the deployment and configuration of the monitoring stack, the basic idea is to deploy Prometheus at the cluster level and additional Prometheus servers for each Rancher project. This approach was fine if you had a small number of projects that didn't need to be controlled via automation. This was mainly done because, initially, all the configurations of the Prometheus server were done by changing configmap. This required a great deal of work to manage the monitoring settings as clusters and applications grew in size and complexity.

With the creation of the Prometheus operator, it all changed. The core idea is that the Prometheus operator monitors a set of **Custom Resource Definitions (CRDs)**. This includes the description of the Prometheus server and its related services such as node-exporter and Alertmanager. It is important to note that monitoring v1 and v2 has built-in rules and dashboards but, most importantly, the configuration of probes, alerts, and other related Prometheus settings, with Prometheus operator handling, creating, and updating the configuration files used by Prometheus.

In October 2020, Rancher 2.5 migrated from monitoring v1 to v2, with v2 being built on the operator model. It is important to note that both Prometheus and Grafana moved to this new model. This also included Rancher using the standard upstream Prometheus and Grafana image instead of the Rancher customized images.

If you are currently running the old v1 monitoring, migrating to the new v2 monitoring is recommended. The official process can be found at `https://rancher.com/docs/rancher/v2.5/en/monitoring-alerting/guides/migrating/`, but the process can be summarized as follows:

1. You need to delete all the current settings and configurations.
2. Then, uninstall the old Prometheus server and its components.
3. At this point, you can install v2 monitoring and reconfigure all the settings.

You must make sure that nothing is left behind from v1 monitoring before installing v2. Luckily, one of the engineers at Rancher named Bastian Hofmann created a script that handles the process of collecting all the alerts and dashboards and migrating them over to v2 (`https://github.com/bashofmann/rancher-monitoring-v1-to-v2`). It is important to note that it is not an official script, and you should take an etcd backup before starting this process.

For deploying monitoring v1, log into the Rancher UI, go to **Tools | Monitoring**, and click the **Enable** button. At this point, the Rancher server will take over deploying the Prometheus server and node exporters. Then, all the monitoring configuration will be done via the Rancher UI. For example, if you wanted to view the CPU usage of a pod, you would browse to the pod in the Rancher UI, and Grafana graphs will be displayed right inside the UI. For additional details about the workload metrics that can be collected, please see the official Rancher documentation at `https://rancher.com/docs/rancher/v2.0-v2.4/en/cluster-admin/tools/cluster-monitoring/cluster-metrics/`.

It is important to note that cluster monitoring is only designed to be used by users that have full view access to the cluster. If you want to scope monitoring to a single project, you'll need to enable project monitoring by going to the project and selecting **Monitoring** from the **Tools** menu. This will cause the Rancher server to deploy an additional Prometheus server with its own namespace inside the project. This Prometheus server is scoped to the project and its namespace:

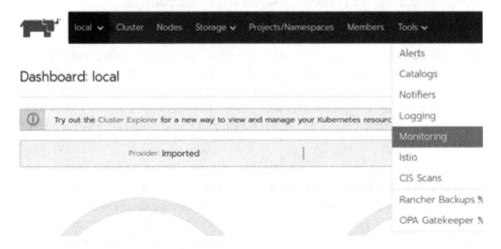

Figure 10.1 – Rancher monitoring v1

For deploying monitoring v2, you have a couple of different options. The first one is to go to **Cluster explorer | Cluster Tools** and click **Install** next to **Monitoring**:

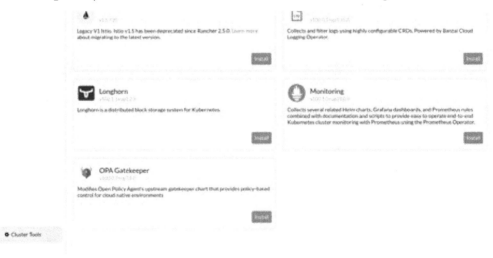

Figure 10.2 – Rancher monitoring v2

This will deploy Rancher's monitoring chart via the app catalog. This chart is just a repackage of upstream images with no code changes. The only real difference is to use Rancher's Docker Hub repositories in place of upstreams. Also, the default namespace is set to `cattle-monitoring-system`, but this can be customized if you so choose. Because monitoring v2 is a Helm chart, you can choose to deploy it directly via the `helm` command, which can be very helpful when managing clusters at scale, using tools such as Rancher's fleet. The following is an example command:

```
helm repo add rancher-charts https://git.rancher.io/charts
helm repo update
helm upgrade –install -n cattle-monitoring-system rancher-
monitoring rancher-charts/rancher-monitoring
```

You can find the complete command and `values.yaml` for installing Rancher monitoring via the `helm` command at `https://github.com/PacktPublishing/Rancher-Deep-Dive/tree/main/ch10/rancher-monitoring-v2`.

The second option is to deploy the upstream Helm chart, commonly called `kube-prometheus-stack`:

```
helm repo add prometheus-community https://prometheus-
community.github.io/helm-charts
helm repo update
helm upgrade –install -n monitoring monitoring prometheus-
community/kube-prometheus-stack
```

It is important to note that, at the time of writing, this chart is still in beta and is subject to change, and Rancher doesn't support all the versions available in the upstream charts. So, it recommends reviewing Rancher's support matrix at `https://www.suse.com/suse-rancher/support-matrix/all-supported-versions/`. You can also find a complete list of the configuration options by viewing the chart value at `https://github.com/prometheus-community/helm-charts/tree/main/charts/kube-prometheus-stack#configuration`.

At this point, you should have Prometheus and Grafana installed on your cluster. It is important to note that it can take approximately 5–10 minutes for all the pods and services that Prometheus needs to start entirely. It is also important to note that, at the time of writing, Rancher does not fully support Prometheus federation – the idea being that you can have a central Prometheus server that scans all other Prometheus servers across your other clusters. If you would like to learn more about this, I recommend looking at the official documentation at `https://prometheus.io/docs/prometheus/latest/federation/`, but I would note that this is still a new feature and still evolving.

Adding custom application metrics to Prometheus

Of course, now that you have Prometheus and Grafana all installed and working, the question becomes, *how do you get metrics from our applications into Prometheus?* In this section, we will cover two main ways of doing this.

The easiest way is to use a community-created chart such as Bitnami's MariaDB chart, including the `metrics.enabled=true` option. This option enables a sidecar that adds `mysqld-exporter` to the deployment, with many community-created charts using this model of having the exporter be a sidecar container to the main container. It is important to note that you should read the documentation for the Helm chart to see if any additional steps need to be taken when enabling metrics in your chart, as some applications will require a service account or permissions to be set for the exporter to work correctly.

Besides enabling the metrics, you'll also see an annotation section with the `prometheus.io/scrape=true` and `prometheus.io/port=9000` key pair. The port might be different, but it is a standard practice to set it to something in this range. These two annotations are significant, as they are what Prometheus uses when discovering all the different pods that should be scraped.

But let's assume that you are using a custom-made application and want to capture metrics from this application. The following are a couple of examples of different applications where the metrics exporter is installed.

With GoLang, Prometheus provides an official library located at `https://github.com/prometheus/client_golang/`. This library handles most of the heavy lifting when generating the metrics output. You can find an example Go application and deployment at `https://github.com/PacktPublishing/Rancher-Deep-Dive/tree/main/ch10/examples/go`. You need to run the `kubectl apply -f deploy.yaml` command in order to deploy the example application. If you curl the pod IP address with the path/metrics, you'll find that the application returns a list of different metrics (for example, curl `10.42.7.23:8080/metrics`). Once the application is up and running, you can send a `GET` request to `/ping`, which will return the word `pong`. Then, inside the application, it will increase a counter called `ping_request_count`, which is a custom metric that is being exposed.

Here is an example of the metrics output:

```
# HELP ping_request_count No of request handled by Ping handler
# TYPE ping_request_count counter
ping_request_count 4
....
```

```
# HELP promhttp_metric_handler_requests_in_flight Current
number of scrapes being served.
# TYPE promhttp_metric_handler_requests_in_flight gauge
promhttp_metric_handler_requests_in_flight 1
# HELP promhttp_metric_handler_requests_total Total number of
scrapes by HTTP status code.
# TYPE promhttp_metric_handler_requests_total counter
promhttp_metric_handler_requests_total{code="200"} 2
promhttp_metric_handler_requests_total{code="500"} 0
promhttp_metric_handler_requests_total{code="503"} 0
```

The full output can be found at `https://github.com/PacktPublishing/Rancher-Deep-Dive/blob/main/ch10/examples/go/output.txt`.

With Apache2, we need to take the sidecar option to add the exporter to the deployment. In our example, we are going to use a popular third-party exporter called `apache_exporter`. You can read more about this project at `https://github.com/Lusitaniae/apache_exporter`. The basic idea behind this project is to act as a translation layer between the Apache `mod_status` module and Prometheus. We need to install/enable the `mod_status` module to the primary web server container in the example deployment. Then, we need to expose the `server-status` page to the sidecar container that hosts the exporter. You can find the example and deployment file at `https://github.com/PacktPublishing/Rancher-Deep-Dive/tree/main/ch10/examples/apache`. You need to run the `kubectl apply -f deploy.yaml` command to deploy the example application.

Here is an example of the metrics output:

```
# HELP apache_accesses_total Current total apache accesses (*)
# TYPE apache_accesses_total counter
apache_accesses_total 6
# HELP apache_connections Apache connection statuses
# TYPE apache_connections gauge
apache_connections{state="closing"} 0
apache_connections{state="keepalive"} 0
apache_connections{state="total"} 1
apache_connections{state="writing"} 0
# HELP apache_cpu_time_ms_total Apache CPU time
# TYPE apache_cpu_time_ms_total counter
apache_cpu_time_ms_total{type="system"} 30
```

```
apache_cpu_time_ms_total{type="user"} 0
# HELP apache_cpuload The current percentage CPU used by each
worker and in total by all workers combined (*)
# TYPE apache_cpuload gauge
apache_cpuload
```

The full output can be found at `https://github.com/PacktPublishing/`
`Rancher-Deep-Dive/blob/main/ch10/examples/apache/output.txt`.

With NGINX, we will use a similar process as we did with Apache, but this time, we will use an exporter provided by NGINX. You can find the example and deployment file at `https://github.com/PacktPublishing/Rancher-Deep-Dive/tree/` `main/ch10/examples/nginx`. You simply need to run the `kubectl apply -f` `deploy.yaml` command.

Here is an example of the metrics output:

```
# HELP nginx_connections_accepted Accepted client connections
# TYPE nginx_connections_accepted counter
nginx_connections_accepted 1
# HELP nginx_connections_active Active client connections
# TYPE nginx_connections_active gauge
nginx_connections_active 1
# HELP nginx_connections_handled Handled client connections
# TYPE nginx_connections_handled counter
nginx_connections_handled 1
# HELP nginx_connections_reading Connections where NGINX is
reading the request header
# TYPE nginx_connections_reading gauge
nginx_connections_reading 0
# HELP nginx_connections_waiting Idle client connections
# TYPE nginx_connections_waiting gauge
nginx_connections_waiting 0
# HELP nginx_connections_writing Connections where NGINX is
writing the response back to the client
# TYPE nginx_connections_writing gauge
nginx_connections_writing 1
# HELP nginx_http_requests_total Total http requests
# TYPE nginx_http_requests_total counter
```

```
nginx_http_requests_total 9
# HELP nginx_up Status of the last metric scrape
# TYPE nginx_up gauge
nginx_up 1
```

The full output can be found at `https://github.com/PacktPublishing/ Rancher-Deep-Dive/blob/main/ch10/examples/nginx/output.txt.`.

At this point, we can monitor the metrics of our different applications, but we're missing the ability to create alerts based on these metrics. In the next section, we'll dive into alert rules for Prometheus.

Creating alert rules in Prometheus

The Prometheus operator defines alert rules via the CRD PrometheusRule. At its core, all an alert is is an expression with a trigger. Let's look at the following example alert. This alert is from Longhorn, which we'll cover in the next chapter. As you can see, the expression is denoted by the `expr` field, which has a formula to take the actual size of the volume, divided by the capacity, and convert it to a percentage. Then, if that value is greater than 90%, the expression is `true`, which will trigger an alert. The `description` section is mainly for the end user. Still, it's important to note that you can have variables inside the description because the alert will contain the same explanation as the summary, typically used for the subject line. For example, when sending an email alert, the email's subject will be set to the subject of the alert, with the body of the email being the description.

Here is an example of an alert:

```
apiVersion: monitoring.coreos.com/v1
kind: PrometheusRule
metadata:
  labels:
    prometheus: longhorn
    role: alert-rules
  name: prometheus-longhorn-rules
  namespace: monitoring
spec:
  groups:
  - name: longhorn.rules
    rules:
```

```
- alert: LonghornVolumeActualSpaceUsedWarning
  annotations:
    description: The actual space used by Longhorn volume
{{$labels.volume}} on {{$labels.node}} is at {{$value}}%
capacity for
        more than 5 minutes.
    summary: The actual used space of Longhorn volume is
over 90% of the capacity.
  expr: (longhorn_volume_actual_size_bytes / longhorn_
volume_capacity_bytes) * 100 > 90
  for: 5m
  labels:
    issue: The actual used space of Longhorn volume
{{$labels.volume}} on {{$labels.node}} is high.
    severity: warning
```

It is important to note that Prometheus will only find rules located in the same namespace as the server by default. This can cause issues, as application teams might need access to the namespace to add/edit/remove their alerts. To work around this issue, you'll need to add the following settings in your `values.yaml` file.

Here is an example of `values.yaml`:

```
prometheusSpec:
  podMonitorNamespaceSelector: {}
  serviceMonitorNamespaceSelector: {}
  ruleNamespaceSelector: {}
```

At this point, we have Prometheus up and running. It's collecting all the data about our cluster, but the built-in UI doesn't give you a way to visualize this data in a useful way. In the next section, we'll be diving into Grafana to bring dashboards to our data.

Creating a Grafana dashboard

At this point, we should have Prometheus and Grafana up and running, with the server collecting all the data about our cluster. Still, you can't see most of the data unless you use Rancher's monitoring charts, including some prebuilt dashboards that are mostly related to the cluster and its core services such as etcd, kube-apiserver, and CoreDNS. But, of course, a question comes up: *How do I create my own?*

The most straightforward answer is to find a premade dashboard and let someone else do all the hard work for you. The Grafana Labs dashboard repository is the most extensive resource, located at `https://grafana.com/grafana/dashboards/`. Their search tool lets you filter results by applications, data sources, and so on. But the coolest part is their dashboard ID system. All dashboards on the official site have an ID number – for example, the NGINX Ingress controller dashboard has an ID of `9614`, and all you need to do to use this dashboard is copy that ID number and go to the Grafana UI. Browse to **Dashboards | Manage | Import**. Note that you might need to log into Grafana using the default login, which is `admin/prom-operator`. Then, paste the ID number in, and you're done.

Of course, Rancher monitoring provides some example dashboards bundled into the rancher-monitoring chart. You can find the raw JSON files at `https://github.com/rancher/system-charts/tree/dev-v2.6/charts/rancher-monitoring/v0.3.1/charts/grafana/dashboards`. Additionally, you can add baseboards by ID too, with some of the most important ones being the component and etcd dashboards, which can be used to provide a great deal of insight into cluster performance issues.

But let's say the application you are deploying is a community-created application that doesn't have a dashboard on the official site. Most repositories will have the dashboard defined as a JSON file. You'll copy and paste it into the UI and import it with this file. But let's say you are deploying a custom in-house application and want to start from zero. I recommend watching the *Getting started with Grafana dashboard design* video at `https://grafana.com/go/webinar/guide-to-dashboard-design/`. I use a lot of community-created dashboards and tune them to my needs. You can click the share button at the top and export a dashboard as a JSON file, at which point you can copy and paste the parts you like. It is also imperative that you save your work when making changes to your dashboard by clicking the save icon at the top-right corner. If you close the page without clicking that icon, all your changes will be lost.

So far in this chapter, we have been talking about monitoring and alerting. In the next section, we will shift gears and focus on the other half of the equation, logging.

What is the Banzai Cloud Logging operator?

Along with migrating to monitoring v2 in Rancher 2.5, Rancher also migrated to logging v2 for mostly the same reasons. In v1, logging is built on Fluentd and uses plugins to ship logs to different logging services such as Elasticsearch, Splunk, Kafka, and Syslog. With v1, the Rancher server was in complete control of the logging deployments, which made customizing and tuning the logging solution complicated. Most of the settings were hard coded inside Rancher. This is where Banzai's Logging operator comes into the picture.

The Logging operator uses the CRD model, just like the Prometheus operator, wherein you'll define your Fluent Bit deployment and its setting via a CRD. The operator takes over pushing out your changes. Because everything is a CRD, including your settings, you can let your application teams define their logging settings. For example, one team might want their logs sent to a cloud log service such as Splunk, while another team might have the legal requirement for everything to stay running on RKE or another K8s cluster hosted on-premises, and you can do this because of the Logging operator. The idea is that you have logging flows that are a set of application pods going to an output, which can be any number of logging servers/services.

What is Fluent Bit and Fluentd?

When talking about logging, two of the questions are, *what is Fluent Bit?* and *what is Fluentd?*

Before diving into Fluent Bit, let's talk about Fluentd, which came first. Fluentd is an open source project written in Ruby by the Treasure Data team back in 2011. Its core idea was that all logs should be JSON objects. With Fluentd and Docker, the basic process used to collect logs from the containers is to use the default Docker log driver that writes the container logs to a file on the disk. Then, Fluentd will read the whole log file and bring forward the events onto the server, at which point Fluentd will open a tail file handler that will hold the log file open and read all writes to it.

It is important to note that Fluentd has a process for handling log rotation, so it is recommended to enable log rotation in Docker Engine. The following is an example configuration. You can find the complete documentation at `https://docs.docker.com/config/containers/logging/configure/`. Docker will wait until the `logs` file is 100 MB before rotating the file in the following example. This is done to prevent the loss of events for applications that create large amounts of events. Fluentd needs to read all the events and forward them to the log server before the rotation.

In the following example, we are defining the log options for the `json-file` log driver, which is built into Docker Engine by default.

Here is an example at `/etc/docker/daemon.json`:

```
{
  "log-driver": "json-file",
  "log-opts": {
    "max-size": "100m",
    "max-file": "3"
  }
}
```

In this case, we are allowing the log file for all containers to reach a maximum size of 100 MB before rotating the file. Then, we'll only be keeping the last three rotated files.

Now, let's go over Fluent Bit. Basically, Fluentd was designed to be a simple tool that is fast and lightweight. Fluent Bit is built on top of Fluentd and is intended to provide the additional filtering and routing that Banzai logging needs. You can find more about the differences at `https://docs.fluentbit.io/manual/about/fluentd-and-fluent-bit`.

Deploying Rancher logging

With Rancher logging, it is recommended to deploy via the Apps and Marketplace in the Rancher UI by going to **Cluster Tools** and clicking **Logging app**. This will deploy the operator in the `cattle-logging-system` namespace. It is important to note that you'll see two applications, `rancher-logging` and `rancher-logging-crd`, in the **Installed** section after the installation is complete. Also, depending on the size of the cluster, it might take 5 to 15 minutes for all the pods to start up and go into the *ready* state. Once Rancher logging is installed on the cluster, we will be able to configure filtering and log flows, which we'll cover in the next two sections.

Because logging v2 is a Helm chart, you can choose to deploy it directly via the `helm` command, which can be very helpful when managing clusters at scale, using tools such as Rancher's Fleet. The following is an example command:

```
helm repo add rancher-charts https://git.rancher.io/charts
helm repo update
helm upgrade –install -n cattle-logging-system rancher-logging
rancher-charts/rancher-logging
```

You can find the full commands and `values.yaml` to install Rancher monitoring via the `helm` command at `https://github.com/PacktPublishing/Rancher-Deep-Dive/tree/main/ch10/rancher-logging-v2`.

Filtering application logs

The first setting that most people configure with Rancher logging is **ClusterFlows** and **ClusterOutput**. ClusterFlow is designed to be scoped to all namespaces and can set the default logging policy for the cluster as a whole. To configure this setting, you'll go to the Rancher UI and browse to **Logging** and then **ClusterFlows**. From there, you'll fill out the form. Then, once that is done, you'll want to define ClusterOutput, where you define the target location for your logs, ElasticSearch, Splunk, Syslog, and so on. For an example of each of the different logging providers, please see Rancher's official documentation at `https://rancher.com/docs/rancher/v2.5/en/logging/custom-resource-config/outputs/`.

Once you have ClusterFlows and ClusterOutput configured, you can call it done. But if you want to customize the logging for an application, you need to repeat the process. Still, this time, you'll be configuring the Flows and Outputs, with the main difference being setting the selector rules or what the documentation calls **matches**, which are a set of `include` or `exclude` labels that you can use to limit the scope of the Flows and Outputs. The following is an example YAML for a NGINX application in the default namespace. It is important to note that Flows are namespace-scoped:

Here is a Flow example:

```
apiVersion: logging.banzaicloud.io/v1beta1
kind: Flow
metadata:
  name: flow-sample
  namespace: default
spec:
  filters:
    - parser:
        remove_key_name_field: true
        parse:
          type: nginx
    - tag_normaliser:
```

```
        format: ${namespace_name}.${pod_name}.${container_name}
localOutputRefs:
  - s3-output
match:
  - select:
      labels:
        app: nginx
```

At this point, we should have logging configured on our cluster and be forwarding the logs to a log server. In the next section, we'll cover a more advanced setup that a number of users use in their environments to log to multiple servers.

Writing logs to multiple log servers

Because you can define as many outputs as you would like, suppose you wanted to send logs to multiple log servers, such as sending to a local Syslog and Splunk server. It is imperative to note that this will duplicate your logs, so this is not recommended as an **High Availability** (**HA**) solution – that is, sending to a production log server or a **Disaster Recovery** (**DR**) log server. It's also vital that you do not dispatch logs to an offline server. Fluent Bit does cache `failed to send` logs, so you can run into memory pressure issues if you have a misconfigured log server or the log server is offline for long periods.

You can find YAML examples in Rancher's official documentation, located at `https://rancher.com/docs/rancher/v2.6/en/logging/custom-resource-config/outputs/`. It's important to note that, as of Rancher 2.6.3, the logging settings in the Rancher UI are still buggy (for example, `https://github.com/rancher/rancher/issues/36516`, where the **ClusterOutput** field is failing to update in the UI), so it's recommended to use YAML files as much as possible.

Summary

In this chapter, we learned about Rancher monitoring and logging. This includes how Prometheus, Grafana, Fluentd, and Fluent Bit work. We learned how to install Rancher monitoring and logging. We finally went into detail about some example dashboards. We ended the chapter by talking about customizing application logging and its flows.

The next chapter will cover Rancher's storage project to provide storage to Kubernetes clusters.

11

Bringing Storage to Kubernetes Using Longhorn

The previous chapters covered monitoring and logging. This chapter will cover Rancher's distributed block storage for Kubernetes called **Longhorn**, including the pros and cons, and how to architect a storage solution using Longhorn. We will then dive into some standard designs for RKE and RKE2 clusters. Then, we will cover the different ways to install Longhorn and upgrade it. Finally, we will close with some maintenance tasks and troubleshooting steps for common issues.

We're going to cover the following main topics in this chapter:

- What is persistent storage and why do we need it in Kubernetes?
- What is Longhorn?
- How does Longhorn work?
- Pros and cons of Longhorn
- Rules for architecting a Longhorn solution

- Installing Longhorn

- How do Longhorn upgrades work?

- Critical maintenance tasks for keeping Longhorn at 100%

- Troubleshooting common Longhorn issues

What is persistent storage and why do we need it in Kubernetes?

After creating a Kubernetes cluster, users will start deploying their applications to the cluster, but the questions always come up, *Where is my data?* or *Where do I store my data?* The philosophical answer is, *You shouldn't be storing any data; all containers should be stateless,* but this is the real world. Some applications need to store data that will be persistent; that is, when the Pod is terminated, the data will become available to its replacement pod. For example, let's say you deployed a MySQL database as a pod. You'll most likely want that data to be persistent so that when the node is rebooted or the deployment is updated, you won't lose all your data.

This persistent data problem has been a problem since containers were created. Docker's first *fix* to this problem was adding bind mounts from earlier OS-level virtualization software, such as jails in FreeBSD back in 2000. With bind mounts being an alternative view of a directory tree, a mount creates a view of the storage device as a directory object in the root tree. Instead, a bind mount takes an existing directory tree and replicates it to a different point. With containers, you have a root filesystem that was created to be isolated from the host filesystem. For example, inside a container, you'll see the filesystem looks like normal Linux server with files, such as binaries and libraries, but what you'll notice is that the root filesystem is not the same directory as the host file's root filesystem.

But, let's say you have a directory on the host, `/mnt/data` for this example, that you want to pass into your container as `/data`. With Docker on Linux, bind mounts are built into the kernel as a feature. So, you would run a command such as `docker run -v /mnt/data:/data Image:Tag` with the critical flag being `-v`, which tells Docker during the container creation process to make the equivalent syscalls as the `mount -bind /mnt/data /var/lib/docker/.../data` command. It is important to note that a bind mount in older *3.x* kernels is indistinguishable. This means that tools such as **df** (short for **disk free**) will see the same device details as the original.

For example, if you are bind mounting a **Network File System** (**NFS**) share into a container, you'll see that the details of the underlying mount point will be visible in df. For example, if you mount an NFS share at /mnt/nfs from the nfs.example.com server then do a bind mount to /data; when you run the df command inside the container, you'll see that an NFS filesystem from the nfs.example.com server is mounted at /data.

In this section, we have managed to understand what persistent storage is and why we need it in Kubernetes. Next, we'll take a look at Longhorn, how it works, and how it can fulfill our storage needs.

What is Longhorn?

Longhorn is a distributed block storage system for Kubernetes clusters. Longhorn is just like Rancher because it is free, open source, and even being developed as an incubating project with the **Cloud Native Computing Foundation** (**CNCF**). Longhorn can be used for providing persistent storage for workloads in a Kubernetes cluster, including providing raw block storage, ReadWriteOnce, and ReadWriteMany volumes. Longhorn offers a backup solution for its volumes and provides cross-cluster disaster recovery of volumes.

But, one of the most remarkable things about Longhorn is that it simplifies distributed block storage. Longhorn does this by being built as a microservice application. Traditional big iron storage subsystems are large blocks of storage with a small number of controllers with application data being provisioned from a shared pool of disks. Longhorn flips that process on its head with the idea that every volume has a dedicated storage controller, which turns into its microservice. This is called the **Longhorn Engine**, which will be covered in the *How does Longhorn work?* section.

One of the other main reasons people love Longhorn is that it brings storage into Kubernetes. Most other external storage providers, such as NFS or cloud-provided storage, require all this work from storage teams to configure and consume. This brings us to another big selling point of Longhorn: you are not tied to a cloud provider for block storage. For example, in **Amazon Web Services** (**AWS**), you might use Amazon's **Elastic Block Store** (**EBS**) or their **Elastic File System** (**EFS**) storage provisioner, which connects to AWS's API, creates EBS volumes for your application, and attaches them to your nodes, which is great until you start hitting **Small Computer System Interface** (**SCSI**) device limits and limitations around moving EBS volumes to different regions. Of course, it's Amazon, so you need to provide your backup solution. Longhorn addresses all these limitations because it doesn't care whether you run Longhorn on physical servers in a data center or VMs up in a cloud.

Of course, with Longhorn being a distributed block storage solution, one of its great strengths is that Longhorn replicates data across disks and hosts. With traditional big iron storage subsystems, you would define **Redundant Array of Independent Disks (RAID)** groups, map out your **Logical Unit Number (LUN)**, and make all these decisions ahead of time that you have to lock-in. On the other hand, Longhorn can be presented on each disk as a single filesystem without RAID and just let node-based replication protect your data. At the same time, you can change your mind, re-layout your storage, and just slide data around without your applications knowing or caring.

This leads us to what makes Longhorn's **high availability (HA)** different. With traditional big iron storage subsystems, you would have a pair of storage controllers running in active/standby or inactive state, which is great until you have a controller failure or need to take a controller offline for maintenance. You are now without redundancy if the other controller has an issue or can't handle the load. A simple software upgrade can take down your whole environment. As someone who was an enterprise storage administrator for years, storage upgrades were always something you had to schedule out and get all these approvals before you were able to do the upgrade late on a Saturday night when no one else was online. Longhorn puts those days behind us because an upgrade is just a new container image that slowly gets rolled out to the environment. We'll be covering this in more detail in the *How do Longhorn upgrades work?* section.

Now that we know what Longhorn is, in the next section, we'll be diving into the nuts and bolts of how Longhorn works, including each of the different components.

How does Longhorn work?

Longhorn can be broken into two layers: the **control plane** and the **data plane**, with Longhorn managers being in the control plane and the engines in the data plane.

The control plane is built on a set of pods called the **Longhorn Manager**. This is a DaemonSet that runs on all nodes in the cluster. Its main job is to handle the cluster's creation and management of volumes. These pods also take the API calls from the Longhorn UI and the volume plugins. Longhorn, of course, follows the same operator model as Rancher, where it uses **CustomResourceDefinitions (CRDs)** that the Longhorn Manager deploys. The Longhorn Manager then connects to the Kubernetes API server and watches volume tasks, such as creating new volumes. It is important to remember that Kubernetes doesn't reach out to Longhorn's API but waits for the Longhorn controllers to detect changes in the spec of the CRD objects.

In addition to watching the Kubernetes API, the Longhorn Manager handles the orchestration on the Longhorn pods. This includes the Longhorn Engine pods, which run on every node in the cluster. The engine pods bridge the control and data plane with them, handling the creation of replicas and presenting the storage to the pod.

If we follow the creation of a volume, first, a user creates a **PersistentVolumeClaim** (**PVC**) with a Longhorn StorageClass. This creation event is seen by the Longhorn Manager pods, which start the volume creation process. The process begins with assigning the new volume to a Longhorn engine. The engine will always be on the same node as the requesting pod for block-based volumes. For the following example, we will assume that the application is assigned to node01 in the cluster. Once the engine has been given a volume, it creates a set of replicas, with each replica being assigned to a node and a disk/filesystem on that node. The default is three replicas, but you can choose to set this to any number you like, including only a single replica. It is essential to know that a replica is just a disk image file on the filesystem. Still, when the Longhorn engine creates this file, it uses the Linux system called **fallocate**, which makes an empty file with the size of the volume but doesn't actually allocate the space on the filesystem. This means you can create a 1 TB replica on a node, but besides some metadata, you don't use any space on the node until you start writing the data, at which point you only consume the blocks that you use; that is, if you write 500 GB to a 1 TB volume, you will only use 500 GB on the node.

You must understand that once a block has been allocated, it is consumed for the life of the volume. If you write a 500 GB file to your volume, delete it. You will still be consuming 500 GB on the filesystem. There is an open feature request to add support for what is called **trimming** or punching holes that would be able to reclaim deleted space. At the time of writing this book, this feature has not been assigned to a release and is still in the planning stage. You can find this feature request at https://github.com/longhorn/longhorn/issues/836. It is also important to note that Longhorn requires Fallocate on the storage disks, which currently are only provided by the **fourth extended filesystem** (**Ext4**) and **Extents File System** (**XFS**). Other filesystems, such as the **Zettabyte File System** (**ZFS**), are adding fallocate support but are still missing the filemap, which Longhorn needs to detect the holes in the file. If you would like to learn more about this issue, please see the *OpenZFS* GitHub issue at https://github.com/openzfs/zfs/pull/10408 to learn more about the current status of this feature, as it is still in active development.

Of course, the creation of replicas happens on a total of three nodes by default, with each replica being a full copy of the data. It is important to note that each replica has its own Linux process inside the Longhorn Engine. In addition, no replica is unique because all read and writes can be sent to any replica. This is because Longhorn uses a process where all writes are sent to all replicas, and the write is not acknowledged to the client, in this case, the pod, until all replicas have acknowledged the write. Longhorn assumes the volume is lost and discards the replicas if a replica times out during this writing process, which will trigger a rebuild. This is because Longhorn doesn't have a transaction log, so there is no way for the Longhorn Engine to know what writes are missing for a replica.

There is a particular case whereby if the pod is located on the same node as its replica, that replica will be given preference for all read requests. This is done by setting the data locality setting, which will try to keep a local replica on the same node as the pod. It is important to note that Longhorn scheduling, by default, is best effort meaning that if possible, it will colocate replicas on the same node but that is not always possible. This is typically caused by the pod being assigned to a node where there is not enough space, incompatible disk tags, or the node is not assigned the role of the storage node.

Now that we have all the replicas created for our volume, we need to expose it to the pod to be consumed. This is done by the Longhorn Engine creating an **Internet Small Computer Systems Interface (iSCSI)** target server that exports the volumes as a SCSI block device. Then, on the node, Longhorn uses the `open-iscsi` package to act as the iSCSI initiator, which then attaches the iSCSI device as a device under `/dev/longhorn/pvc-###`. Longhorn then uses a CSI plugin to take the block device, format it, and mount it on the node at which the kubelet will do a bind mount inside the pod.

In addition to block storage, as of Longhorn v1.1.0, which was released in January 2021, Longhorn supports exporting **ReadWriteMany (RWX)** volumes too. These volumes are built on top of the block storage, with Longhorn creating a share manager pod that mounts the block device and is an NFS server running inside the pod. Then, this pod exports the volumes as an NFS to a cluster. Finally, Longhorn uses its CSI plugin to mount the NFS share and bind mount it into the pod.

Now that we understand how Longhorn works, we'll cover its pros and cons in the next section, including how it stacks up to other storage providers, which we'll cover later in this chapter.

Pros and cons of Longhorn

Let's look at the pros and cons now.

The **pros** are as follows:

- Built-in backup solution. Longhorn supports taking snapshots for operational backups and external backups to an S3 or NFS target.

- Support for cross-cluster disaster recovery volumes that can be backed up on one cluster and restored into another.

- With the release of v1.1.1, Longhorn now supports rebuilding replicas from existing data using system snapshots. You can read more about this feature at `https://github.com/longhorn/longhorn/issues/1304`.

- Scalability. As Longhorn is a microservices application, it can be scaled from three nodes to tens of thousands of nodes.

- Support for both RWO and RWX volumes with the same storage class; the only change that needs to be made is to set the access mode for the volume.

- Infrastructure/cloud provider agnostic, which means you can deploy Longhorn on physical servers, VMware, AWS, and GCP, all with a standardized storage platform, allowing you to move volumes around as you see fit.

- Thin-provisioned by default. With most cloud providers, such as AWS EBS and GCP volumes, you pay for the size of the volume even if you never write a single block of data to it. With Longhorn, you can over-provision your cloud storage and gain some cost savings.

- Longhorn scheduling is region/zone aware, meaning you can define fault domains, such as spanning your cluster across the AWS Availability Zones (for example, us-west-2a, us-west-2b, and us-west-2c) with Longhorn replicas volumes so that you could lose a whole Zone in AWS and not lose any data. You can read more about this at `https://longhorn.io/docs/1.2.3/volumes-and-nodes/scheduling/#scheduling-policy`.

The **cons** are as follows:

- Volumes getting stuck in attaching and detaching status when a new pod is being created or deleted is a very common issue with Longhorn not being sure if the volume is really mounted on the node or not.

- Official support for large volumes, as Longhorn has a hardcoded rebuild limit of 24 hours. There is no hardcoded size limit, but generally, 1~2 TB is the upper limit in volume size.

- Heavy network usage, because all data needs to be written to all replicas. Suppose you were writing 50 MBps to a Longhorn volume from a pod. You can create up to 150 MBps of network traffic between nodes. So, 10 GB network connections between nodes are highly recommended.

- Disk latency can cause volumes/replicas to timeout as Longhorn uses remote acknowledgment. Writes for a volume are only as fast as its slowness replica. So, it's highly recommended to use SSD or tier 1 storage for Longhorn.

- Nested storage virtualization can be wasteful if you deploy Longhorn on VMware with a shared storage subsystem or vSAN. Longhorn will store three copies of the data on your datastores, so 1 TB becomes 3 TB.

> **Note**
>
> It is recommended that if your storage subsystem supports data deduplication, you enable it for Longhorn storage nodes to work around this issue.

At this point, you should understand the pros and cons of Longhorn. We'll use these in the next section to design our Longhorn solution.

Rules for architecting a Longhorn solution

In this section, we'll be covering some standard designs and the pros and cons of each. It is important to note that each environment is unique and will require tuning for the best performance and experience. It's also important to note that all CPU, memory, and storage sizes are recommended starting points and may need to be increased or decreased by your workload and deployment processes.

Before designing a solution, you should be able to answer the following questions:

- What level of availability will this cluster and its applications require?

- Will this cluster be spanning multiple data centers in a MetroCluster environment?

- How much latency will there be between nodes in the cluster?

- If you need storage, do you need only RWO, or will you need RWX?

- Do you have applications that provide their own application data replication/redundancy?

> **Note**
>
> Longhorn has an official performance scalability report published at `https://longhorn.io/blog/performance-scalability-report-aug-2020/`; this report is a little out-of-date but still provides hard numbers to different sizes of the clusters.

Next, we'll be covering the three standard designs (smallest, medium, and large) that you can use as a starting point when designing a Kubernetes cluster with Longhorn.

Smallest

In this design, we'll be deploying the smallest possible configuration of Longhorn but having full **high availability (HA)**. This cluster is based on the RKE small design that we covered in *Chapter 4*, *Creating an RKE and RKE2 Cluster*, which can be found at `https://github.com/PacktPublishing/Rancher-Deep-Dive/blob/main/ch04/standard_designs/rke/01_small_cluster/README.md`.

The **pros** are as follows:

- Full HA, so you can lose any node in the cluster and still have full availability to all storage
- Simple to manage as all nodes will be storage nodes and support Longhorn equally

The **cons** are as follows:

- A Longhorn filesystem will be required on all three nodes.
- Only *N+1* of availability/redundancy (you only have one spare replica), so when doing maintenance tasks like OS patching, you cannot suffer a failure of a node without loss of service. As you already have taken your spare node offline for maintenance.
- Any node maintenance, such as OS patching and reboots, will require a rebuild of all volumes as each node will store one of the third replicas for each volume.

The **hardware requirements** are as follows:

- **Server(s)**: Three physical/virtual servers.
- **CPU**: Six cores per server (two will be dedicated to Longhorn).
- **Memory**: 4~8 GB per server.
- **Disk**: SSD is recommended.
- **Network**: 10 GB between nodes is recommended.

For RKE clusters, please see the following design. The basic idea is that this is a three-node cluster with all nodes sharing all roles. Anything smaller than this design will not be highly available.

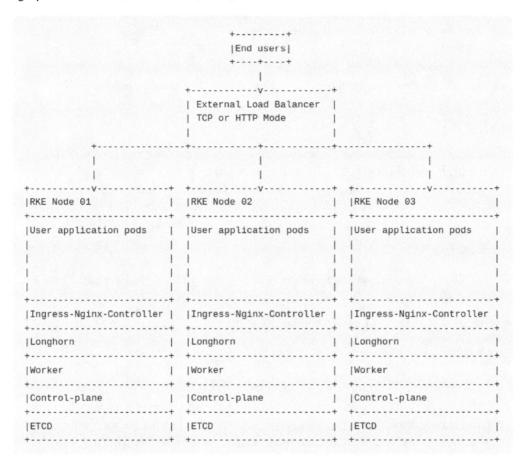

Figure 11.1 – RKE three-node cluster with all nodes, all roles

More information about RKE can be found here: `https://github.com/PacktPublishing/Rancher-Deep-Dive/tree/ch10/ch11/standard_designs/rke/01_small_cluster`For RKE2 clusters.

In RKE2, the basic idea is the same as an RKE cluster but with the master nodes having the `Worker` role assigned to them too.

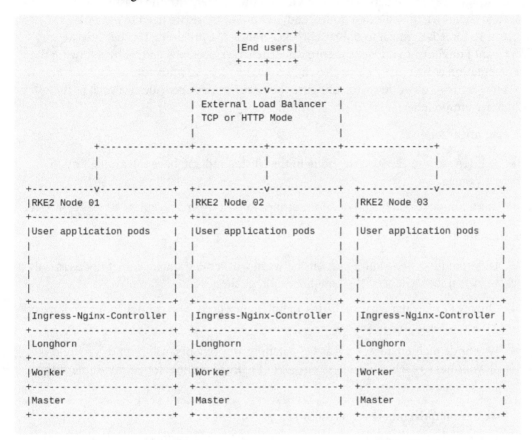

Figure 11.2 – RKE2 three-node cluster, with all nodes being masters or workers

More information about RKE2 can be found here: `https://github.com/PacktPublishing/Rancher-Deep-Dive/tree/ch10/ch11/standard_designs/rke2/01_small_cluster`.

Medium with shared nodes

In this design, we will be deploying an RKE medium cluster with the master services moved to their owned dedicated nodes, and because of these, we need to use node selectors to force Longhorn to only use worker nodes. We are doing this because we don't want Longhorn to impact the core Kubernetes services. We do this by following the documentation at `https://longhorn.io/docs/1.2.3/advanced-resources/deploy/node-selector/` to configure the `nodeSelector` rules for each of the Longhorn components.

The **pros** are as follows:

- Full HA, so you can lose any node in the cluster and still have full availability to all storage.

- The additional load from Longhorn cannot impact the management services for RKE.

The **cons** are as follows:

- Different filesystem configurations between worker and management nodes as only worker nodes will need the Longhorn storage filesystem.

- Only *N+1* of availability, so during maintenance tasks, you cannot suffer a failure of a node without loss of service.

- Any node maintenance, such as OS patching and reboots, will require a rebuild of all volumes as each node will store one of the third replicas for each volume at the worker plane.

The **hardware requirements** are as follows:

- **Node role(s)**: Etcd/Control plane

- **Servers(s)**: Three physical/virtual servers

- **CPU**: Eight cores per server

- **Memory**: 8~16 GB

> **Note**
>
> Worker node sizing should be based on your workload and requirements. You should add two cores to each worker node to support Longhorn.

For RKE clusters, please see the following design. The basic idea is that this cluster has three management nodes with the ETCD and Control-plane roles assigned to them. For the worker nodes, they will also be Longhorn storage nodes. This design is mainly to break out the management services to their nodes to prevent applications from affecting the management services of the cluster.

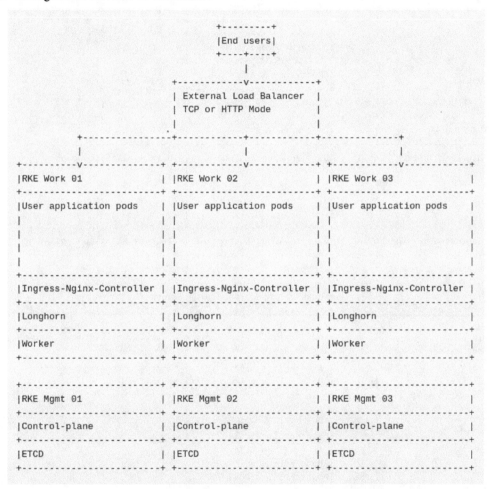

Figure 11.3 – RKE three management nodes with worker nodes being Longhorn storage nodes

More information about RKE can be found here: https://github.com/ PacktPublishing/Rancher-Deep-Dive/tree/ch10/standard_designs/ rke/02_medium_cluster.

For RKE2 clusters, please see the following design. The basic idea is the same as an RKE cluster but with the master nodes having their own load balancer for backend services.

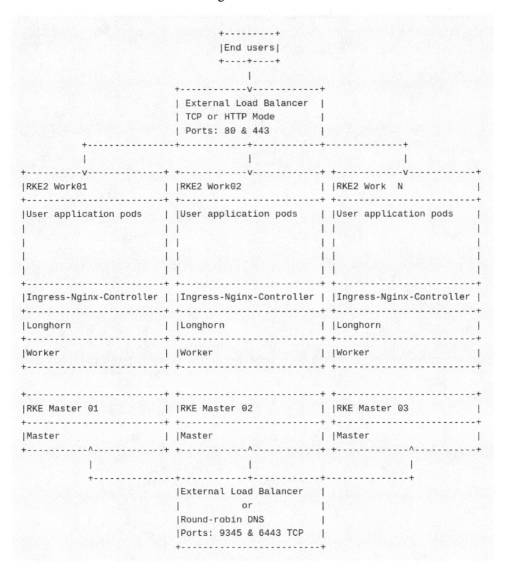

Figure 11.4 – RKE three master nodes with worker nodes being Longhorn storage nodes

More information about RKE2 can be found here: `https://github.com/ PacktPublishing/Rancher-Deep-Dive/tree/ch10/ch11/standard_ designs/rke2/02_medium_cluster`.

Large with dedicated nodes

In this design, we're expanding on the design for a medium cluster but breaking off Longhorn to its own set of dedicated nodes. We're also increasing the number of Longhorn nodes from three to five allow for *N+2* for the Longhorn volumes. You can take down any Longhorn node for maintenance and still lose an additional node without loss of service or redundancy in Longhorn. We'll be using the node selector rules from the medium design, but with further node taints and tolerations. Details on these steps can be found at `https://longhorn.io/docs/1.2.3/advanced-resources/ deploy/taint-toleration/#setting-up-taints-and-tolerations`.

The **pros** are as follows:

- Full HA, so can lose any two Longhorn nodes in the cluster and still have full availability to all storage.

- With dedicated Longhorn nodes, the user application cannot impact Longhorn.

The **cons** are as follows:

- By using dedicated nodes, you can configure them to be pretty static. For example, you might use auto-scaling groups for your worker plane, but for your Longhorn plane, it is recommended that these nodes be added/removed while making sure all volumes have been rebuilt before proceeding to the next node.

- Additional steps are required to force workloads, such as log collectors and monitors, to handle the node taints needed for Longhorn on the Longhorn nodes.

For RKE clusters, you can find an example cluster configuration file at the link listed following this figure:

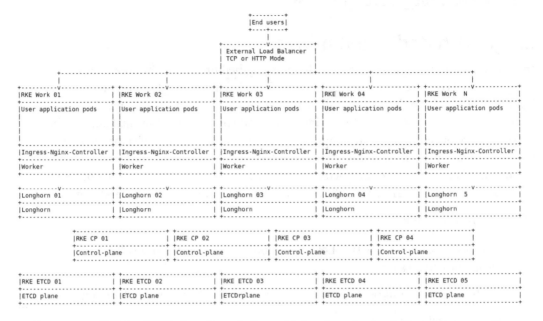

Figure 11.5 – RKE five ETCD, four Control-plane with Longhorn having dedicated storage nodes

(`https://github.com/PacktPublishing/Rancher-Deep-Dive/tree/main/ch11/standard_designs/rke/03_large_cluster.`)

> **Note**
>
> This configuration is designed to be generic and should be customized to fit your needs and your environment.

For an RKE2 cluster, you can find a set of example commands at the URL listed following the next figure. It is important to note that because RKE2 master servers are control-plane and ETCD nodes, the design is different from the RKE design.

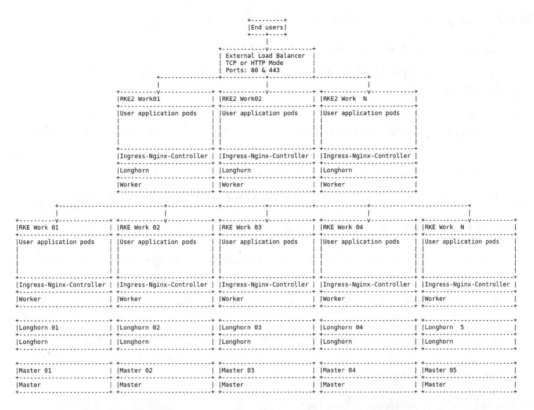

Figure 11.6 – RKE2 three master nodes with Longhorn having dedicated storage nodes

(`https://github.com/PacktPublishing/Rancher-Deep-Dive/tree/main/ch11/standard_designs/rke2/03_large_cluster.`)

At this point, you should do all that you need to create your Longhorn design. We'll use this design to deploy Longhorn in the next section.

Installing Longhorn

There are three ways of deploying Longhorn on a Kubernetes cluster. First, let's cover some of the basic requirements, with each node in the cluster needing to meet the following criteria:

- A compatible runtime, that is, Docker v1.13 or greater.
- The cluster must be running at least Kubernetes v1.18 or greater.

To install Longhorn via the Rancher catalog, follow these steps:

1. Navigate to the cluster where you will install Longhorn.

2. Navigate to **Apps & Marketplace** and search for `Longhorn`, then click the **Install** button.

3. At this point, you can use the default settings. If you would like to customize the values, please see `https://longhorn.io/docs/1.2.3/deploy/install/install-with-rancher/`.

   It will take 5–10 minutes for Longhorn to fully start.

4. You can access the Longhorn UI by clicking on **Longhorn** in the side menu.

To install Longhorn via kubectl, follow these steps:

1. Run the `kubectl apply -f https://raw.githubusercontent.com/longhorn/longhorn/v1.2.3/deploy/longhorn.yaml` command.

2. Wait for the pods to start using the `kubectl get pods -n longhorn-system -w` command.

3. You can then access the Longhorn UI following the steps at `https://longhorn.io/docs/1.2.3/deploy/accessing-the-ui` to create a load balancer or port-forward from your local workstation.

To install Longhorn via Helm, follow these steps:

1. Add the Helm repository using the `helm repo add longhorn https://charts.longhorn.io` command.

2. Update your Helm charts with the `helm repo update` command.

3. Install Longhorn using the `helm install longhorn longhorn/longhorn --namespace longhorn-system --create-namespace` command.

   You can find the full list of Helm values at `https://github.com/longhorn/longhorn/blob/master/chart/values.yaml`.

4. Once Longhorn has started, you can configure the ingress with authentication using the steps located at `https://longhorn.io/docs/1.2.3/deploy/accessing-the-ui/longhorn-ingress`.

At this point, you should have a cluster with Longhorn up and ready to be consumed by applications. In the next section, we'll be covering how to upgrade Longhorn.

How do Longhorn upgrades work?

Upgrading Longhorn is similar to upgrading most Kubernetes applications, but understand that Longhorn is intentionally designed to not be downgradable. Once you start an upgrade, it must be finished. Because of this, you should review the release notes at `https://github.com/longhorn/longhorn/releases`; you should also test all upgrades in a lower environment before upgrading a production/mission-critical environment. Finally, it's imperative that whatever method you used to install Longhorn (the Rancher catalog, kubectl, or Helm) should be used to perform any future upgrades.

Once you start the upgrade process, Longhorn will upgrade the manager pods but not the engines. Upgrading engines are handled by the Longhorn Manager and can be done manually by default using the steps located at `https://longhorn.io/docs/1.2.3/deploy/upgrade/upgrade-engine`, or using the automatic process located at `https://longhorn.io/docs/1.2.3/deploy/upgrade/auto-upgrade-engine`. With engines upgrades, they can be done offline or live. The volume will be detached from its workload and reattached with an offline upgrade. This usually is the faster option but requires a small amount of downtime. The other option is a live upgrade that doubles the replicas, that is, three replicas become six during the upgrade. So, you will be required to have additional capacity on your storage node, and the upgrade requires rebuilding all of your volumes, which will require extra space and I/O.

Critical maintenance tasks for keeping Longhorn at 100%

When running Longhorn, you must complete some additional maintenance tasks to keep Longhorn running in a healthy state.

First, when upgrading/patching storage nodes, you must take the following steps as part of your upgrade. Before starting any OS-level work, the following steps should be taken on each node one at a time:

1. Cordon the node using the following command:

    ```
    kubectl cordon NodeName
    ```

2. Drain the node using the following command:

    ```
    kubectl drain NodeName –ignore-daemonsets
    --pod-selector='app!=csi-attacher,app!=csi-provisioner'
    ```

    This command will cause Longhorn to rebuild replicas on a new node in the cluster.

> **Note**
>
> The draining process will wait for the replicas to be reconstructed.
>
> By default, if there is one last healthy replica for a volume on the node, Longhorn will prevent the node from completing the drain operation, to protect the last replica and prevent the disruption of the workload. You can either override the behavior in the setting or evict the replica to other nodes before draining.

3. At this point, you can perform any node maintenance, including patching and rebooting.

4. Once all node maintenance is done, you'll need to uncordon the node using the following command:

```
kubectl uncordon NodeName
```

Second, Longhorn relies upon the underlying filesystem to detect corruption. You can detect a corrupted replica using the steps located at `https://longhorn.io/docs/1.2.3/advanced-resources/data-recovery/corrupted-replica/`. The process disconnects the volume, takes a checksum of each replica, and compares them. If a single corrupt replica is found, you should remove it via the Longhorn UI and rebuild it. If multiple corrupted replicas are found, you restore the volume from a backup or use the following steps to mount the replicas and review the data manually:

1. First, you'll need to SSH into the node and become root using the command `sudo su` - then run the following commands listed:

```
cd into /var/lib/longhorn/replicas/pvc-...
```

2. Run the following commands:

```
docker run -it -v /dev:/host/dev -v /proc:/host/proc -v
<The replica data path on host>:/volume --privileged
longhornio/longhorn-engine:v1.2.3 launch-simple-longhorn
<volume name> <volume size> &
mkdir /mnt/recovery
mount -o ro /dev/longhorn/pvc-... /mnt/recovery
```

At this point, we have covered the steps for keeping Longhorn healthy, but as we all know, no application is perfect, so in the next section, we'll be covering some common issues and how to resolve them.

Troubleshooting common Longhorn issues

With Longhorn, the two most common failures are running a node until the disk is full, and recovering stuck volumes.

First, a node becomes full because Longhorn uses a shared filesystem such as `root` or `/var` with other applications or pods filling up the space. Note that it's recommended that Longhorn be on its own filesystem for this reason. To recover from this failure, you'll want to use the following steps:

1. Disable the scheduling for the full disk.
2. Expand the current filesystem to bring the used capacity below 80%.
3. If additional storage is not an option, you'll need to delete replicas until the node is no longer in the error state.

The second most common issue is stuck volumes as a pod cannot start if the Longhorn volume is timing out during the `mount` command. To recover from this issue, you'll use the following steps:

1. Start by scaling the workload to zero and deleting the pod.
2. If the volume goes into detached status, retry scaling back up.
3. If the volume is still stuck in attaching, you'll want to try attaching the volume manually to the host using the maintenance flag via the Longhorn UI:

    A. If the volume attaches successfully, try detaching it again and scaling back up.
    B. If the volume won't attach, then there is something broken on the node; usually, rebooting the node resolves it, or you can force the pod to be rescheduled on another node.

At this point, you should be able to resolve most issues with Longhorn and have the tools to keep your data protected.

Summary

In this chapter, we learned about Longhorn, including how it works. We then went over the requirements and limitations in the *Architecting* section. We also went over some common cluster designs by size. We then dove into the different ways to install, upgrade, and customize Longhorn.

In the next chapter, we will cover how to bring security and compliance to your Rancher clusters using OPA Gatekeeper.

12
Security and Compliance Using OPA Gatekeeper

In this chapter, we'll cover bringing security and compliance to our Kubernetes clusters using **OPA Gatekeeper** and why it is needed to manage a cluster at scale. (OPA stands for **Open Policy Agent**.) With so many different teams deploying their applications on your clusters, enforcing standards in your environment (for example, blocking public image registries and blocking deployments that don't follow the rules, such as setting CPU and memory limits on Pods) becomes extremely hard. We'll also cover Rancher's **Center for Internet Security** (**CIS**) scanner, which is required to scan a Kubernetes cluster for known vulnerabilities, along with Rancher's hardening guides applying changes to RKE and RKE2 clusters that enforce extra security standards as defined in the CIS benchmark. We'll also look at how to maintain the cluster on an ongoing basis, and enterprise solutions such as NeuVector.

In this chapter, we're going to cover the following main topics:

- Why should I care about security in Kubernetes?

- How do I enforce standards and security policies in Kubernetes?

- What is OPA Gatekeeper?

- How do I install OPA Gatekeeper from the marketplace?

- Best practices and standard policies.

- How do I scan my cluster for security issues?

- How do I lock down my cluster?

- Deploying the Rancher CIS scan.

- Additional security tools for protecting a cluster.

Why should I care about security in Kubernetes?

One of the questions I get asked a lot is *Why should I care about security? Doesn't containerization fix this?* The short answer is no. Containerization does not solve every IT security problem, but it does change the game if we look back at how we traditionally handled security with servers.

First, we would deploy **antivirus (AV)** software on all our servers to detect and block malware, worms, and Trojan horses, for example, from attacking our servers and stealing our data. Now, containerization throws a big wrench into the works because we virtualize our applications inside another server, and most AV software does not understand nor support running on a server with Docker. This is even discussed in the official Docker documentation at `https://docs.docker.com/engine/security/antivirus/` that recommends excluding the Docker process and its directories from being scanned. In addition, most of the popular AV vendors, such as Symantec Endpoint Protection, block Docker from running altogether. It is important to note that security software, such as Aqua, supports running AV scans at the host level. We'll talk more about this topic later in this chapter.

Second, we would create firewall rules between our servers, giving only the bare minimum access. For example, you might only allow a **Secure Shell (SSH)** protocol from a limited number of jump servers so that if someone compromised a public-facing web server and gained remote access, they wouldn't be able to SSH into other servers, such as the database server. Kubernetes changed this because most **Container Network Interface (CNI)** providers, such as Canal, Calico, and Weave, are open by default, meaning any pod in the cluster can directly connect to any other pod in the cluster. This means if someone compromised the pod running your web server, they could now start directly attacking other pods in the same cluster. It is essential to note that Kubernetes has NetworkPolicies that allow you to bring firewall-like rules into your cluster. However, not all CNI providers support NetworkPolicies. You can find a list of the different CNIs that Rancher supports located at `https://rancher.com/docs/rancher/v2.6/en/faq/networking/cni-providers/#cni-features-by-provider`. This table includes the ones that support the NetworkPolicies resource type as not all CNI providers support this feature.

Third is control over what software is allowed to be installed in your environment. Most enterprise environments do not allow application teams to directly access production servers. They require application teams to document how to install their application and how this process is being reviewed by outside teams such as security and compliance. This was mainly to prevent application teams from making changes to the server that could be a security issue. For example, without controls in place, an application team might just disable the AV software instead of going through the process of whitelisting their processes and fixing security issues with their application. In addition, a team might be using outdated software, such as Java, that has known vulnerabilities, with most security teams blocking this. Containerization flips the script because an application team builds their images; that is, if needed, they can install the software and libraries they want, including outdated and vulnerable software.

Fourth, we come to patching. Most translational server environments have regular patching schedules, such as applying OS patches every month. Because of this, known vulnerabilities are regularly removed from your environment. Containerization, by default, makes a task such as monthly patching not a thing. One of the core concepts with containers is that your images should be static and can only change with a re-deployment.

For example, an application team deploys a pod running a currently patched Ubuntu-based image. They then leave it untouched for six months. Now, the Ubuntu-based image is out of date and needs to be updated. You can, of course, connect to the pod and run `apply patches` by running `apt upgrade` but your changes will be wiped out as soon as that pod gets rescheduled. You need to rely on application teams to keep the images up to date by redeploying the application on a set schedule, and we all know how that will work out, as they don't want to change anything if it's working. It's important to note that this problem is solved by adding image scanning to your pipeline, and we'll be covering this topic later in this chapter.

Last, but not least, is limiting access in a traditional enterprise environment. Access to production servers is limited, with application teams not being allowed access. But, with Kubernetes, it is typical for organizations to get started on their Kubernetes journey to give developers access to the production clusters for speed and efficiency.

In the next section, we'll dive into how we start solving these issues, mainly focusing on OPA Gatekeeper and Rancher CIS scans.

How do I enforce standards and security policies in Kubernetes?

Of course, now that we know about all these security issues/limitations, we need to ask what can we do about them?

First is the AV software issue, with the question being, why do we need AV software in the first place? We need it because we need to detect when rogue software runs in our environment. For example, a hacker compromises a web server by finding a vulnerability that gives them **Remote Code Execution (RCE)**, also known as **Arbitrary Code Execution (ACE)**. Then, the hacker will start installing a **Remote Access Tool (RAT)** to start moving laterally to other servers, trying to gain more access. Containerization addresses this issue by shrinking the attack surface. For example, it's tough to get a remote shell on a server if it doesn't have a shell. This is why it's expected that most container images contain only the absolute minimum software packages and libraries. Kubernetes also addresses this issue by running containers with non-privileged accounts. For example, we might run Apache as a non-root user. So, even if someone gains access to the pod, they wouldn't have permission to install additional software and libraries. This also includes if they were to find a way to break out of the container, they would still be running as an account with little to no permissions.

The second is firewall rules, as discussed in the previous section. Kubernetes, by default, is open between pods but because you need to expose ports and services to the outside world explicitly, you get the benefit of being secure to the outside world by default. For example, if we are running an Apache server as a pod in our cluster, by default, we are not opening that pod directly to the world. But still, you are exposing it via an ingress-controller where you can enable security settings such as **ModSecurity**, which is a **Web Application Firewall** (**WAF**) that can protect you from cross-site scripting, SQL injections, and sessions. You can find out more about ModSecurity by visiting `https://github.com/SpiderLabs/ModSecurity`, and you can find the details around enabling ModSecurity with Ingress NGINX located at `https://kubernetes.github.io/ingress-nginx/user-guide/nginx-configuration/annotations/#modsecurity`.

The third issue is control of the deployed software. We would manage the software on the endpoints, or servers, in translational environments. Containerization moved this process from the endpoint into your build pipeline. This is done by integrating software such as Clair into your build scripts. The idea with Clair is that you run your `docker build` command, then pass the image over to Clair, where it will be downloaded and scanned for known vulnerabilities inside the image. Clair will create a report listing the vulnerabilities, **CVE** (**Common Vulnerabilities and Exposures**) number, and severity level. Depending on your **continuous integration/continuous deployment** (**CI/CD**) software, you can choose to block a build if the image has too many vulnerabilities.

The fourth issue is application patching. Unfortunately, there isn't an easy way to solve this problem; the proper way is to regularly update your containers as part of your ongoing development process. But, as we know, regular patching of images can fall behind. So, what some people do is set up scheduled builds in their pipeline. For example, you might create a scheduled task to rebuild your application image every month using the current code versions and automatically deploy and test it in your environment. By doing this, you are *patching* your containers every month, just like we do with our servers.

Finally, we have the issue of access. The easy way is to give everyone access to deploy into production and make any changes they want. But, this will provide you with unwanted problems and security, because it's always easier to just turn off protection when it's in your way than to fix the reason it's being blocked. To prevent this behavior, it is recommended to force all changes via a CI/CD pipeline to be tracked and controlled using tools such as GitHub/GitLab **pull request** (**PR**) approvals and not give anyone access to production outside cluster administrators. Rancher can address this issue using its Fleet product, which you can learn more about by visiting `https://fleet.rancher.io`. In addition, as of Rancher v2.6, Fleet is built into Rancher itself.

At this point, we should know about the basic concepts around translating traditional IT security requirements into their Kubernetes counterparts. In the next section, we'll be diving into OPA Gatekeeper to enforce our clusters' security standards.

What is OPA Gatekeeper?

OPA is an open source policy engine that has been built for the cloud. In addition, OPA is a **Cloud Native Computing Foundation** (**CNCF**) graduated project like a number of the other tools we covered. OPA uses declarative language to enforce policies across your environment. The basic idea is everything should call OPA and ask, *Hey can I do XYZ?* At which point, OPA will evaluate the request against its policies to approve or reject the request. It is important to note that OPA is designed to be generic to be integrated with Kubernetes and other systems, such as Terraform, Docker, and SSH.

Of course, the question comes up, what is Gatekeeper then? In short, OPA Gatekeeper is a Kubernetes controller that allows you to define your OPA policies as Kubernetes objects. This mainly includes constraints and constraint templates. This enables users to define their policies as YAML and apply them to their cluster just like another Kubernetes deployment. For the rest of this chapter, we'll focus on OPA Gatekeeper.

Now that we know what OPA Gatekeeper is, the next question to answer is *How does it work?* The best way to answer that question is to follow a request through the process. Please see the following diagram to understand this process.

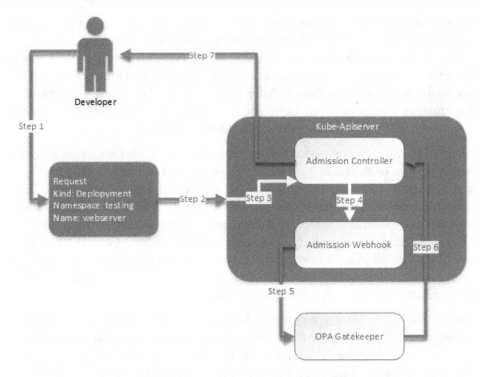

Figure 12.1 – OPA Gatekeeper request flow diagram

Let's look at these steps in detail next:

- **Step 1**: A developer creates a request, and in this case, the request is for a new Deployment called **webserver** in the **testing** namespace.

- **Step 2**: The developer submits the request to **Kube-Apiserver** as a YAML or JSON file.

- **Step 3**: **Kube-Apiserver** receives the request and starts processing by verifying if the user has valid credentials, the request has valid syntax, and the user has permissions to access the requested resources. At this point, usually, **Kube-Apiserver** would respond to the developer accepting or denying the request. But, because we deployed OPA Gatekeeper to this cluster, the request follows a different path.

- **Step 4**: **Admission Controller** takes the incoming requests and uses a set of rules called `ValidatingAdmissionWebhook` to route some requests to a defined webhook. It is important to note that not all requests are forwarded to the webhook. For example, a `kubectl get pods` request is a read-only request, so it would not be forwarded to the webhook. But, a request for creating a pod would be because it's a change to the environment. In this case, OPA Gatekeeper has added `ValidatingAdmissionWebhook` into **Kube-Apiserver**.

- **Step 5**: The request is forwarded via the webhook to the OPA Gatekeeper service, which defaults to `https://gatekeeper-webhook-service.cattle-gatekeeper-system:443` with Rancher's OPA Gatekeeper deployment. The forwarded request has the complete payload minus the user authentication. This includes items such as image paths, labels, and security context. At this point, the OPA Gatekeeper server pods take over and review the request to see if it violates any of the defined policies or constraints. For example, you might have a constraint requiring all namespaces to have a label such as `billing-code`, which you can use for charge-back to your application teams.

- **Step 6**: Once OPA Gatekeeper reviews the request, it will approve or reject it. If we use the example in *Step 5*, if someone tries to deploy a namespace without the `billing-code` label, the creation will be blocked, and the rejection will be forwarded to the next step. But, assuming that the request was approved, OPA Gatekeeper will respond with an HTTP success code of `200`.

- **Step 7**: At this point, **Kube-Apiserver** takes over the request and will use the HTTP success code to decide what it should do with the request. It is important to note that upstream OPA Gatekeeper is set to `fail close by default` by default. What this means is if the request is anything but `200`, it is assumed to be a denial, and the request will be rejected. Even valid deployments will be rejected if the OPA Gatekeeper pods are down or unavailable. This means your cluster is blocked, and no pod will spin up. So, Rancher's OPA Gatekeeper deployment switches the default policy to `failurePolicy: Ignore`, which states if the webhook request receives an error such as a timeout. The Admission Controller will fail to open, which means that the controller will assume the request would have been approved if OPA Gatekeeper is ever offline. You should review this setting with your security team and confirm if availability is more important than potentially allowing a deployment that doesn't meet the standards during an outage.

Finally, at this point, the end user will receive a response to their request. Because of the steps listed previously, the user might see additional latency during a deployment. But, this usually is so quick that it becomes background noise for most environments. It is also important to note that this process applies to both end users and internal requests from other controllers inside the cluster, such as kube-scheduler.

At this point, you should understand how a request flows through kube-apiserver into the Admission Controller, then forwarded on to OPA Gatekeeper, then finally back to the developer via kube-apiserver. In the next section, we are going to dive into the process of installing OPA Gatekeeper in your cluster.

How to install OPA Gatekeeper from the marketplace

With Rancher, there are two main ways to deploy OPA Gatekeeper, these being via the App marketplace in Rancher and via the Rancher Helm Chart. Of course, you can deploy upstream OPA Gatekeeper directly without Rancher. It is typically recommended to deploy OPA Gatekeeper via the App marketplace simply for convenience. The steps for installing OPA Gatekeeper are listed in this section for each of the major Rancher releases.

Before we discuss the installation steps, here's a list of the prerequisites to have ready for the installation:

- You should have the global role Administrator or Cluster Owner permissions to the cluster.

- OPA Gatekeeper requires Kubernetes v1.16 or higher.

- You should review the official support matrix at `https://www.suse.com/suse-rancher/support-matrix/all-supported-versions/` to confirm that you are deploying a fully compatible and validated system solution.

To install OPA Gatekeeper in Rancher v2.4, follow these steps:

1. In the Rancher UI, go to the **Cluster** dashboard.

2. Go to the **Tools** menu and select **OPA Gatekeeper** from the drop-down menu; refer to *Figure 12.2*:

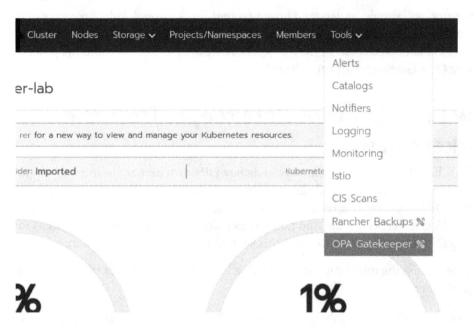

Figure 12.2 – Rancher v2.4 installing OPA Gatekeeper from the Tools menu

3. It is normally recommended to use the default settings, which can be found at `https://rancher.com/docs/rancher/v2.0-v2.4/en/cluster-admin/tools/opa-gatekeeper/`.

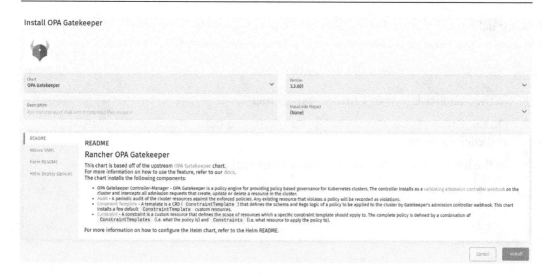

Figure 12.3 – Rancher v2.4 OPA Gatekeeper install wizard

Next, let's look at the installation steps for Rancher v2.5:

1. In the Rancher UI, go to **Cluster Explorer**.

2. Click on the **Apps & Marketplace** option.

3. Select the **OPA Gatekeeper** chart.

Figure 12.4 – Rancher v2.5 installing OPA Gatekeeper from Apps & Marketplace

It is normally recommended to use the default settings, which can be found at `https://rancher.com/docs/rancher/v2.5/en/opa-gatekeper/`.

Now, we'll discuss the installation for Rancher v2.6:

1. In the Rancher UI, go to **Cluster Management**.

2. On the **Clusters** page, go to the cluster where you want to enable OPA Gatekeeper and click **Explore**.

3. In the left navigation bar, click **Apps & Marketplace**.

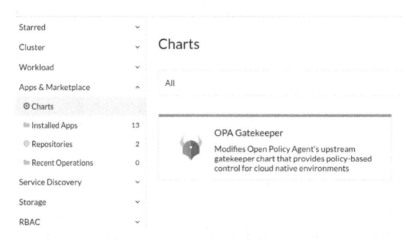

Figure 12.5 – Rancher v2.6 installing OPA Gatekeeper from Apps & Marketplace

4. Click **Charts**, then click **OPA Gatekeeper** and click **Install**.

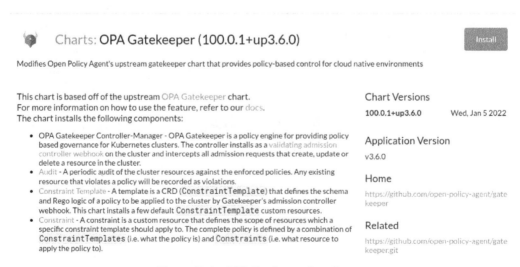

Figure 12.6 – OPA Gatekeeper Install page

5. It is usually recommended to use the default settings, which can be found at `https://rancher.com/docs/rancher/v2.6/en/opa-gatekeper/`.

Figure 12.7 – Rancher v2.6 OPA Gatekeeper Install options

At this point, we should have OPA Gatekeeper installed in our environment but without constraints, it won't do much. In the next section, we are going to cover some standard constraint templates that you can use to get started.

Best practices and standard policies

Now that we have OPA Gatekeeper installed, it's time to start creating templates and applying them to your cluster. In this section, we are going to cover some of the most popular templates. It is important to note that most of these templates come from upstream OPA Gatekeeper.

I like to deploy the first one called `containerlimits`, a template rule that ensures that all pods have CPU and memory limits set. You can find the template at `https://github.com/open-policy-agent/gatekeeper-library/tree/master/library/general/containerlimits`. The main idea here is that, by default, all pods are given unlimited CPU and memory, meaning a single pod can steal all the resources on a node forcing out other pods and even causing nodes to lock up and then crash. This causes what I call a *runaway app* that will consume a node, cause it to crash, then move to another node and repeat the process until you run out of nodes. You can find an example of this kind of application at `https://github.com/mattmattox/Kubernetes-Master-Class/tree/main/disaster-recovery/run-away-app`.

This link also includes how to resolve a runaway app issue. This template makes sure that it's set to a valid value. It could be 1 MB of memory, meaning the pods will never be scheduled, or it could be 100 TB, meaning the pod will never be scheduled because there is no node big enough for it to start. This also has the benefit of giving you insight into the capacity required for your clusters, because if you see that your cluster is reporting 100% allocation, it means one of two things:

- Your limits are being set too high, and you are wasting resources.

- You need to start adding nodes, because you will run out of resources.

OPA Gatekeeper can protect us from runaway apps by blocking pods/deployments that are missing CPU and memory limits, which means a runaway app can never make it into the cluster in the first place.

> **Note**
> We'll be covering scaling in the next chapter.

To apply this template, simply run the following command:

```
kubectl apply -f https://raw.githubusercontent.com/open-
policy-agent/gatekeeper-library/master/library/general/
containerlimits/template.yaml
```

But, make sure you test this in a non-production cluster first.

Another template I like to use is called `requiredlabels`, which is a template that allows you to force all namespaces to have a label. For example, you might want to move all namespaces to have a billing code so you can do show-back and charge-back. Or maybe, you want to force the namespaces to have a technical contact listed to make it easier to contact the application team when deployments are misbehaving.

To apply this template, simply run the following command:

```
kubectl apply -f https://raw.githubusercontent.com/open-policy-
agent/gatekeeper-library/master/library/general/requiredlabels/
template.yaml
```

> **Note**
> This will only apply to newly created namespaces, so you will have to go back and set the label for existing namespaces.

Full details about this template can be found at `https://github.com/open-policy-agent/gatekeeper-library/tree/master/library/general/requiredlabels`.

Finally, the template that I see many security teams asking for is `httpsonly`, which forces all ingresses to have the `kubernetes.io/ingress.allow-http = false` annotation, meaning all ingresses must have an SSL certificated defined in the ingress configuration under the **TLS** (**Transport Layer Security**) section. Many security teams require all traffic, including backend services, to be HTTPS only.

To apply this template, simply run the following command:

```
kubectl apply -f https://raw.githubusercontent.com/open-policy-agent/gatekeeper-library/master/library/general/httpsonly/template.yaml
```

Full details about this template can be found at `https://github.com/open-policy-agent/gatekeeper-library/tree/master/library/general/httpsonly`. It is important to note that, by default, Rancher clusters come with a self-signed certificate for ingresses to default to when another certificate is not defined.

There are, of course, more templates that the open source community has created, which can be found at `https://github.com/open-policy-agent/gatekeeper-library`. I also recommend using these templates as a base for creating your custom templates.

At this point, you should have OPA Gatekeeper installed in your cluster and some rules defined, allowing you to enforce your standards. In the next section, we'll be diving into taking the next step of locking down your cluster to prevent security-related issues.

How do I scan my cluster for security issues?

Rancher has a Rancher CIS scan or Rancher-cis-benchmark tool built on top of kube-bench, an open source software from Aqua Security. kube-bench is designed to scan a Kubernetes cluster and review the settings on the components of Kubernetes such as kube-apiserver, etcd, and kubelet. kube-bench uses the CIS Benchmark report from the non-profit organization CIS, which creates a standard list of best practice settings for protecting your Kubernetes cluster. These reports are made after the most significant changes to Kubernetes and are designed to be as vendor-neutral as possible. You can learn more about CIS and its reports by going to `https://learn.cisecurity.org`. But, because this report is intended to be vendor-neutral, some settings don't apply to Rancher and its cluster. So, Rancher publishes a self-assessment and hardening guide that addresses all the items in the report. This assessment is designed so that it can be handed over to your security team/auditors when they start asking questions.

But, it is important to note that, by default, Rancher and its cluster will not pass the CIS report without making changes to your environment and nodes, with some of these steps requiring manual steps. In the next section, we'll be diving into how to make Rancher pass the report.

You can find Rancher's reports and assessment at `https://rancher.com/docs/ rancher/v2.5/en/security/rancher-2.5/`. It is important to note that these guides change over time as Kubernetes and Rancher are upgraded, and additionally, as security issues are found; thus, it is recommended to review these assessments on a scheduled basis.

How do I lock down my cluster?

In the previous section, we talked about the CIS scan and Rancher's self-assessments, but of course, the question of *What can I do about this report?* comes up, and Rancher's answer to this question is what Rancher calls its **hardening guides**. These guides cover the three Kubernetes distributions that Rancher owns: RKE, RKE2, and k3s. We won't be going into too much detail in this section, as Rancher already has this process documented. Here, we'll be linking to guides for each cluster type.

For RKE clusters, the hardening guide is tied to the Rancher server and Kubernetes version. The following are the high-level steps:

1. Configuring the Linux kernel to safely handle **Out-Of-Memory (OOM)** and kernel panics.

2. Creating a local user and group to be used by etcd to isolate the database from other processes to protect the data.

3. Disabling the default service accounts being mounted to every pod.

4. Enabling a `NetworkPolicy` default to limit all pod-to-pod traffic, requiring that you open rules as you need them.

5. Turning on secret encryption wherein, by default, secrets are stored in etcd in plain text, but with etcd encryption enabled, the secrets will be encrypted at rest.

6. Finally, ending by turning on `PodSecurityPolicy` to limit pod security settings, such as blocking pods from running as root.

The complete guide can be found at `https://rancher.com/docs/rancher/ v2.5/en/security/rancher-2.5/1.6-hardening-2.5/`.

This process is much easier for RKE2 clusters, as RKE2 is secure by default, but you still need to apply a few changes, which are listed here:

1. Setting the same Linux kernel parameters as RKE.

2. Creating an etcd user.

3. Finally, we just need to turn on the CIS profile that we would like on the master servers by adding the `profile: cis-1.5/6` option.

The complete guide can be found at `https://docs.rke2.io/security/hardening_guide/`.

The hardening process for k3s clusters is similar to RKE2 but still requires a few extra steps:

1. Setting the same Linux kernel parameters as RKE2

2. Skipping the etcd steps, as k3s doesn't use etcd by default

3. Turning on `PodSecurityPolicy` to limit pod security settings, such as blocking pods from running as root

It is important to note that k3s doesn't have the CIS profiles like RKE2 and is not secure by default as it's designed to be lightweight and fast.

The complete guide can be found at `https://rancher.com/docs/k3s/latest/en/security/hardening_guide/`.

At this point, assuming you have followed the guides listed previously, you should be able to move to install the Rancher CIS scan and be able to pass it.

Deploying Rancher CIS scan

The only recommended way of installing Rancher CIS scan is via **Apps & Marketplace** inside Rancher. But first, let's cover some of the basic requirements:

*   Rancher v2.4 or greater.

*   Cluster owner permissions to the downstream cluster(s) or global role Administrator permissions.

*   The downstream cluster must be an RKE, RKE2, EKS, or GKE cluster for full support.

> **Note**
> A generic profile can be used for other clusters, but there might be false positives or other permissions issues.

Here is how to install `rancher-cis-benchmark` with Rancher v2.4.x and v2.5.x via the Cluster Explorer:

1. In the Rancher UI, go to **Cluster Explorer**.
2. Click **Apps**.
3. Click **rancher-cis-benchmark**.
4. Click **Install**.

To install the CIS Benchmark with Rancher v2.6.x via the **Cluster Management** pane, do the following:

1. In the Rancher UI, go to **Cluster Management**.
2. Navigate to the cluster where you will install the CIS Benchmark.
3. In the left navigation bar, click **Apps & Marketplace | Charts**.
4. Click **CIS Benchmark**.
5. Click **Install**.

> **Note**
> For Rancher-created clusters, you should use the *default* settings. For generic clusters, please review the example settings at `https://github.com/rancher/cis-operator/tree/master/examples`.

At this point, you should have your cluster locked down, and Rancher's CIS scan running in your cluster to confirm that the cluster stays locked over time. In the next section, we're going to dive into some additional tools for protecting your cluster, including some paid solutions.

Additional security tools for protecting a cluster

We have mostly been talking about OPA Gatekeeper in this chapter, as it is one of the most popular open source solutions. But, of course, there are other paid solutions, such as NeuVector, which provides image and cluster scanning.

> **Note**
>
> With **SUSE** (German: **Software- und System-Entwicklung**) buying NeuVector,
> it has been announced that NeuVector's container runtime security platform
> will be released to the public under the Apache 2.0 license on GitHub at
> `https://github.com/neuvector/neuvector`.

In addition, the Aqua Platform is ubiquitous for paying customers, as it is a closed source product that requires licensing.

For NeuVector, I recommend watching the master class *PCI Compliance and Vulnerability Management for Kubernetes* on YouTube (`https://www.youtube.com/watch?v=kSkX5MRmEkE`) to learn more about NeuVector and how to integrate it into Rancher.

I also recommend watching the master class *Kubernetes Master Class Preventive Security for Kubernetes Enterprise Deployments* for Aqua, found here: `https://www.youtube.com/watch?v=2Phk7yyWezU`.

> **Note**
>
> Both the YouTube videos are hosted on Rancher's YouTube channel and
> include links to their slides and scripts.

Summary

This chapter taught us about some of the security and compliance issues that containers and Kubernetes have addressed. We went over what OPA Gatekeeper is and how it works. We then dove into some of the best practices and standard templates. We learned how OPA Gatekeeper enforces different rules for your cluster by deploying these templates. This is important because this skill is necessary to create your own rules that suit your environment and its requirements. We then covered how to lock down your cluster and ensure it stays locked down using Rancher CIS scans.

The next chapter will cover how to bring scaling to your clusters for both pods and nodes, including all the limitations and concerns with scaling your clusters.

13
Scaling in Kubernetes

In this chapter, we'll be covering scaling your Kubernetes cluster. We'll go over the three main ways of doing so: with the **Horizontal Pod Autoscaler (HPA)**, **Vertical Pod Autoscaler (VPA)**, and Cluster Autoscaler. We will cover the pros and cons and some examples of each of these ways, as well as diving into the best practices for each method.

In this chapter, we're going to cover the following main topics:

- What is an HPA?
- What is a VPA?
- What is Kubernetes Cluster Autoscaler?

What is an HPA?

An HPA is a controller within a controller manager. An HPA automatically scales pods in replication controllers, deployments, replica sets, or stateful sets based on CPU usage (or custom metrics). Objects that cannot be scaled, such as DaemonSets, are not affected by horizontal pod autoscaling. With a default value of 15 seconds, the `horizontal-pod-autoscaler-sync-period` flag in the controller manager determines how often the HPA runs. Every cycle, the controller manager checks resource utilization on the workload in question. The controller uses a custom metrics endpoint along with the metrics server to gather its statistics.

In essence, the HPA monitors current and desired metric values, and if they do not match the specification, it takes action. The HPA follows the following algorithm:

```
desiredReplicas = ceil[currentReplicas * ( currentMetricValue /
desiredMetricValue )]
```

For example, let's say you have an application to keep the CPU usage at 50%. Currently, this deployment has a CPU request of 1000 m (millicores), which equals one core on the node. It is important to note that the HPA uses the CPU and memory request metrics and not the limits. The HPA computes the `currentMetricValue` object type by dividing the request value by the current usage, which outputs a percentage. HPA does this calculation for every pod in the deployment, then averages them to create a `currentMetricValue` object type for the deployment. The HPA then compares the `currentMetricValue` object type to the `desiredMetricValue` object type, which is 50% for both, so that the HPA won't make a change. But if the ratio is too high (1.0 is the target), it will trigger a scale-up event, which will add more pods. It is important to note that *not ready* or *terminating* pods are not counted. By default, the metrics for the first 30 seconds of a pod's life are ignored as defined by the `horizontal-pod-autoscaler-initial-readiness-delay` flag. Also, the HPA can scale by more than one pod at a time, but usually, this requires a significant ratio difference, so most of the time, the workload is only scaled by one.

At this point, we know how HPAs work, including how the HPA makes its decisions to scale up and down workloads. Of course, the next question we need to ask is when you should and shouldn't use HPAs for your workload, and in the next section, we will dive into that topic.

When should you use an HPA?

Now that we know how an HPA works, let's dive into when you should use one. An example application of an HPA is a web server. The question is, why is it a great example? The answer is that, traditionally, even before Kubernetes, web servers were designed in a way that you could remove or add them at any time without impacting your application.

The following is a list of characteristics of an application that it would make sense to use with an HPA:

- **Stateless** – The application must be able to be added and removed at any time.
- **Quick startup** – Generally, your pods should start up and be ready for requests within 30 seconds.
- **HTTP-based** – Most applications that will use HPAs are HTTP-based because we want to leverage the built-in load balancing capabilities that come with an ingress controller.
- **Batch jobs** – If you have batch jobs that can be run in parallel, you can use an HPA to scale up and down the number of worker pods based on the load, for example, having a pod that grabs an item out of a queue, processes the data, then publishes the output. Assuming multiple jobs can be run at once, you should set up an HPA based on the length of the queue to scale up and down the number of workers, that is, deployment.

Next, let's learn about when to not use an HPA.

When should you not use an HPA?

Of course, it doesn't make sense to have an HPA on all applications, and having an HPA can break them, for example, a database cluster, where you do not want pods being added and removed all the time because it could cause application errors. It is important to note that HPAs support scaling StatefulSets, but you should be careful as most applications that require StatefulSets do not like being scaled up and down a lot. There, of course, are other reasons why you might not want to use an HPA with your applications and the following are a few of the most common reasons:

- **StatefulSets** – Applications such as databases that require storage and orderly scaling tend to not be compatible with an HPA adding and removing pods as it sees fit.

- **Pods that require storage** – Applications that require a **PersistentVolumeClaim** (**PVC**) are generally not recommended for the fact that provisioning and attaching storage can require a reasonable amount of time to complete and can break over time.

- **Applications that require reconfiguration when scale changes** – A great example of this kind of workload is a Java app that uses database connection pooling with an external database. This is because any time a pod is created, Java will need to develop several new connections, which can be a heavy load on the database server and cause connection exhaustion as the database runs out of connections, which will cause the pod to fail. This, in turn, will generate a new pod to be created and at the same time, the load on the pods can go up due to the database running slowly, causing more scaling. The problem just runs away, creating more and more pods, which eventually causes a cluster outage.

- **Workloads that burst** – If you have an application that sits at very low utilization most of the time and then jumps to high utilization for a short time, it doesn't make sense to use an HPA because the HPA will scale down the deployment until it needs the resources. The issue happens during short-lived bursts as by the time the HPA reacts and spins up new pods, the event has already passed, making the HPA worthless.

> **Note**
> You can set a crazily high minimum scale but at that point, the question needs to be asked, why do you need an HPA if it's never going to scale up or down?

We have covered the pros and cons of an HPA in this section. It is important to note that every application is different, and you should work with the application developer to decide whether adding an HPA could help. Let's look at an example.

Example – simple web server with CPU utilization

To deploy this example, please run the following command:

```
kubectl apply -f https://raw.githubusercontent.com/
PacktPublishing/Rancher-Deep-Dive/main/ch13/examples/simple/
deploy.yaml
```

This command will deploy a namespace called `hpa-example-simple` with a test app called `hello-world` and an HPA that will trigger a CPU utilization of 50%. We can test the HPA using the `load-generator` deployment, which is set to a scale of 0 by default.

To create a load on the `hello-world` app, simply run the following command to turn on the load:

```
kubectl -n hpa-example-simple scale deployment load-generator
--replicas=1
```

Run the following command to turn it back off:

```
kubectl -n hpa-example-simple scale deployment load-generator
--replicas=0
```

If you run the `kubectl -n hpa-example-simple describe hpa hello-world` command, you can see the following events and actions taken by the HPA:

```
Reason                          Age                        From                        Message
------                          ---                        ----                        -------
SuccessfulRescale               11m                        horizontal-pod-autoscaler   New size: 8; reas
SuccessfulRescale               11m                        horizontal-pod-autoscaler   New size: 10; rea
SuccessfulRescale               10m (x2 over 11m)          horizontal-pod-autoscaler   New size: 4; reas
SuccessfulRescale               9m53s                      horizontal-pod-autoscaler   New size: 8; reas
SuccessfulRescale               9m37s                      horizontal-pod-autoscaler   New size: 10; rea
FailedGetResourceMetric         4m19s                      horizontal-pod-autoscaler   failed to get cpu
FailedComputeMetricsReplicas    4m18s                      horizontal-pod-autoscaler   invalid metrics (
ics returned from resource metrics API
FailedGetResourceMetric         3m18s (x6 over 10m)        horizontal-pod-autoscaler   failed to get cpu
FailedComputeMetricsReplicas    3m18s (x6 over 10m)        horizontal-pod-autoscaler   invalid metrics (

SuccessfulRescale               3m3s                       horizontal-pod-autoscaler   New size: 1; reas
```

Figure 13.1 – HPA events

In this section, we covered scaling our workload in the horizontal direction, that is, adding and removing pods. In the next section, we will go in the other direction, vertically.

What is a VPA?

If there is an HPA, is there a VPA? Yes, there is. A VPA is similar to an HPA, but instead of scaling the pod count up and down, the VPA automatically sets the resource request and limit values based on the actual CPU usage. The main goal of a VPA is to reduce the maintenance overhead associated with managing resource requests and limits for containers and to improve cluster utilization.

Even though a VPA is similar to an HPA, it's important to know that VPAs have a different way of working, which we'll be covering in the next section.

How does a VPA work?

There are three different components that make up a VPA:

- **VPA admission hook** – Each pod submitted to the cluster is examined with this webhook to see whether its parent object references the pod (a replication set, a deployment, and so on).

- **VPA recommender** – Connections to the metrics-server application give recommendations for scaling up or down the requests and limits of the pods based on historical and current usage data (CPU and memory) for each pod with VPA enabled.

- **VPA updater** – Each minute the VPA updater runs, it will evict the running version of a pod that is not in the recommended range, so the pod can restart and go through the VPA admission webhook to adjust the CPU and memory settings before starting.

  This means that if you are running something such as Argo CD, the VPA updater will not detect any changes in the deployment, and the two won't be fighting to adjust the specifications.

Next, let's learn why we need a VPA.

Why do you need a VPA?

We need to cover the resource request and limit before diving deeper into VPAs. When kube-scheduler assigns a pod to a node, it does not know how much memory and CPU it will need. There is only 16 GB of free RAM on the node, but the pod needs 64 GB. As soon as the pod starts, it runs out of memory, evicting pods. A cluster node with the correct amount of memory might support that pod. Here is where resource requests are put in play, where we specify that kube-scheduler should give this pod X amount of CPU and memory on a specific node. By adding this intelligence into the scheduling process, kube-scheduler can make a more informed decision about where to schedule pods. We also have resource limits, which act as hard limits for throttling or killing pods if they exceed their limits.

Of course, setting the resource request and limits can require a lot of work because you need to load test your application and review the performance data, and set your requests and limits. Then you have to keep monitoring this over time to tune these settings. This is why we see many environments where everything is set to unlimited, and the cluster administrator will just throw hardware at the problem. This is where a VPA comes into the picture by setting our requests for us and fine-tuning them over time.

For example, we can build a pod with the following settings:

```
requests:
  cpu: 50m
  memory: 100Mi
limits:
  cpu: 200m
  memory: 250Mi
```

The VPA recommender determines that you will need 120 MB of CPU power and 300 MB of memory to make your pod function properly. The recommended settings are as follows:

```
requests:
  cpu: 120m
  memory: 300Mi
limits:
  cpu: 480m
  memory: 750Mi
```

There will also be an increase in the limits because the VPA will scale them proportionally. Therefore, it is imperative to set your limits to something realistic rather than something crazy such as 1 TB of memory if your nodes are only equipped with 128 GB each. As a starting point, set your limits by doubling your request size, for example, if your request is 100 MB, your limit should be 200 MB. But don't forget that your limits are meaningless because the scheduling decision (and therefore, resource contention) will always be based on the requests. Limits are helpful only when there is resource contention or to avoid uncontrollable memory leaks.

How to write VPA manifests

You should never define more than one VPA for the same Pod/ReplicaSet/Deployment/ StatefulSet – the behavior becomes unpredictable in such cases. A VPA should not be used on the same pod as an HPA.

You first need to create a VPA object with `updateMode: off` for the target application, which puts the VPA in a dry run mode (which is the recommendation mode).

The following is an example VPA with the minimum required settings:

```
apiVersion: autoscaling.k8s.io/v1beta2
kind: VerticalPodAutoscaler
```

```
metadata:
  name: hello-world
spec:
  targetRef:
    apiVersion: "apps/v1"
    kind: Deployment
    name: hello-world
  updatePolicy:
    updateMode: "Off"
```

After about 5 minutes, you will be able to query the data and start to see some of the recommendations:

```
kubectl describe vpa hello-world
```

As you can see in the following screenshot, the `status` section gives us some recommendations for our targets, and following the screenshot is a complete breakdown of what each of these sections means:

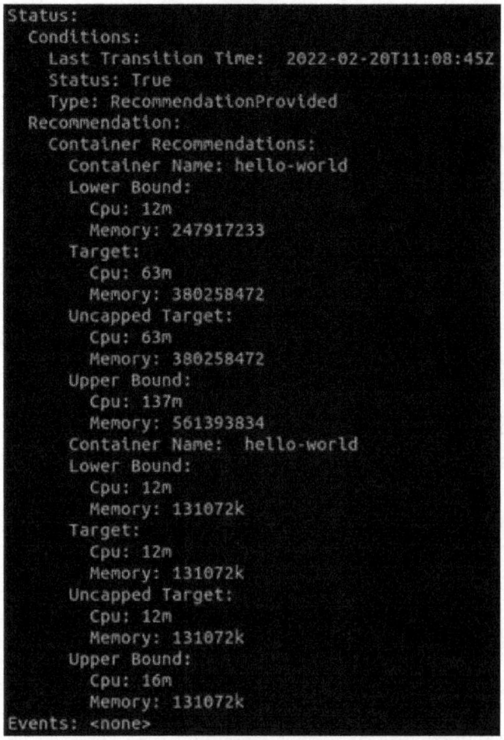

Figure 13.2 – Example VPA description

You can find the complete output at `https://raw.githubusercontent.com/ PacktPublishing/Rancher-Deep-Dive/main/ch13/vpa/describe-vpa. yaml`. To break down this output, you'll see the following sections:

- `Uncapped Target`: When upper limits are not configured in the VPA definition, the resource request on your pod will be uncapped.

- `Target`: This is the amount that will be configured on the subsequent execution of the admission webhook. If it already has this configuration, no changes will happen (your pod won't be in a restart/evict loop). Otherwise, the pod will be evicted and restarted using this target setting.

- `Lower Bound`: When your pod goes below this usage, it will be evicted and downscaled.

- `Upper Bound`: When your pod goes above this usage, it will be evicted and upscaled.

At this point, you can just use this information to create and set the request limits of your deployments. But if you want to use automatic predictions, you need to change the `updateMode` value to `Auto`.

Now, if you want to set minimum and maximum limits for the VPA, you can add the following section to your VPA config:

```
minAllowed:
  cpu: "300m"
  memory: "512Mi"
maxAllowed:
  cpu: "1800m"
  memory: "3600Mi"
```

So far, we have focused on scaling pods, but the other half of the picture is scaling the nodes. In the next section, we are going to dive into node autoscaling.

What is Kubernetes Node Autoscaler?

As new workloads and pods are deployed, all the cluster worker nodes' resources can be exhausted. This will result in pods not being scheduled on existing workers. In some cases, pods can sit in a pending state, awaiting resource allocation and possibly causing an outage. Manually adding or removing worker nodes can, of course, solve this problem, as Cluster Autoscaler increases or decreases the size of a Kubernetes cluster based on pending pods and node utilization metrics.

Now that we know what a Node Autoscaler is, it's essential to know when it should or shouldn't be used, which we'll cover in the next section.

When should you use a Kubernetes Node Autoscaler?

There are two main reasons to set up a Node Autoscaler in Rancher/Kubernetes environments:

- **Cost controls/efficiency** – When moving workloads into the cloud, a big mistake many people make is to treat cloud VMs just like they treated on-prem VMs. What I mean by this is on-prem, if you provision an eight-core VM but are only really using four cores of resources, the cost in physical hardware is only the four cores that are actually in use. But in the cloud, for example, if you provision an eight-core VM in AWS, your bill will be the same if you use 100% of the CPU or zero. Because of this, we want to keep our nodes as close to 100% utilization as possible without impacting applications. The general rule of thumb is 80% CPU and 90% memory. This is because these are the default node pressure limits. Node autoscaling can allow you to add just enough nodes to your cluster to meet your needs when you need them. This is very helpful for workloads that vary throughout the day. For example, your application might just be very busy between 8 A.M. and 5 P.M. from Monday to Friday but have a very low utilization after hours. So autoscaling and spinning up your nodes early in the morning and spinning them down at night will help to cut costs.

- **Node patching/upgrading** – Node rehydration is one of the side effects of autoscaling your nodes. You have to create a process to easily add and remove nodes from your cluster, instead of patching/upgrading your nodes in place, which means you need to drain and cordon your nodes one at a time, then apply any OS patches and upgrades, then finally reboot the node. You need to wait for the node to come back online and uncordon the node. Then repeat this process for each node in the cluster. This, of course, requires scripting and automation along with checks and tests. With autoscaling, you just need to update the base VM image and verify its health. Then, just trigger a rolling update on the node pool. At this point, the autoscaling takes over.

Next, let's learn about when to not use a Kubernetes Node Autoscaler.

When should you not use a Kubernetes Node Autoscaler?

Node Autoscaler has some practical limitations and best practices that can cause instability in your cluster if not followed:

- **Kubernetes and OS matching** – Kubernetes is an ever-evolving platform, with new features and releases being released regularly. To ensure the best performance, ensure that you deploy the Kubernetes Cluster Autoscaler with the recommended version. To keep Kubernetes in lockstep with your OSs, you have to upgrade them regularly. For a list of recommended versions, visit Rancher's support matrix at `https://www.suse.com/suse-rancher/support-matrix/all-supported-versions/`.

- **Your nodes must be the right size** – The Cluster Autoscaler will only function properly if your node pools have nodes of the same capacity. Among the reasons is the underlying assumption of the Cluster Autoscaler that each node in the node group has the same CPU and memory capacity. Autoscaling decisions are made based on the template nodes for each node group. Therefore, the best practice is to ensure that all nodes and instances in the instance group being autoscaled are the same type. This might not be the best approach for public cloud providers such as AWS, as diversification and availability factors dictate having multiple instance types.

- **A pod disruption budget can be specified** – By default, the Cluster Autoscaler will scale down nodes without disrupting an application. For instance, an Autoscaler might remove three nodes from a cluster, and your application might be unlucky and run all its pods on those three nodes. If nodes violate the policy, for example, having a `PodDisruptionBudget` flag prevents them from being drained. You can specify the disruption budgets by setting the `.spec.minAvailable` and `.spec.maxUnavailable` fields. As an absolute or a percentage value, `.spec.minAvailable` specifies the minimum number of pods available after the eviction. In the same way, `.spec.maxUnavailable` specifies the number of pods that will be unavailable after eviction, either as an absolute number or as a percentage.

At this point, we have covered what node autoscaling is and why you would want to use it. In the next section, we will cover how to set up node autoscaling in Rancher.

How to set up autoscaling with Rancher-managed clusters

At present, Rancher supports only AWS Auto Scaling groups. The details can be found in Rancher's official documentation located at `https://rancher.com/docs/rancher/v2.5/en/cluster-admin/cluster-autoscaler/amazon/`. It is crucial to note that autoscaling etcd and control plane nodes can be risky as removing and adding multiple management nodes simultaneously can cause cluster outages. Also, you must configure etcd S3 backups because the etcd backups are stored locally on the etcd nodes by default. This can cause you to lose your backups if you recycle your etcd nodes. Details on configuring S3 backups can be found at `https://rancher.com/docs/rancher/v2.5/en/cluster-admin/backing-up-etcd/`.

How to set up autoscaling with hosted clusters

Rancher does not focus on autoscaling clusters for hosted clusters, but all Kubernetes providers support Cluster Autoscaler. Visit `https://github.com/kubernetes/autoscaler/tree/master/cluster-autoscaler#deployment` for the list of supported providers.

At this point, you should be able to autoscale your Rancher-managed and hosted clusters, allowing you to add and remove nodes from your cluster with ease.

Summary

This chapter went over the three main ways of scaling your Kubernetes cluster: with HPA, VPA, and Cluster Autoscaler. For the HPA, we dove into how it works and when it should be used to scale your workloads by adding and removing pods. We then covered how VPAs are like HPAs but are used to add and remove resources from pods, closing out the chapter by covering Cluster Autoscalers for adding and removing nodes from the cluster, including the different autoscalers and when it makes sense to use them.

In the next chapter, we'll cover the topics of load balancers and SSL certificates, which are very important for publishing our applications to the outside world. And in that chapter, we'll be covering the different technicalities for accomplishing this task.

14
Load Balancer Configuration and SSL Certificates

In this chapter, we'll be covering the very important task of how to publish our applications that are being hosted inside Kubernetes to the outside world using load balancers and ingress rules. We'll be going over the four main techniques: round-robin DNS, passive external load balancer, active external load balancer, and an integrated load balancer. We'll look at the pros and cons along with an example of each technique, and we'll dive into the best practices for each method. Finally, we will cover how to bring SSL certificates to your cluster.

In this chapter, we're going to cover the following main topics:

- Why do we need an external load balancer to support a Kubernetes cluster?
- Rules for architecting a solution
- Configuring F5 in TCP and HTTP mode
- Configuring HAProxy in TCP and HTTP mode

- Installing and configuring MetalLB

- What is ingress in Kubernetes?

- How to add an SSL certificate to an ingress

Why do we need an external load balancer to support a Kubernetes cluster?

After building a Kubernetes cluster and deploying your first application, the next question that comes up is how do my users access my application? In a traditional enterprise environment, we would deploy our application on a server and then create a DNS record and firewall rules to expose our application to the outside world. Of course, we want our applications to be **high availability (HA)**, so we would usually deploy our application on multiple servers and then create a load balancer that would sit in front of our application's servers. We use a load balancer to distribute traffic across multiple servers and increase the availability of our application by allowing us to add and remove servers from the load balancer as needed.

For Kubernetes clusters, we still have this same problem. We need to deploy our applications across multiple nodes and provide a single point of contact, that is, a **virtual IP (VIP)** address for our application. Our end users will use it to connect to our application. There are, of course, a few different ways to solve this problem, and in the next section, we will dive into these solutions.

Rules for architecting a solution

This section will cover the four main ways of exposing the applications hosted inside our Kubernetes cluster to the outside world.

Round-robin DNS

The most straightforward load balancing technique is **round-robin DNS**, which creates a DNS record containing a list of IP addresses instead of just one. For example, let's say you had a three-node cluster with the nodes having IP addresses of 1.1.1.1, 2.2.2.2, and 3.3.3.3, and you want to publish your application, hello-world.example.com. You would create three A records with the name hello-world.example.com with the IP address of each node. By doing this, when a client initially attempts to connect to your application, the client will make a DNS query to their DNS server, which will respond with a list of IP addresses. Most clients will simply attempt to connect to the first IP address in the list, and if that server fails to respond, it will try the following IP address until it runs out of IP addresses. It's essential to note that most DNS servers/providers only allow up to six IP addresses in response.

The following is an example of how requests from different end users follow into the cluster when using round-robin DNS:

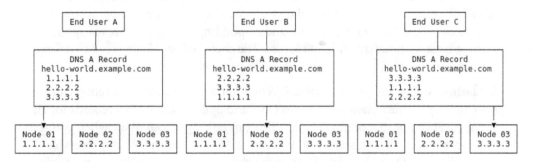

Figure 14.1 – Round-robin DNS with a three-node example

Next, let's have a look at the list of pros and cons that this design offers.

The **pros** are as follows:

- **Simplicity** – Round-robin DNS is by far the easiest way to load balance an application in your cluster because you already need to create a DNS record for your application, so it's not much work to add multiple IP addresses to that record.

- **No additional servers/hardware needed** – Because we are just using our DNS infrastructure to be our load balancer, you don't need additional servers/hardware in front of the cluster to balance the load for your cluster.

- **Cost** – Load balancers are not free; for example, a simple **Elastic Load Balancing (ELB)** service in AWS can cost around $16/month. Most DNS solutions (such as AWS Route53) are almost free ($0.04/month for 100k requests), and even providers such as CloudFlare are free; you just pay if you want more features.

The **cons** are as follows:

- **Caching** – DNS is designed to have multiple caching layers, including all the DNS servers between you and your client, and even your end users' machines have caching built-in. You only have control of the **time-to-live** (**TTL**), which tells the DNS server how long to cache a query before requesting a new one. This can help by setting it to as low as 1 second, but now you will put a considerable load on your DNS servers as you effectively turn off caching for that record.

- **No actual load balancing** – Round-robin DNS is merely just rotating the IP list each time the DNS server is queried. Because of this, factors such as server load, response times, or server uptime are not accounted for when routing traffic to different nodes. This means that if a server crashes or is overloaded, traffic will still be routed to that server until the clients stop trying to use that server and failover to another server. And for some clients, this can take up to 5 minutes to happen.

- **Only hard failures count** – DNS has no idea about the health of a server if a server has a failure, such as running out of disk space or having a connection problem to a database where the server is still up and responding to requests. So, the request is coming back to the client with 500 errors. The client will still keep using that server even though the next server in the list might be totally fine.

- **Updating DNS when nodes change** – Whenever a node is added or removed from the cluster, you must manually go into DNS and update all the DNS records for all the applications hosted on that cluster. This can be a significant issue when you start looking at autoscaling clusters. But, you can address this issue by using a service such as ExternalDNS to update DNS as the cluster changes over time dynamically. You can find out more about ExternalDNS by visiting the official documentation at `https://github.com/kubernetes-sigs/external-dns`.

- **No security outside the cluster** – Because we are just using DNS to route our traffic, we can't do more advanced features, such as forcing HTTPS, blocking SQL injection attacks, and blocking insecure cryptography.

> **Note**
>
> Most large-scale applications use a type of round-robin DNS called **global server load balancing** (**GSLB**), which does bring intelligence into the DNS by doing health checks and responding to requests based on server load, response times, and location. But, this is typically done on top of a load balancing service to provide server-level redundancy, with GSLB providing data center-level redundancy.

It is important to note that round-robin DNS is not recommended due to all the listed cons vastly outweighing the pros.

Passive external load balancer

Sometimes called a **dumb load balancer**, in this setup, you create a **Transmission Control Protocol** (**TCP**) load balancer in front of the cluster. Now, this load balancer doesn't handle any high-level functions of your traffic, that is, routing based on hostname, SSL offloading, caching, and **web application firewall** (**WAF**). This is because anything higher than layer 4 in the OSI model is not handled by the load balancer and is provided by the Kubernetes cluster/application. Generally, you would create a node pool with all the worker nodes in this design. Then, you would make a VIP on the load balancer and map it to the node pool.

> **Note**
> We'll be covering an HAProxy example in the next section.

The following is an example of how end user traffic is routed through the load balancer and onto the nodes in the cluster:

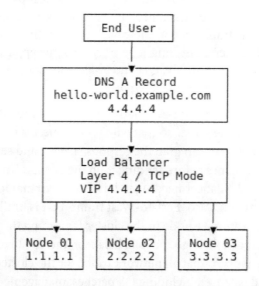

Figure 14.2 – Example of a load balancer in TCP mode with three nodes

Next, let's have a look at the list of pros and cons that this design offers.

The **pros** are as follows:

- **Low barrier of entry** – Most on-premises and cloud environments already have load balancers in place to support other non-Kubernetes applications. So, requesting an additional VIP address and node pool to the existing load balancer can be very easy and add little to no cost to the project.

- **Single point of contact of the cluster** – Most enterprise load balancers support what's called `port 0` mode, which binds all the TCP/UDP ports on the load balancer to the nodes. This can be helpful when exposing non-HTTP applications using the node port. For example, you might publish a MySQL server on port `31001` on all nodes, which becomes available on the VIP using the same port.

- **Simple ongoing maintenance** – Once the VIP address and node pool have been created, there is no need to update certificates or site names on the load balancer as new applications are added and removed.

The **cons** are as follows:

- **Source IP transparency** – With the load balancer in TCP mode, it has two options when the load balancer forwards a request to the server. The first is to leave the source IP address (the end user's IP address) alone and just pass it along the server. The server will process the request and response because the source IP address is the client's IP address. The traffic will not flow back through the load balancer but will be sent directly to the client. This might be okay for some applications, but other applications, such as HTTP(S), MySQL, and SMTP, can have problems with the server's IP address changing during a request.

  The other option is what's called NAT mode, which turns the load balancer into the default gateway for the server so that when the request is being sent back to the client, the load balancer can grab the response packet and set the IP addresses back to their original values before sending it on the clients. This, of course, has the downside of your load balancer needing to be in every **virtual local area network (VLAN)** in your network. Also, East-to-West traffic, that is, traffic going from one node in the cluster to another node in the cluster (assuming they are on the same subnet), will not go back through the load balancer, thereby breaking the source IP address. This also means that all network traffic for the cluster will need to go through the load balancer, including OS patches, management software, and monitoring tools.

- **Each cluster needs its load balancer/VIP address** – With the load balancer in TCP mode, we can't do any host-based routing; each cluster will need its node pool and VIP address. This, of course, costs you additional IP addresses, and most cloud-based load balancers do not support the addition of IP addresses, so you'll need to create a load balancer for each cluster, which will increase your costs.

- **Limited security outside the cluster** – We are just passing traffic between the end users and the cluster. We can't do more advanced features such as forcing HTTPS, blocking SQL injection attacks, and blocking insecure cryptography.

- **Only basic health checks** – With this mode, the load balancer only checks whether the port is open and responding but doesn't check whether the server is healthy.

It is important to remember that there are a number of drawbacks to using a passive load balancer and it should really only be used if you can't use an active external load balancer, which we'll be covering in the next section.

Active external load balancer

In this design, we build a passive external load balancer on top but add intelligence to the chain by moving from layer 4 to 7 instead of blindly forwarding traffic between the clients and servers. The load balancer acts as a virtual server that accepts the request and decodes it, including decrypting the SSL encryption, which allows the load balancer to make decisions on the request, such as routing to different servers/clusters based on the hostname of the request. For example, `dev.example.com` and `staging.example.com` share the same public IP address but are routed to two clusters. Or, you can enforce additional security software such as ModSecurity, which can block a wide range of attacks. In the following figure, you can see an example setup with end users' traffic flowing to the DNS A record, to the load balancer, and then finally to the nodes:

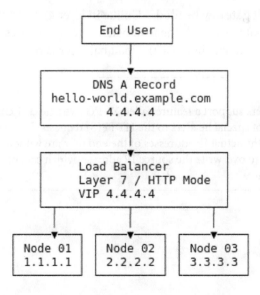

Figure 14.3 – Load balancer in HTTP mode with three nodes example

Next, let's have a look at the list of pros and cons that this design offers.

The **pros** are as follows:

- **Control** – With the load balancer in HTTP/layer 7 mode, you have more control over the traffic because the load balancer is making a *man-in-the-middle attack* between the clients. The server allows the load balancer to inspect and modify the request as it sees fit.

- **Wild card certificates** – In this mode, we can have a single IP address that can be shared across many different applications. For example, `www.example.com` and `api.example.com` might be two separate applications, but they can share the same IP address and wildcard certificate, that is, `*.example.com`. We can even expand it more by using a multi-domain wildcard SSL, which allows us to have a certificate for `*.example.com`, `*.example.net`, and so on. All of these can save money and simplify management, as now we have one certificate for all the applications in one spot.

- **Better health checks** – In layer 7 mode, the load balancer runs tests such as sending an HTTP request to a known good endpoint to test and verify the server's health. For example, with an ingress-nginx controller, the load balancer can send an HTTP request to port `80` with the `/healthz` path, which only responds with `200 OK` if the ingress is up and healthy. If a server is unhealthy, the chances of being gracefully removed from the load balancer are much better.

- **No NAT or default gateway needed** – Unlike in layer 4 mode, the traffic doesn't need to be force routed through the load balancer as the source IP address will always be the load balancer because the load balancer is repackaging the request.

> **Note**
>
> Most load balancers support a feature called `X-Forwarded-For` headers, which adds a set of special headers to the HTTP(S) requests that tell the application what the actual IP addresses of the end user are without needing the load balancer to overwrite the source IP address, which can, of course, cause routing issues.

The **cons** are as follows:

- **Additional configuration for new sites** – Because the load balancer is SSL offloading, host-based routing, and more, we need to tell the load balancer about sites/applications that we are adding. If we have a certificate covering `*.example.com`, we add a new application called `test.example.net`. We have to make sure that our current SSL certificate and rules cover this new domain; if not, we need to update them. This is not usually an issue if all of your applications can be covered under wildcard rules such as `*.example.com`. But, if you are doing nested domains such as `qa1.api.example.com` and `dev.docs.example.com`, these two nested domains will not be covered by the `*.example.com` wildcard and will require multiple certificates or a multi-domain wildcard SSL that includes `*.api.example.com` and `*.docs.example.com`.

- **End-to-end SSL requires more work** – In layer 4 mode, we are doing the SSL offloading at the ingress-nginx controller level, meaning we only need an SSL certificate in one spot. But, if we move that SSL offloading to the load balancer, we need to decide whether we are okay downgrading to having non-SSL traffic between the load balancer and our cluster, which is the most straightforward option because we just route the backend request to port `80` and call it done. However, if we need to keep the traffic encrypted using SSL, we need to configure an SSL certificate at the ingress-nginx controller and the load balancer. We can now make it easy by default by using the built-in fake certificate with an ingress-nginx controller and configuring the load balancer to ignore the invalid certificate. It's important to review this with your security team to confirm acceptance.

- **Speed** – DNS and layer 4 are fast because they are simple. Most enterprise load balancers can do layer 4 using specialized chips rather than software, meaning they can operate at very high speeds. For example, A10's 7655S ADC can do 370 Gbps in layer 4 mode but drops to 145 Gbps in layer 7 with SSL. It is important to note that this gap is closing over time because of faster CPUs and better hardware integration.

This approach should be used in environments where the process of updating and configuring the external load balancer is automated because the load balancer will need to be updated as applications are added to your clusters.

Integrated load balancer

The previous solution lacked integration with the Kubernetes clusters management plane, meaning that the management of the cluster and its application is not connected directly to the management of the load balancer and its configuration. This is, of course, addressed by using the load balancer that supports Kubernetes natively. For example, in Amazon's EKS, you can deploy the *AWS Load Balancer Controller,* which connects the EKS cluster directly to Amazon's load balancer with the controller handling management of the load balancers as cluster objects. For example, you can create an ingress in your cluster, and the controller will detect this change and take care of provisioning the load balancer for you. It's important to note that most hosted Kubernetes clusters provide these kinds of solutions to integrate with their own hosted load balancers. For the on-premises environments, load balancers such as F5 have started providing Kubernetes integration solutions that help bridge that gap, including replacing the ingress-nginx controller altogether and having the load balancer join the cluster directly, giving it direct access to pods inside the cluster. In the following figure, you'll see that traffic flows from the end user to the DNS A record, then to the load balancer, which handles the layer 7 session management, and finally forwards the traffic to the backend nodes. However, the essential item here is the controller pod that pushes changes back to the load balancer to keep the cluster and the load balancer in sync.

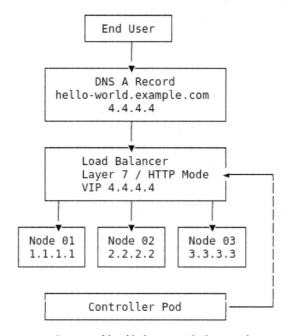

Figure 14.4 – Integrated load balancer with three nodes example

Next, let's have a look at the list of pros and cons that this design offers.

The **pros** are as follows:

- **Simple ongoing management** – We add a controller that sits between the cluster and the load balancer from a management layer. The two will now stay in lockstep with each other. There is no need for users to manually push out load balancers as application teams deploy and change their applications.

- **Speed** – Some load balancers replace the ingress-nginx controller with the load balancer, directly removing that additional overhead.

The **cons** are as follows:

- **Control** – Application teams can now push changes to a production load balancer, meaning they could push an unsafe change such as disabling SSL without the networking/load balancer team seeing that change and stopping it.

- **One app can break another** – Some of the controllers, such as AWS's controller, by default, allow a user to create two different ingress rules for the same hostname, which could allow a bad actor to hijack the traffic from another application by creating an ingress in their namespace, such as the same hostname as the actual application. This can, of course, happen by accident, too. For example, the application team forgets to change the hostname on ingress and accidentally starts routing production traffic to the application's dev or QA instance. It is important to note that newer controllers are adding safeguards to prevent duplicate ingress.

This is the preferred option if your environment supports it. It is important to note that in most cloud environments, this can increase your costs as they will create different load balancers for each application.

At this point, we should have a good idea of what kind of load balancer we want/need. In the next section, we'll be covering installing and configuring some of the most common load balancers.

Configuring F5 in TCP and HTTP mode

F5's BIG-IP (generally shortened to just **F5**) load balancer is popular for enterprise customers. Because of this, it is pretty common for Kubernetes clusters to use F5 as their external load balancer. This section will cover the two most common configurations, TCP and HTTP mode.

It is important to note that we will not be covering installing and configuring the F5 hardware/appliance for this section, as that would be out of scope for a Kubernetes/ Rancher administrator. If you would like to learn more, I recommend reading F5's official documentation at `https://www.f5.com/services/resources/deployment-guides`. I would also recommend working with your networking/load balancer teams to customize the following setups to best match your environment.

TCP mode

We will start by creating the server pool, which should contain your cluster's worker nodes:

1. From the F5 web interface, go to **Local Traffic | Pools | Pool List** and click **Create**.
2. Give the pool a name. I usually name the pool the cluster name, followed by the port.
3. For the **Health Monitors** option, select **http**.
4. Go to the **Resources** section and enter the details for each worker in the cluster:

   - **Node Name**: Hostname of the node (this is just a label)
   - **Address**: IP address of the node
   - **Service Port**: `80`
   - **Service**: HTTP

5. Click **Finish** when done.

6. You'll want to repeat this process for port 443.

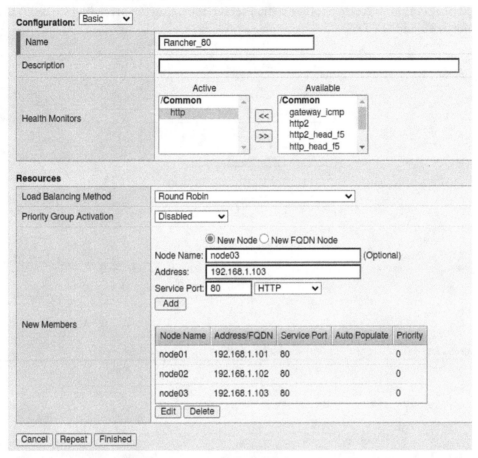

Figure 14.5 – F5 node pool configuration example

We also need to create the frontend, or what F5 calls the virtual server:

1. From the F5 web interface, go to the **Local Traffic | Virtual Servers | Virtual Server List** page and click **Create**.

2. Give the virtual server a name. I usually name it the same as the pool.

3. For the **Type** option, select **Performance (Layer 4)**.

4. You'll need to enter a VIP address assigned to the load balancer for the **Destination Address/Mask** field.

5. For the **Service Port** section, enter port 80 with a service type of **HTTP**.

6. The rest of the settings can be left to the default values, and you should click the **Repeat** button to create another virtual server, repeating the preceding steps but for port 443 and **HTTPS**.

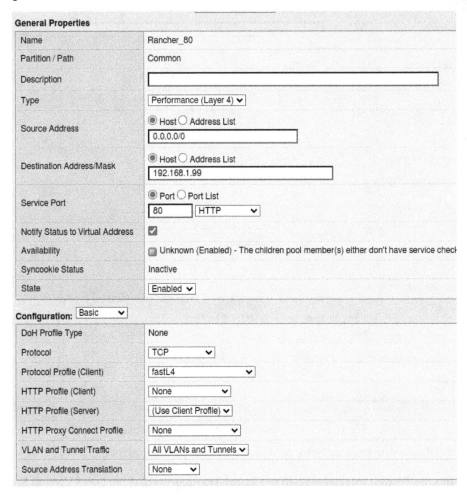

Figure 14.6 – F5 virtual server settings

At this point, we need to link the frontend (virtual server) to the backend (pool):

1. Go to the virtual server and click the **Resources** tab.

2. Set the **Default Pool** value to be the port 80 pool in the **Load Balancing** section, and click **Update** to apply the change.

3. Repeat this process for port 443.

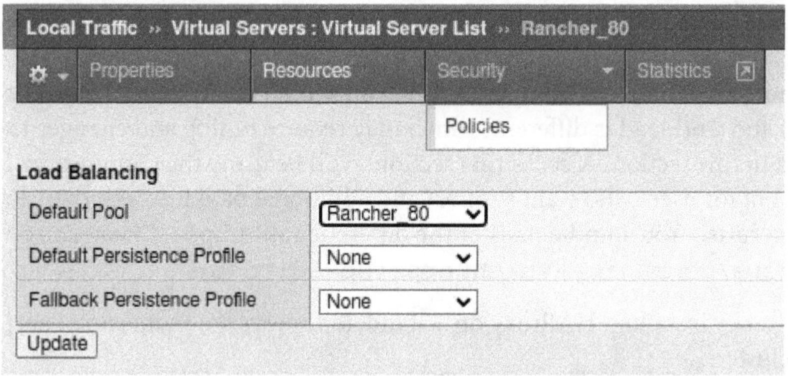

Figure 14.7 – F5 Binding pool and virtual server together

At this point, you should be able to access your Kubernetes/Rancher cluster via the VIP address. It is imperative to remember that this is TCP mode, so F5 is just passing traffic, meaning the ingress controller needs to handle items such as SSL.

HTTP mode

We'll follow the same steps for creating the pool as we covered in TCP mode for HTTP mode. The only changes that we need to make are in the virtual server:

- For the **Virtual Server** type, please select **Performance (HTTP)** instead of **Performance (Layer 4)** and click **Finish**.

- Repeat this process for port 443, but this time, select the server type as **Standard** and set **SSL Profile (Client)** to point to your SSL certificate.

At this point, you should be able to access your cluster just like in TCP mode, but with the difference being that the load balancer handles SSL for you, and you won't have the source IP address issues that we talked about in the previous section.

In the next section, we will cover another popular load balancer software called HAProxy.

Configuring HAProxy to work with Kubernetes

This section will cover installing and configuring HAProxy for internal and external deployments. It is essential to note the examples listed in this section are generalized to cover the most common environments. Still, you should understand that every environment and workload is different, which may require tuning and changes to the designs listed in this section. Also, in this section, we'll be using the Community Edition of HAProxy, but for users who want support and additional paid features, they do offer HAProxy Enterprise. You'll find details of the difference at `https://www.haproxy.com/products/community-vs-enterprise-edition/`.

First, we will cover installing HAProxy on a standalone server(s) that is not a part of the Kubernetes clusters.

> **Note**
>
> Before starting this process, we assume you already have the server(s) built, the latest patches applied, and your `root`/`sudo` access to the server(s). Also, as of writing, v2.5 is the current latest stable release. You should review release notes and version recommendations at the official HAProxy community site at `https://www.haproxy.org/`.

Installing HAProxy on Ubuntu/Debian systems

For Ubuntu and Debian-based systems, the HAProxy bundled in the default package repository lags behind the current release by a minor version or two, but more importantly, can be missing significant security until the next major release. Because we are dealing with a load balancer that might be publicly accessible and will be a valuable target for attackers, we'll want to make sure that we are running the latest versions with the most up-to-date security patches. So, we are going to use a **Personal Package Archive** (**PPA**) repository for this installation.

We need to generate our install steps by going to `https://haproxy.debian.net/` and filling out the form. This will create two sets of commands, with the first set being to add the PPA repository and the second command installing HAProxy.

Debian/Ubuntu HAProxy packages

The Debian HAProxy packaging team provides various versions of HAProxy packages for use on different Debian or Ubuntu systems. The following wizard helps you to find the package suitable for your system.

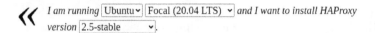 *I am running* Ubuntu ✓ Focal (20.04 LTS) ✓ *and I want to install HAProxy version* 2.5-stable ✓ .

Instructions for latest release

You need to enable a dedicated PPA with the following command:

```
# apt-get install --no-install-recommends software-properties-common
# add-apt-repository ppa:vbernat/haproxy-2.5
```

Then, use the following command:

```
# apt-get install haproxy=2.5.\*
```

You will get the *latest* release of HAProxy 2.5 (and stick to this branch).

Figure 14.8 – PPA and Install wizard

At this point, we should have HAProxy installed on our Ubuntu server. In the next section, we'll be covering the steps for Red Hat/CentOS servers.

Red Hat/CentOS

Just like Ubuntu and Debian based systems, the HAProxy bundled in the default package repository lags behind the current release by a minor version or two, but more importantly, can be missing significant security until the next major release. Because of this, it usually is recommended to build HAProxy from the source steps, which can be found here:

1. Install the prerequisites to compile the binaries by running the following command:

    ```
    yum install gcc pcre-static pcre-devel -y`
    ```

2. Download the source code using the following command:

    ```
    cd /opt; wget https://www.haproxy.org/download/2.5/src/
    haproxy-2.5.4.tar.gz"
    ```

    > **NOTE**
    > You should review the recommended versions before choosing a version.

3. Run the following commands to build and install HAProxy:

    ```
    make clean
    make -j $(nproc) TARGET=linux-glibc USE_OPENSSL=1 USE_
    LUA=1 USE_PCRE=1 USE_SYSTEMD=1
    make install
    mkdir -p /etc/haproxy
    mkdir -p /var/lib/haproxy
    touch /var/lib/haproxy/stats
    ```

At this point, we should have HAProxy installed, and now we need to create a config file for which we'll use the example listed in the following sections as a starting point.

TCP mode

In this section, we'll be covering some example configuration files that can be used as a starting point for your environment for a TCP load balancer. It is important to note that this is the most basic configuration.

The full configuration can be found at `https://github.com/PacktPublishing/Rancher-Deep-Dive/main/ch14/example-configs/haproxy/tcp-mode.cfg`. But, the critical part is listed in the following example, which binds to the ports `80` and `443`, and just passes traffic to the backend server nodes 01/02/03:

```
frontend http_frontend
    mode tcp
    bind :80
    default_backend http_backend

backend http_backend
    mode tcp
    balance leastconn
    server node01 192.168.1.101:80 check
    server node02 192.168.1.102:80 check
    server node03 192.168.1.103:80 check

frontend https_frontend
    mode tcp
    bind :80
    default_backend https_backend

backend https_backend
    mode tcp
    balance leastconn
    server node01 192.168.1.101:443 check
    server node02 192.168.1.102:443 check
    server node03 192.168.1.103:443 check
```

Figure 14.9 – HAProxy TCP mode

As we can see in the config file, we are creating a frontend and backend for both ports `80` and `443` with both configs in TCP mode, as we want the load balancer to pass traffic directly from the frontend port to the backend ports.

HTTP mode

In this section, we'll be covering some example configuration files that can be used as a starting point for your environment for an HTTP load balancer.

The full configuration can be found at `https://github.com/PacktPublishing/` `Rancher-Deep-Dive/main/ch14/example-configs/haproxy/http-mode.` `cfg`. The critical part in this config file is the fact that there is a single frontend for both `80` and `443` ports. Then, in the frontend, we define the SSL certificate, which is stored in `/etc/haproxy/certs/star.example.com.pem`. Then, following that, we have a set of **access control lists** (**ACLs**) that allows us to route traffic to different clusters in this case. Non-production traffic goes to the `rke-cluster-npd` cluster, with the production traffic going to `rke-cluster-prd`. This configuration also includes an example backend configuration that is running SSL.

This is the frontend section of the configuration:

```
frontend frontend:
    bind *:80
    bind *:443 ssl crt /etc/haproxy/certs/star.example.com.pem
    http-request redirect scheme https unless { ssl_fc }
    mode http

    acl host_rke-cluster-npd hdr(host) -i dev.example.com
    acl host_rke-cluster-npd hdr(host) -i qas.example.com
    use_backend rke-cluster-npd-https if host_a1-rke-cluster-npd

    acl host_rke-cluster-prd hdr(host) -i example.com
    acl host_rke-cluster-prd hdr(host) -i www.example.com
    use_backend rke-cluster-prd-https if host_a1-rke-cluster-prd
```

Figure 14.10 – HAProxy HTTP mode frontend

It is important to note that because we are using HTTP mode, we can have multiple clusters and applications sharing a single load balancer. As we can see in the preceding example, we have both `dev.example.com` pointing to the non-production cluster and `example.com` pointing to the production cluster.

These are the backend settings:

```
backend rke-cluster-npd-https
    mode http
    option httpchk HEAD /healthz HTTP/1.0
    server node01 192.168.1.101:443 check weight 1 maxconn 1024 ssl verify none
    server node02 192.168.1.102:443 check weight 1 maxconn 1024 ssl verify none
    server node03 192.168.1.103:443 check weight 1 maxconn 1024 ssl verify none

backend rke-cluster-prd-https
    mode http
    option httpchk HEAD /healthz HTTP/1.0
    server node04 192.168.1.104:443 check weight 1 maxconn 1024 ssl verify none
    server node05 192.168.1.105:443 check weight 1 maxconn 1024 ssl verify none
    server node06 192.168.1.106:443 check weight 1 maxconn 1024 ssl verify none
```

Figure 14.11 – HAProxy HTTP mode backend

As you can see, we are creating two different backends with one for each cluster. We are also sending all backend traffic to port 443 (SSL) as the `http-request redirect scheme https unless { ssl_fc }` frontend rule handles redirecting all HTTP traffic to HTTPS.

At this point, we should have HAProxy up and running and be able to access applications that are hosted on our Kubernetes clusters. In the next section, we'll be covering MetalLB, which removes the need for a load balancer.

Installing and configuring MetalLB

Of course, the question always comes up – what if I don't want to deal with an external load balancer, but I still want my cluster to be highly available? This is where a tool called MetalLB comes into the picture. MetalLB is a load balancer for Kubernetes clusters running on bare metal using standard routing protocols. The project is still in its infancy. It should be treated as a beta version. That is explained on the *Project Maturity* page located at `https://metallb.universe.tf/concepts/maturity/`.

MetalLB can be configured in two modes. The first one we will cover is layer 2 mode, which is the most straightforward configuration, with **Border Gateway Protocol** (**BGP**) being the second mode, which is commonly being used by more advanced users/ environments; for both modes, the installation steps are the same.

Run the following two commands to create the namespace and install the MetalLB controller:

```
kubectl apply -f https://raw.githubusercontent.com/metallb/
metallb/v0.12.1/manifests/namespace.yaml
kubectl apply -f https://raw.githubusercontent.com/metallb/
metallb/v0.12.1/manifests/metallb.yaml
```

> **Note**
>
> You can find more details about customizing this installation for non-Rancher clusters located at `https://metallb.universe.tf/installation/`, including how to use the Helm chart.

For layer 2 mode, we need to configure a range of IP addresses for MetalLB to use. It is important that this range is in the same subnet as the rest of your nodes.

Simply create the following configmap:

```yaml
apiVersion: v1
kind: ConfigMap
metadata:
  namespace: metallb-system
  name: config
data:
  config: |
    address-pools:
    - name: default
      protocol: layer2
      addresses:
      - 192.168.2.2-192.168.2.125
```

Figure 14.12 – MetalLB layer 2 configmap

You can find the following details of this configuration in the official documentation located at `https://metallb.universe.tf/configuration/#layer-2-configuration`.

For BGP mode, we need a router that supports BGP that MetalLB can connect to, an **autonomous system (AS)** number for MetalLB to use, and a network CIDR prefix for the cluster. The BGP configuration is also configured with a configmap; an example can be found in the following figure:

```
apiVersion: v1
kind: ConfigMap
metadata:
  namespace: metallb-system
  name: config
data:
  config: |
    peers:
    - peer-address: 10.0.0.1
      peer-asn: 64501
      my-asn: 64500
    address-pools:
    - name: default
      protocol: bgp
      addresses:
      - 192.168.10.0/24
```

Figure 14.13 – MetalLB BGP configmap

You can find the full details for this configuration in the official documentation located at `https://metallb.universe.tf/configuration/#bgp-configuration`.

At this point, we should have MetalLB up and running. To use an IP address from MetalLB, we need to create a service record with the `LoadBalancer` type, at which point MetalLB takes care of the rest. You can find the full details at `https://metallb.universe.tf/usage/`.

What is ingress in Kubernetes?

A Kubernetes ingress is a standard object that defines a set of rules for routing external traffic into a Kubernetes cluster. This includes setting the SSL certificate, name, or path-based routing to different pods. The ingress rules were designed around HTTP and HTTPS traffic.

The following is an example config with the central area of the config being the `rules` section, which, in this example, is `foo.bar.com`. This rule directs the traffic to the `server1` service. It is important to note that the `rules` section is simple and very generic. This section must follow the Kubernetes standard. This allows you to swap out ingress controllers; for example, RKE1/2 comes with nginx by default, but you can choose to replace nginx with Traefik.

But, of course, if you need to customize the ingress more than the `rules` section allows, you can use annotations; for example, adding `nginx.ingress.kubernetes.io/ ssl-redirect=true` to an ingress nginx will direct all non-SSL traffic to the SSL port of that ingress. You can find all the annotations in the official documentation at `https://kubernetes.github.io/ingress-nginx/user-guide/nginx- configuration/annotations/`.

An example ingress config is as follows:

```yaml
apiVersion: networking.k8s.io/v1
kind: Ingress
metadata:
  name: ingress-wildcard-host
spec:
  rules:
  - host: "foo.bar.com"
    http:
      paths:
      - pathType: Prefix
        path: "/bar"
        backend:
          service:
            name: service1
            port:
              number: 80
  - host: "*.foo.com"
    http:
      paths:
      - pathType: Prefix
        path: "/foo"
        backend:
          service:
            name: service2
            port:
              number: 80
```

Figure 14.14 – Ingress example YAML

As you can see, we are defining an ingress for two hostnames, `foo.bar.com` and `*.bar.com`, with each hostname routing traffic to a different backend service, such as deployment. At this point, we should have an ingress set up and be able to access the test application over HTTP. But, as we know, companies and browsers require sites to support SSL as they'll throw warning messages about being insecure. So, in the next section, we'll be covering how to add an SSL certificate to this ingress.

How to add an SSL certificate to an ingress

To use an SSL certificate with your ingress, you must create a particular type of secret called `kubernetes.io/tls`, an example of which will be shown in a moment. It is important to note that values must encode in `base64` from the PEM format. You can let kubectl handle this for you by running the following command:

```
kubectl create secret tls test-tls --key="tls.key" --cert="tls.
crt"
```

It is recommended that you include the complete certificate chain in `tls.crt`. Also, this secret must be located in the same namespace as the ingress rule:

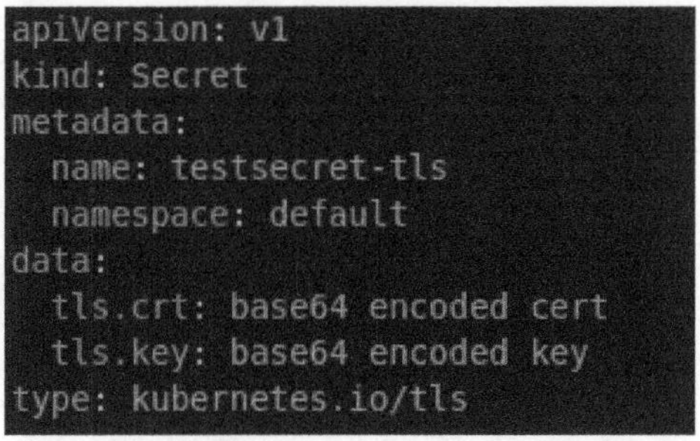

```yaml
apiVersion: v1
kind: Secret
metadata:
  name: testsecret-tls
  namespace: default
data:
  tls.crt: base64 encoded cert
  tls.key: base64 encoded key
type: kubernetes.io/tls
```

Figure 14.15 – TLS example YAML

Once the secret has been created, you only need to add the following section to your ingress config, which includes the secret name and the hostnames that this secret covers. You can define multiple certificates and hosts for a single ingress rule, but typically, it's recommended to keep ingresses limited to a single application:

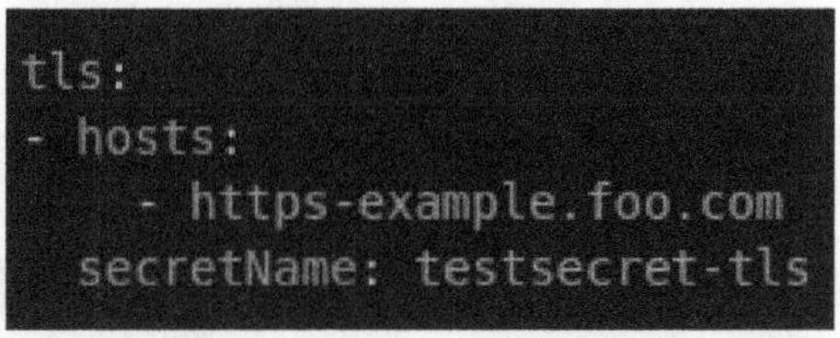

```yaml
tls:
- hosts:
    - https-example.foo.com
  secretName: testsecret-tls
```

Figure 14.16 – Adding TLS to ingress

At this point, we should be able to publish our applications that are hosted inside our cluster to the outside world using an ingress rule, while providing SSL support for our application.

Summary

This chapter went over the four main load balancer designs: round-robin DNS, passive external load balancer, active external load balancer, and an integrated load balancer. We then covered the pros and cons and some examples for each design, including making the most sense, at which point we dove into configuring a TCP and HTTP mode load balancer in an F5. We then went over the installation steps for creating an HAProxy server, including some example configs. We also covered some new software called MetalLB, which replaces a load balancer altogether. We then wrapped up the chapter by covering what an ingress is and how to make one. This is very important, as most applications that are hosted inside Kubernetes need to be published to the outside world and we need to do it in a highly available way.

In the next chapter, we'll be diving into troubleshooting Rancher and Kubernetes clusters, including how to fix some common issues and how to set up lab environments that you can use to practice recovering from these issues.

15
Rancher and Kubernetes Troubleshooting

In this chapter, we'll explore the master components of Kubernetes, their interactions, and how to troubleshoot the most common problems. Next, we'll explore some common failure scenarios, including identifying the failures and resolving them as quickly as possible, using the same troubleshooting steps and tools that Rancher's support team uses when supporting Enterprise customers. Then, we'll discuss recovery from some common cluster failures. This chapter includes scripts and documentation for reproducing all of these failures in a lab environment (based on actual events).

In this chapter, we're going to cover the following main topics:

- Recovering an RKE cluster from an etcd split-brain
- Rebuilding from etcd backup
- Pods not being scheduled with OPA Gatekeeper
- A runaway app stomping all over a cluster

- Can rotating kube-ca break my cluster?
- A namespace is stuck in terminating
- General troubleshooting for RKE clusters

Recovering an RKE cluster from an etcd split-brain

In this section, we are going to be covering what an etcd spilt-brain is, how to detect it, and finally, how to recover from it.

What is an etcd split-brain?

Etcd is a leader-based distributed system. Etcd ensures that the leader node periodically sends heartbeats to all followers in order to keep the leader lease. Etcd requires a majority of nodes to be up and healthy to accept writes using the model **(n+1)/2** members. When fewer than half of the etcd members fail, the etcd cluster can still accept read/write requests. For example, if you have a five-node etcd cluster and lose two nodes, the Kubernetes cluster will still be up and running. But if you lose an additional node, then the etcd cluster will lose quorum, and the remaining nodes will go into read-only mode until a quorum is restored.

After a failure, the etcd cluster will go through a recovery process. The first step is to elect a new leader that verifies that the cluster has a majority of members in a healthy state – that is, responding to health checks. The leader will then return the cluster to a healthy state and begin accepting `write` requests.

Now, another common failure scenario is what we call a **network partition**. This is when most or all nodes in the etcd cluster lose access to one another, which generally happens during an infrastructure outage such as a switch failure or a storage outage. But this can also occur if you have an even number of etcd nodes – for example, if you have three etcd nodes in data center *A* and three etcd nodes in data center *B*.

> **Important Note**
> Having etcd running across two data centers is not recommended.

Then, the network connection between the data center fails. In this case, this means that all etcd nodes will go into read-only mode because of quorum loss.

You should rarely run into a split-brain cluster if you have an odd number of nodes in the preceding scenario. But it still can happen. Of course, the question that comes up is, what is a **split-brain cluster**? The essential thing to understand is that etcd uses a cluster and member IDs to track the state of the cluster. The first node to come online creates the cluster ID, sometimes called `initial-cluster-token`. As nodes join that cluster, they will each be assigned a unique member ID and sent the cluster ID. At this point, the new node will be syncing data from other members in the cluster.

There are only three main reasons why the cluster ID would be changed:

- The first is data corruption; this is a rare occurrence (I have only seen it once before, during an intentional data corruption test), that is, using the `dd` command to write random data to the drive storing the etcd database filesystem. Most of the time, the safeguards and consistency checks built into etcd prevent this.

- A misconfiguration is the second reason, which is more common when someone is making a cluster change. For example, when an etcd node fails, some users will try to add a new etcd node without removing the broken node first, causing the new etcd node to fail to join correctly, putting the cluster into a weird broken state. The new node sometimes generates a new cluster ID instead of joining the existing nodes.

- The third reason is a failed etcd restore. During the etcd restore process, a new etcd cluster is created, with the first node being used as a bootstrap node to create a new etcd cluster, with the original data being injected into this new cluster. The rest of the etcd node should join the *new* etcd cluster, but this process can fail if the connection between Rancher and the cluster/nodes is unstable, or if there is a bug in `Rancher/RKE/RKE2`. The other reason is that the restore fails partway through, leaving some etcd nodes running on older data and some nodes running on *newer* data.

Now we know how etcd can get into a split-brain state. In the next section, we are going to cover how to identify this issue in the real world, including common error messages that you should find.

Identifying the common error messages

When etcd goes into a split-brain state, it is typically found when a cluster is found offline – that is, a request to the kube-apiserver(s) start failing, which generally shows itself as a cluster going offline in the Rancher UI.

You should run the following commands for RKE (1) clusters and review the output:

```
Error messages in etcd logs:
`docker logs --tail 100 -f etcd`


```

```
2021-05-04 07:50:10.140405 E | rafthttp: request cluster ID
mismatch (got ecdd18d533c7bdc3 want a0b4701215acdc84)
2021-05-04 07:50:10.142212 E | rafthttp:
request sent was ignored (cluster ID mismatch:
peer[fa573fde1c0b9eb9]=ecdd18d533c7bdc3,
local=a0b4701215acdc84)
2021-05-04 07:50:10.155090 E | rafthttp:
request sent was ignored (cluster ID mismatch:
peer[fa573fde1c0b9eb9]=ecdd18d533c7bdc3,
local=a0b4701215acdc84)
```

Note in the output that the fa573fde1c0b9eb9 member responds with a cluster ID different from the local copy in the following command; we are jumping into the etcd container and then connecting the etcd server using the etcd command-line tool. Finally, we are running the member list sub-command to show all the nodes in this etcd cluster:

```
Unhealthy members in etcd cluster:
`docker exec -e ETCDCTL_ENDPOINTS=$(docker exec etcd /bin/sh -c
"etcdctl member list | cut -d, -f5 | sed -e 's/ //g' | paste
-sd ','") etcd etcdctl member list`


```

```
15de45eddfe271bb, started, etcd-a1ublabat03,
https://172.27.5.33:2380, https://172.27.5.33:2379, false
1d6ed2e3fa3a12e1, started, etcd-a1ublabat02,
https://172.27.5.32:2380, https://172.27.5.32:2379, false
68d49b1389cdfca0, started, etcd-a1ublabat01,
https://172.27.5.31:2380, https://172.27.5.31:2379, false
```

Note that the output shows that all etcd members are in the `started` state, which would make you think that they are all healthy, but this output may be misleading, particularly that the members have successfully joined the cluster:

```
Endpoint health:
`docker exec -e ETCDCTL_ENDPOINTS=$(docker exec etcd /bin/sh -c
"etcdctl member list | cut -d, -f5 | sed -e 's/ //g' | paste
-sd ','") etcd etcdctl endpoint health`


```
```
https://172.27.5.31:2379 is healthy: successfully committed
proposal: took = 66.729472ms
https://172.27.5.32:2379 is healthy: successfully committed
proposal: took = 70.804719ms
https://172.27.5.33:2379 is healthy: successfully committed
proposal: took = 71.457556ms
```

Note that the output shows that all etcd members are reporting as healthy even though one of the members has the wrong cluster ID. This output reports that the etcd process is up and running, responding to its health check endpoint.

You should run the following commands for RKE2 clusters and review the output:

```
Error messages in etcd logs:
`tail -f /var/log/pods/kube-system_etcd-*/etcd/*.log`
```

Note that the output is very similar to the output for the RKE1 cluster, with the only difference being that etcd runs as a Pod instead of a standalone container. In the following commands, we are doing a `for` loop, going through each etcd server and testing the endpoint. This endpoint will tell us whether the etcd server is healthy or having issues:

```
Unhealthy members in etcd cluster:
`for etcdpod in $(kubectl -n kube-system get pod -l
component=etcd --no-headers -o custom-columns=NAME:.metadata.
name); do echo $etcdpod; kubectl -n kube-system exec $etcdpod
-- sh -c "ETCDCTL_ENDPOINTS='https://127.0.0.1:2379' ETCDCTL_
CACERT='/var/lib/rancher/rke2/server/tls/etcd/server-ca.crt'
ETCDCTL_CERT='/var/lib/rancher/rke2/server/tls/etcd/server-
client.crt' ETCDCTL_KEY='/var/lib/rancher/rke2/server/tls/
etcd/server-client.key' ETCDCTL_API=3 etcdctl --write-out=table
endpoint health"; echo ""; done;`
```

In the following screenshot, we can see that we are testing a total of five etcd servers, with each server reporting health that equals `true`, along with output showing how long each server took to respond to this health check request. Finally, the last block will show us whether there are any known errors with the etcd server:

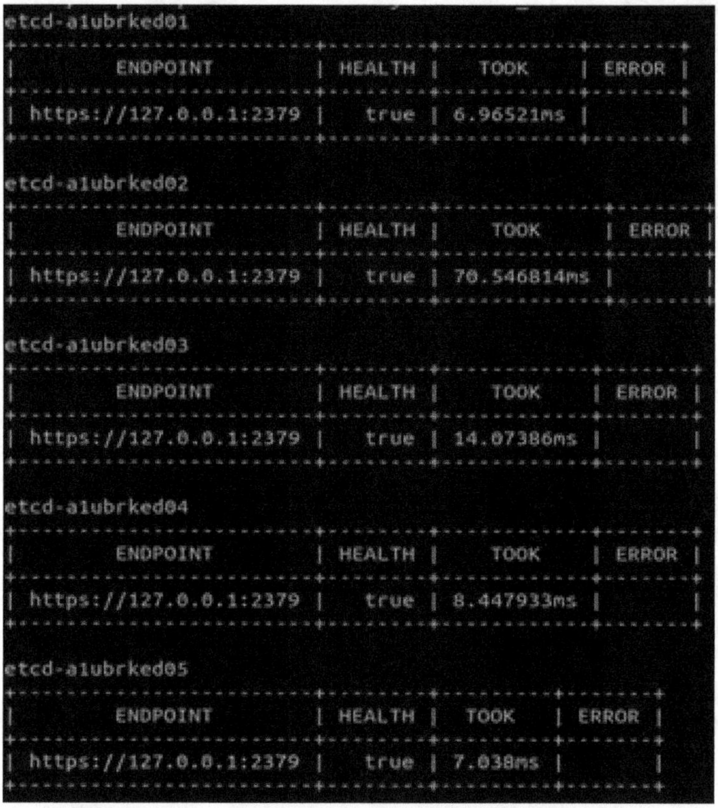

```
etcd-a1ubrked01
+------------------------+--------+-----------+-------+
|        ENDPOINT        | HEALTH |   TOOK    | ERROR |
+------------------------+--------+-----------+-------+
| https://127.0.0.1:2379 |   true | 6.96521ms |       |
+------------------------+--------+-----------+-------+

etcd-a1ubrked02
+------------------------+--------+-------------+-------+
|        ENDPOINT        | HEALTH |    TOOK     | ERROR |
+------------------------+--------+-------------+-------+
| https://127.0.0.1:2379 |   true | 70.546814ms |       |
+------------------------+--------+-------------+-------+

etcd-a1ubrked03
+------------------------+--------+-------------+-------+
|        ENDPOINT        | HEALTH |    TOOK     | ERROR |
+------------------------+--------+-------------+-------+
| https://127.0.0.1:2379 |   true | 14.07386ms  |       |
+------------------------+--------+-------------+-------+

etcd-a1ubrked04
+------------------------+--------+-------------+-------+
|        ENDPOINT        | HEALTH |    TOOK     | ERROR |
+------------------------+--------+-------------+-------+
| https://127.0.0.1:2379 |   true | 8.447933ms  |       |
+------------------------+--------+-------------+-------+

etcd-a1ubrked05
+------------------------+--------+---------+-------+
|        ENDPOINT        | HEALTH |  TOOK   | ERROR |
+------------------------+--------+---------+-------+
| https://127.0.0.1:2379 |   true | 7.038ms |       |
+------------------------+--------+---------+-------+
```

Figure 15.1 – The RKE2 endpoint health output table

Note that the output shows the health status of each of the master nodes. It is crucial to note that this script uses `kubectl` to execute into each etcd Pod and runs the `etcdctl endpoint health` command, which checks itself.

If `kubectl` is unavailable, you can SSH into each of the master nodes and run the following command instead:

```
```

export CRI_CONFIG_FILE=/var/lib/rancher/rke2/agent/etc/crictl.
yaml
etcdcontainer=$(/var/lib/rancher/rke2/bin/crictl ps --label
io.kubernetes.container.name=etcd --quiet)
```
```

```
/var/lib/rancher/rke2/bin/crictl exec $etcdcontainer sh -c
"ETCDCTL_ENDPOINTS='https://127.0.0.1:2379' ETCDCTL_CACERT='/
var/lib/rancher/rke2/server/tls/etcd/server-ca.crt' ETCDCTL_
CERT='/var/lib/rancher/rke2/server/tls/etcd/server-client.
crt' ETCDCTL_KEY='/var/lib/rancher/rke2/server/tls/etcd/server-
client.key' ETCDCTL_API=3 etcdctl endpoint health --cluster
--write-out=table"
```

The command directly connects to the container process.

To recover from this issue in an RKE(1) cluster, you'll want to use try the following steps:

1. Triggering a cluster update process by running the `rke up --config cluster.yml` command, or for Rancher-managed RKE(1) clusters, you'll need to change the cluster settings.

2. If the `rke up` command fails, use `etcd-tools`, found at `https://github.com/rancherlabs/support-tools/tree/master/etcd-tools`, to rebuild the etcd cluster manually.

3. If `etcd-tools` fails, you need to restore the cluster from an etcd snapshot.

At this point, we know how to resolve an etcd failure such as this. We now need to take steps to prevent these issues from happening again. In the next section, we are going to go over some common steps that you can take to protect your cluster.

Here are the preventive tasks to take:

-   If hosted in VMware, use **VM Anti-Affinity** rules to make sure that etcd nodes are hosted on different **ESXi** hosts. The **VMware Knowledge Base** can be found at `https://docs.vmware.com/en/VMware-vSphere/7.0/com.vmware.vsphere.resmgmt.doc/GUID-FBE46165-065C-48C2-B775-7ADA87FF9A20.html`.

-   If hosted in a cloud provider such as **AWS**, use different availability zones – for example, `etcd1` in `us-west-2a` and `etcd2` in `us-west-2b`.

-   Only apply patching in a rolling fashion. An example script can be found at `https://github.com/mattmattox/Kubernetes-Master-Class/blob/main/disaster-recovery/etcd-split-brain/rolling_reboot.sh`.

To reproduce this issue in a lab environment, you should follow the steps located at `https://github.com/mattmattox/Kubernetes-Master-Class/tree/main/disaster-recovery/etcd-split-brain#reproducing-in-a-lab`. Note that this process only applies to RKE(1) clusters, as finding a repeatable process for RKE2 is very difficult due to the built-in self-healing processes that are part of RKE2.

At this point, we have handled a broken etcd cluster and will need to restore the cluster in place. We, of course, need to take this to the next step, which is how to recover when the cluster is lost and we need to rebuild. In the next section, we are going to cover the steps for rebuilding a cluster from zero.

Rebuilding from an etcd backup

Cluster data, including Deployments, Secrets, and configmap, is stored in etcd. Using RKE1/2, we can take an etcd backup and seed a cluster using the backup. This feature can be helpful in cases of disasters such as a large-scale storage outage or accidental deletion of data for a cluster.

For RKE v0.2.0 and newer versions, etcd backups are turned on by default. Using the default setting, RKE will take a backup every 12 hours, keeping 6 copies locally on each etcd node, located at `/opt/rke/etcd-snapshots`. You can, of course, customize these settings by overriding the values in `cluster.yaml` in the Rancher UI details, which can be found at `https://rancher.com/docs/rke/latest/en/etcd-snapshots/recurring-snapshots/#configuring-the-snapshot-service-in-yaml`.

The most important settings are the Amazon **Simple Storage Service** (**S3**) settings that allow you to store the etcd snapshots in an S3 bucket instead of locally on the etcd nodes. This is important because we want to get the backups off the server that is being backed up. Note that RKE uses a standard S3 GO library that supports any S3 provider that follows the S3 standard. For example, you can use **Wasabi** in place of AWS S3, but you cannot use **Azure Blob**, as it's not fully S3 compatible. For environments where sending data to the cloud is not allowed, you can use some enterprise storage arrays such as **NetApp** and **EMC**, as they can become an S3 provider.

RKE can restore an etcd snapshot up into the same cluster or a new cluster. For restoring etcd, run the `rke etcd snapshot-restore --name SnapshotName` command, with RKE taking care of the rest. Restoring a snapshot into a new cluster is slightly different because the etcd snapshot restores all the cluster data, including items such as the node object for the *old* nodes. In addition, the Kubernetes certificates are regenerated. This causes the service account tokens to be invalided, breaking several services such as `canal`, `coredns`, and `ingress-nginx-controllers`. To work around this issue, I created a script that deleted all the broken service account tokens and recycled the services and nodes. This script can be found at `https://github.com/mattmattox/Kubernetes-Master-Class/tree/main/disaster-recovery/rebuild-from-scratch#restoringrecovering`.

You can find more details about the backup and restore process in Rancher's official documentation, located at `https://rancher.com/docs/rke/latest/en/etcd-snapshots/`.

In the RKE2 cluster, you can restore an etcd snapshot using the built-in `rke2` command on the master nodes, using the following steps:

1. Stop `rke2` on all master nodes using the `systemctl stop rke2-server` command.

2. Reset a cluster on one of the master nodes using the `rke2 server --cluster-reset` command. This command creates a new etcd cluster with only a single node one.

3. Clean the other master nodes using the `mv /var/lib/rancher/rke2/server/db/etcd /var/lib/rancher/rke2/server/db/etcd-old-%date%` command.

4. Then, rejoin the other master nodes to the cluster by running `systemctl start rke2-server`.

You can find more details on this process in the official RKE2 documentation at `https://docs.rke2.io/backup_restore/`.

At this point, you should be able to take an etcd backup and rebuild a cluster using just that backup. This process includes both the RKE1 and RKE2 clusters.

How to resolve Pods not being able to be scheduled due to OPA Gatekeeper

As we covered in *Chapter 12, Security and Compliance Using OPA Gatekeeper*, **OPA Gatekeeper** uses `ValidatingWebhookConfigurations` to screen updates requests sent to kube-apiserver to verify whether they pass OPA Gatekeeper policies. If OPA Gatekeeper Pod(s) are down, these requests will fail, which will break kube-scheduler because all the update requests will be blocked. This means that all new Pods will fail to be created.

> **Important Note**
>
> OPA Gatekeeper can be set to `fail open` – that is, if OPA Gatekeeper is down, assume that it would have been approved and move forward. I have seen in larger clusters that the delay caused by OPA Gatekeeper timing out caused a ton of load on the kube-apiservers, which caused the cluster to go offline.

You can identify this issue by reviewing the kube-scheduler logs using the following commands:

1. For RKE(1) clusters, run the `docker logs --tail 10 -t kube-scheduler` command if the output looks like the following. It's telling us that the kube-scheduler is having issues connecting the OPA Gatekeeper service endpoint:

    ```
    2021-05-08T04:44:41.406070907Z E0508 04:44:41.405968
    1 leaderelection.go:361] Failed to update lock: Internal
    error occurred: failed calling webhook "validation.
    gatekeeper.sh": Post "https://gatekeeper-webhook-service.
    gatekeeper-system.svc:443/v1/admit?timeout=3s": dial tcp
    10.43.104.236:443: connect: connection refused
    ```

2. By running the following command, you can discover which RKE server is currently hosting the kube-scheduler leader:

    ```
    NODE="$(kubectl get leases -n kube-system kube-scheduler
    -o 'jsonpath={.spec.holderIdentity}' | awk -F '_' '{print
    $1}')"
    echo "kube-scheduler is the leader on node $NODE"
    ```

3. For RKE2 clusters, it's a little different because kube-scheduler runs as a pod instead of a standalone container. You can use the following command to show the logs for all the kube-scheduler Pods:

```
kubectl -n kube-system logs -f -l component=kube-
scheduler
```

To recover from this issue, you need to restore the OPA Gatekeeper Pods, but this is a problem because all new Pod creations are being blocked. To work around this issue, we need to remove the webhook, allowing OPA Gatekeeper to restart successfully before restoring the webhook:

1. First, try setting the failure policy to open using the following command:

```
kubectl get ValidatingWebhookConfiguration gatekeeper-
validating-webhook-configuration -o yaml | sed 's/
failurePolicy.*/failurePolicy: Ignore/g' | kubectl apply
-f -.
```

2. If the open policy doesn't work, backup and remove all Gatekeeper admission checks, using the following commands:

```
kubectl get validatingwebhookconfigurations.
admissionregistration.k8s.io gatekeeper-validating-
webhook-configuration -o yaml > webhook.yaml
```

```
kubectl delete validatingwebhookconfigurations.
admissionregistration.k8s.io gatekeeper-validating-
webhook-configuration.
```

3. Monitor the cluster and wait for the cluster to stabilize.

4. Restore the webhook using the `kubectl apply -f webhook.yaml` command.

At this point, you should be able to recover from an OPA Gatekeeper outage. In addition, you should be able to use these steps for recovery of other software that uses webhooks in your cluster.

A runaway app stomping all over a cluster

One question that comes up a lot is, *How can a single app bring down my cluster?*

Let's say an application was deployed without CPU and memory limits. Pods can consume so much of a node's resources that the node becomes unresponsive, causing the node to go into an unschedulable state – that is, not ready. kube-scheduler is configured to reschedule the Pods running on the node after 5 minutes (default). This will break that node, and the process will repeat until all nodes are broken.

> **Important Note**
>
> Most of the time, the node will crash and self-recover, meaning you'll only see nodes flipping up and down as the Pods are bouncing between nodes. But I have seen environments where the nodes become locked up but don't restart.

You can identify this issue by reviewing the cluster event using the `kubectl get events -A` command, which shows the Pod events for all namespaces. And what we are looking for is a large number of Pod evictions, which is Kubernetes moving the Pods from the dying/dead node. You can also review the current CPU and memory of the present running Pods by using the `kubectl top Pod -A` command, which breaks the usage by the Pod. It's also recommended that you review any monitoring software such as **Prometheus** to watch the node resource usage over time.

To recover from this issue, you need to disable the Pod/workload, with an example being to scale the deployment to zero using the `kubectl -n <namespace> scale deployment/<deployment name> --replicas=0` command, and then to prevent the issue from happening again, you should add resource limits and a request to all workloads by adding the following settings:

```
resources:
limits:
  cpu: "800m"
  mem: "500Mi"
requests:
  cpu: "500m"
  mem: "250Mi"
```

It is important to note that in *Chapter 12*, *Security and Compliance Using OPA Gatekeeper*, we covered how to use OPA Gatekeeper to enforce these settings on all Pods in your cluster, and it is highly recommended that you use that policy, which can be found at `https://docs.rafay.co/recipes/governance/limits_policy/`.

To reproduce this issue in the lab, you can find an example application, located at `https://github.com/mattmattox/Kubernetes-Master-Class/tree/main/disaster-recovery/run-away-app`.

At this point, you should be able to detect a runaway application in your cluster. Then, you should be able to apply resource requests and limits to stop the application from damaging your cluster. Finally, we covered how to use OPA Gatekeeper to prevent this issue in the future.

Can rotating kube-ca break my cluster?

What is kube-ca, and how can it break my cluster?

Kubernetes protects all of its services using SSL certificates, and as part of this, a **Certificate Authority (CA)** is needed in order to work correctly. In the case of Kubernetes, kube-ca is the root certificate authority for the cluster and handles signing all the different certificates needed for the cluster. RKE then creates key pairs for kube-apiserver, etcd, kube-scheduler, and more, and signs them using kube-ca. This also includes service account tokens, which `kube-service-account-token` certificate signs as part of the authentication model. This means that if that chain is broken, kubectl and other Kubernetes services will choose the safest option and block the connection as that token can no longer be trusted. And of course, several services such as `canal`, `coredns`, and `ingress-nginx-controller` use `service-account-token` in order to communicate and authenticate with the cluster.

Typically, with RKE1/2, the kube-ca certificate is valid for 10 years. So typically, there is no need for this certificate ever to be rotated. But it can be for a couple of reasons, the first being because of cluster upgrade. Sometimes, during a Kubernetes upgrade, cluster services change to different versions, requiring new certificates to be created. But most of the time, this issue is accidentally caused when someone runs the `rke up` command but it is missing, or has an out-of-date `cluster.rkestate` file on their local machine. This is because the `rkestate` file stores the certificates and their private keys. When RKE defaults to generating these certificates, i.e., starts building a new cluster if this file is missing. This process typically fails, as some services such as `kubelet` are still using the old certificates and tokens so never go into a healthy state, causing the `rke up` process to error out. But RKE will leave the cluster in a broken state.

At this point, you should have a better understanding of what kube-ca is and how rotating it can affect your cluster. In addition, you should be able to fix the cluster using the `rke up` command.

How to fix a namespace that is stuck in terminating status

Why is my namespace stuck in termination?

When you run `kubectl delete ns <namespace>` on a namespace, `status.phase` will be set to `Terminating`, at which point the kube-controller will wait for the finalizers to be removed. At this point, the different controllers will detect that they need to clean up their resources inside the namespace.

For example, if you delete a namespace with a PVC inside it, the volume controller unmaps and deletes the volume(s), at which point the controller will remove the finalizer. Once all the finalizers have been removed, the kube-controller will finally delete the namespace. This is because finalizers are a safety mechanism built in Kubernetes to ensure that all objects are cleaned up before deleting the namespace. This whole process can take a few minutes. The issue comes into play when a finalizer never gets removed.

We'll see some of the common finalizers and how to resolve them:

- Rancher-created namespaces getting stuck.
- Custom metrics causing all namespaces to be stuck.
- The Longhorn system is stuck terminating.

Rancher-created namespaces getting stuck

In this example, when disabling/uninstalling monitoring in Rancher, the finalizer, `controller.cattle.io/namespace-auth`, is left behind by Rancher. And because of this, the namespace will get stuck in `Terminating` and will never self-resolve. You can confirm this issue by running the `kubectl get ns NamespaceName -o yaml` command.

It is important to note that this issue has mostly stopped since **Rancher v2.4** but still comes up if Rancher is unhealthy or disconnected from the cluster. In the following screenshot, you'll see a YAML output for a stuck namespace. The most important part that we want to look into is the `spec.finalizers` section, which tells us what finalizers are currently assigned to this namespace:

```
apiVersion: v1
kind: Namespace
metadata:
  annotations:
    cattle.io/status: '{"Conditions":[{"Type":"InitialRolesPopulate
      resource quota","LastUpdateTime":""},{"Type":"ResourceQuotaIn
    field.cattle.io/creatorId: u-zbw65mdtej
    field.cattle.io/projectId: c-x8rzf:p-pr7zr
    field.cattle.io/resourceQuota: "null"
  creationTimestamp: "2022-03-19T14:00:17Z"
  deletionTimestamp: "2022-03-19T14:02:05Z"
  labels:
    cattle.io/creator: norman
    field.cattle.io/projectId: p-pr7zr
  name: cattle-logging
  resourceVersion: "5872"
  selfLink: /api/v1/namespaces/t
  uid: 6a975c42-0396-11e9-bd3b-aaaaaaaaaa4a
spec:
  finalizers:
  - kubernetes
status:
  phase: Terminating
```

Figure 15.2 – An example of a stuck namespace YAML output

To resolve this issue, you have two options:

- Manually remove the finalizer using the `kubectl edit namespace NamespaceName` command, delete the line containing `controller.cattle.io/namespace-auth`, and save the edit.

- If you need to make a mass change for all namespaces in the cluster, you can run the following command:

```
kubectl get ns | awk '{print $1}' | grep -v NAME
| xargs -I{} kubectl patch namespace {}  -p
'{"metadata":{"finalizers":[]}}' --type='merge' -n {}
```

Custom metrics causing all namespaces to be stuck

A common reason for a namespace getting stuck is the custom metrics endpoint. Prometheus adds an API resource called `custom.metrics.k8s.io/v1beta1`, which exposes Prometheus metrics to the Kubernetes services such as **Horizontal Pod Autoscaling (HPA)**. In this case, the `kubernetes` finalizer will be left behind, which is not a very helpful status. You can confirm this issue by running the following command:

```
kubectl get ns NamespaceName  -o yaml.
```

In the following screenshot, you'll see a namespace with `finalizer kubernetes`:

```
apiVersion: v1
kind: Namespace
metadata:
    creationTimestamp: 2022-03-19T18:48:30Z
    deletionTimestamp: 2022-03-19T18:59:36Z
    name: test-namespace
    resourceVersion: "1385077"
    selfLink: /api/v1/namespaces/test-namespace
    uid: b50c9ea4-ec2b-11e8-a0be-fa163eeb47a5
spec:
    finalizers:
    - kubernetes
status:
    phase: Terminating
```

Figure 15.3 – A namespace stuck terminating with the Kubernetes finalizer

To resolve this issue, you have a couple of different options.

- Fix Prometheus because as long as it is up and running, the finalizer should be removed automatically without issue.

- If Prometheus has been disabled/removed from the cluster, you should clean up the leftover `custom.metrics` endpoint using the following commands:

  - Run `kubectl get apiservice|grep metrics` to find the name.

  - Delete it using the `kubectl delete apiservice v1beta1.custom.metrics.k8s.io` command.

- You can also remove the finalizer by running the following command:

  ```
  for ns in $(kubectl get ns --field-selector status.
  phase=Terminating -o jsonpath='{.items[*].metadata.
  name}'); do  kubectl get ns $ns -ojson | jq '.spec.
  finalizers = []' | kubectl replace --raw "/api/v1/
  namespaces/$ns/finalize" -f -; done
  ```

  It is important to note that this command is used to *fix* all the namespaces that are stuck in `Terminating`. Also, this does not fix the root cause but is more like a workaround to recover a broken cluster.

- You can use a tool called **knsk**, which can be found at `https://github.com/thyarles/knsk`. The aim of this script is to fix stuck namespaces and clean up broken API resources.

The Longhorn system is stuck terminating

Another common issue is the `longhorn-system` namespace being stuck in `Terminating` after uninstalling Longhorn. This namespace is used by Longhorn and stores several **Custom Resource Definitions (CRDs)** (`CustomResourceDefinition`). You can confirm this issue by running the `kubectl get ns longhorn-system -o json` command.

In the following screenshot, you'll see the JSON output for the `longhorn-system` namespace, which is the default namespace for Longhorn:

```json
{
    "apiVersion": "v1",
    "kind": "Namespace",
    "metadata": {
        "annotations": {
            "cattle.io/status": "{\"Conditions\":[{\"Type\":\"InitialRo
            "field.cattle.io/creatorId": "user-sw4mg",
            "field.cattle.io/projectId": "c-gkz6s:p-48tst",
            "kubectl.kubernetes.io/last-applied-configuration": "{\"api
            "lifecycle.cattle.io/create.namespace-auth": "true"
        },
        "creationTimestamp": "2022-03-01T17:17:20Z",
        "deletionTimestamp": "2022-03-18T12:30:14Z",
        "labels": {
            "cattle.io/creator": "norman",
            "field.cattle.io/projectId": "p-48tst"
        },
        "name": "longhorn-system",
        "resourceVersion": "15206257",
        "selfLink": "/api/v1/namespaces/longhorn-system",
        "uid": "9673789f-14fb-11e9-ba68-005056b171b1"
    },
    "spec": {
        "finalizers": [
            "kubernetes"
        ]
    },
    "status": {
        "phase": "Terminating"
    }
}
```

Figure 15.4 – longhorn-system stuck terminating with the Kubernetes finalizer

To resolve this issue, you have various options:

- Run the **Longhorn cleanup script**, which can be found at `https://longhorn.io/docs/1.2.4/deploy/uninstall/`. This script cleans up all the other CRD resources used by Longhorn.

- Run the following command to cycle through all the `api-resource` types in the cluster and delete them from the namespace:

```
kubectl api-resources --verbs=list --namespaced -o name
| xargs -n 1 kubectl get --show-kind --ignore-not-found
-n longhorn-system,
```

At this point, you should be able to clean up a namespace that is stuck in `terminating` by finding what finalizer is assigned to it. Then, you should be able to resolve that finalizer or remove it.

General troubleshooting for RKE clusters

This section will cover some common troubleshooting commands and scripts that can be used to debug issues. All these commands and scripts are designed around standard RKE clusters.

Find the current leader node by running the following listed script. This script will review the `kube-scheduler` endpoint in the `kube-system` namespace, which includes an annotation used by the leader controller.

This is the script for finding the kube-scheduler leader Pod: `curl https://raw.githubusercontent.com/mattmattox/k8s-troubleshooting/master/kube-scheduler | bash`.

Here is an output example of a healthy cluster:

```
```
kube-scheduler is the leader on node alubk8slab103
```
```

Suppose that this node is unhealthy or overlay networking isn't working correctly. In that case, the kube-scheduler isn't operating correctly, and you should recycle the containers by running `rke up`. And if that doesn't resolve the issue, you should stop the container on the leader node and allow another node to take over.

In order to show the etcd cluster members list, we'll use the following command:

```
docker exec etcd etcdctl member list
```

With the preceding command, you can see the current list of members – that is, the nodes in the etcd cluster.

Here is an output example of a healthy cluster from the preceding command:

```
```
2f080bc6ec98f39b, started, etcd-alubrkeat03,
https://172.27.5.33:2380, https://172.27.5.33:2379,ht
tps://172.27.5.33:4001, false
9d7204f89b221ba3, started, etcd-alubrkeat01,
https://172.27.5.31:2380, https://172.27.5.31:2379,ht
tps://172.27.5.31:4001, false
bd37bc0dc2e990b6, started, etcd-alubrkeat02,
https://172.27.5.32:2380, https://172.27.5.32:2379,ht
tps://172.27.5.32:4001, false
```
```

If this list does not match the cluster – that is, it has a node that should have been removed and a duplicate node – then you know that the etcd cluster is currently misconfigured and needs to be synced using RKE and etcd tools.

To expand the member list command, you can run the following command to show the health status of each etcd node:

```
curl https://raw.githubusercontent.com/mattmattox/etcd-
troubleshooting/master/etcd-endpoints | bash
```

It is important to note that this health check only shows that etcd is up and running, as the node might be having other issues, such as a full filesystem or low memory, but may still be reporting as healthy.

From the preceding command, this is an output example of a healthy cluster:

```
```
Validating connection to https://172.27.5.33:2379/health
{"health":"true"}
Validating connection to https://172.27.5.31:2379/health
{"health":"true"}
```
```

```
Validating connection to https://172.27.5.32:2379/health
{"health":"true"}
```

Finally, we will wrap up this section and go over some common errors and what they mean:

- The following error tells us that the etcd is failing to make a connection with the etcd node on port 2380. So, we need to verify that the etcd container is up and running. Your first step is to review the logs of the etcd container:

  ```
  `health check for peer xxx could not connect: dial tcp
  IP:2380: getsockopt: connection refused`
  ```

- This error means that the etcd cluster has lost quorum and it is trying to establish a new leader. Typically, this occurs when the majority of the nodes running etcd go down or cannot be reached – for example, if two out of three etcd nodes are down. This message usually appears following an outage, but if this message is reported multiple times without rebooting etcd nodes, it should be taken seriously. This means that the leader is switching nodes due to etcd timing out leader leases, which should be investigated. This is known by the following error:

  ```
  `xxx is starting a new election at term x`
  ```

- The following error means that the TCP connection to an etcd node is timing out and the request that was sent by the client never received a response. This can be because the node is offline or that a firewall is dropping the traffic:

  ```
  `connection error: desc = "transport: Error while dialing
  dial tcp 0.0.0.0:2379: i/o timeout"; Reconnecting to
  {0.0.0.0:2379 0 <nil>}`
  ```

- The etcd service stores the etcd node and cluster state in a directory (/var/lib/etcd). If this state is wrong for any reason, the node should be removed from the cluster and cleaned; the recommended way to run the cleanup script can be found at https://github.com/rancherlabs/support-tools/blob/master/extended-rancher-2-cleanup/extended-cleanup-rancher2.sh. Then, the node can to readded to the cluster. The following error shows this:

  ```
  `rafthttp: failed to find member.`
  ```

You can find more scripts and commands at https://github.com/mattmattox/Kubernetes-Master-Class/tree/main/troubleshooting-kubernetes.

At this point, you should be able to detect and resolve the most common failures that can happen with your RKE cluster. In addition, we covered how to prevent these kinds of failures from happening.

Summary

This chapter went over the main parts of an RKE1 and RKE2 cluster. We then dove into some of the common failure scenarios, covering how these scenarios happen, how to find them, and finally, how to resolve them.

We then closed out the chapter by covering some common troubleshooting commands and scripts that can be used to debug other issues.

In the next chapter, we are going to dive into the topic of CI/CD pipelines and image registries, including how to install tools such as Drone and Harbor. Then, we'll be covering how to integrate with our clusters. Finally, we'll be covering how to set up our applications to use the new pipelines.

Part 5 – Deploying Your Applications

This part will cover setting up a CI/CD pipeline for deploying applications into a Rancher cluster, including a supporting service such as an image registry and Helm charts. In addition, we will cover how to expose applications to the outside world using ingress rules, including SSL certificates to protect communication between applications. Finally, we will cover how performance capacity planning and management can be applied and enforced in Rancher.

This part of the book comprises the following chapters:

- *Chapter 16, Setting Up a CI/CD Pipeline and Image Registry*
- *Chapter 17, Creating and Using Helm Charts*
- *Chapter 18, Resource Management*

16
Setting Up a CI/CD Pipeline and Image Registry

This chapter covers **Continuous Integration/Continuous Delivery (CI/CD)** pipelines and how they work with Rancher to deploy applications in standardized and controlled processes, including how injecting secrets such as database credentials into a deployment allows the application to use them without giving application teams access to the raw credentials. Then, this chapter covers how to set up and configure Harbor as a Docker image repository, including how to configure Harbor as a pull-through cache to work around the Docker Hub pull limits. And finally, we'll look at how to integrate Harbor as a private registry in place of the Docker defaults.

In this chapter, we're going to cover the following main topics:

- What is a CI/CD pipeline?
- Rules for architecting a solution
- How to deploy Drone and its runners in Kubernetes with Rancher

- Injecting secrets into a pipeline
- What is an image repository, and rules for architecting a solution
- How to deploy Harbor in Kubernetes
- Integrating a private registry into Kubernetes

What is a CI/CD pipeline?

CI refers to a coding philosophy and practices that encourage developers to frequently commit code to version control systems in software development. The goal is your applications and environment are defined as code commonly called **Infrastructure as Code (IaC)** or **Platform as Code (PaC)**. As applications move from traditional monolithic architecture to more cloud-native microservice architecture, building, packaging, and testing applications become more complex. CI addresses this issue by focusing on being consistent and automated. This is done by moving these steps into a software framework such as Drone, which we'll be covering in this chapter.

Of course, CI is only the first half of the solution, with the other half being CD. The idea is that once an application has been compiled, tested, and packaged, we need a way to publish the application and its changes to our environments in a consistent and repeatable fashion. Because Kubernetes uses a desired state-driven technology, we only need to modify the desired configuration if we want to change something about our cluster. Kubernetes takes care of making the current state match the desired state. We covered how this process works back in *Chapter 2, Rancher and Kubernetes High-Level Architecture*. CD takes advantage of Kubernetes by allowing an application developer to define their application as a YAML file or Helm chart. We can deploy to our cluster in a repeatable way.

Of course, it's common to put both parts (CI/CD) together into what we call a pipeline, and the best way I have found to walk through a pipeline from start to finish is shown here.

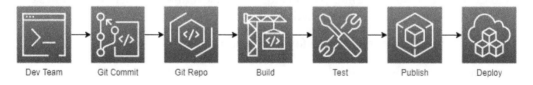

Dev Team   Git Commit   Git Repo   Build   Test   Publish   Deploy

Figure 16.1 – Example CI/CD pipeline

These are the high-level steps for most CI/CD pipelines with a description of each step:

Step 1 (Dev Team): The process starts with a developer checking the code for the repo (GitHub, GitLab, Git server) and making a change to the code, that is, fixing a bug, adding a feature, and so on. At this point, the developer might run the application locally to test their changes. But when developers are ready, they'll commit their changes to the repo.

Step 2 (Git Commit): In this step, a developer would generally create a branch for their new feature or bug fix. Depending on the setup, the developer might fork the repository and push their changes into the fork instead of the main repository. But the critical part of understanding this step is that the Git commit is the only way to make changes to your code, application, deployment, and infrastructure.

Step 3 (Git Repo): Once the Git commit has been pushed into the repository, the repository takes over. The first step is to validate that the developer has permission to push changes into the repository. For example, they might have permission to commit changes to the feature branch but not to the main/master branch. Then, typically, the next step would be to create a **Pull Request (PR)**, which initiates a request to merge the changes from one branch/fork into another. For example, you might create a PR to merge your feature into the main branch. It's common at this point for the CI/CD software to come into the picture. For example, you are using GitHub and Drone. Once you create a PR request, GitHub will send an HTTP request, called a webhook, to your Drone server, which initiates the next step.

Step 4 (Build): This step is where stuff starts happening. We will continue the Drone example where the Drone server has received a webhook from GitHub, which includes some details about the change to the repo. For example, it consists of the repo name, branch, commit hash, and commit message. But it is important to note that it doesn't include the code.

> **Note**
>
> If you would like to see what is included in the webhook payload, please see GitHub's official documentation at `https://docs.github.com/en/developers/webhooks-and-events/webhooks/webhook-events-and-payloads`.

The process might change depending on your pipeline software, but in general, the first step is to clone the code repository into a temporary location. This is why your pipeline server needs access to your code repository. The second step is to load the pipeline configuration file for Drone, which is `.drone.yml`. This file stores the steps that will be used during the build process. An example might be pulling down any dependencies and running some commands to compile your binaries. It is important to note that most pipeline software includes prebuilt plugins/modules for compiling common languages such as Go, npm, C++, and so on. For Drone, you can find a list at `https://plugins.drone.io`, but one of the nice things about modern pipeline software such as Drone and GitHub Actions is they use containers for these plugins/modules, so making your custom steps can be a straightforward process.

You may ask, where does this build step run? The answer to that question depends on the software and where it's hosted. For example, this whole process might be in a cloud using something such as GitHub Actions, or if you are using self-hosted Drone, it'll be running on your own computer. These are typically called **runners** because they run your code. For the example we will cover later in this chapter, we will deploy Drone's runners in a Kubernetes cluster where it will create temporary pods for each build with sidecars for each step.

Step 5 (Test): So far, we have the application built, but we need to test it and verify whether it's working as planned. This step can be as simple as being compiled at the end of testing, or it can be as complex as deploying to a test cluster, then simulating end users using the application, and everything in-between. This step depends on your application and programming language. For example, Go has built-in testing for writing tests directly into the application. Like a LAMP (Linux, Apache, MySQL, and PHP) stack, applications might need a couple of different components, including a database, to start. At the same time, there's the question of how easily you can test your application. For example, do you already have scripts to test logging in, running a report, making a test sale, and more? If you do, then in this step, you'll want to create a process to run these tests. The idea is that you want to verify that whatever changes are part of this commit will not disrupt production.

Step 6 (Publish): Once all our testing is done and we're ready to start spinning up our application in our Kubernetes cluster(s), we need to make the container images that we just created available to our clusters. We do this by publishing them to a Docker registry of some kind. Of course, there are several different solutions to this problem, some of which we'll be covering later in this chapter. But the key thing to understand here is we need a location to publish images, whether that is Docker Hub, a simple private registry, or a more enterprise solution such as Harbor.

This step is pretty straightforward for Drone and most CI/CD software, mainly tagging the image(s) with a version/build number, then running the `docker push image...` command to your registry of choice. As part of publishing the images to our registry, it's common to do security scans looking for known vulnerabilities. For example, you might want to block all images that include software versions that are vulnerable to the Log4j (CVE-2021-44228) issue with most CI/CD software using a tool such as Clair, which handles this process and will alert or block images depending on the number of CVEs found and their severity.

Step 7 (Deploy): Once everything is ready, the fun part of deploying the application to our Kubernetes clusters comes into the picture. This step mainly is to create/prepare our deployment files, which could be as simple as a YAML file or as complex as a Helm chart, or even a mix of both. We will not dive too deep into Helm charts in this chapter, as we'll cover that topic in the next chapter. This process mainly includes updating the image tags in our deployment file for the newly created images.

At this point, our CI/CD starts the process of publishing our application to the cluster. This can, of course, be as simple as running the `kubectl apply -f deploy.yaml` command or can be as complicated as deploying a public Helm chart for the database, that is, `helm install mysql`, then verifying that the database is up and ready before running a Kubernetes job (a single-use pod that only runs once) to create the database, and finally loading our data from an S3 bucket. Then, eventually, we run `kubectl apply` to spin up our application and run some test commands to verify everything is working as expected. The essential item to understand about this step is that this step is how we give our developers access to our production Kubernetes cluster in a safe and controlled manner without giving them direct access to the cluster.

At this point, the pipeline is done, and we will start all over again for the next feature or bug fix. The big idea is that pipelines are designed to make this process repeatable and controllable, allowing developers to move fast but not break our clusters. In the next section, we will dive into creating a CI/CD solution, followed by an installation.

Rules for architecting a solution

Now that we understand what CI/CD is, we will go over designing a solution, including the pros and cons of standard designs. It is important to note that each environment/application is unique and will require tuning for the best experience.

Before designing a solution, you should be able to answer the following questions:

- Does your application team already have a CI/CD solution that supports Kubernetes?
- Will a single team use this CI/CD solution, or will multiple teams share it?
- How many pipelines/builds do you think will be created?
- What kind of deployment schedules do your developers follow?
- Will they be making changes at any time, or will it be in big patches, that is, every Friday is *build day*?
- How important is speed to the pipeline process? Is it okay if a pipeline takes an hour or should it run in minutes?
- Will you be using a self-hosted or **Software as a service** (**SaaS**) offering?
- What software stack will you be deploying (Go, LAMP, Node.js, DotNet, and so on)?
- What kind of tools/packages will you need to build your applications?
- Do your build tools require special licensing?
- What CPU architecture and OS family do you need to build on (Linux, Windows, AMD64, ARM)?
- Is your code private or public?
- Will the build processes and output need to be publicly accessible (most open source projects do)?
- Will only internal employees create commits and publish them or is this a public project so outside users might be triggering builds?
- What is your budget for both software and hardware?

Once we have answers to many of these questions, we can evaluate solutions.

Drone

Drone is a Go-based application that performs all actions that are done within containers. Thus, it is a perfect fit for platforms such as Kubernetes, where launching containers is a breeze. Drone uses a server for management and orchestration, with runners handling the creation of containers for build tasks.

The **pros** are as follows:

- Free for open source projects.

- Verified good integration with GitHub, Bitbucket, and GitLab.

- The Drone server and its runners are lightweight and can be deployed on low-end hardware such as a Raspberry Pi.

- Pipelines as code, meaning your pipeline becomes part of your application development. There is no need to change your pipeline configurations outside your source control.

- Both internal and external secret management via Vault, KMS, and third parties.

- Easy to use as the UI is easy to understand.

- All plugins are containers meaning if you want to write your own, just create a Docker image to do whichever task you want.

- The cloud and on-premise software are the same, so migration between the two is effortless.

- Scalability is built-in because all the builds run as containers that can easily be scaled out thanks to Kubernetes.

- Drone was built to be on the public internet because many open source projects use Drone. Because of this and the fact that Drone is based on containers, it is safe and normal to have a Drone server publicly exposed, allowing better transparency with the public.

- The Drone CLI has built-in support for local builds, which allows you to trigger a build locally on your machine without connecting to the Drone server. Because every task is a container, the Drone CLI just makes the same API calls to Docker as the runner would.

The **cons** are as follows:

- Build caching is not a thing with Drone. Because every build is a new container/ pod, items from the previous builds are not available, meaning if you need to download a set of dependencies to run your build, you'll be downloading the same dependencies every time. Plugins such as drone-cache can help with this, but they are not the most reliable solutions and can force you to limit how you run builds.

- It suffers from the big empty box problem because Drone is built to support almost any language/application stack. Everything is empty when you first get started with little to no framework guiding you. Some examples can be found in the Drone documentation, but you'll mostly be starting from zero.

- Drone has a reasonably active community but is still a newcomer to the CI/CD market, being created in 2014, but finding people with administrator knowledge can be difficult.

- There are no authentication providers outside your repository, meaning you can't point it to your Active Directory, LDAP, or SAML provider for authentication.

- Having a public Drone server instance is normal…but safety is relative. There are settings that can be used to restrict access to a specific GitHub organization, and also settings on access to secrets so that they can't be stolen by a malicious user via a rogue repository. These settings aren't configured out of the box.

- Drone has code maintenance issues as it takes quite a bit of patching and custom plugins to support specific workloads. For example, the default Kubernetes plugin is minimal, with users needing to create their custom plugins, such as `https://github.com/SupportTools/kube-builder`. There is even a community fork of Drone called Woodpecker to address these issues.

- There is no **High Availability** (**HA**) for the Drone server as the server uses an in-memory queue system. The Drone server will rely on Kubernetes to provide HA, that is, restarting and rescheduling a failed pod. As of writing, an HA feature is currently in beta, details of which can be found at `https://docs.drone.io/server/ha/overview/`.

Typically, I recommend Drone for cloud and Kubernetes native applications built with containers in mind from the start and a team that wants a GitOps workflow, as with open source projects that need public access.

Jenkins

Jenkins is a Java-based CI/CD tool that is built around automating the running of scripts and is sometimes called an automation platform that can support CI/CD.

The **pros** are as follows:

- It has a deep history in DevOps and the CI/CD marketplace as it is the oldest tool in this list. It was created in 2011 under Oracle before being forked in 2014 to become Jenkins.

- Because of the history of Jenkins, it has become the default when it comes to CI/CD, meaning a lot of software, plugins, and workflows are built around Jenkins first and then are adapted to other CI/CD tools.

- Jenkins has an extensive list of plugins (1,000+ at the time of writing) ranging from integrations into Nagios for monitoring, to Puppet for configuration management, to hooks into Jira for issue tracking.

- Because Jenkins is written in Java, it is portable, meaning the server can run on Windows or Linux, depending on your requirements.

- Jenkins has excellent plugins for test automation, such as `TestComplete Support`, which can simulate user actions such as opening a web page, running a desktop application, and so on. It is important to note that this is a third-party plugin.

- Jenkins has built-in support for some enterprise authentication providers, such as Active Directory, LDAP, SAML, and others.

- Jenkins has built-in HA support using an active-standby setup.

- Enterprise/paid plugins typically come with excellent documentation and support.

The **cons** are as follows:

- Jenkins is built to be an enterprise product, meaning it assumes that it will have administrators to care for and feed it, that is, someone to kill stuck jobs, monitor resources, restart it when it gets stuck, and so on.

- Community/free plugins typically come with little to no documentation and no option for paid support.

- Jenkins has runners for Kubernetes to allow you to run tasks as pods in your cluster, but setting up and using this kind of runner can be challenging and requires the use of details that can be found at `https://plugins.jenkins.io/kubernetes/`.

- Jenkins does have local builds, but you are running a local copy of the Jenkins server, meaning you have to go through all the work of setting it up and match your local configuration with your real Jenkins server.

- There's no SaaS/cloud-hosted option, meaning you'll need to install and manage the Jenkins server.

- The UI is clunky, not very user-friendly, and looks like a Java application from 10 years ago.

Typically, I recommend Jenkins for two reasons. The first reason is that it's already deployed and used in the customer's environment. This is because switching between pipelines can require a large amount of work, with the process being that you need to start over. The second reason is enterprise plugin support. Writing your own plugins can take time and resources that are better spent elsewhere. So, it's common for enterprise customers just to buy commercial plugins that work out of the box.

> **Note**
>
> Rancher did have its own pipeline solution called Rancher Pipelines, but as of Rancher v2.5, this feature has been deprecated and replaced by Fleet. Rancher Pipelines was built on top of Jenkins but integrated into Rancher. You can still enable it using the steps at `https://rancher.com/docs/rancher/v2.6/en/pipelines/example-repos/`, but it is highly recommended not to use it.

GitHub Actions

GitHub Actions was launched back in 2018 as a workflow automation tool that can also do CI/CD. It shares the core item of all tasks being containers like Drone does, but with the big difference that it's a cloud solution sold as an add-on to your GitHub subscription.

The **pros** are as follows:

- It's easy to use for GitHub users as their repositories are just built into the platform, which just needs to be enabled.

- You can use self-hosted runners to work around costs by providing your own hardware details, which can be found at `https://docs.github.com/en/actions/hosting-your-own-runners/about-self-hosted-runners`.

- Nearly unlimited scale – as a cloud-based solution, you can run as many parallel builds as possible without needing to spin up additional servers/nodes, depending on your GitHub subscription, details of which can be found at `https://docs.github.com/en/billing/managing-billing-for-github-actions/about-billing-for-github-actions`.

- Tight integration with GitHub events allows you to customize your pipelines based on the type of event. For example, you might run one workflow to create a new issue and another one to create a pull request.

- Built-in caching for the GitHub repo means that if you have a large repository with lots of changes, you can assume that the clone will take little to no time. This is because everything is being done inside the GitHub network.

- GitHub has a marketplace for Actions, meaning it's effortless to add plugins to your workflow. For example, if you need a K3s cluster to test, just go to `https://github.com/marketplace/actions/setup-k3d-k3s` and click the **Use the latest version** button, then copy and paste the text into your flow.

The **cons** are as follows:

- Actions are sold by the minute. For example, if your task runs for 5 mins, you are billed for 5 mins of usage. GitHub does provide some amount of free usage depending on your subscription and repository type (private versus public).

- GitHub Actions has been a popular target for hackers and crypto miners to steal resources for public projects. For example, if you run a build on every pull request, what is to stop someone from running a bitcoin miner as part of the workflow? This, in turn, runs up your bill and has cost users thousands of dollars. You can read more about these kinds of attacks at `https://www.bleepingcomputer.com/news/security/github-actions-being-actively-abused-to-mine-cryptocurrency-on-github-servers/`.

- GitHub has a lot of the same cons as Drone when it comes to commercial plugins, called Actions, as it simply hasn't been around for a long time.

- GitHub Actions mainly runs in the cloud, so accessing on-premise resources such as databases, servers, and Kubernetes clusters can be difficult without publishing them on the internet. You can work around this using local runners.

- Running builds locally on your laptop is limited to third-party tools such as `https://github.com/nektos/act`.

- Limited build environments again, because GitHub hosts the VMs for you. You can only choose the OS and versions they tell you. For example, ARM is not available without self-hosted runners. You can find the current list of supported environments at `https://github.com/actions/virtual-environments`.

Typically, I recommend GitHub Actions for small one-off projects that need a simple build script; just run the `make` command. Doing higher-level testing such as user simulation gets very difficult.

Rancher does have a product called Fleet that kind of fits into this space as it is a CD-only tool and does not do CI. You can't do a Docker build, application testing, or anything like that as part of Fleet. It's only designed to push changes to your environment. Of course, you can use Fleet as part of publishing your applications to clusters. Still, it is not recommended as Fleet doesn't have a rollback or failback feature, meaning if you push out a change and it breaks your application, you need to update your Git repo and push out a new change.

For the rest of this chapter, we will assume that you have chosen Drone for your CI/CD pipeline, but most of these steps can easily be translated for other tools.

How to deploy Drone and its runners in Kubernetes with Rancher

This section will break the process into three parts: deploying the Drone server, standing up a Kubernetes runner, and connecting a pipeline to an external Rancher cluster.

Prerequisites

The following are the items that you'll need to have set up before starting to install Drone and its runners:

- A Kubernetes cluster with permissions to create cluster-level resources (cluster admin is preferred)

- Persistent storage (please see *Chapter 11, Bringing Storage to Kubernetes Using Longhorn*, for more details)

- A hostname for publishing the Drone web UI

- A publicly signed SSL certificate (internally or self-signed certs can cause issues)

- Permissions in GitHub to create an OAuth application

- A publicly accessible URL from GitHub (for example, `https://drone.example.com`)

- kubectl and Helm access to the cluster where the Drone server will be installed.

Installation steps

In this section, we'll cover installing PostgreSQL before installing Drone. Then, finally, we'll install the runner.

PostgreSQL

The Drone server needs a backend database to store its settings, configuration, and so on. For this, we'll be using PostgreSQL as it's the only supported database for self-hosted deployments. You can skip this step and use an externally managed database such as Amazon RDS for PostgreSQL if you so choose.

To install PostgreSQL, you need to run the following commands:

1. The first command is to create a namespace.
2. It is then followed by a `helm` command to add the `bitnami` repo.

3. Then, finally, we run the `helm install` command to deploy the PostgreSQL server with additional options to set the username and password.

Here's the result:

```
## Create drone namespace
kubectl create ns drone --dry-run=client | kubectl apply -f

## Setup helm repo
helm repo add bitnami https://charts.bitnami.com/bitnami

## Install the chart
helm install drone-db bitnami/postgresql -n drone \
--set global.storageClass=longhorn \
--set global.postgresql.auth.postgresPassword=drone \
--set global.postgresql.auth.username=drone \
--set global.postgresql.auth.password=drone \
--global.postgresql.auth.database=drone
```

Figure 16.2 – PostgreSQL install steps

You can find the complete commands at `https://github.com/PacktPublishing/Rancher-Deep-Dive/tree/main/ch16/drone/postgresql/install_commands.md`. You can also find a full breakdown of the Helm chart options at `https://github.com/bitnami/charts/tree/master/bitnami/postgresql/`.

Note

We are setting the password to `drone` for this example. This should be set to something more secure.

The Drone server

In this section, we will install the Drone server. But before installing Drone, you should follow the steps located at `https://docs.drone.io/server/provider/github/` to create your OAuth2 app on GitHub. To install the Drone server, you need to follow these steps:

1. We create a new namespace and add the Drone `helm repo` using the commands listed in Figure 16.3.

2. We then create the SSL secret for the RPC secret which is used by Drone and its runners for authentication.

3. Next, we make an RPC secret, which is used to authenticate runners.

4. Finally, we use the `helm install` command with a number of settings.

    The first section defines the ingress settings followed by storage, then we set up the database connection string. Then, the final section is for integrating into GitHub for our authentication.

```
## Setup helm repo
helm repo add drone https://charts.drone.io
helm repo update

## Upload ssl cert
kubectl -n drone create secret tls ssl-cert --key="tls.key" --cert="tls.crt"

## Create RPC Secret
openssl rand -hex 16
bea26a2221fd8090ea38720fc445eca6

## Install the chart
helm install drone-server drone/drone -n drone \
--set ingress.enabled=true \
--set ingress.hosts[0].host=drone.example.com \
--ingress.tls.[0].hosts=drone.example.com \
--set ingress.tls.[0].secretName=ssl-cert \
--set persistentVolume.enabled=true \
--set persistentVolume.storageClass=longhorn \
--set env.DRONE_SERVER_HOST=drone.example.com \
--set env.DRONE_SERVER_PROTO=https \
--set env.DRONE_DATABASE_DRIVER=postgres \
--set env.DRONE_DATABASE_DATASOURCE="postgres://drone:drone@drone-db:5432/drone?sslmode=disable" \
--set env.DRONE_RPC_SECRET=bea26a2221fd8090ea38720fc445eca6 \
--set env.DRONE_GIT_ALWAYS_AUTH=true \
--set env.DRONE_GITHUB_CLIENT_ID=your-id \
--set env.DRONE_GITHUB_CLIENT_SECRET=github-secret \
--set env.DRONE_USER_CREATE=username:Your-GitHub-Username,admin:true \
--set env.DRONE_USER_FILTER=Your-GitHub-ORG
```

Figure 16.3 – Drone server install steps

You can find the full commands at `https://github.com/PacktPublishing/Rancher-Deep-Dive/tree/main/ch16/drone/server/install_commands.md`. You can also find a full breakdown of the Helm chart options at `https://github.com/drone/charts/blob/master/charts/drone/`.

At this point, you should be able to log in to your Drone server by visiting the web UI.

The Drone Kubernetes runner

In this section, we will install the Drone Kubernetes runner. This can be installed on the same cluster as the Drone server if you so choose. Also, in the following example, we'll be using the default namespace for running our temporary pods. You can customize this if you so desire.

To install the runner, you need to run the following steps:

1. Create a new namespace.

2. Add the drone `helm` `repo`.

3. Then, finally, install `drone-runner`.

    It is important to note that we are pointing this runner to our Drone server and using the RPC secret to authenticate.

```
## Create drone namespace
kubectl create ns drone-runner --dry-run=client | kubectl apply -f

## Setup helm repo
helm repo add drone https://charts.drone.io
helm repo update

## Install the chart
helm install kube-runner drone/drone -n drone-runner \
--set env.DRONE_SERVER_HOST=drone.example.com \
--set env.DRONE_SERVER_PROTO=https \
--set env.DRONE_RPC_SECRET=bea26a2221fd8090ea38720fc445eca6
```

Figure 16.4 – Drone runner installation steps

You can find the full commands at `https://github.com/PacktPublishing/` `Rancher-Deep-Dive/tree/main/ch16/drone/runner/install_` `commands.md`. You can also find a full breakdown of the Helm chart options at `https://github.com/drone/charts/tree/master/charts/drone-` `runner-kube`.

At this point, you should be able to run builds in your Drone server. In the next section, we'll connect Drone to our Kubernetes cluster so we can deploy our apps.

Connecting to Rancher

In this section, we will create a service account in another Kubernetes cluster to add it as a secret to the Drone server. In this command, we create a service account, assign it cluster-admin permissions, and finally grab the token for this account.

```
## Create a ServiceAccount and assign it ClusterAdmin permissions
kubectl -n kube-system create serviceaccount drone
kubectl create clusterrolebinding --clusterrole=cluster-admin --serviceaccount=kube-system:drone
TOKENNAME=`kubectl -n kube-system get serviceaccount/drone -o jsonpath='{.secrets[0].name}'`
TOKEN=`kubectl -n kube-system get secret $TOKENNAME -o jsonpath='{.data.token}'| base64 --decode`
echo $TOKEN
```

Figure 16.5 – Create a Drone service account

You can find the full commands at `https://github.com/PacktPublishing/Rancher-Deep-Dive/tree/main/ch16/drone/external-cluster/rbac.md`.

Next, we need to grab the cluster server URL by logging into the Rancher UI, browsing the cluster in question, and clicking the **Download KubeConfig** button. You should get a file that looks like the following example. We need the server value, which in this example is `https://rancher.example.com/k8s/clusters/c-m-abcdefgj`.

```
apiVersion: v1
kind: Config
clusters:
- name: "example-cluster"
  cluster:
    server: "https://rancher.example.com/k8s/clusters/c-m-abcdefgj"

users:
- name: "example-cluster"
  user:
    token: "kubeconfig-user-abcdefgj:1234678912346789123467891234678912346789"

contexts:
- name: "example-cluster"
  context:
    user: "example-cluster"
    cluster: "example-cluster"

current-context: "example-cluster"
```

Figure 16.6 – KubeConfig example

Now, we can add the credentials as a secret so it can be consumed by a pipeline, which we'll cover in the next section.

Injecting secrets into a pipeline

In this section, we are going to cover adding a secret to a pipeline. In this example, we will use the Kubernetes credentials that we created in the last section.

We will start by browsing a repository and clicking the **Activate repository** button. Then we need to go to the **Settings** tab and select **Secrets** from the side menu.

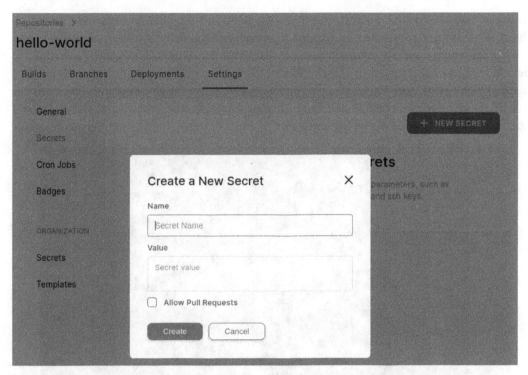

Figure 16.7 – Creating a secret wizard

We are going to create the following secrets and their values. It is important to note that if you are using a public repository, someone could access your secret if you check the **Allow Pull Requests** box.

> **Important Note**
>
> Once a secret has been added to Drone, it can never be retrieved again. So, it is recommended that you have a copy stored somewhere outside Drone such as a password manager.

```
docker-username: DockerHub-Username
docker-password: DockerHub-PAT
kubernetes_server: https://rancher.example.com/k8s/clusters/c-m-abcdefgj
kubernetes_token: abcdefghiklmnopqrstuvwxyz1234567890.......
```

Figure 16.8 – Example secrets

Now that we have created our secrets, we can use them in a pipeline. The essential item in the example is the `from_secret` command, which ties the secret's value to a setting for the plugin, which is an environment variable inside the container. This pipeline uses the default Docker plugin to run the Docker build, then uses a custom plugin I created called `supporttools/kube-builder` for running kubectl and Helm commands. You must run the `bash /usr/local/bin/init-kubectl` command first as it handles setting up the `kubeconfig` file inside the container.

```yaml
kind: pipeline
type: kubernetes
name: Example-App

steps:
  - name: Docker-Build
    image: plugins/docker
    settings:
      tags:
        - ${DRONE_BUILD_NUMBER}
        - ${DRONE_COMMIT_BRANCH}
        - latest
      username:
        from_secret: docker-username
      password:
        from_secret: docker-password

  - name: Deploy-to-k8s
    image: supporttools/kube-builder:latest
    settings:
      kubernetes_server:
        from_secret: kubernetes_server
      kubernetes_token:
        from_secret: kubernetes_token
    commands:
      - bash /usr/local/bin/init-kubectl
      - kubectl create ns hello-world --dry-run=client | kubectl apply -f
      - kubectl apply -n hello-world -f deploy.yaml
```

Figure 16.9 – Example pipeline

At this point, we have a pipeline up and running and should be able to build and deploy our applications. In the next section, we will dive into setting up a private image repository for storing our Docker images outside Docker Hub.

What an image repository is and the rules for architecting a solution

One of the critical things with containerization is the concept of images. An image is a read-only file that contains all the files, libraries, and executables that make up a container. Once you create a container image, you need to store it someplace where it will be available to download from your Kubernetes nodes. This place is called a registry, container registry, or image repository. For this chapter, we are going to call it an image repository. There are, of course, three main types of image repositories: Docker Hub, third-party, and self-hosted.

But before designing a solution, you should be able to answer the following questions:

- Will this be an air-gapped environment, that is, do all images have to come from a registry we control?

- Are all your images public, or will you be using a private repo?

- What is your budget for both software and hardware?

- Will multiple data centers/sites need access to your registry?

- Do you have any security/regulatory requirements for keeping data in a location, that is, on-premise only, in your country, and so on?

- Are you planning on scanning images and limiting what images are allowed in your environment?

Once we have answers to most of these questions, we can evaluate solutions.

Docker Hub

This is the official/default image repository for most Kubernetes distributions, including Rancher. Because it is the default, most deployments, open source projects, and software vendors use Docker Hub.

The **pros** are as follows:

- It's the default and accessible for public images, with you only needing to pay for private images.

- **Trust**: Pulling an image from a random third-party image repository can throw up red flags for an open source project as there is no telling who is hosting it. Are they injecting malicious software into the images? Docker Hub addresses this issue by doing security scans of all public images, including flagging images that contain viruses and other malicious code. It is important to note that this system is not perfect and does not catch everything.

- **Speed**: Docker Hub, of course, is the largest image repository, and it uses Cloudflare as its CDN along with AWS to provide the backend S3 storage. Pulling images from Docker Hub is very fast, with the limiting factor almost always being on your end, unless you are rate limited by Docker Hub. You can find out by querying their API details, which can be found at `https://www.docker.com/blog/checking-your-current-docker-pull-rate-limits-and-status/`.

- **Data redundancy / availablity**: Again, the images are stored in AWS S3 with Amazon's official documentation stating that S3 object durability is 99.999999999 (11 nines) for a year. So, the chance of losing your images due to data loss is almost zero.

The **cons** are as follows:

- **Security requirements**: Some organizations require that all source code and data stay on-premises. Docker Hub accounts have been attacked and private images have been leaked before.

- Docker images are stored as plain text and are not encrypted in Docker Hub, meaning someone with access to the repository would be able to download an image and extract data/source code from it. This includes Docker Hub itself as it does scans of images uploaded to its sites. An example is the Log4js issue where Docker Hub triggered a scan of all images hosted on its site. Details of which can be found at `https://docs.docker.com/security/#log4j-2-cve-2021-44228`.

- **Pull limits**: Docker Hub added rate limits to images in November 2021, details of which can be found in their official documentation located at `https://docs.docker.com/docker-hub/download-rate-limit/`. You can, of course, buy a Docker Hub subscription, which has no limits for your clusters. You can also read about this change in my Kubernetes Master Class – *Docker Hub Limits: Addressing the Amount of Pull Requests in Rancher*, which can be found at `https://github.com/mattmattox/Kubernetes-Master-Class/tree/main/docker-hub-limits`.

I usually recommend using Docker Hub for all public projects and paying a few dollars per month to host private images unless you store sensitive data inside your images or have a limited internet connection.

Image repositories managed by third parties

These platforms act as a central point of access for your own container images, making it easier to store, manage, and secure them without the operational hassle of running your own registry on-premises. Several third-party registry offerings support Docker images, including Amazon ECR, Azure Container Registry, and Google Container Registry.

The **pros** are as follows:

- **Control**: These image repositories are customarily hosted inside your current cloud environment – that is, AWS, Azure, GCP – and because of this, you have control over the data.

- **Managed service**: Because the cloud provider manages all these image repositories, you don't have to upgrade them, patch them, or back them up. You can get just let them handle it for you.

- **Pricing**: Most of the cloud providers charge little to nothing for traffic going to and from the image repository. And storage costs usually are just passed through to the S3/object storage storing the data.

The **cons** are as follows:

- **Not cost-effective for public images**: Because most cloud providers charge extra for traffic being egressed (going out to the public internet), hosting a public image can become very expensive.

- **Authentication**: Most cloud providers use their own authentication sources to control access to the image repository. This causes problems as Docker is built around basic authentication (a static username and password), and services such as AWS ECR only provide a good password for 6 hours. This means that you need to use a tool such as `https://github.com/SupportTools/ecr-helper` to handle updating that password on schedule.

I usually only recommend using a third-party image repository with hosted Kubernetes clusters where you need to store private images but don't want to manage the service. For example, if you deploy an EKS cluster on Amazon, you should use ECR.

Self-hosted repo

An organization may prefer to host container images on their own on-premises infrastructure for various reasons, including security, compliance concerns, or low-latency requirements.

The **pros** are as follows:

- **Control**. You are in complete control because you are hosting the images. You can choose to have everything open to the world or all images locked down and everything in-between.

- **Bandwidth**: Because the images are hosted in your data center, your nodes no longer need to reach out to the public internet to pull images. For example, if you have a 100-node cluster, each node needs to pull down a 1 GB image. You need to download 100 GB of data through your internet connection versus downloading that data for a local server.

- **Security**: Using tools such as Harbor, we can integrate image scanning into our registry and set up rules such as blocking the uploading of images with too many high/critical vulnerabilities.

- **Required in air-gap environments**: Private image repositories are required in air-gapped environments that cannot pull images for external image repositories.

The **cons** are as follows:

- **Management**: Because you are now hosting the registry, you are directly responsible for securing, patching, and upgrading tasks of that software.

- **Changes to your deployments**: Most deployments assume that you'll use Docker Hub as your image repository. So, you'll need to copy the images from the public repository into your private registry.

I normally only recommend self-hosted repositories in air-gapped environments and in cases where pulling large amounts of data over the internet can be an issue, that is, low-speed internet or large numbers of nodes sharing a connection.

At this point, you should be able to pick which image repository works best for your environment. In the following sections, we will assume that you'll be going with the self-hosted option.

How to deploy Harbor in Kubernetes

In this section, we will install Harbor in our Kubernetes cluster. It is important to note that this will only be a basic setup as Harbor can be installed in several different ways.

The following are the prerequisites:

- A Kubernetes cluster with permissions to create cluster-level resources (cluster admin is preferred)

- Persistent storage (please see *Chapter 11*, *Bringing Storage to Kubernetes Using Longhorn*, for more details)

- Two hostnames for publishing the main Harbor URL and the notary service

- A publicly signed SSL certificate (internally or self-signed certificates can cause issues)

- kubectl and Helm access to the cluster where the Drone server will be installed

To install Harbor, we are going to run the following commands:

1. First, add the Harbor `helm repo`.

2. Next, create the Harbor `namespace`.

3. Then, upload the `ssl certificate` secret for the ingress.

4. Then, finally, we run `helm install` for the Harbor chart.

It is important to note that this includes some settings: the first part is to set up the ingress and the second half is to set up the storage class, which is Longhorn.

```
## Setup helm repo
helm repo add harbor https://helm.goharbor.io
helm repo update

## Create a namespace
kubectl create ns harbor --dry-run=client | kubectl apply -f

## Upload ssl cert
kubectl -n harbor create secret tls ssl-cert --key="tls.key" --cert="tls.crt"

## Install the chart
helm upgrade --install harbor harbor/harbor -n harbor \
--set expose.type=ingress \
--set expose.tls.secret.secretName=ssl-cert \
--set expose.tls.secret.notarySecretName=ssl-cert \
--set expose.ingress.hosts.core=harbor.example.com \
--set expose.ingress.hosts.notary=harbor-notary.example.com \
--set persistence.enabled=true \
--set persistence.persistentVolumeClaim.registry.storageClass=longhorn \
--set persistence.persistentVolumeClaim.chartmuseum.storageClass=longhorn \
--set persistence.persistentVolumeClaim.jobservice.storageClass=longhorn \
--set persistence.persistentVolumeClaim.database.storageClass=longhorn \
--set persistence.persistentVolumeClaim.redis.storageClass=longhorn \
--set persistence.persistentVolumeClaim.trivy.storageClass=longhorn
```

Figure 16.10 – Harbor install commands

You can find the full commands at `https://github.com/PacktPublishing/ Rancher-Deep-Dive/tree/main/ch16/harbor/server/install_ commands.md`. You can also find a full breakdown of the Helm chart options at `https://github.com/goharbor/harbor-helm`.

At this point, you should have Harbor up and running and be ready to start uploading images and use them in your environment. In the next section, we will configure Kubernetes to use a private registry.

Integrating a private registry into a Kubernetes cluster

Now that you have your own private registry, you now need to add it to your Rancher and Kubernetes clusters so you can start consuming it.

For this section, we will assume that you are using Harbor as your private registry, which will be an air-gapped setup, meaning our nodes cannot pull images from the public internet. We need to do three things for this task:

- Collect/publish images
- Set the Rancher global registry
- Update RKE/RKE2

Collect/publish images

For this part, we need to collect all the images we will need for Rancher and its clusters. Luckily, Rancher supports an install type called air-gapped and has created a script published as part of the Rancher release that takes care of this process. You can find the details of this process in Rancher's documentation located at `https://rancher.com/ docs/rancher/v2.6/en/installation/other-installation-methods/ air-gap/populate-private-registry/`.

But the short answer is Rancher has a file called `rancher-images.txt`, which contains a list of the images that Rancher might need. Rancher then has a script called `rancher- save-images.sh`, which will walk through that list, pulling down all the images using a workstation/server with internet access. It will output a `tar` file that can be physically copied to an air-gapped server. The last step is to run `rancher-load-images.sh`, which takes all those images and pushes them to your private registry.

This list is updated as part of every Rancher release, and this process should be run every time you are going to upgrade Rancher to grab the new/updated images. Also, some customers have a server/workstation that sits between the internet and the air-gapped environment and have chosen to modify this process to do both steps on the same server. They do this by editing `rancher-save-images.sh` and commenting on the last line, `docker save`. This skips the creation of the `tar` file. Then, in `rancher-load-images.sh`, they remove `docker load` as the images are already on the server.

> **Note**
>
> It is recommended that you keep the same registry structure, that is, `docker.io/rancher/rancher` should become `registry.example.com/rancher/rancher`. It is also recommended that the Rancher repos be set to public, which means that anyone can pull them without authenticating. This makes the process easier and replicates Docker Hub for these images.

Rancher global registry

Now that we have all our images, we need to point Rancher to the private registry. For this process, we need to follow the steps located at `https://rancher.com/docs/rancher/v2.6/en/admin-settings/config-private-registry/`. The basic idea is to go to the Rancher UI's **Global Settings** tab, edit `system-default-registry`, and update the value to your private registry. Suppose you have a private registry that needs credentials to pull images from the rancher repos. You would need to take additional steps by adding the credentials to each cluster.

Update RKE/RKE2

Now that you have Rancher using the new private registry, you now need to tell RKE and RKE2 to use that registry too. For RKE, it's as simple as updating the `cluster.yaml` file to include the `private_registries` section and running `rke up`. You can find the details of this change at `https://rancher.com/docs/rke/latest/en/config-options/private-registries/`. RKE2 is the same but with some additional settings if you need them. You can find details at `https://docs.rke2.io/install/containerd_registry_configuration/`.

> **Note**
>
> For both RKE and RKE2 clusters, this can be set up after the cluster has already been created, but it is highly recommended that you test this process in a lab/sandbox cluster as you might run into issues with firewall rules, missing images, misconfigured deployments, and so on, which can break your cluster. So, we want to test this process and make sure it's rock-solid before applying it to a production cluster.

At this point, we should have our clusters pulling images from our registry instead of from Docker Hub. We also went over how to force redirect all images at the host level and how to force a registry change at a deployment level as well.

Summary

This chapter went over what CI/CD is and how it works. We then dove into designing and installing Drone to become our CI/CD system. We then shifted gears and covered the topic of image repositories and the different types. At which point, we designed and installed Harbor to become our private registry. Finally, we closed out this chapter by covering how to configure Rancher, RKE, and RKE2 to consume this new private registry.

In the next chapter, we will build upon what we learned in this chapter to bring our deployment to the next level with Helm charts.

17
Creating and Using Helm Charts

This chapter covers Helm, how Helm is used as a package manager for a Kubernetes cluster, and how it works. We then will be diving into creating a Helm chart from scratch, after which we'll be covering how to publish our new chart to a Kubernetes cluster. Finally, we'll cover taking a publicly available chart and customizing it to fit your needs.

In this chapter, we're going to cover the following main topics:

- What is a Helm chart?
- How does Helm work?
- How do I create a Helm chart?
- Deploying a Helm chart
- Customizing a public Helm chart

What is a Helm chart?

Helm is a package management tool for Kubernetes deployments. Helm is similar to packagers such as **RPM Package Manager** (**RPM**) for Red Hat/CentOS-based systems or deb/dpkg for Debian/Ubuntu-based systems. In that sense, a Helm chart is a set of Kubernetes deployment files that have been packaged into a single templatized file. In this section, we will cover why we need Helm and how it works behind the scenes.

One of the questions that come up a lot when people start working with Kubernetes and Rancher is this: *Why do we need Helm?* But to answer this question, we need to understand how deployment was carried out before Helm, which was to have our developments as **YAML Ain't Markup Language** (**YAML**) files in a Git repository. This process works fine for static deployment whereby you repeatedly deploy the same thing —for example, if you are deploying ingress-nginx on all your clusters using the same settings, images, and so on. Having that as just a flat YAML file that you deploy using kubectl apply -f deployment.yaml may work fine.

The issue that comes into play is this: what happens if one of your clusters is different? For example, you have a **Google Kubernetes Engine** (**GKE**) cluster and a **Rancher Kubernetes Engine** (**RKE**) cluster that might require different images; that is, GKE will use the public Docker Hub image, with your on-premises RKE cluster needing to come from a private registry. Without Helm, you are now going to need two different YAML files while also ensuring that they both stay in sync. Of course, you'll need more than two different deployment files in the real world, so managing these files and keeping them in sync can become a nightmare.

Some people tried to solve this problem by writing scripts to find and replace values in deployments before deploying them—for example, your master deployment files might have their image value being set to something such as ImageTagPlaceHolder. Then, the script would look for this value and replace it using the sed command, like so: sed 's/ImageTagPlaceHolder/my-private-registry/g`. This process works okay if you only update a couple of values, but the process starts breaking down once you need to do more complicated customizations. For example, an ingress for your **development** (**dev**) environment might not have a **Secure Sockets Layer** (**SSL**) setup and might only have dev.example.com defined in the host section, but in your production environment, you'll need SSL certificate-defined, multiple hosts—that is, www.example. com, example.com, and so on. Doing this with Bash scripting becomes too crazy and, more importantly, error-prone.

Helm addresses this issue by having you define your deployment files as YAML files but with variables and `if` statements. The point is that you don't hardcode something such as your image tag in your deployment files; instead, you set it as a variable (that is, the `image` tag). Then, at the time of deployment, you feed values for those variables, and Helm takes care of building the final YAML files and then publishing them to the cluster. At the same time, Helm gives us the ability to define `if` statements in our deployment file, allowing us to modify the deployment based on user and cluster input. We'll be covering how this works in the next section.

How does Helm work?

I have found that the best way to understand how Helm works is to start by understanding the directory structure, but first, we need to remember that most public Helm charts come as TGZ files, which is a compressed directory. Helm's first step is to download this file from a repository and decompress it into the directory structure shown in *Figure 17.1*. Note that we'll be covering more about public Helm charts later in this chapter under the *Customizing a public Helm chart* section, but in this section, we will cover what each of the four directories and files is for. We'll then tie them together and walk through how Helm uses them to deploy applications.

You can view an example of a Helm chart directory structure here:

```
hello-world/
  charts/            # A directory containing any charts upon which this chart depends.
  Chart.yaml         # A YAML file containing information about the chart
  values.yaml        # The default configuration values for this chart
  templates/         # A directory of templates that, when combined with values,
                     # will generate valid Kubernetes manifest files.
```

Figure 17.1 – Helm chart directory structure

`Chart.yaml` is a file that defines a chart as a whole, including the name of the chart, its version, a description, and more. You can find an example in *Figure 17.2* and at `https://github.com/PacktPublishing/Rancher-Deep-Dive/tree/main/ch17/hello-world/Chart.yaml`. As we can see, this file is mainly used to set the metadata for the chart, including the name of the chart, a description, keywords, sources, maintainers, and an icon. Rancher uses all this data to build its catalog page, which allows you to search by keyword and see icons for each chart in a repository. Rancher also expands this file using a set of annotations under the `catalog.cattle.io` path to add data such as `catalog.cattle.io/certified: rancher`, which tells the user that this is a certified chart that is covered under Rancher's **service-level agreement (SLA)** and support. You can find an example of Rancher's monitoring chart at `https://github.com/rancher/charts/blob/release-v2.6/charts/rancher-monitoring/100.1.2%2Bup19.0.3/Chart.yaml`.

Have a look at the `Chart.yaml` example shown here:

```yaml
apiVersion: v2
name: hello-world
description: hello-world
type: application
version: 0.1.0
appVersion: 1.0.0
keywords:
  - hello-world
sources:
  - https://github.com/SupportTools/hello-world
maintainers:
  - name: Matthew Mattox
    email: mmattox@support.tools
    url: https://github.com/mattmattox/
icon: https://raw.githubusercontent.com/SupportTools/hello-world/main/img/logo.svg
```

Figure 17.2 – Chart.yaml example

The `templates` directory is one of the most critical parts of a Helm chart because this directory is where Helm stores all the template files for an application. It is important to note that all files inside this directory should be YAML files. Mixing other files into this directory has been known to cause weird bugs in Helm. By default, this directory is flat, with each object type being its own file—for example, you might have a file called `services.yaml` that includes all service records that need to be created, and another file called `ingress.yaml`.

It is important to note that resources in a file need to be separated by three hyphens (`---`) per the YAML standard. This is great for simple deployments with one or two resources per type, but having all your resources in a single file can be challenging to manage at scale because the Helm/kubectl errors you get will have a line number; still, that line number will not be the line file in the file but will be the line number for that section. For example, suppose you have 10 ingresses defined in a single file, making the total file around 100 lines. Suppose you have an issue with the third ingress on *line 2* of that section. Your error message is only going to say `error located on line 2`, but you won't know which line 2. Because of this, it is common to break up your template files into nested directories.

For example, you might create a folder for each resource type and then create a file for each resource (please see *Figure 17.3* for an example). Another example is breaking our folders down by component—we might create a folder for our frontend application and then have all resources that have made up that component: deployment, service, service account, **persistent volume claim** (**PVC**), and so on (please see *Figure 17.4*). I prefer sorting by component for any multi-tier application so that when I'm working on that component, everything for that component is in one spot. It also makes adding new components easy because I'll just clone that whole folder, then go into the folder and start running find and replace commands but scoped to the folder.

In the following example, you can see that in this Helm chart we are grouping by component type, meaning that all deployments are in the same folder together, the same with all ingresses, and so on:

Figure 17.3 – Helm folder structure by resource type

In the following example, you'll see that instead of grouping by *type*, we are grouping the different parts of the application. For example, we have the `apiserver` folder, which includes all resources that make up that component—that is, the deployment, ingress, and service. Then, we are repeating this process for each of these components of the application—that is, the frontend and the reporting service in this example. Personally, this is how I build Helm charts as I find it much easier to read, along with making it much easier to copy a component from one application to another. For example, I might reuse the frontend **user interface** (**UI**) in another application; so, by using this structure, I can simply copy the `frontend` folder into a new chart and start customizing it to fit the new application. The grouping-by-resource-type folder structure requires me to go into each folder and find all resources that make up that component. This process is, of course, error-prone as I might miss a resource.

You can view the structure here:

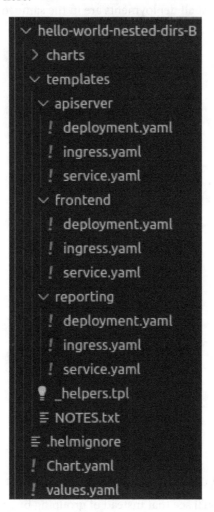

Figure 17.4 – Helm folder structure by component

The file you will be using the most as an end user is `values.yaml`; this is because this file sets the default values for the chart. Of course, this can range from setting global values such as the repository and the image pull policy to custom settings, such as setting database connection strings that will become a secret. We'll be covering this file more in the next section, but the key thing to understand is that this file is the configuration file for the chart, and therefore having good documentation inside this file is very important. Also, this file is designed to be customizable, meaning you can add your own sections and settings. For example, you might add a section for each component—that is, for `frontend`, `apiserver`, `reporting`, and so on, as illustrated in the following screenshot:

```
frontend:
  image: supporttools/hello-world
  tag: v0.1.2

  ingress:
    enabled: true
    hosts:
      - host: hello-world.example.local
        paths:
          - path: /
            pathType: ImplementationSpecific

apiserver:
  image: supporttools/hello-world-api
  tag: v0.1.1-rc1

  ingress:
    enabled: false
    hosts:
      - host: chart-example.local
        paths:
          - path: /
            pathType: ImplementationSpecific
```

Figure 17.5 – Helm custom values for each component

Finally, the last important directory is `charts`. This directory greatly expands Helm's abilities by allowing you to define dependencies for other charts. For example, if we go back to our three-tier application and need a MySQL database as part of our deployment, we don't want to write and manage all the different resource files that a database running in Kubernetes might need when someone else has done all that work for us already. So, in the `charts` directory, we can add the official MySQL chart as a subfolder. This sub-folder is handled just like a normal Helm folder, meaning it has `Chart.yaml`, `templates`, `values.yaml`, and so on. You can, of course, define a dependency inside the `Chart.yaml` file using the `helm dependency` command, which handles downloading and updating subcharts in the `charts` directory, and this is the preferred method over manually merging changes from an external repository into your Helm chart, which—of course—is error-prone and time-consuming.

It is important to remember that if you need to customize a chart outside the `values.yaml` file—that is, changing a template file to work around a bug—then the `helm dependency` command will overwrite your changes, so it is recommended in that case to download the chart into that folder manually.

At this point, we understand the different parts that make up a Helm chart. Now, it's time to walk through a deployment to understand how Helm works. This is what happens:

1. Helm takes the `values.yaml` file and uses that as a base for its variables, at which point any command-line values using the `--set` option will overwrite those variables. The critical item here to understand is that any command-line setting overwrites anything with `values.yaml` and is only used for settings not set via the command-line options.

2. Helm then starts processing the template files, replacing all variables with static values. As a part of this step, any `if` statements will be resolved.

3. Helm resolves any flow controls, including if/else statements. This allows you to add/remove sections of your configuration files using if statements. For example, you might wrap your ingress configuration in an if statement, allowing you to disable and enable it via the values.yaml file. Note that for ingresses, this is very common in most public charts. The other most common if statement is around Kubernetes versions as Kubernetes **application programming interface** (**API**) versions and formatting have changed over time. So, with Helm, you can create if statements, such as the following: if the Kubernetes version is v1.19 or below, use this section; else, use this section. This allows your chart to support a wide range of Kubernetes versions. You can see an example of this in action by looking at Rancher's official chart template https://github.com/rancher/rancher/blob/release/v2.6/chart/templates/ingress.yaml or by looking at the following screenshot. I would also recommend looking at Helm's official documentation, located at https://helm.sh/docs/chart_template_guide/control_structures/:

```
{{- if .Values.ingress.enabled }}
{{- if or (.Capabilities.APIVersions.Has "networking.k8s.io/v1/Ingress") (not (.Capabilities.APIVersions.Has "networking.k8s.io/v1beta1/Ingress")) }}
apiVersion: networking.k8s.io/v1
{{- else }}
apiVersion: networking.k8s.io/v1beta1
{{- end }}
kind: Ingress
metadata:
```

Figure 17.6 – Rancher server Helm chart ingress example

4. Helm is ready to start making changes to your cluster, but it is important to note if you do an air-gapped deployment, it will simply output all the YAML files into a directory. You can find an example of this kind of deployment in the Rancher install documentation, located at https://rancher.com/docs/rancher/v2.6/en/installation/other-installation-methods/air-gap/install-rancher/. But if you are carrying out a standard install, Helm will start applying changes to the cluster in a set order, which can be found at https://github.com/helm/helm/blob/release-3.0/pkg/releaseutil/kind_sorter.go#L27.

The vital part of understanding this step is to understand that Helm uses a set of ownership labels/annotations to know which objects are under the control of that Helm release. Helm automatically applies an `app.kubernetes.io/managed-by:` label and `meta.helm.sh/release-name` and `meta.helm.sh/release-namespace` annotations to every resource it creates. If these are missing or different from Helm's expectations, Helm will error out with an error message such as the one listed in the following screenshot. If you get this error, you have conflicts somewhere between charts—that is, two charts are trying to *own* the same object, which is not supported. To resolve this, you'll need to update the labels and annotations to the correct release to modify your charts to prevent future conflicts:

```
"Error: UPGRADE FAILED: rendered manifests contain a resource that already exists.
Unable to continue with update: Deployment "sentry-relay" in namespace "infra-sentry" exists and cannot
be imported into the current release: invalid ownership metadata; label validation error: missing key
"app.kubernetes.io/managed-by": must be set to "Helm"; annotation validation error: missing key
"meta.helm.sh/release-name": must be set to "sentry"; annotation validation error: missing key
"meta.helm.sh/release-namespace": must be set to "infra-sentry"
```

Figure 17.7 – Helm ownership error message

5. After Helm has run the equivalent of `kubectl apply`, your application should start. You can run a post-install hook that runs a job or creates a ConfigMap/Secret with most charts running a job that might ping their application in a loop until it comes online, at which point the job will complete successfully. You can read more about this process in the official documentation at `https://helm.sh/docs/topics/charts_hooks/`.

Now that we understand how an install works, the only other item is a Helm upgrade, which follows the same process but allows the object that already exists without erroring out. However, I usually recommend running Helm with the `helm upgrade -i` and `--install` flags, which allows you to use the same command to install and upgrade a Helm chart.

At this point, we understand how a Helm chart works. In the next section, we are going to create a Helm chart, and in the section after that, we are going to deploy the chart.

How do I create a Helm chart?

Helm makes creating charts very easy by using the `helm create mychart` command.

This command will create all base files needed to run a basic Helm chart. You can find an example output listed here:

Figure 17.8 – helm create mychart command creates an example chart

By default, this command will create a directory with the same name as the chart. When adding a Helm chart to a Git repository, it is widespread to rename this directory just `chart`, or if this application will have multiple charts from the same repository, you'll want to create a `charts` directory and move your new chart into that directory, keeping the name something easy to read/understand. This, of course, is a personal preference, with some teams choosing to move their Helm charts to their own repository.

At this point, your job is to start moving your deployment files into the template files. This is where you need to set all your variables that look like `{{ .Values.image. repository }}`. This variable suggests starting with the root `values` file. Then, go to the `image` section and grab the value for the repository `undertake` section. You can, of course, hardcode these values in the template file, but it is highly recommended to limit hardcoding values whenever possible and have the values defined in your `values. yaml` file. This is a must for any public Helm charts as there will be someone who needs to customize these values for their environment, and hardcoding the values just makes it harder for them. This is one of the reasons that default template files have a lot of settings defined. For example, the `nodeSelector` and `tolerations` settings are set up, even though a good number of people will never use these settings.

Of course, the default template files do not cover all the different types of resources, so you might need to create your own. The process that I usually follow is to find a public chart with the resource type that I need, then simply copy and paste and modify it to suit my needs. Of course, as you create your chart, you'll need to test it, which is what we'll be covering in the next section.

Deploying a Helm chart

As we covered in the last section, now that we have created our Helm chart, we need to deploy it to our cluster. This is done in two different ways, with the first one being a local chart and the second one being a remote chart—both of which we'll be covering in this section.

Before publishing it, we need to have the chart files downloaded for local Helm charts, which are commonly used while testing a new chart. You'll run a command such as `helm upgrade --install mychart ./chart --namespace mynamespace -f ./chart/values.yaml`. The important part of this command is the `./chart/` part, which tells Helm where the chart is located—in this example, it can be found in the `./chart/` directory. This, of course, should be the root directory of the chart—that is, where the `chart.yaml` file, `values.yaml` file, and so on are located. This kind of install is also common for use in **continuous integration/continuous deployment** (**CI/CD**) pipelines where you want to use Helm to templatize your deployments but don't need to publish them for public/end-user consumption. An example of this is being used in the Drone pipeline shown in the following screenshot. As you can see, it is using an overwrite value of the Drone build number to set the image tag and pass the ingress host as a variable set at the pipeline level:

```
echo "Deploying Portal"
helm upgrade --install portal ./chart \
--namespace ${namespace} \
-f ./chart/values.yaml \
--set image.tag=${DRONE_BUILD_NUMBER} \
--set ingress.host=${ingress}
```

Figure 17.9 – Helm install locally in a Drone pipeline

For example, consider the Drone pipeline using the Helm command listed in *Figure 17.9*. For this step, I'm using a custom image that I have created called `supporttools/kube-builder`, which handles setting up `kubeconfig` and includes some standard tools such as `kubectl` and `helm`. You can see an illustration of this in the following screenshot:

```
- name: Deploy-to-Dev
  image: supporttools/kube-builder:latest
  environment:
    DOCKER_USERNAME:
      from_secret: harbor-username
    DOCKER_PASSWORD:
      from_secret: harbor-password
  settings:
    kubernetes_server:
      from_secret: k8s_dev_server
    kubernetes_token:
      from_secret: k8s_dev_token
  commands:
    - bash deploy.sh dev ${TAG}
```

Figure 17.10 – kube-builder example Drone step

You can find the complete example pipeline at `https://github.com/PacktPublishing/Rancher-Deep-Dive/tree/main/ch17/drone-pipeline-example`.

The other Helm deployment type is a remote chart. The main difference is the fact that you'll be pointing Helm to a repository (Git or **Hypertext Transfer Protocol Secure** (**HTTPS**)) such as `https://charts.bitnami.com/bitnami` and telling Helm to download the chart files from the repository instead of using a local file. The rest of the process is the same as a local install. This process is mainly used to deploy public charts such as Rancher Server charts, Prometheus charts, and so on. This has the benefit of pulling the latest charts and releases simply by running the `helm repo update` command. Now, in the next section, we'll be covering how to customize a public Helm chart.

Customizing a public Helm chart

One of the tasks that everyone has to do someday when working with public Helm charts is to customize them to add some feature or setting that you need, or—in a more likely scenario—fix a bug. For example, some public Helm charts don't include the required settings to support **Pod Security Policy** (**PSP**) as enterprises and high-secure environments are mainly the only ones that use PSPs in the first place. It's something that some community members just don't test. There are, of course, many ways to make these kinds of changes to a public Helm chart.

But the primary way that I recommend is to fork the GitHub repository, create a new branch, and apply any needed changes. In this example, you'll want to add a section in the deployment to configure the `securityContext` section of the deployment(s) files and add the required **role-based access control** (**RBAC**) to assign a PSP to the required workload. Of course, it's recommended not to change the default behavior, so it's common to have `rbac.enable=false` and/or `psp.enabled=false` in the `values.yaml` file to allow users to enable and disable this feature as needed. Then, once you have made these changes, you'll want to create a **pull request** (**PR**) to merge this into the upstream repository. But in the meantime, you can deploy using the Helm local install option.

The idea is to give back to the open source community when the PR is merged. Switching back to the public chart is a simple edit to the Helm command by swapping out the local path of the repository name. Of course, make sure you are updating documentation and command examples as part of your PR request.

Summary

This chapter went over what Helm is and how it takes template files along with a set of values to create final deployment files that Helm can publish to a cluster. We then dove into creating a Helm chart and some of the best practices for structuring your chart for ease of use. We then went over how to install our newly created chart and integrate this process into a Drone pipeline. We then covered the topic of public Helm charts and how to customize them.

The next chapter will cover cluster resource management and capacity planning; as we all know, running **development-operations** (**DevOps**) workloads can quickly get out of control in terms of resource spending, and in the next chapter will cover how to monitor and control costs in Kubernetes.

18
Resource Management

In this final chapter of our book, we will cover the topic of resource management, which includes several items. The first is Pod resource limit and quota, which allows you to control your resource spend at a Pod level. We will cover how these limits are applied and enforced in a cluster. We will then work our way up the chain by covering the topic of namespace limits and quotas and will then move up another level by covering how Rancher project limits work. Finally, we will cover how to use kubecost to monitor our Kubernetes costs over time.

In this chapter, we're going to cover the following main topics:

- How to apply resource limits and quotas to a Pod
- How namespace limits/quotas are calculated
- How to use tools such as Kubecost to track usage and cost over time

Let's get started!

How to apply resource limits and quotas to a Pod

The physical resources in a Kubernetes cluster are limited. Resources are measured based on the number of **central processing unit (CPU)** cores or **random-access memory (RAM)** allocated per worker node. For example, you might have 10 worker nodes with 4 cores per node, meaning this cluster has 40 cores available to use. This kind of cluster is acceptable until you start running out of resources. As we know, CPU and memory are not free, so we can't just keep throwing resources at a cluster.

With Kubernetes, by default, all workloads and namespace have unlimited resources, meaning nothing stops an application from consuming all the CPU and memory in a cluster. For example, an application team could push out a new workload with a misconfigured **Horizontal Pod Autoscaler (HPA)** with a very high upper scale limit. It is important to note that HPAs do not allow unlimited maximum replicas, but nothing is stopping you from setting it very high. If the HPA metrics were set too low, Kubernetes starts scaling up the workload until it hits the max replica count or the cluster runs out of resources. Of course, this can cause an outage in Kubernetes clusters that are shared between environments—that is, non-production and production—or between application teams. We don't want one application/team to cause an outage for another team.

To protect our clusters, we need to set up resource limits and quotas around our workloads and namespaces to prevent this kind of outage. We do this at two levels.

The first level is at the workload/Pod level where we want to set resource limits and requests. This applies to all workload types (deployments, statefulsets, cronjobs, daemonsets, and so on); however, limits are not applied at the workload level but at the Pod level. If I set a one core limit for deployment, that limit applies to each Pod in that deployment, meaning each Pod can consume one core. You can't limit resources at the workload level; for example, you can't—say—only use one core across all Pods in a workload.

Here is a **YAML Ain't Markup Language (YAML)** output of a Pod with the section that we want to focus on being the resources. In that section, you'll see that we are setting both the request and limits. In this case, we are setting a CPU request (minimum) of a quarter core with a limit (maximum) of a half core. For the memory, we are setting a request of 64 **mebibytes (Mi)** and a limit of 128 Mi:

```
apiVersion: v1
kind: Pod
metadata:
  name: hello-world
spec:
  containers:
  - name: webserver
    image: supporttools/hello-world
    resources:
      requests:
        memory: "64Mi"
        cpu: "250m"
      limits:
        memory: "128Mi"
        cpu: "500m"
```

Figure 18.1 – Pod resource request and limit YAML example

Looking at the preceding example, we want to focus on the `resources` section. In this section, we define requests and limits for this Pod. The `request` values are setting the required resources for this Pod. This example tells Kubernetes that the Pod needs 64 Mi of memory and a quarter core (1,000 **millicores (m)** = 1 core). `kube-scheduler` uses these values to find a node with the required available resources in the Pod scheduling process. For example, if we had a database running inside a Pod, we might set the memory request to something such as 16 **gibibytes (Gi)** as that is what the database will need to perform correctly. When `kube-scheduler` builds its list of candidate nodes, it will filter out nodes without the required resources. If a Pod requests more memory than any one node has available, it will get stuck in scheduling. It is important to note that Kubernetes will not rebalance the cluster to make room for this Pod. An unofficial tool called `descheduler`, found at `https://github.com/kubernetes-sigs/descheduler`, tries to do this. Once the Pod is scheduled on a node, kubelet will reserve the requested resources on that node.

The other part of the resource section is `limits`. This is where we are setting much of the resources on the node this Pod is allowed to use. For example, we might only allow this Pod to use 1 **gigabyte (GB)** of memory. The first setting is for the memory, which tells kubelet if this Pod uses more than the set amount of memory. It is important to note that selecting a memory limit on a Pod doesn't change the amount of memory presented to the Pod. For example, if you set a 1 GB limit, open a shell to the Pod, and run the `free -g` command, you'll see that the amount of free memory will be available to the node. If the node has 16 GB of free memory, the Pod will have 16 GB of free memory. This is why it is crucial to have memory limits on your applications and your Pod limits.

The classic example is the Java heap size because older versions of Java (before 8u191) weren't aware of memory and CPU limits for containers. Java would overrun its memory and CPU limits simply because Java thought it had more resources available, so items such as garbage collection weren't running to reduce memory usage. Red Hat published a great blog about this topic and went into great detail about this issue and how Java 10 added the **+UseContainerSupport** settings (enabled by default) to solve this problem. You can find that blog at `https://developers.redhat.com/blog/2017/03/14/java-inside-docker`.

But to get back to memory limits, kubelet/Docker has no way of reclaiming memory —that is, taking it back from the Pod; only the application can release used memory. kubelet/Docker can only take **out of memory (OOM)** action to kill a Pod. CPU limits are handled differently because if you assign one core to a Pod, that Pod can only consume one CPU's worth. A CPU ceiling defines the maximum CPU time that a container can use. During each scheduling interval (time slice), the Linux kernel checks to see if this limit is exceeded; if so, the kernel waits before allowing that **control group (cgroup)** to resume execution. A cgroup is a feature of the Linux kernel that allows a parent process and its child processes to be isolated and limited in terms of the number of resources it can consume. This will show as `WAIT` time in programs such as `top`.

Kubernetes expands on limits and requests by adding **quality of service (QoS)** classes, which allows you to prioritize Pod evictions. If a node goes into CPU or memory pressure, kubelet will start evicting the Pod with the lowest priority first, which is the `BestEffort` class. This type of priority is used for Pods that are batch processing or reporting, or for other jobs that can be stopped at any time without impacting end users. The next class is `Burstable`, and its primary difference is that it allows the Pod to consume more resources than the defined limits, but only if a node has the available resources. Typical usage of this class is when a Pod is relatively static, such as a database, so we want to allow it to use more resources for a short period of time. However, at the same time, we don't want to use statefulsets because doing so would mean that we can't move around this Pod in the cluster. The other main reason is for applications that are using in-memory sessions where a Pod going down would cause disruptions. If this Pod gets evicted, the sessions are dropped, and users have to log back in. The following section will cover how namespace limits and quotas build on top of Pod requests and limits.

How namespace limits/quotas are calculated

One of the nice things about setting CPU and memory requests/limits for all Pods is that you can define namespace limits and quotas, which allows you to specify the total amount of memory and CPU used by all Pods running in a namespace. This can be very helpful when budgeting resources in your cluster; for example, if application *A* buys 16 CPUs and 64 GB of RAM for their production environment, you can limit their namespace to make sure they can't consume more than what they have paid for. This, of course, can be done in two modes, with the first being a hard limit that will block all new Pod creation events for that namespace. If we go back to our earlier example, the application team has purchased 64 GB of RAM for our cluster. Suppose you have four Pods, each with a limit of 16 GB of RAM. When they try to start up a fifth Pod, it will be stuck in scheduling until the quota increases or another Pod in the namespace releases the space, with CPU limits and requests being handled in the same way.

Of course, a namespace can have both limits and requests, just as with a Pod, but it's essential to understand how limits and requests are calculated. `kube-scheduler` simply adds up all limits and requests for Pods under a namespace, which means it does not use current metrics to decide if a Pod should be allowed to be scheduled in a namespace or not. It is essential to note that this only applies to hard limits. Soft limits use the metrics server to calculate currently used resources for each Pod.

The biggest issue that most people run into is allowing Pods without requests and limits into their cluster, as in the case of hard limits. Those Pods need not be a part of the calculation as their values will be zero. On the other hand, soft limits apply to all Pods as long as the metrics server runs. Because of this, it is typically recommended to set both a hard and a soft limit for your namespace.

The other important part is understanding that limits and quotas are not defined as part of the namespace definition (that is, the namespace YAML), but are defined by the ResourceQuota kind, an example of which can be found here:

```yaml
apiVersion: v1
kind: ResourceQuota
metadata:
  name: compute-resources
spec:
  hard:
    requests.cpu: "1"
    requests.memory: 1Gi
    limits.cpu: "2"
    limits.memory: 2Gi
    requests.nvidia.com/gpu: 4
    configmaps: "10"
    persistentvolumeclaims: "4"
    pods: "4"
    replicationcontrollers: "20"
    secrets: "10"
    services: "10"
    services.loadbalancers: "2"
```

Figure 18.2 – ResourceQuota YAML example with more options

However, one of the cool things is that you can set quotas on more than just CPU and memory but can also limit things such as **graphics processing units** (**GPUs**), Pods, load balancers, and so on. If you look at *Figure 18.2*, we specify this namespace to only allow four Pods. This is very low for most clusters/environments, but it is important to note that there is no free lunch. For example, a namespace with 100 Pods with 64 GB of total memory and another namespace with only four Pods using the same amount of memory are two different workloads. The 100 Pods put a much larger workload on the node and cluster management services than just four Pods. The same is true with a namespace that stores a lot of data in the form of secrets versus configmaps as a secret is customarily encrypted and stored in memory on the kube-apiservers. Because they are encrypted, they tend to be uncompressible, as opposed to configmaps, which are stored in plain text and are generally compressible. The other common limit users put on a namespace is a load balancer. In many cloud environments, when you deploy a load balancer in Kubernetes, you are typically deploying a load balancer in the cloud provider, which costs money.

> **Note**
> This covers a Layer-4 load balancer and not an ingress, which is usually a
> shared resource.

One of the nice things about Rancher is it builds on top of namespace limits and quotas by allowing you to define project-level limits and requests. This will enable you to define limits for a team that might have multiple namespaces. A classic example is a non-production cluster where an application team might buy X amount of CPU and RAM and then choose how to distribute it across environments.

For instance, they might assign half of it to DEV and QAS most of the time, but during load testing, they might want to spin down their DEV and QAS namespaces to shift those resources to their TEST namespace and then back, after their testing is done. As a cluster administrator, you don't care about nor need to make any changes as long as they stand under their project limits. It is important to note that projects are Rancher objects because the downstream cluster has no idea what a project is. Rancher controls projects and uses namespace labels, annotations, and Rancher controllers to synchronize settings between Rancher and the downstream cluster.

In the next section, we will cover using tools such as Kubecost to build on top of resource quotas to allow you to do things such as show back and charge back to recover costs in your cluster.

How to use tools such as Kubecost to track usage and cost over time

One of the essential things about Kubernetes is it enables application teams to move fast and consume resources with very few limits by default. This means that many environments early on in their Kubernetes journey tend to have a lot of spending. The perfect example is what is covered in *Chapter 13*, *Scaling in Kubernetes*, allowing you to auto-scale both your cluster and workloads. This means an application team can make a change that increases your costs by a significant number without you knowing until the bill comes, and now you have to go back and find out what changed, and—of course—it becomes tough to pull back resources after Kubernetes has been used for some time.

We can address this issue by using Kubecost, an open source cost monitoring, and reporting tool. Note there is a free community edition and a paid commercial product that expands on the open source project. Kubecost connects your cloud provider—such as **Amazon Web Services (AWS)**, Azure, or **Google Cloud Platform (GCP)**—to get the current cost of your resources, then ties that cost to the Pods consuming it in the cluster. For example, you use the latest and greatest CPU on some nodes with old CPU (cheaper) versions on other nodes. Kubecost allows you to tie the different costs back to the Pod. Because of this, you can choose to switch to newer high-performance CPUs as your applications/Pods run better on them and use fewer resources than slower CPUs.

Kubecost is deployed using a Helm chart or a YAML manifest inside the monitoring cluster. Currently, Kubecost doesn't support remote monitoring, meaning it must be deployed on each cluster in your environment. In addition, Kubecost uses Prometheus to collect metrics in your cluster that can be deployed as part of the Helm chart; the same applies to Grafana for presenting dashboards. Kubecost has its own network metrics collector for collecting traffic costs for different kinds of traffic; for example, some cloud providers charge you more for traffic outside your region than local traffic. The highest price is for egressing out to the public internet, which can be very expensive. The saying is that AWS wants you to bring data into their environment at little to no cost but will charge you an arm and leg to get it back out.

The steps can be as simple as executing the `helm install` command with a token that ties your install to your Kubecost account for installing Kubecost, an example of which you can find in the following screenshot. A complete list of Helm chart options can be found at `https://github.com/kubecost/cost-analyzer-helm-chart/blob/master/README.md#config-options`. These options allow you to customize your deployment:

```
kubectl create namespace kubecost
helm repo add kubecost https://kubecost.github.io/cost-analyzer/
helm install kubecost kubecost/cost-analyzer --namespace kubecost --set kubecostToken="abc123......"
```

Figure 18.3 – ResourceQuota YAML example with more options

In the preceding example, we install Kubecost with the default settings, which will deploy its own instances of Prometheus, Node Exporter, and Grafana. It is highly recommended to reuse your current Rancher monitoring **version 2 (v2)** deployment as the two will conflict. This is done by setting the `global.prometheus.enabled=false`, `prometheus.kube-state-metrics.disabled=true`, and `prometheus.nodeExporter.enabled=true` options. I would also recommend reading through the Kubecost documentation at `https://guide.kubecost.com`, which includes adding external resources such as **Simple Storage Service (S3)** and **Relational Database Service (RDS)**. In addition, their guide walks you through the steps needed to allow Kubecost to query your billing information for any custom pricing; for example, larger AWS customers can get a disconnect on their accounts for some resource types.

Finally, Kubecost has an experimental hosted offering, which can be found at `https://guide.kubecost.com/hc/en-us/articles/4425132038167-Installing-Agent-for-Hosted-Kubecost-Alpha-`. Also, Kubecost is not the only player in town as products such as Datadog can provide cost monitoring and reporting. The essential item is that we want to track our costs over time to know when something changes, and—of course—because we understand how much each Pod costs, we can create reports for management to show where the money is going so that they can turn around and go after application teams to pay for their resources. We do this to budget our **information technology (IT)** spending, allowing us to be proactive instead of reactive.

Summary

This chapter went over what Pod limits and requests are and how they are enforced by Kubernetes, including how they are calculated. We then covered how to use resource quotas at the namespace level to limit these to the team/application level, as well as limiting other resources such as load balancers, secrets, and so on. We then worked our way up the chain by covering the topic of Rancher projects, allowing us to set limits across a namespace. Finally, we covered how to use Kubecost to monitor our Kubernetes costs over time, including how to install and customize it, but more importantly, we covered why we want to monitor and track our costs over time. In addition, we covered some additional solutions such as Datadog.

The journey we have undertaken together is coming to a close. I want to congratulate you on finishing this book, as well as thank you for taking the time to learn about Rancher and Kubernetes. My final note is to remember that Rancher and Kubernetes are an ever-evolving ecosystem. It would be best if you always kept learning more, with Rancher's official events being an excellent resource for learning about new features in both Rancher and Kubernetes. You can find out more about this at `https://rancher.com/events`.

Index

A

access control lists (ACLs) 286
Active Directory (AD) 32
active external load balancer
  about 273
  cons 275
  pros 274
Alertmanager 25
alert rules
  creating, in Prometheus 205, 206
Amazon AWS 28
Amazon EBS 21
Amazon EBS CSI driver
  reference link 152
Amazon EC2 24
Amazon EFS CSI driver
  reference link 152
Amazon Elastic Container Service for
      Kubernetes (Amazon EKS)
  about 152, 156
  cons 153
  creating 110-112
  design limitations and
      considerations 98, 99
  load balancer, creating 112

prerequisites 98, 111, 156
pros 152
reference link 149
setup permissions 157
Amazon Machine Image (AMI) 164
Amazon's API Gateway private endpoint
  reference link 156
Amazon Simple Storage Service (S3) 300
Amazon Web Services (AWS)
  about 124, 131, 215, 364
  cons 133
  etcd/controlplane node sizing 133
  pros 133
AMD64 nodes 19
antivirus software, Docker
  reference link 236
Apache Kafka 26
application
  stomping, over cluster 304
application deployment 11-13
Application Load Balancer (ALB) 152
application logs
  filtering 210, 211
application programming
      interface (API) 170, 351

Apps and Marketplace 23
Aqua Security 26
Arbitrary Code Execution (ACE) 238
ARM64 nodes 19
automatic cluster upgrade
    reference link 155
autonomous system (AS) 289
availability zone (AZ) 103
AWS 299
AWS CLI v2
    reference link 111
AWS EKS 22
Azure Active Directory (Azure AD) 155
Azure Blob 300
Azure Kubernetes Service (AKS)
    about 155, 160, 176
    cons 155
    creating 114, 115
    design limitations and
        considerations 100
    load balancer, creating 116
    logging into 115
    prerequisites 100, 160, 161
    pros 155
    reference link 149
    setup permissions 161, 162

B

backup and restore process, Rancher
    reference link 301
backup and restore process, RKE2
    reference link 301
Banzai Cloud Logging operator 26, 208
Bitbucket 25
BoltDB 33
bootstrap agent 125
Border Gateway Protocol (BGP) 93, 287

Borg
    about 7
    features 7, 8
bring your own nodes 29-31

C

Cattle 17, 60
cattle agents 27
CATTLE_CA_CHECKSUM variable 177
cattle-cluster agent 27
cattle-node agent 27, 28
central processing unit (CPU) 172, 358
Certificate Authority (CA) 305
chart hooks
    reference link 352
CI/CD pipeline
    about 318
    Build 319, 320
    Deploy 321
    Dev Team 319
    Git Commit 319
    Git Repo 319
    Publish 320
    secret, adding 332, 334
    Test 320
CI/CD solution, architecting rules
    about 321-335
    Drone 322
    GitHub Actions 326, 327
    Jenkins 324
CIS
    reference link 249
CIS benchmarks 19
cloud credentials
    reference link 137, 158
Cloud Native Computing Foundation
        (CNCF) 17, 169, 196, 215

cloud provider
  Amazon EKS 156
  Azure Kubernetes Service (AKS) 160
  Google Kubernetes Engine (GKE) 159
  preference link 136
  preparing 156
cluster
  deploying, with node pools 144
  locking down 250, 251
  maintenance tasks 144-146
  scanning, for security issues 249
  security tools, for protection 252
cluster agent tool
  reference link 126
Cluster Autoscaler
  reference link 266
cluster designs, for Amazon EKS
  small clusters 102
  small clusters, node sizing 103
  small clusters, pros and cons 102, 103
  typical cluster size, node sizing 104
  typical cluster size, with availability
    zone (AZ) redundancy 103, 104
cluster designs, for Azure's AKS
  small clusters 108
  small clusters, node sizing 109
  small clusters, pros and cons 108, 109
  typical cluster size, with zone
    redundancy 109, 110
cluster designs, for Google's GKE
  small clusters 104
  small clusters, node sizing 106
  small clusters, pros and cons 105, 106
  typical cluster size, node sizing 107
  typical cluster size, with AZ
    redundancy 106, 107
ClusterFlows 210

cluster metrics
  reference link 199
ClusterOutput 210
clusters
  importing 169
command-line interface (CLI) 125
Common Vulnerabilities and
    Exposures (CVE) 239
configure logging drivers
  reference link 208
containerd 19
Container Network Interface (CNI)
  about 44, 152
  reference link 237
Container Runtime Interface (CRI) 66
continuous integration/continuous
    deployment (CI/CD) 239, 354
control group (cgroup) 360
controller for controllers 34
control plane 216
CoreOS 32
corrupted replica detection
  reference link 232
CrashLooping 38
current state 37, 38
custom application metrics
  adding, to Prometheus 202-205
Custom Resource Definition (CRD) 6, 26

D

DaemonSet 27
Datadog Cluster Agent 23
data plane 217
desired state 37, 38
DigitalOcean 29
Disaster Recovery (DR) 211
disk free (df) tools 214

Docker Hub
  about 335
  cons 336
  pros 336
Docker Kubernetes Service (DKS) 169
Docker machine 24
Docker Swarm
  versus Kubernetes 10-12
Domain Name System (DNS) 170
Drone
  about 322
  connecting, to Rancher 331, 332
  cons 323
  deploying 328
  prerequisites 328
  pros 323
Drone Continuous Integration (CI) 19
Drone installation
  about 328
  Drone Kubernetes runner 330, 331
  Drone server 329, 330
  PostgreSQL 328
dumb load balancer 271
Dynamic Host Configuration
        Protocol (DHCP) 129

E

eksctl
  reference link 111
EKS private-only endpoints
  reference link 150
Elastic Block Storage (EBS) 133
Elastic Container Registry (ECR) 98

Elastic File System (EFS) 152, 215
Elastic Kubernetes Service (EKS) 170
Elastic Load Balancing (ELB) 269
EMC 300
endpoints controller 34
ESXi hosts 299
etcd backup
  about 182
  configuring, for RKE2/k3s clusters 190
  configuring, for RKE clusters 189
  for RKE2/k3s clusters 191
  for RKE clusters 191
  need for 182, 183
  protecting, significance 188
  rebuilding 300, 301
  restoring, to RKE2/k3s clusters 192
  restoring, to RKE clusters 192
  working, for RKE2/k3s clusters 184, 185
  working, for RKE clusters 183, 184
  working with 183
etcd cluster 32
etcd object 32
etcd restore
  need for 186, 188
  working, for RKE2/k3s clusters 186
  working, for RKE clusters 185, 186
  working with 185
etcd-snapshot service options
  reference link 145
etcd split-brain
  about 294
  common error messages,
      identifying 295-300
  RKE cluster, recovering from 294

exporter
  and integrations, reference link 197
  in Prometheus 197
  writing, reference link 197
Extents File System (XFS) 217
ExternalDNS
  reference link 270
external load balancer (HAProxy)
  configuring 89
  HTTP/HTTPS mode 92
  need for 268
  TCP mode 90-92
externally managed RKE
  about 173
  cons 173
  pros 173

F

F5
  about 278
  configuring, in HTTP mode 281
  configuring, in TCP mode 278-281
fallocate 217
Federal Information Processing
      Standards (FIPS) 19
Fluent Bit
  about 208
  reference link 209
Fluentd
  about 26 , 208
  reference link 209
fourth extended filesystem (Ext4) 217
Fully Qualified Domain
      Name (FQDN) 62

G

General Availability (GA) 4
gibibytes (Gi) 359
gigabyte (GB) 359
GitHub 23
GitHub Actions
  about 326, 327
  cons 327
  pros 326
GitLab 25
GKE private endpoints
  reference link 150
global server load balancing (GSLB) 270
Google Cloud Platform
      (GCP) 130-135, 364
Google Kubernetes Engine (GKE)
  about 153, 159, 170, 344
  Cloud Shell, setting up 113
  cons 154
  creating 113
  design limitations and
      considerations 100
  load balancer, creating 114
  pros 153, 154
  prerequisites 113
  reference link 149
  requirements 99
  setup permissions 159, 160
Grafana 25, 196, 197
Grafana dashboard
  creating 207
  design, reference link 207
Grafana Labs dashboard repository
  reference link 207
graphics processing unit (GPU) 173

H

HA cluster, migration
  about 53, 54
  cleaning up/rolling back 57
  Rancher Server, backing up 54, 55
  Rancher Server, backing up
    to new cluster 56
HAProxy
  about 282
  configuring, for Kubernetes 282
  HTTP mode configuration 286, 287
  installing, on Ubuntu/Debian
    systems 282, 283
  TCP mode configuration 285
  URL 283
HAProxy community and Enterprise
  reference link 282
Harbor
  deploying, in Kubernetes 338-340
  prerequisites 338
hardening guides 250
Helm
  reference link 111
  used, for installing Longhorn 230
  reference link 230
Helm chart
  about 11, 344
  creating 353, 354
  deploying 354, 355
  working 345-352
helmsman 7
High Availability (HA) 211
Horizontal Pod Autoscaler (HPA)
  about 25, 256, 358
  avoiding 257, 258

need for 257
web server, with CPU
  utilization 258, 259
hosted cluster
  design consideration 150, 171, 172
  design limitation 171, 172
  managing, with Rancher 148, 149
  requisites 149, 170, 171
hosted cluster, installation steps
  about 162
  AKS 165
  Amazon EKS 163, 164
  GKE 164
hosted Kubernetes cluster
  about 96
  Amazon EKS, creating 110
  Azure's AKS, creating 114
  creating 110
  Google's GKE, creating 113
  limitations 96, 97
Hosted Kubernetes Providers
  reference link 149
HPA characteristics
  batch jobs 257
  HTTP-based 257
  quick startup 257
  stateless 257
HTTP/HTTPS mode 92
HTTP mode, F5
  configuring 281
HTTP model, HAProxy
  configuring 286, 287
Hypertext Transfer Protocol
  Secure (HTTPS) 355
HyperText Transfer Protocol/
  Secure (HTTP/S) 171

I

Identity and Access Management
    (IAM) 156
image repository
  cons 337
  pros 337
  secret, adding 335
  third party management 337
imported cluster
  about 168
  accessing, in Rancher 176-178
  need for 169
  Rancher, usage 170
imported K8s clusters 32
information technology (IT) 365
Infrastructure as Code (IaC) 318
ingress 289
ingress-nginx
  about 22
  reference link 290
integrated load balancer
  about 276
  cons 277
  pros 277
Internet Protocol Security (IPsec) 4
Internet Small Computer Systems
    Interface (iSCSI) 218
IP Address Management (IPAM) 129

J

Jenkins
  about 25, 324
  cons 325
  pros 324

K

k3s cluster
  about 174
  cons 175
  pros 175
  reference link 174
Kasten 165
Key Management Service (KMS) 97
Kiali 26
knsk
  reference link 308
kube-apiserver 33
Kube-ca
  about 86, 305
  used, for breaking cluster 305
Kubecost tool
  used, for tracking usage and
    cost over time 363, 365
kubectl
  reference link 111
  used, for installing Longhorn 230
kubelet 36
kube-prometheus-stack 201
Kubernetes
  about 7
  external load balancer, need for 268
  Harbor, deploying 338-340
  persistent storage, using 214
  reasons, for enforcing standards
    and security policies 238, 239
  security 236, 237
  trying, to solve issues 9
  versus Docker Swarm 10-12
  versus OpenShift 13
Kubernetes as a Service (KaaS) 96, 152
Kubernetes cluster
  private registry, integrating into 340

Kubernetes ingress
  about 289, 290
  SSL certificate, adding 291
Kubernetes Node Autoscaler
  about 263
  autoscaling, setting up with
      hosted clusters 266
  autoscaling, setting up with
      Rancher-managed clusters 266
  avoiding 265
  need for 264
Kubernetes runner
  deploying, with Rancher 328
Kubernetes services
  etcd 44
  Kube-apiserver 44
  Kube-controller-manager 44
  kubelet 44
  Kube-proxy 44
  Kube-scheduler 44
kubernetes-the-hard-way
  about 169, 174
  cons 174
  pros 174
  reference link 169
kube-scheduler 36

L

lab environment
  setting up, to test common
      failure scenarios 193
large with dedicated nodes
      design, Longhorn
  about 227, 228
  cons 227
  pros 227

latency 134
Lightweight Directory Access
      Protocol(LDAP) 23
Linode 28
Linux/Unix 18
liveness probes 37
load balancing 12
local cluster
  in Rancher 168
  need for 168
Logical Unit Number (LUN) 216
logs
  writing, to multiple log servers 211
Longhorn
  about 215, 216
  cleanup script, reference link 310
  cons 219
  critical maintenance tasks 231, 232
  installing 229
  installing, via Helm 230
  installing, via kubectl 230
  installing, via Rancher catalog 230
  issues, troubleshooting 233
  performance scalability report,
      reference link 221
  pros 219
  scheduling policy, reference link 219
  working 216-218
Longhorn Engine 215
Longhorn layers
  control plane 216
  data plane 216
Longhorn solution, architecting rules
  about 220
  large with dedicated nodes
      design 227, 228
  medium with shared nodes design 224
  smallest design 221

Longhorn upgrade
  reference link 231
  working 231
Long-Term Evolution (LTE) 21

M

mebibytes (Mi) 358
medium with shared nodes
      design, Longhorn
  about 224-227
  cons 224
  hardware requisites 224
  pros 224
MetalLB
  about 287
  configuring 93, 94, 287-289
  installation 93, 287
  reference link 93, 287, 288
millicores (m) 359
ModSecurity
  reference link 239
multiple log servers
  logs, writing to 211
multiversion concurrency
      control (MVCC) 33
MySQL 21, 23

N

namespace
  custom metrics, for stuck
      namespace 307, 308
  fixing, in terminating status 306
  limits, calculating 361-363
  Longhorn system stuck, in
      terminating 309, 310

stuck namespace, resolving 306, 307
  quotas, calculating 361-363
NetApp 300
Network Address Translation (NAT) 127
Network File System (NFS) 188, 215
networking 11-13
Network Interface Controller (NIC) 127
Network Load Balancer (NLB) 152
network partition 294
node controller 35
node drivers 124
node pools
  used, for deploying cluster 144
nodes
  limitations 130
  preparing, to join Rancher 135, 136
  requisites 129
node selector
  reference link 224
node templates
  reference link 140
non-volatile memory express
      (NVMe) 133
non-volatile memory (NVM) 131
Norman 16

O

Okta 23
ongoing maintenance tasks 165, 166
OPA Gatekeeper
  about 13, 240, 302
  best practices 247-249
  installation, ways 243
  installing, in Rancher v2.4 244
  installing, in Rancher v2.5 245
  installing, in Rancher v2.6 246, 247
  prerequisites 243

reference link 171
request flow 241, 242
standard policies 247-249
OPA Gatekeeper Pods
　issue, identifying 302
　issue, resolving 303
Open Policy Agent (OPA) 171
Open Policy Agent (OPA) Gatekeeper 19
OpenShift
　reference link 169
　versus Kubernetes 13
Open vSwitch 13
out of memory (OOM) 360
Outputs and ClusterOutputs
　reference link 210, 211
OVHcloud 28

P

PagerDuty 25
passive external load balancer
　about 271
　cons 272, 273
　example 271
　pros 272
persistent storage
　about 214
　using, in Kubernetes 214
PersistentVolumeClaim (PVC) 188, 217
PersistentVolume (PV) 188
Personal Package Archive (PPA) 282
pilot 7
plans 169
Platform as Code (PaC) 318
pod
　about 7
　resource limits, applying 358-360
　resource quotas, applying 358-360

Pod networking
　reference link 152
Pod Security Policy (PSP) 171, 356
Postgres 21
PostgreSQL 328
Privacy Enhanced Mail (PEM) 49
private registry
　collect/publish images 340, 341
　integrating, into Kubernetes cluster 340
　Rancher global registry 341
　RKE/RKE2, updating 341
probes 37
Prometheus
　about 23, 25, 196, 197, 304
　alert rules, creating 205, 206
　custom application metrics,
　　adding to 202-205
Prometheus Adapter 25
Prometheus federation
　reference link 201
Prometheus Operator 25
public Helm chart
　customizing 356
Pull Request (PR) 319

Q

quality of service (QoS) 360

R

Rackspace 29
Rancher
　backing up, with
　　Rancher-Backup-Operator 117
　core design principles 5, 6
　imported cluster, accessing 176-178

infrastructure provider, preparing
    for 136, 138-140
installing 116
local cluster 168
monitoring stack, deploying 198-201
nodes, preparing to join 135, 136
provisioning, clusters 28
provisioning, nodes 28
reference link 169
support matrix, reference link 201
upgrading 116, 117
usage, in imported cluster 170
used, for creating RKE cluster 141-143
used, for deploying Kubernetes
    runner 328
used, for managing hosted
    cluster 148, 149
Rancher agent options
    reference link 127
Rancher API 16
Rancher Authentication Controller 23
Rancher-Backup-Operator
    about 117
    backup, creating 118
    installation 118
Rancher catalog
    used, for installing Longhorn 230
Rancher Catalog Controller 23, 24
rancher-cis-benchmark 26
Rancher CIS scan
    deploying 252
    requisites 251
Rancher CIS Scan Controller 26
Rancher Cluster Controller 24
Rancher-created clusters
    with hosted provider 31

Rancher-created managed nodes
    limitations 129
    requisites 128
Rancher-created nodes 28-31
RancherD 22 69
Rancher installation
    reference link 351
Rancher Istio Controller 26
Rancher Kubernetes Engine (RKE)
    about 17, 168, 344
    Golang application 18
Rancher Labs
    about 4, 5
    history, as company 4
Rancher logging
    deploying 209, 210
Rancher Logging Controller 26
Rancher Longhorn 23
Rancher-machine 28
Rancher-managed cluster
    about 124-128
    defining 124
    limitations 128
    nodes, managing 124
    requisites 128
Rancher Monitoring Controller 25
Rancher Node Controller 24
Rancher Pipeline Controller 25
Rancher requirements
    Azure's AKS 100, 101
    Google's GKE 99, 100
    on Amazon EKS 98, 99
Rancher server 16
Rancher server pods, controllers
    Rancher Authentication Controller 23
    Rancher Catalog Controller 23, 24
    Rancher CIS Scan Controller 26
    Rancher Cluster Controller 24

Rancher Istio Controller 26
Rancher Logging Controller 26
Rancher Monitoring Controller 25
Rancher Node Controller 24
Rancher Pipeline Controller 25
Rancher v2.4
  about 306
  OPA Gatekeeper, installing in 244
Rancher v2.5
  migration, reference link 199
  OPA Gatekeeper, installing in 245
Rancher v2.6
  OPA Gatekeeper, installing in 246, 247
Rancher v2.6.3
  reference link 125, 170
Rancher v2.6.5
  reference link 265
random-access memory (RAM) 358
Raspberry Pi 19
readiness probe 37
ReadWriteMany (RWX) 218
Read Write Once (RWO) 73, 131, 173
Red Hat/CentOS
  HAProxy, installing 284
Redundant Array of Independent
    Disks (RAID) 216
Relational Database Service (RDS) 365
Remote Access Tool (RAT) 238
Remote Code Execution (RCE) 238
ReplicaSet 34
replication controller 34
reports and assessment, Rancher
  reference link 250
RESTful API 16
RKE2 cluster
  about 66-68, 175
  cons 176

design limitations and
    considerations 71, 72
installation steps 87-89
pros 176
requirements 69-71
RKE2 cluster, designs
    81
  large clusters 86
  medium clusters 84, 85
  single-node clusters 81, 82
  small three-node clusters 82, 84
RKE2 cluster, medium clusters
  about 84
  cons 85
  pros 85
RKE2 cluster, single-node clusters
  about 81
  cons 82
  pros 81
RKE2 cluster, small three-node clusters
  about 82
  cons 83
  pros 83
RKE2/k3s clusters
  etcd backup 191
  etcd backups, configuring 190
  etcd backup, working for 184, 185
  etcd restore, working for 186
  restoring, from etcd backup 192
RKE cluster
  about 60
  creating, with Rancher 141-143
  design limitations and
    considerations 71, 72
  etcd backup 191
  etcd backups, configuring 189
  etcd backup, working for 183, 184
  etcd restore, working for 185, 186

import, need for 169
installation steps 86, 87
origin 60
recovering, from etcd split-brain 294
restoring, from etcd backup 192
requirements 69-71
troubleshooting 310-313
working with 60-65
RKE cluster, designs
  about 74
  large clusters 79, 80
  medium clusters 77, 78
  single-node clusters 74, 75
  small three-node clusters 76, 77
RKE cluster, large clusters
  about 79, 80
  pros and cons 79, 80
RKE cluster, medium clusters
  about 77
  pros and cons 78
RKE cluster, single-node clusters
  about 74
  pros and cons 74, 75
RKE cluster, small three-node clusters
  about 76, 77
  pros and cons 76, 77
role-based access control (RBAC) 33, 356
round-robin DNS
  about 269
  pros and cons 269, 270
  with three-node example 269
RPM Package Manager (RPM) 344

S

S3 backup
  reference link 266
scalability 10

script 145
Secure Hash Algorithm 256
    (SHA256) 177
Secure Shell (SSH) protocol 237
Secure Sockets Layer (SSL) 344
security, Kubernetes 236, 237
self-bootstrapping 19
self-hosted repository
  about 337
  cons 338
  pros 338
service account and token controller 35
service-level agreement (SLA) 154, 345
SHA-256 28
Simple Storage Service (S3) 365
single node Rancher
  architecture rules 46, 47
  cons 46
  installing 44
  limitations 45
  migrating, to HA cluster 53, 54
  pros 46
  Rancher server, implementing 51-53
  requisites 44
single node Rancher, installation steps
  about 47
  Docker, installing 47, 49
  SSL certificates, prepping 49-51
Slack 25
Small Computer System
    Interface (SCSI) 215
smallest design, Longhorn
  about 221-223
  cons 221
  hardware requisites 221
  pros 221
Software as a service (SaaS) 322
software development kit (SDK) 31

solid-state drive (SSD) 33, 133
solution architect, rules
    about 101, 130, 151, 172, 173
    active external load balancer 273-275
    Amazon EKS 152
    Azure Kubernetes Service (AKS) 155
    externally managed RKE 173
    Google Kubernetes Engine (GKE) 153
    integrated load balancer 276, 277
    k3s cluster 174
    passive external load balancer 271-273
    RKE2 cluster 175
    round-robin DNS 269, 270
speaker 93
split-brain cluster
    about 295
    reasons, for changing 295
Splunk 26
SQLite3 21
SSL certificate
    adding, to ingress 291
standards and security policies
    enforcing in Kubernetes,
        reasons 238, 239
startup probe 37
static pods 19
Swarmpit 12
Syslog 26
systemd 17
System Upgrade Controller
    about 169
    reference link 169

T

TCP mode, F5
    about 90-92
    configuring 278-281
TCP mode, HAProxy
    configuring 285
time-to-live (TTL) 270
Transmission Control Protocol
        (TCP) load balancer 271
trimming 217
troubleshooting
    RKE cluster 310-313
two-factor authentication (2FA) 63

U

Ubuntu/Debian systems
    HAProxy, installing 282, 283
Uniform Resource Locator (URL) 177
user interface (UI) 16, 170, 347

V

Velcro 165
version matching 174
Vertical Pod Autoscaler (VPA)
    about 259
    manifests, writing 261-263
    need for 260, 261
    working 260
Virtual IP Address (VIP) 90
virtual local area network (VLAN) 272
Virtual Machines (VMs) 124

Virtual Machine Disk (VMDKs) 21
Virtual Private Cloud (VPC) 152
VM Anti-Affinity rules 299
VMware 21
VMware Knowledge Base
  reference link 299
VPA admission hook 260
VPA components
  VPA admission hook 260
  VPA recommender 260
  VPA updater 260
VPA recommender 260
VPA updater 260
vSphere 21

W

Wasabi 300
Web Application Firewall (WAF) 239
webhooks 23
WebSocket 27
Windows Agent Node installation
  reference link 176
WordPress 23
worker node 224

Y

YAML Ain't Markup Language
    (YAML) 344, 358

Z

Zettabyte File System (ZFS) 217

Packt>

Subscribe to our online digital library for full access to over 7,000 books and videos, as well as industry leading tools to help you plan your personal development and advance your career. For more information, please visit our website.

Why subscribe?

- Spend less time learning and more time coding with practical eBooks and Videos from over 4,000 industry professionals

- Improve your learning with Skill Plans built especially for you

- Get a free eBook or video every month

- Fully searchable for easy access to vital information

- Copy and paste, print, and bookmark content

Did you know that Packt offers eBook versions of every book published, with PDF and ePub files available? You can upgrade to the eBook version at packt.com and as a print book customer, you are entitled to a discount on the eBook copy. Get in touch with us at customercare@packtpub.com for more details.

At www.packt.com, you can also read a collection of free technical articles, sign up for a range of free newsletters, and receive exclusive discounts and offers on Packt books and eBooks.

Other Books You May Enjoy

If you enjoyed this book, you may be interested in these other books by Packt:

The Kubernetes Bible

Nassim Kebbani | Piotr Tylenda | Russ McKendrick

ISBN: 9781838827694

- Manage containerized applications with Kubernetes
- Understand Kubernetes architecture and the responsibilities of each component
- Set up Kubernetes on Amazon Elastic Kubernetes Service, Google Kubernetes Engine, and Microsoft Azure Kubernetes Service
- Deploy cloud applications such as Prometheus and Elasticsearch using Helm charts
- Discover advanced techniques for Pod scheduling and auto-scaling the cluster
- Understand possible approaches to traffic routing in Kubernetes

Go for DevOps

John Doak | David Justice

ISBN: 9781801818896

- Understand the basic structure of the Go language to begin your DevOps journey
- Interact with filesystems to read or stream data
- Communicate with remote services via REST and gRPC
- Explore writing tools that can be used in the DevOps environment
- Develop command-line operational software in Go
- Work with popular frameworks to deploy production software
- Create GitHub actions that streamline your CI/CD process
- Write a ChatOps application with Slack to simplify production visibility

Packt is searching for authors like you

If you're interested in becoming an author for Packt, please visit authors.packtpub.com and apply today. We have worked with thousands of developers and tech professionals, just like you, to help them share their insight with the global tech community. You can make a general application, apply for a specific hot topic that we are recruiting an author for, or submit your own idea.

Share Your Thoughts

Now you've finished *Rancher Deep Dive*, we'd love to hear your thoughts! Scan the QR code below to go straight to the Amazon review page for this book and share your feedback or leave a review on the site that you purchased it from.

https://packt.link/r/180324609X

Your review is important to us and the tech community and will help us make sure we're delivering excellent quality content.

Printed in the USA
CPSIA information can be obtained
at www.ICGtesting.com
LVHW081629151123
763729LV00044BA/81

9 781803 246093